THE
SECRET
U.S. PLAN
TO OVERTHROW
THE BRITISH EMPIRE

WAR PLAN RED

Graham M Simons

The Secret U.S. Plan To Overthrow The British Empire
War Plan Red

First published in Great Britain in 2020 by Frontline Books,
an imprint of Pen & Sword Books Ltd, Yorkshire - Philadelphia

Copyright © Graham M Simons
ISBN: 978-1-47389-236-1

Typeset in 10 pt Times by GMS Enterprises, Peterborough.
Printed and bound by TJ International, Padstow, Cornwall.

Pen & Sword Books Ltd incorporates the imprints of Pen & Sword Archaeology,
Air World Books, Atlas, Aviation, Battleground, Discovery, Family History,
History, Maritime, Military, Naval, Politics, Social History, Transport, True
Crime, Claymore Press, Frontline Books, Praetorian Press, Seaforth Publishing
and White Owl.

For a complete list of Pen & Sword titles please contact:

PEN & SWORD BOOKS LTD
47 Church Street, Barnsley, South Yorkshire, S70 2AS, UK.
E-mail: enquiries@pen-and-sword.co.uk
Website: www.pen-and-sword.co.uk

Or

PEN AND SWORD BOOKS,
1950 Lawrence Road, Havertown, PA 19083, USA
E-mail: Uspen-and-sword@casematepublishers.com
Website: www.penandswordbooks.com

Contents

Acknowledgements

A book of this nature would not have been possible without the help of many people and organisations.

My thanks go to - in no particular order - David Lee; Simon Peters, John Hamlin, Sydney Craner-Hargrove, Dr Harry Friedman, Martin Mace, Russell Plummer, 'Paddy' Porter, Ian Frimston, Phil McCraken the staff of the National Archives and Records Administration, Jeff Duford, Roger Deere, Laura Hirst, Amy Jordan, Lori Jones, Jon Wilkinson, Charles Hewitt and all the staff at Pen & Sword.

I am indebted to many people and organisations for providing photographs for this story, but in some cases it has not been possible to identify the original photographer and so credits are given in the appropriate places to the immediate supplier. If any of the pictures have not been correctly credited, please accept my apologies.

Introduction

This book starts around the turn of the 20th century when Vittorio Emanuele Cuniberti (1854 – 1913) an Italian military officer and naval engineer envisioned the concept of the all big gun battleship. He recorded his thoughts in an article he wrote for *Jane's Fighting Ships* in 1903. The vessel Cuniberti envisaged would be nothing less than a colossus of the seas. His main idea was that this ship would carry only one calibre of gun - the twelve-inch - the largest available.

This heavily armoured titan would be impervious to all but the twelve-inch guns of the enemy. Cuniberti saw the enemy's small calibre guns as having no effect on his design. Cuniberti's vessel had twelve large calibre guns and would have a significant advantage over the then-standard four of the enemy ship. His ship would be fast so that she could choose her point of attack. Cuniberti saw this ship able to discharge such a massive broadside, all of one large calibre, that she would engulf first one enemy ship, then move on to the next, and the next, disdainfully destroying an entire enemy fleet. He conjectured that the effect of a squadron of six colossi would give a fleet such overwhelming power as to deter all possible opponents.

At this time the political atmosphere in Britain was explosive; for the first time since Trafalgar, there was a severe challenge to the Royal Navy. A short distance across the North Sea, the German Navy, was building a powerful fleet. Behind that fleet lay the overwhelming power of the German Army. Behind Britain's, sea shield lay the numerically small British Army.

The challenge to Britain was serious. Admiral Sir John 'Jacky' Fisher, Royal Navy, was the driving force behind the revolutionary HMS *Dreadnought*. The ship was completed in a year and day and was launched in 1906. *Dreadnought's* speed was ensured by using the revolutionary turbine engines devised by Sir Charles Parsons.

Immediately this vessel defined the era. Thereafter all battleships following its design would be referred to, generically, as 'dreadnoughts'.

Jacky Fisher never gave any credit to Cuniberti or any foreigner for that matter. The Americans were publishing articles about potential designs and the General Board was reviewing several options, but USS *South Carolina* and USS *Michigan* were not authorised until March 1905 and neither were laid down until December 1906. Neither were the Japanese building the Satsuma class, which wasn't ordered until 1904 and laid down in 1905.

To say the threat from the dreadnought concept worried other nations is an understatement - it petrified them! It was now a race to match, and hopefully beat the British Royal Navy - then came the Great War which brought forth even more advances.

The horrors of the war brought forth campaigns for peace, at the same time as there were clamourings within certain quarters that America should consider itself first. The 1920s were to become a battle between disparate groups - hawks, doves, imperialists, isolationists, politicians, military men - all had vested interests, and all had a drum to bang. There were calls from the so-called 'Isolationists' for keeping out of any future conflicts with what was seen as 'the old world'. Within the American politico-military establishment was a growing body of opinion termed 'Imperialists' who thought that they - the United States of America - could and should be the world's only superpower. Coupled with this was the anti-British emotions stirred up by convicted criminal and jail escapee Éamon de Valera.

Throughout the 1920s there was a whole series of peace and re-armament conferences in which the Imperialists metaphorically fought with the Isolationists for control over hearts, minds and the military-industrial complex. If the Imperialists within the US Navy won this clandestine battle, then they would achieve their aims to become the world's super-power.

It became clear as the decade wore on that the Imperialists were not going to gain a clear-cut victory, so other, more direct means would be needed - and it is at this point that the story moves from being an entrée to the main course. The majority of this book has been compiled using just three contemporary, primary-source sets of documents from NARA - the National Archives & Records Administration. The first is what was called War Plan Red, a scheme for the USA to invade Canada and the Caribbean and then destroy the Royal Navy which in turn would destroy the British Empire. The second is a group of files called 'SPOBS - The Special Observers Group', an organisation that evolved from a large number of Military Attachés based in and operating out of the American Embassy in Grosvenor Square, London. This group, in turn, developed into what was recorded in the third set of files, detailing what was termed the USAFBI - the United States Armed Forces in the British Isles. With the eventual coming of American troops to the UK, this was to become the ETO - European Theater of Operations.

The linking item between War Plan Red and the SPOBS is the evolution of many extreme right-wing groups, individuals and organisations who had literally millions of followers and supporters who were able to sway public opinion in the USA to persuade the military men to shelve War Plan Red and use different tactics to achieve their aim.

As early as 1939 the American military establishment created an intelligence-gathering machine of ever-growing dimensions within their Embassy in London under the ambassadorship of Joseph Patrick Kennedy Snr.

This was well before the creation of the Office of Strategic Services (OSS) which was the wartime intelligence agency of the USA during World War Two, and a predecessor of the modern Central Intelligence Agency (CIA). The OSS was formed as an agency of the Joint Chiefs of Staff (JCS) to gather intelligence and to coordinate espionage activities for all branches of the US Armed Forces. Other OSS functions included the use of propaganda, subversion, and post-war planning.

The difficulty here is in trying to determine if the Military Attachés and SPOBS activities could be termed as 'spying', for according to the discovered documents, they were operating - at least in the early days in Great Britain - with the full permission and knowledge of British Prime Minister Neville Chamberlain and Lord Halifax, the Foreign Secretary. This, of course, goes against the definition of the word - a spy being a person employed by a government or other organisation to obtain information on an enemy or competitor secretly. That said, their intelligence-gathering activities spread out from Great Britain as far as the Middle East, Africa, South America, Russia and Asia - far beyond the terms of the original brief. It also did not cease with the outbreak of peace in 1945. The advent of the 'Cold War' between East and West brought forth a whole new range of subterfuge and behind the scenes activities by the CIA that had been formed on 18 September 1947.

The USA and the Soviet Union fought a whole series of wars by proxy around the world, ranging from The Far East, through Africa to Central and Southern America - often in countries that were formerly part of the British Empire. Although the subject of many books in its own right, this too is investigated to put things in context.

So, were the Americans allies — or spies? Certainly the SPOBS bled Great Britain white of data and information, sending it all back to the War Department in Washington under the guise of preparing to help. It was also something of a blueprint that America was to use in one form or another to 'encourage' regime change around the world through the seventy years or so after World War Two, and continues on today.

Writing this has proved to be challenging - reading it may be the same. The difficulties, as usual with much of my work, springs from the differences of our so-called 'common language'. Color becomes colour, program becomes programme, and of course, American phrasing is often different from English. Then there is the dreaded use of plane instead of aircraft; I don't care what anyone says, a plane is a cutting tool used to smooth wood in my books!

This was further complicated - especially in the latter part of this work - by using primary source documents written by Americans, but at least typed out in part by British civilians, resulting in the strange mix of British and American spellings and phrasing appearing on the same carbon copy! It is a standard convention that quotes are sacrosanct, so these anomalies remain untouched.

Graham M Simons
Peterborough
25 December 2019.

Chapter One

War Plan Red - And Other Machinations.

The joint Army and Navy Basic War Plan Red was one of a series of colour-coded war plans created by the United States armed forces in the late 1920s and early 1930s to estimate the requirements for a war - hypothetical or otherwise - with the United Kingdom.

Termed the 'Red' forces - one suspects because the standard coding for the British Empire on all maps and globes was that colour, War Plan Red discussed the potential for fighting a war with the British Empire and outlined those steps necessary to defend the Atlantic coast against any attempted invasion of the United States of America.

The use of colours for US war planning originated from the desire for the Army and Navy to use the same symbols for their plans. At the end of 1904, the Joint Board adopted a system of colours, symbols, and abbreviated names to represent different countries. Many war plans became known by the colour of the country to which they were related, a convention that lasted through World War Two.

The plan outlined those actions that would be necessary if the US and the UK went to war with each other. It assumed that the British would initially have the upper hand due to the strength of their

Royal Navy. The plan further assumed that Britain would probably use its base in Canada as a springboard from which to initiate an invasion of the United States. The assumption was taken that at first Britain would fight a defensive battle against invading American forces, but that the US would eventually defeat the British by blockading Britain and cutting off its food supplies.

War Plan Red was developed by the United States Army following the 1927 Geneva Naval Conference and approved in May 1930 by Secretary of War, Patrick J. Hurley and Secretary of Navy, Charles Francis Adams III. The Plan appears to have been updated over the period 1934-35; but seems not to have been presented for congressional or presidential approval. Only the US Congress has the power to declare war.

The plans, developed by the Joint Planning Committee - which later became the Joint Chiefs of Staff - were officially withdrawn in 1939. That year, on the outbreak of World War Two, a decision was taken that no further planning was required but the plan would be retained.

The 1930 edition of War Plan Red was not even partially declassified until 1974, when it was sold to the

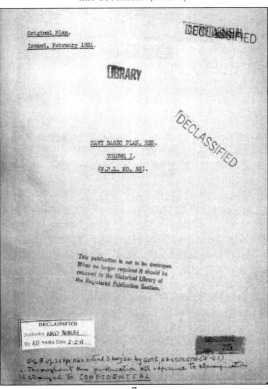

The title page of the 1931 edition of Navy Basic Plan, Red, more commonly known as War Plan Red. Remarkably, it took thirty-seven years to declassify this document. *(NARA)*

general public by the American politico - military machine as little more than part of a series of strategic planning exercises involving a number of 'what if' scenarios, drawn up and continually updated by low-ranked officers as 'make-work', none of which had ever been seriously considered. It was claimed that given the state of international relations in the 1920s, the war plans were extremely unlikely to happen and were just in keeping with the military planning of other nation-states.

Franklin Delano Roosevelt [D] (*b*. 30 January 1882, *d*. 12 April 1945), often referred to by his initials FDR, was an American statesman and political leader who served as the 32nd President of the United States from 1933 until his death in 1945. *(NARA)*

The War Plans were described in a rainbow of colours: Blue denoted the USA, Crimson was Canada, India was Ruby, Australia was Scarlet, New Zealand was Garnet, Ireland was Emerald. Newfoundland - for some reason separated from Canada and classed as Red. The rest of the British Empire - mostly, but not the African continent - not coded otherwise was coloured pink.

By 1974 the general public may have been sold the idea that this was just a 'what if' planning exercise and that it only involved Canada - even by 2011, when the 1931 edition was declassified, nothing like the full picture was emerging.

It was not until more material surfaced in the new millennium that something approaching the complete story started to surface that could be said to change the previously known timeline and events of World War Two. Far from starting in 1930, events can be traced back to the latter days of the Great War, when the USA was studying its policies in virtually every area of the globe.

Outside influences and a Special Relationship?
Even in 1918, there was a strong contingent of 'Imperialists', 'non-interventionalists' and

'isolationists' operating within the American political system. There were also outside influences at work, such as an eighteen-month sojourn in the US by convicted criminal and jail escapee Éamon de Valera, who did much to sway public opinion. Then there was the massive upwelling of support for Germany's *'National-sozialismus'* or National Socialism - the Nazis.

These events need investigating in detail and context as well as looking at War Plan Red and how this plan evolved into a whole series of nefarious ramifications that created spies, lies and deception which impacted on World War Two and the so-called 'special relationship'!

The Special Relationship is an unofficial term often used to describe the political, diplomatic, cultural, economic, military, and historical relations between Great Britain and the United States. The origins of the phrase have always been attributed to British Prime Minister Winston Spencer Churchill. Indeed, the first recorded use by Churchill of the term 'special relationship' was on 16 February 1944, when he said it was his *'...deepest conviction that unless Britain and the United States are joined in a special relationship, another destructive war will come to pass'*.

The two nations have been close allies during many conflicts in the 20th and 21st centuries, including World War One, World War Two, the Korean War, the Cold War, the Gulf War, and the War on Terror.

Although both governments have close relationships with many other nations, the level of cooperation between the UK and the US in trade and commerce, military planning, execution of military operations, nuclear weapons technology, and intelligence sharing has been described as unparalleled among major world powers.

But was that a relationship between two nations - or two men? When Winston Churchill entered the office of Prime Minister, the UK had already entered World War Two.

Before Churchill's premiership, Roosevelt had secretively been in regular communication with him, since their correspondence had begun in September 1939, at the very start of World War Two.

In these supposedly private letters, the two had been discussing ways in which the United States might support Britain in their war effort, but details of this had been passed over to the Germans by Tyler Kent, a spy in the US Embassy in London.

Sir Winston Leonard Spencer-Churchill (*b*.30 November 1874, *d*. 24 January 1965) was a British politician, statesman, army officer, and writer, who was Prime Minister of the United Kingdom from 1940 to 1945 and again from 1951 to 1955.

It seems that things had not always been like that. Roosevelt had only met Churchill face-to-face once previously as he is supposed to have confided to Joseph P Kennedy, on his appointment to the post of ambassador to Great Britain: '*I have always disliked him since that time I went to England in 1918. He acted like a stinker at a dinner I attended, lording it over us*'.

Joseph Kennedy was not to remain popular for long with FDR, especially with antics like this. Early in 1939, Joe Kennedy angered FDR by responding positively to a request from Helmuth Wohlthat, an economic advisor to Reichmarschall Hermann Goring who requested a meeting with Kennedy to consider an American gold loan to Germany. Kennedy's request to see the man was turned down by a horrified FDR. Kennedy repeated the request, and again the President refused. Kennedy then, in direct contradiction of FDR's orders, allowed Wohlthat to meet with him in London.

In December, after the war had begun,

Kennedy returned to Washington, where he delivered to the President his blunt opinion of Churchill. The then First Lord of the Admiralty, he told FDR, was '*...ruthless and scheming*' and was in touch with an American clique eager to embroil the United States in Europe's war, '*...notably, certain strong Jewish leaders*'. Kennedy also visited the State Department on 1 February 1940, to see another visiting ambassador, William C 'Bill' Bullitt, FDR's envoy to France. There, Kennedy interrupted an interview that Bullitt was having with Joseph M. Patterson and Doris Fleeson, respectively the publisher and Washington reporter of the *New York Daily News*. Bullitt later described his astonishment at Kennedy's bad manners to Interior Secretary Harold Ickes. According to accounts, Kennedy was saying that Germany would win, that everything in France and Great Britain would go to hell, and that his one interest was in saving his money for his children. He began to sharply criticise the President whereupon Bullitt took issue. The argument became so heated that Patterson and Fleeson discreetly withdrew. Kennedy continued to berate the President, and Bullitt told him that he was disloyal and that he had no right to say what he had before Patterson and Fleeson. Kennedy's language offended Bullitt, to which Kennedy supposedly responded that he '*...would say what he goddamned pleased before whom he goddamned liked*'.

When Winston Churchill assumed the office of Prime Minister of Great Britain on 10 May 1940, Roosevelt was nearing the end of his second term and making considerations of seeking election to an unprecedented third term. He would make no public pronouncements at all about this until the Democratic National Convention that year. From the US experience during the First World War, Roosevelt judged that involvement in the Second World War was likely to be an inevitability. This was a key reason for Roosevelt's decision to break from tradition and seek a third term, for he desired to be President when the USA would finally be drawn into entering the conflict. However, in order to win a third term, Roosevelt made the American people a promise that he would keep them out of the war.

The title page of a set of files called 'SPOBS - The Special Observers Group'. *(NARA)*

In November 1940, upon Roosevelt's victory in the presidential election, Churchill sent him a congratulatory letter containing the thoughts *'I prayed for your success... we are entering a sombre phase of what must inevitably be a protracted and broadening war'*.

Having promised the American public to avoid entering any foreign war, Roosevelt went as far as public opinion allowed in providing financial and military aid to Britain, France and China. In a talk given to the nation on 29 December 1940 - the so-called Arsenal of Democracy Speech - Roosevelt told the country *'This is not a fireside chat on war. It is a talk about national security'*.

He went on to declare US support of Britain's war effort, framing it as a matter of national security for the US. As the American public opposed involvement in the conflict, Roosevelt sought to emphasise that it was critical to assist the British to prevent the conflict from reaching American shores. He described the British war effort as beneficial to the United States by arguing that they would contain the Nazi threat from spreading across the Atlantic.

'If Great Britain goes down, the Axis powers will be in a position to bring enormous military and naval resources against this hemisphere... We are the Arsenal of Democracy. Our national policy is to keep war away from this country'.

To assist the British war effort, Roosevelt enacted the Lend-Lease policy and drafted the Atlantic Charter with Churchill. The USA ultimately joined the war effort in December 1941, under Roosevelt's leadership.

Clearly Roosevelt and Churchill had a relative fondness of one another. They connected on their shared passions for tobacco and liquors, and their mutual interest in history and battleships. Churchill later wrote, *'I felt I was in contact with a very great man, who was also a warm-hearted friend, and the foremost champion of the high causes which we served.'*

Between 1939 and 1945, Roosevelt and Churchill exchanged an estimated 1700 letters and telegrams and met with one another 11 times. On Churchill's 60th birthday, Roosevelt wrote to him, *'It is fun to be in the same decade as you.'*

There may have been something of a mutual love-in going on between the two leaders that were breathlessly reported in the media - at least, it certainly was within the Great Britain - but on the sidelines, politicians, military men and government officials were all actively plotting to destroy the British Empire.

Chapter Two

Rule, Britannia!

Rule, Britannia! Britannia, rule the waves!
Britons never, never, never shall be slaves.

The immediate cause of the United States' entry into the Great War in April 1917 was the German announcement of renewed unrestricted submarine warfare and the subsequent sinking of ships with American citizens on board. However, US President Woodrow Wilson's war aims went beyond the defence of maritime interests. In his war message to Congress, Wilson declared that the United States' objective was '...to vindicate the principles of peace and justice in the life of the world.' In many speeches earlier that year, Wilson sketched out his vision of an end to the war that would bring a 'just and secure peace', not merely what he called 'a new balance of power'. Clearly this was a not-very-well disguised reference of American dreams to depose the Great Britain's Royal Navy as the number one naval power.

What then followed was ten years of wrangling between the leading maritime nations, with turgid discussions, political machinations and much bargaining which appeared never to get anywhere. To the casual reader, this may all seem almost irrelevant and pointless, but I feel one has to read through it to understand exactly why the Americans took their action. As someone once said: 'Stick with me kid, and I'll show you the world'.

President Wilson subsequently initiated a series of secret studies named The Inquiry, primarily focused on Europe, and carried out by a group in New York which included geographers, historians and political scientists; Colonel Edward M House, an influential diplomat, politician, and presidential advisor directed the group. House became an advisor to Wilson particularly in the area of foreign affairs. He functioned as Wilson's chief negotiator in Europe during the negotiations for peace (1917–1919) and as chief deputy for Wilson at the Paris Peace Conference.

The Inquiry's job was to study Allied and American policy in virtually every region of the globe and analyse economic, social, and political facts likely to come up in discussions during the peace conference. The group produced and collected nearly 2,000 separate reports and documents plus at least 1,200 maps. The studies culminated in a speech by Wilson to Congress on 8 January 1918, where he articulated America's long-term war objectives - it was an address that was the most explicit expression of intention made by any of the belligerent nations, and it projected Wilson's progressive domestic policies into the international arena.

The speech, which became known as the Fourteen Points, was developed from a set of strategic points by Wilson and territorial aspects drafted by the Inquiry's general secretary, Walter Lippmann, and his three colleagues, Isaiah Bowman, Sidney Mezes, and David Hunter

Left: Thomas Woodrow Wilson [D] (*b*. 28 December 1856, *d*. 3 February 3, 1924) was the 28th President of the USA, serving two terms in office, from 4 March 1913 to 4 March 1921.

Right: Edward Mandell House [D] (*b*. 26 July 1858, *d*. 28 March 1938) was a powerful American diplomat, Democratic politician, and presidential advisor, commonly known by the courtesy title Colonel House, although he had no military experience. *(both NARA)*

Left: Newton Diehl Baker, Jr. [D] (*b*. 3 December1871, *d*. 25 December 1937) was an American lawyer, politician and government official. He served as the 37th mayor of Cleveland, Ohio from 1912 to 1915 and as US Secretary of War from 1916 to 1921.

Right: John Maynard Keynes, 1st Baron Keynes CB FBA (*b*. 5 June 1883, *d. 21* April 1946), was an English economist whose ideas fundamentally changed the theory and practice of macroeconomics and the economic policies of governments. *(both NARA)*

Miller. Lippmann's draft territorial points were a direct response to the secret treaties of the European Allies, which Secretary of War Newton D. Baker had shown Lippman. Lippman's task according to House was '*...to take the secret treaties, analyse the parts which were tolerable, and separate them from those which we regarded as intolerable, and then develop a position which conceded as much to the Allies as it could, but took away the poison. ... It was all keyed upon the secret treaties.*'

In the speech, Wilson directly addressed what he perceived as the causes for the world war by calling for the abolition of secret treaties, a reduction in armaments, an adjustment in territorial claims in the interests of both native peoples and colonists, and freedom of the seas. Wilson also made proposals that would ensure world peace in the future. He proposed the removal of economic barriers between nations, the promise of self-determination for national minorities, and a world organisation that would guarantee the '*...political independence and territorial integrity of great and small states alike*' - a League of Nations.

Though Wilson's idealism pervaded the Fourteen Points, he also had more practical objectives in mind. He hoped to keep Russia in the war by convincing the Bolsheviks that they would receive a better peace from the Allies, to bolster Allied morale, and to undermine German war support. The address was well received in the United States and Allied nations, and even by Bolshevik leader Vladimir Ilyich Ulyanov, better known by the alias Lenin, as a landmark of enlightenment in international relations.

Wilson subsequently used the Fourteen Points as the basis for negotiating the Treaty of Versailles, one of a number of treaties that ended the state of war between Germany and the Allied powers. It was signed on 28 June 1919, exactly five years after the assassination of Archduke Franz Ferdinand. The other Central powers on the German side of the Great War were dealt with in separate treaties. Although the armistice, signed on 11 November 1918, ended the actual fighting, it took six months of negotiations at the Paris Peace Conference to conclude the peace treaty.

Of the many provisions in the treaty, one of the most important and controversial required '*...Germany* [to] *accept the responsibility of Germany and her allies for causing all the loss and damage*' during the war. This article, Article 231, later became known as the War Guilt clause. The treaty forced Germany to disarm, make substantial territorial concessions, and pay reparations to certain countries that had formed the Entente powers. In 1921 the total cost of these reparations was assessed at 132 billion Marks (then \$31.4 billion or £6.6 billion). At the time John Maynard Keynes, the 1st Baron Keynes, was an English economist whose ideas fundamentally changed the theory and practice of macroeconomics and the economic policies of governments. He built on and greatly refined earlier work on the causes of business cycles and is widely considered to be one of the most influential economists of the 20th century and the founder of modern macroeconomics. His ideas are the basis for the school of thought known as Keynesian economics and its various offshoots. Keynes predicted that the treaty was too harsh and said the reparations figure was excessive and counter-productive. On the other hand, prominent figures on the Allied side such as French Marshal Ferdinand Foch criticised the treaty for treating Germany too leniently.

The result of these competing and sometimes conflicting goals among the victors was a compromise that left no one content: Germany was neither pacified nor conciliated, nor was it permanently weakened. The problems that arose from the treaty would lead to the Locarno Treaties, which improved relations between Germany and the other European Powers, and the renegotiation of the reparation system resulting in the Dawes Plan, the Young Plan, and the indefinite postponement of reparations at the Lausanne Conference of 1932.

President Wilson at first considered abandoning his Fourteen Points speech after Lloyd George delivered a speech outlining British war aims, many of which were similar to Woodrow Wilson's aspirations, at Caxton Hall, London on 5 January 1918. Wilson was persuaded by his adviser Colonel House to go ahead, and his speech overshadowed Lloyd George's and is better remembered by posterity.

In his speech to Congress on 18 January, President Woodrow Wilson declared fourteen points which he regarded as the only possible basis of enduring peace. They were according to him:

I. Open covenants of peace, openly arrived at, after which there shall be no private international understandings of any kind but diplomacy shall proceed always frankly and in the public view.

II. Absolute freedom of navigation upon the seas, outside territorial waters, alike in peace and in war, except as the seas may be closed in whole or in part by international action for the enforcement of international covenants.

III. The removal, so far as possible, of all economic barriers and the establishment of an equality of trade conditions among all the nations consenting to the peace and associating themselves for its maintenance.

IV. Adequate guarantees given and taken that national armaments will be reduced to the lowest point consistent with domestic safety.

V. A free, open-minded, and absolutely impartial adjustment of all colonial claims, based upon a strict observance of the principle that in determining all such questions of sovereignty the interests of the populations concerned must have equal weight with the equitable government whose title is to be determined.

VI. The evacuation of all Russian territory and such a settlement of all questions affecting Russia as will secure the best and freest cooperation of the other nations of the world in obtaining for her an unhampered and unembarrassed opportunity for the independent determination of her own political development and national policy and assure her of a sincere welcome into the society of free nations under institutions of her own choosing; and, more than a welcome, assistance also of every kind that she may need and may herself desire. The treatment accorded Russia by her sister nations in the months to come will be the acid test of their good will, of their comprehension of her needs as distinguished from their own interests, and of their intelligent and unselfish sympathy.

VII. Belgium, the whole world will agree, must be evacuated and restored, without any attempt to limit the sovereignty which she enjoys in common with all other free nations. No other single act will serve as this will serve to restore confidence among the nations in the laws which they have themselves set and determined for the government of their relations with one another. Without this healing act the whole structure and validity of international law is forever impaired.

VIII. All French territory should be freed and the invaded portions restored, and the wrong done to France by Prussia in 1871 in the matter of Alsace-Lorraine, which has unsettled the peace of the world for nearly fifty years, should be righted, in order that peace may once more be made secure in the interest of all.

IX. A re-adjustment of the frontiers of Italy should be effected along clearly recognizable lines of nationality.

X. The people of Austria-Hungary, whose place among the nations we wish to see safeguarded and assured, should be accorded the freest opportunity to autonomous development.

XI. Romania, Serbia, and Montenegro should be evacuated; occupied territories restored; Serbia accorded free and secure access to the sea; and the relations of the several Balkan states to one another determined by friendly counsel along historically established lines of allegiance and nationality; and international guarantees of the political and economic independence and territorial integrity of the several Balkan states should be entered into.

XII. The Turkish portion of the present Ottoman Empire should be assured a secure sovereignty, but the other nationalities which are now under Turkish rule should be assured an undoubted security of life and an absolutely unmolested opportunity of autonomous development, and the Dardanelles should be permanently opened as a free passage to the ships and commerce of all nations under international guarantees.

XIII. An independent Polish state should be erected which should include the territories inhabited by indisputably Polish populations, which should be assured a free and secure access to the sea, and whose political and economic independence and territorial integrity should be guaranteed by international covenant. XIV. A general association of nations must be formed under specific covenants for the purpose of affording mutual guarantees of political independence and territorial integrity to great and small states alike.

The speech was made without prior coordination or consultation with Wilson's counterparts in Europe. Georges Benjamin Clemenceau, the French Prime Minister from 1906 to 1909 and from 1917 to 1920, upon hearing of the Fourteen Points, was said to have sarcastically claimed *'Le Bon Dieu n'en avait que dix!'* (The good Lord only had ten!). As a major public statement of war aims, it became the basis for the terms of the German surrender at the end of World War One. After the speech, Colonel House worked to secure the acceptance of the Fourteen Points by Entente leaders. On 16 October 1918, President Woodrow Wilson

and Sir William Wiseman, had an interview. When in 1915 Wiseman was gassed and invalided out of the army, he was entrusted with the setting up Britain's Secret Intelligence Service's first section in America. He had been instructed to subvert German interests and counter Irish and Indian nationalist plots to undermine the British war effort. His network of spies in New York included some dubious characters like the occultist and self-proclaimed 'Great Beast 666', Aleister Crowley, and 'ace of spies', Sidney Reilly. But Wiseman was adept at cultivating influential American allies, including President Woodrow Wilson's friend and confidential advisor, Colonel Edward House.

The report was made as negotiation points, and later the Fourteen Points, were accepted by both France and Italy on 1 November 1918. Britain later signed off on all of the points except the freedom of the seas. The United Kingdom also wanted Germany to make reparation payments for the war and thought that that should be added to the Fourteen Points. The speech was delivered ten months before the Armistice with Germany and became the basis for the terms of the German surrender, as negotiated at the Paris Peace Conference in 1919.

It was not long after the Great War ended that a significant number of Americans started wondering whether their country's involvement in that conflict had not been a grave mistake. To many liberals, the Treaty of Versailles made a mockery of President Wilson's idealistic war aims. Instead of concluding a just settlement that would reform the international system and make future wars unlikely, the Allies, they concluded, had simply just expanded their empires at the expense of their defeated foes. They began to question whether the loss of more than 120,000

Left: David Lloyd George, 1st Earl Lloyd-George of Dwyfor, OM, PC (*b*. 17 January 1863, *d*. 26 March 1945) was a British Liberal politician and statesman. He was British Prime Minister from 1916 to 1922.

Right: Sir William George Eden Wiseman, 10th Baronet CB (*b*. 1 February 1885, *d*. 17 June 1962) was a British intelligence agent and banker. He was also the first Head of the British Intelligence Service section in America.

Left: Georges Benjamin Clemenceau (*b*. 28 September 1841, *d*. 24 November 1929) was a French politician, physician, and journalist who was Prime Minister of France during the First World War.

Right: Sidney George Reilly MC (*b*. 1873, *d*. 5 November 1925), known as the 'Ace of Spies', was a Russian-born adventurer and secret agent employed by Special Branch and later by the Foreign Section of the British Secret Service Bureau, the precursor to the modern British Secret Intelligence Service (MI6/SIS). The picture is Reilly's 1918 German passport issued under the alias of George Bergmann.

dead, and nearly a quarter million wounded - not to mention the more than half a million Americans who died in the pandemic of Spanish Flu, which soldiers returning from Europe brought with them - was justified by this apparent return to 'business as usual'

The presidential election of 1920 was the 34th quadrennial presidential election, held on Tuesday, 2 November. The Republicans nominated newspaper publisher and Ohio Senator Warren G. Harding, while the Democrats chose newspaper publisher and Ohio Governor James M. Cox. Incumbent President Woodrow Wilson, a Democrat, in poor health, chose not to run for a third term. Former President Theodore Roosevelt had been the front-runner for the Republican nomination, but his health collapsed in 1918. He died in January 1919, leaving no obvious heir to his progressive legacy. As a result, both major parties ultimately turned to little-known dark horse candidates from the electoral-vote-rich state of Ohio. To help his campaign, Cox chose future president Franklin D. Roosevelt - a fifth cousin of Theodore - as his running mate. Harding virtually ignored Cox and essentially campaigned against Wilson, calling for a return to normalcy'. With an almost four-to-one spending advantage, Harding won a landslide victory by winning thirty-seven states.

The election was dominated by the social and political environment in the aftermath of the Great War and a hostile response to specific policies of Woodrow Wilson, as well as the massive reaction against the reformist zeal of the Progressive Era - a period of widespread social activism and political reform across the United States, from the 1890s to 1920s. The primary objective of the Progressive movement was the elimination of corruption in government. It primarily targeted political machines and their bosses. By taking down these corrupt representatives in office, a further means of direct democracy would be established. They also sought regulation of monopolies and corporations through anti-trust laws.

The wartime economic boom had collapsed, and politicians were arguing over peace treaties and the question of America's entry into the League of Nations, which was overturned because of the return to a non-interventionist opinion, a continuation of the nation's opinion since the early 1800s.

Non-interventionism, the diplomatic policy whereby a nation seeks to avoid alliances with other nations in order to avoid being drawn into conflicts not related to direct territorial self-defence, has had a long history of popularity in the government and among the people of the United States. The Treaty of Versailles, and thus, United States' participation in the League of Nations, even with reservations, was rejected by the Republican-dominated Senate in the final months of Wilson's presidency. A group of senators known as the Irreconcilables, identifying with both William Borah and Henry Cabot Lodge, had great objections regarding the clauses of the treaty which compelled America to come to the defence of other nations. Lodge, echoing Wilson, issued fourteen reservations regarding the treaty; among them, the second argued that America would sign only with the understanding that: *'Nothing compels the United States to ensure border contiguity or political* independence of any nation, to interfere in foreign domestic disputes regardless of their status in the League, or to command troops or ships without Congressional declaration of war'. While some of the sentiment was grounded in adherence to Constitutional principles, some of the sentiment bore a reassertion of nativist and inward-looking policy.

The Lodge Reservations gave a lot of power back to the United States in control over how it interacted with other nations, and how they interacted with it. Almost all of the Reservations granted the United States more authority over its place within the League of Nations, or when the League of Nations was allowed to make decisions involving the United States.

'Reservation One: The United States reserves the right to determine when it can withdraw from the League'.

'Reservation Two: Nothing compels the United States to ensure border contiguity or political independence of any nation, to interfere in foreign domestic disputes regardless of their status in the League, or to command troops or ships without Congressional declaration of war. To apply this would be to destroy the mutual security provided by articles 10–17 in the Treaty of Versailles'.

Articles 10–17 ensured 'independence and territorial integrity' by stating that any attack on a League nation would be seen as an attack on all League nations. This would highly discourage any League or non-League nations from attacking the League nations. In this way, the sections of the Treaty of Versailles that dealt with the right to declare war themselves '...were almost ironclad guarantees of mutual security...'. However, these articles would also take constitutional rights away from Congress, in the form of the right to declare war, which was given to Congress by article 1 section 8 of the Constitution. Instead, the power to declare war would be given to the League of Nations, which would, if a League nation was attacked, automatically blockade the offending country, using the armies and navies of the League nations.

'Reservation Three: The United States retains sole control over foreign issues'.

'Reservation Four: The United States retains its right to decide which questions are within its own domestic jurisdiction and says that all political and domestic questions relating to its internal affairs - immigration, labour, coastal traffic, the tariff, commerce, the suppression of traffic in women, children, and dangerous drugs such as opium - are purely within the jurisdiction of the United States and are not to be required to be reviewed or approved by the League of Nations'.

'Reservation Five: The United States is not to be questioned about the Monroe Doctrine, or its interpretation of the Monroe Doctrine'.

'Reservation Six: The United States reserves the right to take either side if China and Japan start a war against each other'.

'Reservation Seven: Congress will elect US Representatives in the League of Nations and have total control over any representatives'.

'Reservation Eight: Trade between Germany and the United States can only be interfered with approval from Congress'.

'Reservation Nine: The United States is not obligated to pay any money to the League of Nations'.

'Reservation Ten: If the United States builds down its military might because of an order by the League of Nations, it can at any time, without warning, build up again if threatened'.

'Reservation Eleven: The United States reserves the right to allow peoples of states which break the Treaty of Versailles who live in the United States to continue their lives in the United States'.

'Reservation Twelve: Nothing in the Treaty of Versailles shall approve of anything illegal or compromise the rights of US citizens'.

'Reservation Thirteen: If the League of Nations is to create any future organisations, the United States is not bound to join, no matter as to how the League of Nations wishes concerning their involvement. Instead, Congress has the right to make the decision as to whether or not the United States chooses to be involved and the terms of their involvement'.

'Reservation Fourteen: The United States will not be bound by any vote in the League of Nations in which a nation has voted twice. Neither will it be bound by a vote which concerns and affects a voting party'.

Overseas, there were wars and revolutions. At home, 1919 was marked by major strikes in the meat-packing and steel industries, and large-scale race riots in Chicago and other cities. Anarchist attacks on Wall Street produced fears of radicals and terrorists. The Irish Catholic and German communities were outraged at Wilson's foreign policy which in turn brought pressure to bear. His political position was critically weakened after he suffered a severe stroke in 1919 that rendered him unable to speak on his own behalf.

The Irish Issue and Influence.

It seems that when Irish-Americans talk about identifying with the Irish, they mean the Irish who came to settle in the United States and their descendants, not those of currently living in Ireland. For at least the last one hundred and thirty years, Ireland itself, the country, is an abstract, romanticised receptacle of dreams and green fields, and the place that will soothe a lifelong ache. With it, goes an almost partisan dislike of the English. The scale of this dislike had a considerable impact on the thinking of the military and politicians alike - and on the mentality of a particular father of a future American President, but more of that later.

At the turn of the century by force of circumstance, when one left Ireland without having learned its history of oppression, a countryman in America would gladly provide the remedial instruction. He also had the opportunity of learning the story of Ireland through the letters from his friends and relatives who were still living under English rule. The Irish of this era did not usually return to farming; instead, they settled in or near the metropolitan areas - Boston, New York and San Francisco were the destinations of many. As time passed, the immigrant, his sons and his grandson's became a vital part in local and state political organisations. Their political representatives were continuously aware of their British grievances. In time also, the Irish rose to positions of leadership themselves.

The Irish-American leaders of the post World War One era missed few opportunities to cause agitation for the cause of Ireland. In spite of this agitation, however, they did, with a few exceptions, manage to elude the classification of being rabble-rousers. Leaders who arose from this group played prominent and distinguished roles in public and professional life which went far beyond Irish circles. Their ranks included judges, governors, mayors, doctors, bankers, clergymen, college professors and university presidents.

In 1919, the Irish-Americans were united and organised. The Ancient Order of Hibernians and The Ladies Auxiliary boasted of having more than half a million members devoted to the cause of Ireland. This boisterous group greatly displeased the Wilson administration. Whenever judge Daniel F Cohalan of the New York Supreme Court spoke, he pointed out that he spoke not for himself alone but twenty million Irish in the United States through an organisation called 'The Friends of Irish Freedom' (FOIF), Judge Cohalan was acknowledged as the voice of Irish-America. The Friends had branches in every city of size in the USA, and its members held positions ideally suited to greatly influence local politics and public opinion. The Envoy of the 'Irish Republic', Dr Patrick McCarton, believed that Judge Cohalan was in complete control of the Friends and that before America had entered World War One, he had used this national organisation in an attempt to defeat Wilson and to have Charles Evans Hughes elected President in 1916.

Throughout his life, Cohalan remained a staunch supporter of the Irish nationalist cause. Cohalan's grandfather and father left Cork at the height of the Famine in 1847 and, like the descendants of many Irish emigrants to America, harboured a deep hatred of the British Empire. Paradoxically, the hate was matched by an intense devotion to American principles of government and institutions. Cohalan's father, Timothy had joined the Fenians in the 1860s, and Daniel himself joined Clan Na Gael in the 1890s. Although never a member of the Clan executive, he soon gained the confidence of Devoy, who valued Cohalan for his political and social connections. The Clan was a source of funding and Cohalan played a crucial role in raising such funds. Knowing his importance, Irish nationalists of all hues, including Patrick Pearse and Douglas Hyde, beat a well-worn path to his door seeking funds and support. Cohalan, along with Devoy, helped coordinate Clan support for the 1916 uprising and also met with Roger Casement before his mission to Germany. Cohalan was a crucial figure in the launch of the FOIF, just a few weeks before the 1916 Rising. After the war, the FOIF claimed 275,000 members and had been described as the '...*most effective propaganda machine in Irish-American history*'.

Judge Daniel Cohalan, Éamon de Valera and another member of the Friends of Irish Freedom (FOIF) leadership, Judge John Goff. The photograph taken on the roof of the Waldorf Astoria Hotel, 23 June 1919, shortly after the arrival of de Valera in the USA. *(Library of Congress)*

During this time, the Friends of Irish Freedom received help from a variety of sources for an even greater variety of reasons. Cooperating with and supporting the work of the Friends were many small, local propaganda committees of limited interests, athletic clubs and youth organisations. The influence thrown behind the Irish cause by the clergy was vast. The effect of the various newspapers, even today, is unmeasurable. Many politicians on the national, state and local levels sincerely worked for the cause of Ireland while others supported it as a means of embarrassing the President and defeating his peace treaty and the proposed League of Nations.

Unlike their cousins in Ireland, the Irish in America could well afford to propagate the cause of freedom. The Irish organisations in America were financially secure. After large expenses incurred during 1919, the treasury of the Friends was still over the million dollar mark. Sentiment for the Irish cause had never been higher, and voluntary contributions were so easy to obtain that the Hibernians and Ladies Auxiliary felt that it would be unnecessary to go beyond their organisation to raise five million dollars for Irish freedom.

Yes, as long as the Irish-Americans remained united in their actions, any pressure which they would bring to bear for the cause of Ireland could not easily be disregarded or minimised. Theirs was a force to be taken into consideration.

These Irish-Americans had always been sympathetic to the perennial cause of the old country. Easter Week 1916 brought this emotion to the fore as never before. After the British put down the revolt, their treatment of the Patriots so aroused the ire of Irish-Americans that the participants became martyrs to the cause of freedom. These were fresh atrocities by the English to add to the history of burnings, lootings and killings. Had the Patriots received different treatment at the hands of the UK, more Americans would have been inclined to see them as radicals trying to capitalise on the UK's preoccupation with the war on the continent. After all, Ireland's Parliamentary representative, with or without popular support, had declared that Ireland would fight for the Allies.

Irish propagandists had been active in America for some time. They saw the Sinn Féin landslide victory of 1918 as a decisive event and feared their British counterparts would attempt to explain the triumph as merely a factional victory over the rival party. British propagandists did not adopt this line of attack, preferring to assail the Sinn Féin membership as: '..*idealistic, ill-balanced fanatics and mischief-makers*'.

Early in 1919, the average Irish-American did not understand what the exact nature of Ireland's political demand should be. In general, they wanted freedom for Ireland. Some saw it as recognition of the 'Irish Republic' by the United States Government; others saw it as self-determination for Ireland. The public at large made little distinction between the two. Both embodied their hopes and dreams. Even some of the leaders of the movement in America lost sight of the fact that a drive for recognition of the 'Irish Republic' elevated the issue to the international level, while a fight for self-determination might limit the scope of the subject to merely a domestic question for settlement within the United Kingdom. In the view of the many, it was a red herring: which often obliterated the real issues, so this confusion is quite understandable.

By organising sympathy, enthusiasm, and devotion to the Irish cause, it was hoped that enough pressure could be brought to bear as to force a settlement which would be favourable to the Irish. But no matter which avenue one chose, cultivation of favourable public opinion seemed to be a necessary step in America.

The campaign to bring the issue before the people of the USA and to utilise their voices in the fight for Irish freedom was gaining momentum and nothing demonstrated the breadth and depth of pro-Irish and anti-British feeling in the USA than the arrival of Éamon de Valera in New York. The New York-born de Valera made quite a favourable impression on the American public. Though his scholarly stoop seemed to detract from his total height, de Valera was, nonetheless, much taller than the average American of the day. His high forehead gave the impression that his black hair was receding. Americans thought his nose rather prominent but found that his glasses and deep-set eyes contributed to his dignity.

Éamon de Valera (*b*.14 October 1882, *d*.29 August 1975) was a prominent statesman and political leader in Ireland. De Valera's original birth certificate was registered in New Jersey, his name is given as George de Valero, and his father is listed as Spaniard Vivion de Valero.

Taken to Ireland at the age of two, he received a good education; in 1904, he graduated in mathematics from the Royal University of Ireland. He then studied for a year at Trinity College Dublin but, owing to the necessity of earning a living, did not proceed further and returned to teaching, this time at Belvedere College.

While he was already involved in the Gaelic Revival, de Valera's involvement in the political revolution began on 25 November 1913, when he joined the Irish Volunteers. The organisation was formed to oppose the Ulster Volunteers and ensure the enactment of the Irish Parliamentary Party's Third Home Rule Act won by its leader John Redmond. After the outbreak of World War One in August 1914, de Valera rose through the ranks and was elected captain of the Donnybrook branch. Preparations were pushed ahead for an armed revolt, and he was made commandant of the Third Battalion and adjutant of the Dublin Brigade. He took part in the Howth gun-running. Thomas MacDonagh swore De Valera into the oath-bound Irish Republican Brotherhood, which secretly controlled the central executive of the Volunteers. He opposed secret societies, but this was the only way he could be guaranteed full information on plans for the Rising.

On 24 April 1916, the Easter Rising began. Forces commanded by de Valera occupied Boland's Mill on Grand Canal Street in Dublin. His chief task was to cover the southeastern approaches to the city. After a week of fighting, the order came from Pádraig Pearse to surrender. One man's freedom fighter was another man's terrorist, so De Valera was court-martialled, convicted, and sentenced to death, but the sentence was commuted to penal servitude for life.

However, De Valera was among the few Republican leaders the British did not execute. It has been argued that his life was saved by four facts. First, he was one of the last to surrender and he was held in a different prison from other leaders, thus his execution was delayed by practicalities. Secondly, due to him being a US citizen, the US Consulate in Dublin made representations before his trial while the full legal situation was clarified. The UK was trying

Eamon de Valera in custody after the Easter Rising. *(Library of Congress)*

to bring the US into the war in Europe at the time, and the Irish American vote was important in US politics, though this did not prevent the execution of Tom Clarke who had been a naturalised American citizen since 1905. Third, when Lt Gen Sir John Maxwell reviewed his case he said, '*Who is he? I haven't heard of him before. I wonder would he be likely to make trouble in the future?*' On being told that de Valera was unimportant, he commuted the court-martial's death sentence to life imprisonment. De Valera had no Fenian family or personal background and his MI5 file in 1916 was very slim, detailing only his open membership in the Irish Volunteers. Fourth, by the time de Valera was court-martialled on 8 May, political pressure was being brought to bear on Maxwell to halt the executions; Maxwell had already told British Prime Minister H H Asquith that only two more were to be executed, Seán Mac Diarmada and James Connolly, although they were court-martialled the day after de Valera. His late trial,

representations made by the American Consulate, his lack of Fenian background and political pressure all combined to save his life, though had he been tried a week earlier he would probably have been shot.

After imprisonment in Dartmoor, Maidstone and Lewes prisons, de Valera and his comrades were released under an amnesty in June 1917. On 10 July he was elected a Member of Parliament for East Clare (the constituency which he represented until 1959) in a by-election caused by the death of the previous incumbent Willie Redmond. In the 1918 general election he was elected both for that seat and Mayo East. Because most other Irish rebellion leaders were dead, in 1917 he was elected President of Sinn Féin, the party which had been blamed incorrectly for provoking the Easter Rising. This party became the political vehicle through which the survivors of the Easter Rising channelled their republican ethos and objectives. The previous President of Sinn Féin, Arthur Griffith, had championed an

Anglo-Irish dual-monarchy based on the Austro-Hungarian model, with independent legislatures for both Ireland and Britain.

Sinn Féin won a huge majority in the 1918 general election, largely thanks to the British executions of the 1916 leaders, the threat of conscription with the Conscription Crisis of 1918 and the first-past-the-post ballot. They won 73 out of 105 Irish seats, with about 47 per cent of votes cast. 25 seats were uncontested. On 21 January 1919, 27 Sinn Féin MPs (the rest were imprisoned or impaired), calling themselves Teachtaí Dála, assembled in the Mansion House in Dublin and formed an Irish parliament - translatable into English as the Assembly of Ireland - known as Dáil Éireann. A Ministry or Aireacht was formed, under the leadership of the Príomh Aire (also called President of Dáil Éireann) Cathal Brugha. De Valera had been re-arrested in May 1918 and imprisoned and so could not attend the January session of the Dáil. He escaped from Lincoln Gaol in England in February 1919. As a result he replaced Brugha as Príomh Aire in the April session of Dáil Éireann.

In the hope of securing international recognition, Seán T O'Kelly was sent as envoy to Paris to present the Irish case to the Peace Conference convened at the end of World War One. When it became clear by May 1919 that this mission could not succeed, de Valera decided to visit the United States. The mission had three objectives: to ask for official recognition of the Irish Republic, to float a loan to finance the work of the Government (and by extension, the Irish Republican Army, the IRA), and to secure the support of the American people for the republic. His visit lasted from June 1919 to December 1920 and had mixed success. One negative outcome was the splitting of the Irish-American organisations into pro- and anti- de Valera factions.

De Valera managed to raise $5,500,000 from American supporters, an amount that far exceeded the hopes of the Dáil. Of this, $500,000 was devoted to the American presidential campaign in 1920, helping him gain wider public support there. In 1921 it was said that $1,466,000 had already been spent, and it is unclear when the net balance arrived in Ireland. He also had difficulties with a number of Irish-American leaders, such as John Devoy and Judge Daniel F. Cohalan, who resented the dominant position he established, preferring to retain their control over Irish affairs in the United States.

Meanwhile in Ireland, conflict between the British authorities and the Dáil (which the British declared illegal in September 1919) escalated into the Irish War of Independence. De Valera left day-to-day government, during his eighteen-month absence in the United States, to Michael Collins, his 29-year-old Minister for Finance.

Throughout his stay in America, de Valera appeared often wearing a high collar with a wide tie which was tied in a large knot. Besides this, it was noted that, contrary to the style of the day, he disliked wearing a hat. Generally, he appeared intellectual and distinguished. His personal appearance went far to prevent him from being painted as a red-shirted agitator who advocated seizure of private property, murder or bloody revolution. De Valera seemed too much the poet and scholar to be a Lenin or a Trotsky.

He first came to public attention by his participation in the Easter Week Rising. It is worth noting that although the Wilson administration was not sympathetic to Irish agitation, the State Department let it be known that de Valera would '...*not be interfered with unless he violated American laws or runs contrary to our treaty stipulations*'. His activities in America were never hampered by official interference even though it seems he had no passport.

In bringing his case to the people of America de Valera addressed mass meetings in fifty-six cities from New York to San Diego. The majority of these visits were officially requested by the local mayors. De Valera was the man of the hour and local politicians were eager to be seen at his side and gladly lauded the justice of the Irish cause.

To his huge American audiences, de Valera was the symbol of the nationalist movement and was wildly cheered wherever he spoke. The galleries and aisles of Madison Square Garden were filled long before the 'President of the Irish Republic' was scheduled to make his appearance on the night of 10 July 1919.

Twenty-sixth and Twenty-fifth Streets along with Madison and Fourth Avenues were packed solid when the fire chief ordered the doors to the Garden closed. The ardour of the crowd was stimulated by Irish pipers and a second band, both of which played familiar old Irish melodies. Everyone was provided with a Sinn Féin flag, and when de Valera rose to speak the Garden became a sea of tossing green, white, and gold. The crowd stood roaring with applause for ten and a half minutes. Finally, it was necessary to stop the bands so that the feverish applause might wear itself down.

This reception was hostile when compared with the demonstration given by 25,000 cheering Chicagoans at the Cubs National League baseball park. They, however, had the advantage of being warmed up before their thirty-one-minute ovation by Frank Walsh. His flair for oratory had not been dampened by an unsuccessful, earlier mission to Versailles in behalf of Ireland. Before the crowd shouldered the American and Irish flag-waving de Valera and carried him to the speakers' platform, Walsh had dwelled on the revolution-breeding conditions he said existed in the slums of London. He went on to tell how America's Secretary of State, Robert Lansing, dined at Buckingham Palace on $100,000 gold plate service while English workers were planning the destruction of the monarchy.

In this speech, the names of President Wilson and Prime Minister Lloyd George were freely hissed by the audience. The proposed League of Nations was scorned and Clemenceau was hooted. This type of action was not only in poor taste but was definitely detrimental to the objectives the Irish themselves were trying to achieve in America at this time. This was hardly the type of public response that would influence President Wilson in any decision to recognise the 'Irish Republic.'

De Valera put a stop to this behaviour when it became his turn to speak. The 17,000 at Madison Square Garden had booed and hissed Wilson for three minutes, but after de Valera spoke at Chicago, this behaviour was no longer a problem. The 25,000 at the Cubs' ball park listened to the schoolmaster and took their scolding. He told them: *'I would be deeply humiliated if my presence in your country and my advocacy of the just and reasonable claims of the Irish people should be made the occasion of any demonstration of hostility to your President. He is your President, and whilst as Americans, you have the right no doubt to criticise, you will forgive me for saying I feel it is not in good taste before a stranger. I am here*

to get the aid of all lovers of liberty in America, and they embrace all sections. Those who would identify us with any section and those who act unworthily of what is a holy cause are, even though it be unconsciously, the worst enemies of Ireland'.

De Valera concluded cleverly: *'...one or two in a meeting can make a great noise, and it would be a very obvious device for those who are opposed to our cause to send agents for that purpose.'*

This minor knuckle rapping was sufficient to suffocate the anti-Wilson outbursts, but had no adverse effect on de Valera's personal popularity nor on the popularity of his cause.

A few days after de Valera's successful Chicago speech the *San Francisco Examiner* saluted him *'as the rightful representative and head of your people and their free nation! God save the Republic of Ireland!'*

But even before he reached the City Hall in San Francisco, de Valera received honours and a public demonstration. Flowers and girls seemed to be the order of the day. Little girls in Irish costumes strewed his path with flowers and placed a crown of roses on his head. Another girl, older and very attractive, presented de Valera with a wreath. At the start of de Valera's ride from the Ferry Building, Irish sympathisers overpowered his driver and with a rope tied to the bumper dragged the vehicle victoriously up Market Street and on to the Saint Francis Hotel a dozen blocks away.

The press did do its duty for de Valera. The cause of the Irish people was so well brought before the common people that British propaganda was rebutted even before it reached the public. The airing of the British point of view was virtually restricted to a few periodicals which would have few ordinary men among their subscribers. If the public at large had so desired, the best way to become acquainted with opposing opinions would have been to check the articles blasted by the pro-Irish writers, who seem to have combed the literary journals for inspiration.

With general anti-League and isolationist sentiments on the rise at this same time, the Irish campaign made vast strides. William Randolph Hearst was still re-fighting the Revolution. Since 8 June he had had George Creel, Wilson's director of Public Information, writing a series of articles on the importance of the Irish question. They appeared in the *San Francisco Examiner* on Sundays, Wednesdays, and Fridays during June of 1919.

The last of the series, appearing on 2 July held the front page. Creel listed the persons on Royal pensions and the large amounts paid by Ireland to fortune-amassing British officials. The Lord Lieutenant had his salary listed as $100,000 per year plus a $225,000 allowance to cover household expenses and another $25,000 to keep him in uniforms and equipment. The *Examiner* readers were informed that petty judges got more for their services than United States Supreme Court Justices. The annual tribute to Great Britain in the form of rents, interest and salaries was put at $55,000,000; and since the Act of Union, *'England extorted two billion dollars'* from Ireland.

After overpowering the reader with these damning charges, Creel concluded: *'Today, no less than in every wretched, blood-stained day for seven long, terrible centuries, Ireland wants to be free'.*

For a week before de Valera reached the San Francisco Bay Area, the front page of the Examiner carried Irish headlines. Two of the more prominent were a report on the atrocious conditions existing in Ireland and one titled 'Britain Denies Erin's Rights to Self-Rule'. The rival *San Francisco Chronicle* was not to be outdone by Hearst in championing the Irish cause. It covered the Irish question being debated in the British House of Commons between Andrew Bonar Law, representing the loyalist position, and Joseph Devine of more liberal sentiments. Needless to say, the cause of a free Ireland emerged victoriously.

The Monitor, the house magazine of the Archdiocese of San Francisco had a permanent column devoted to 'Irish Views' and contained numerous other articles of interest to the Irish of the San Francisco Bay area. But Archbishop Edward J. Hanna went to sources much deeper than the *Monitor* for his sermon to the Ancient Order of Hibernians at San Francisco's Saint Mary's Cathedral. He pointed to the debt America owed the Irish for their participation in US military history, for their contribution to

Left to right: Harry Boland, Liam Mellows, Éamon de Valera, John Devoy (seated), Dr Patrick McCartan and Diarmuid Lynch. Photograph taken on the roof of the Waldorf Astoria, 23 June 1919. *(Library of Congress)*

American qualities of mind and the belief in God that gives America permanent greatness, for their spread of education and beneficence, and for their toilers who helped build America.

The Monitor presented the cause of Ireland with pale moderation compared with Reverend Peter C. Yorke, who was pastor of Saint Peter's Church in San Francisco and long time champion of labour, Catholic, and Irish causes. Father Yorke aired his positive views from the pulpit and when aroused often preached at every Sunday Mass. He spared no honours when de Valera attended Mass at St. Peter's. With de Valera sitting inside the sanctuary, he was treated as might be the official head of a foreign nation. From the pulpit, Father Yorke prayed God's blessing: *'O God of our Fathers... save thy servant, Edmone, the President of the Irish Republic, here present. May he be to his people as Moses and as Peter and as Patrick, a leader sent by Thee to lead them* [the Irish people] *like Moses out of the house of bondage, to establish them like Peter on the impregnable rock of liberty...'*

As supercharged as the American champions of the Irish cause were, they did not overshadow the activities of de Valera. He was a young man of thirty-seven, inspired by the cause of freedom for his people. The *Monitor* claimed 200,000 had heard him speak on various occasions in the San Francisco area. His three days in the Bay Area were so filled with engagements that many of them overlapped.

Following the official greeting by the Mayor at the San Francisco City Hall, de Valera addressed the convention of the Ancient Order of Hibernians at the Civic Auditorium. The same night, Friday, 18 July he returned to the auditorium to participate in a mass meeting with Archdeacon James Grattan Mythen, who was the active head of the Protestant Friends of Ireland; Archbishop Hanna; Supervisor Gallagher; Father Yorke and Father Augustine, from The Order of Saints Francis and Clare, the Franciscan who had ministered to the Irishmen who were executed for their participation in the Easter Week Rising.

The police found it impossible to clear the aisles, for an overflow crowd of 12,000 had succeeded in gaining admission. Thousands filled the streets, while inside de Valera made his appeal to the people for recognition of the 'Irish Republic'.

De Valera did not permit the ardour of public opinion to cool. At ten o'clock on Saturday morning, he received an honorary Doctor of Philosophy degree at Saint Ignatius College from Father President, Patrick J. Foote, SJ. This was one of three honorary degrees given him on his American tour. The others were Doctors of Laws given by De Paul University and the University of Valparaiso in Indiana.

After receiving his degree at Saint Ignatius College, de Valera hurried back to the St. Francis Hotel where a reception for the priests of the Archdiocese was being held. From there, he went to an 11:30 am reception for the nuns at the Young Men's Institute Building. Prior to his afternoon motor trip through the city, he was able to confer with prominent Irish leaders of the city back at the hotel. The official appearances of the day were rounded out by his Letterman Hospital speech and the Hibernian banquet at the Civic Auditorium.

On the following day, between his noon address in Golden Gate Park and the main meeting at the Oakland Auditorium, he found time to combine his business with a bit of pleasure at an Irish picnic for the benefit of the Jesuit Fathers. Besides his scheduled speeches, de Valera took advantage of any opportunity to present his case to the people. He spoke to several thousand at the Union Iron Works and at the Bethlehem ship plant. He spoke in Gaelic to a few of the old folks under the care of the Little Sisters of the Poor at their home in San Francisco. Some of them had taken part in the uprising in 1867. De Valera expressed his wish that they would all live to see Ireland free.

From the fact that the 'Irish Republic' was not recognised by the Wilson administration it cannot be concluded that the American campaign for public opinion was so much wasted motion. It was not. War-weary and ally-seeking Great Britain were made acutely aware of the ill will felt towards her in America. At Versailles and immediately after, Britain dealt with a President who needed her cooperation in order to realise his own personal dream - the League of Nations. Britain, therefore, could afford to ignore American public opinion at that time. This, however, would not always be the case.

Wilson and his League were then and there. The Irish Question had generated anti-British feeling in America even before Eire was created. The ill-feeling was widespread and long-lasting: it clearly influenced the politicians and military alike.

Naval Expansion

In general, the naval policy of the USA in the period 1919–1932 was the maintaining of a maritime establishment equal to that of Great Britain and more substantial than that of Japan.

Immediately after the Great War, the UK had the world's largest and most powerful navy, followed by the USA and more distantly by Japan. The three nations had been allies for the war, but now a naval arms race appeared to be in the offing and began in the United States. President Woodrow Wilson's administration announced successive plans for the expansion of the US Navy from 1916 to 1919 that would have resulted in a massive fleet of fifty modern battleships. At the time, it was engaged in building six battleships and six battle-cruisers.

To understand the naval policy of the United States, it is necessary, first, to summarise the facts and events brought about by the US maritime expansion programme and, second, to analyse the motives behind this building plan.

It was in 1916 that the United States decidedly became sea-minded. For half a century the American people had thought very little about the sea, for there were more natural ways of earning a living in this country than by the hard, self-denying labour of the sea. The resources of our country made our people much more interested in agriculture and internal improvements. The USA became highly industrialised - factories were built at strategic sites, and the great cities came into being. People became imperialistic; prestige demanded that the USA become a world power with outlying possessions of their own. Probably the outstanding aspect of this increased nationalism was a desire for power on the ocean.

Modern US navalism dated back to 1880 although its seeds had been sown some twenty years earlier when the first experiments with iron side armour and turret mountings, as well as with steam propulsion had introduced the machine age into naval warfare.

In 1880 the amount spent on the navy was at a low point, but by 1890, there was an extraordinary rise in expenditure, while the 1900 figure more than doubled the 1890 amount. Since that time it rose almost steadily until it reached its abnormal peak in the world war years.

It was in the administration of President Chester A Arthur that a modest expansion of the navy was begun. There was no thought of disputing the 'dominion of the sea' with Great Britain's fleet, and America's naval policy at the time was decidedly not maritime expansion. As late as 1894, they were content to stand about sixth on the list of naval powers. The idea of parity with the large British fleet would hardly have been advanced by the most ambitious naval expansionist. Only ten years later a significant change had taken place.

By 1904, America had built a fleet that was the second largest in the world, surpassed only by that of Great Britain.

Just what events had occurred that made naval defence such an ongoing issue? First, there was the Samoan affair that stirred the national honour. In March 1889, it was rumoured that a German ship had sunk an American vessel.

The Samoan Crisis was a standoff between the USA, Imperial Germany, and the United Kingdom from 1887 over control of the Samoan Islands during the Samoan Civil War. The incident involved three US Navy warships (the sloop-of-war USS *Vandalia*, the screw steamer USS *Trenton*, and the gunboat USS *Nipsic*) and three Imperial German Navy warships (the gunboats SMS *Adler* and SMS *Eber* and the corvette SMS *Olga*), keeping each other at bay over several months in Apia harbour, which was monitored by the British corvette HMS *Calliope*.

A wave of excitement and patriotic fervour swept over the country as the historian, and Harry Thurston Peck recorded in his book *Twenty Years of the Republic*, published by Dodd Mead and Company, New York, 1920. '*In San Francisco, great crowds filled the streets and massed themselves about the newspaper offices, awaiting the posting of further bulletins. The tone of the press was one of intense hostility to Germany. The government at Washington began preparing for an emergency that might arise. All the vessels of the Pacific squadron were notified to be in readiness.*'

At last the real news came. The rumour had been false - a typhoon had wrecked the ships - yet, the Americans began to realise that a navy was necessary. Second, there was the

Wrecked vessels at Apia Harbor, Upolu, Samoa, during salvage efforts soon after the storm. The view looks about northward, with USS *Trenton*, the sunken USS *Vandalia* to the left and the beached German corvette *Olga* at right.Wreckage just off *Trenton's* stern may be from the German gunboat *Eber*, which was destroyed when she struck the harbour reef during the hurricane. *(USN)*

Venezuelan affair with Great Britain, which brought home clearly the fact that if the American government were to assert authority that implied war, the provision would have to be made for fighting the war.

Even though it was discovered that Great Britain was mainly right in her demands on Venezuela, this did not alter the psychological force behind naval expansion.

Third, there was the victorious war with Spain which generated great enthusiasm for the navy. The American Navy had covered itself with glory in the war, and the nation was very proud of it. It was not difficult to prove to the people and Congress that US naval power must be expanded since there were also the Philippine Islands and Porto Rico to protect. The nation started to realise that they were becoming a significant world power.

Theodore Roosevelt was mainly responsible for the big navy idea. In his address before the Naval War College in June 1897, he paid tribute to peace at the same time that he advocated a big navy: *'In all our history there has never been a time when preparedness for war was any menace to peace. On the contrary, again and again, we have owed peace to the fact that we were prepared for war. Arbitration is an* excellent thing, but ultimately those who wish to see this country at peace with foreign nations will be wise if they place reliance upon a first-class fleet of first-class battleships, rather than on any arbitration treaty which the wit of man can devise. A really great people, proud and high-spirited, would face all the disasters of war rather than purchase that base prosperity which is bought at the price of national honor. We ask for a great navy partly because we feel that no national life is worth having if the nation is not willing, when the need shall arise, to stake everything on the supreme arbitrament of war, and to pour out its blood, its treasure, and tears like water rather than to submit to the loss of honor and renown.'*

The rise of the battleship.

It was an Italian engineer who first came up with the idea of a battleship. Vittorio Cuniberti reasoned way back in 1903 that soon naval vessels would not only have to face attack from the surface. Torpedoes would make them vulnerable from below and, who knows, one day bombs could be dropped by 'aero craft' making ships susceptible from above as well.

His solution was simple. The modern naval vessel, he considered, would have to be fast, incredibly well armoured and fitted only with massive guns. No more pea-shooters for close-range stuff, just lots and lots of monsters. That way, the battleship could use its speed to get to the right place while its armour resisted any attack from above or below. And then, when it was in the right position, the enemy could be bombarded with a hail of twelve-inch, or better still sixteen-inch shells.

Cuniberti thought there was no point fitting smaller supplementary guns. Those just confused things - the splashes made when their shells missed the target would obscure the view for the main armament and make life difficult for the loaders in the magazines. If there was only one type of shell in there, the chance of sending the wrong type to the wrong gun was eliminated.

It was sound military reasoning- but there was another advantage to such a huge and powerful ship. In a word, prestige. Let the world know you have a 'battleship' and suddenly you are a force to be reckoned with.

Japan was the first nation to start building such a vessel but, inevitably, it was the British who got theirs into the water first. It was constructed in just one hundred days, it was christened by King Edward VII and it would give its name to every battleship that ever there

was. It was called HMS *Dreadnought*.

At this time, Great Britain and Germany entered into a naval race that ended in the ruin of Germany. Great Britain, alarmed by the growth of the German Navy, brought out in 1906 HMS *Dreadnought,* the first ever all-big-gun battleship, planned to make obsolete at a stroke the whole German Navy. The design succeeded; but unfortunately, it also made obsolete the rest of the British Navy and every other navy as well. The battleship fleet built up during the Roosevelt administration was now only a second-string defence. The superiority of the British fleet had been removed; all the nations could start at an equal point in the new race for dreadnought tonnage, which had become the only thing that counted. The Germans and British plunged ahead, but the Americans held back, their expenditures increasing steadily though not spectacularly.

By 1914, at the end of the next ten-year period, the British had built forty-six dreadnoughts and cruisers, the Germans had twenty-eight, and even Japan had ten. The United States had only twelve. The second power standard had been dropped, but still the competitive idea was in the minds of the people, and just a few years later the USA was asserting its right to a navy at least equal to that of the

HMS *Dreadnought* of the British Navy, as seen in 1906. This was the battleship that changed the face of naval warfare.
(Russell Plummer Collection)

USS *Olympia* was a protected cruiser that saw service in the United States Navy from her commissioning in 1895 until 1922. This vessel became famous as the flagship of Commodore George Dewey at the Battle of Manila Bay during the Spanish–American War in 1898. The ship was decommissioned after returning to the US in 1899 but was returned to active service in 1902 until being decommissioned in 1922. *(USN)*

strongest power on the seas and greater by one third than the next most powerful fleet.

This seems to have come about by historical accident. The outbreak of the war in Europe added to the excitement of the Vera Cruz landing and the Mexican border trouble had naturally awakened great interest in the state of America's military machinery. During the neutral years, unusual changes in commerce and finances in the United States had taken place. Large groups and interests turned their attention to maritime affairs. Decreased production in Europe made increased demands on American goods, and shipping and commercial interests made huge dividends. As a nation, the USA became highly nationalistic, and so their navy plans were transformed. President Woodrow Wilson in his annual message of December 1911, declared *'A powerful navy we have always regarded as our proper and natural means of defense.'*

The European War promised to give practically for the first time, a sort of laboratory trial of the effectiveness of the machine-age navy. For a time, the belief had gained ground that the submarine had significantly reduced the importance of the big ship, but, at Jutland in May 1916, the success of the heavily armoured vessel with large-calibre guns had disposed naval men to return to their faith in the powerful

capital ship. Indeed, in a report, the Secretary of the Navy for 1920 clearly stated that the all-big-gun ship was the best.

After the submarine sinking of the *Lusitania,* the great campaign of the naval building began. The naval bill of 1915 carried increased appropriations, but that was only a beginning. The Republicans were not satisfied and referred to the weak-kneed attitude of the Wilson administration on defence. They asked for the old second power standard, which seemed a simple demand, hallowed by precedent. The *New York Times* of 10 November 1915 reported that the Secretary of the Navy, Josephus Daniels, had asked the General Board to prepare a five-year programme that would make the US Navy second to Great Britain's. This he felt would be the correct answer to the critics who said the Wilson administration was neglecting national defence.

President Wilson was in favour of it, and when Congress reopened in December 1915, diplomatic tension and patriotic fervour became so great that his entire message was devoted to the subject of national defence. *'I have spoken today, gentlemen, upon a single theme, the thorough preparation of the nation to care for its security, and to make sure of entire freedom to play an important role in this hemisphere and in the world which we all believe to have been providentially assigned to it.'*

Wilson gave further credence to the programme, when at the beginning of 1916 he went on a tour of the USA, speaking on behalf of preparedness and his re-election. It ended in St. Louis on 3 February. In an afternoon speech, Wilson had portrayed the horrors of the war in Europe, but at the St. Louis Coliseum that evening, his subject was preparedness. At first, the audience seemed unfriendly, but as he made his plea stronger and stronger, he carried his listeners to emotional heights. Possibly, in response to this emotionalism, he too was carried away, for he cried that the American navy '*...ought in my judgement be incomparably the most adequate navy in the world'.*

Thus the idea that the United States Navy was not merely as the second power of the Mc-Kinley and Roosevelt days, but as the supreme naval nation was introduced into the body of American naval policy.

The Naval Act of 1916 was a milestone in the naval expansion. In its final form the programme enacted by Congress did not authorise a navy 'incomparably the most adequate in the world', but it did provide for the building within three years of 813,000 tons of naval vessels, calling for ten battleships with twelve sixteen-inch guns, and six battlecruisers, armed with eight sixteen-inch guns and capable of a thirty-four knot speed. Also, the programme planned for ten scout cruisers, fifty destroyers, sixty-seven submarines, and some lesser types, the whole estimated to cost from $544,000,000.

Actual appropriations could be made for one year alone, therefore in the first year it provided for four battleships, four battlecruisers, four light cruisers, and a few of the lesser vessels.

The Act of 1916 would have given the United States a great preponderance in massive ships. A forecast of the anticipated naval situation of 1923, made prior to the Washington Conference by Congressman Frederick A Britten of the House Committee on Naval Affairs, showed that altogether the American fleet would have possessed thirty-three capital ships as compared with thirty-five in the British navy, but the American ships would have been larger and would have had greater gun power. This comparison led Hector Bywater, the British naval writer, to observe in 1921 in his book *Sea Power in the Pacific: 'On the basis of modern armoured vessels completed, building, and authorised the British navy has already declined to the second rank. And in this connection, it is important to note that the modern armoured vessel - the capital ship - remains in the reasoned opinion of the British Admiralty the unit on which sea power is built up'.*

The 1916 programme was never completed. In a few months, the USA was at war with Germany, and the programme was cast aside as useless. What was required to fight the Germans was not battleships or battlecruisers, it was merchant ships to carry food and light men-of-war capable of dropping depth bombs on submarines. Of the eight leviathans which were to have been commenced by July 1917, the

The USS *Maine* (BB-10), the lead ship of her class of pre-dreadnought battleships, was the second ship of the United States Navy to be named in honour of the 23rd state. *Maine* was laid down in February 1899 at the William Cramp & Sons shipyard in Philadelphia. She was launched in July 1901 and commissioned into the fleet in December 1902. *(USN)*

HMS *Lord Nelson* was a pre-dreadnought battleship launched in 1906 and completed in 1908. She was the Royal Navy's last pre-dreadnought. The ship was the flagship of the Channel Fleet when World War One began in 1914. *Lord Nelson* was transferred to the Mediterranean Sea in early 1915 to participate in the Dardanelles Campaign. She remained there, becoming the flagship of the Eastern Mediterranean Squadron, which was later redesignated the Aegean Squadron. After the Ottoman surrender in 1918, the ship moved to the Black Sea where she remained as flagship before returning to the UK in May 1919. *Lord Nelson* was placed into reserve upon her arrival and sold for scrap in June 1920. *(Russell Plummer Collection)*

USA laid down just one, but the destroyer programme had been significantly increased. By 1919, the USA had built five times as many destroyers as had been authorised by the 1916 programme. Of the ten battleships planned, they had started only two; only two of the ten light cruisers were laid down, and of the six battle cruisers, not one was started.

The 1916 naval programme set in motion programmes and counter programmes. It gave rise to suspicions and alarms and finally led to a series of remarkable international conferences.

Motives Behind the Expansion Programme
American naval policy had its roots deep in national history. Once free of Great Britain, the chief purpose of American politicians for many years was to keep out of European affairs, especially out of the Napoleonic wars waging between Great Britain and France.

At the same time, commercial interests were trying to trade with all the European nations, regardless of their state of belligerency. Naval policy evolved fundamentally out of this state of affairs. America looked upon itself as neutrals and insisted upon rights as a neutral. America claimed the right in time of war to carry everything except military supplies to both

belligerents unless the belligerent port was actively blockaded. The outbreak of the world war in 1914 found the two countries firmly supporting their traditional doctrines. Great Britain paid little attention to American demands. In carrying out her plan to starve Germany into submission, Great Britain often stopped American ships at sea and this interference, justifiable from the British point of view, crystallised the demand in this country for a navy second to none.

In an article in the *New York Times*, James T. Shotwell, Professor of History at Columbia University, wrote: '*All through American history, there has been one supreme principle of naval rights which has remained an ideal unattained, and that is freedom of the seas. On the other hand, the British have almost as consistently opposed this principle. The reason for the two national attitudes lies chiefly in the fact that the preemption of the United States has been that in most wars it would be neutral; therefore it was but natural that it should be the champion of neutral rights against belligerents*'.

On the other hand, Great Britain involved as it was in the maintenance of a worldwide empire, had been more likely to think in belligerent terms and was more likely to be drawn into conflicts that were arising almost anywhere throughout the world.

George Young, an adviser on international affairs to the British Labour party, formed in 1900, claimed that the two policies — freedom of the seas and control of the seas — were merely points of view of the same thing. He explained that Great Britain, fighting for the freedom of the seas refused her by the Papal Bull dividing the seas between Spain and Portugal, acquired command of the seas and predicted that the same outcome was inevitable in the case of America. To gain freedom of the seas, America would very likely also gain command of the seas, unless something different was definitely planned. *'This belief in our neutral rights and in the freedom of the seas is fundamental in our creed and has been a most useful argument for the advocating of large navies'.*

Rear Admiral William L Rodgers declared: *'The principal diplomatic service of the American navy will always be found in its support of neutrality and the neutral rights of commerce.*

'This support is a fundamental policy which directs the shipbuilding programme of the Navy Department. For the navy must be adequate to guard its commerce when other nations are at war'.

'As an outgrowth of this policy our freedom of the seas, it has naturally developed in our naval policy that our navy should be strong enough to protect our commerce'.

This was strikingly emphasised while debating the Cruiser Bill of 1929 by Senator William Edgar Borah, one of the isolationalists: *'So Mr President,... we have in our minds the sole question of how we are going to protect our commerce. I do not think many think of the use of the Navy in any other light. The moving, controlling question is how to protect our commerce against the inroads of those whom be engaged in war'.*

Congressman Frederick A Britten objected strenuously to what he said was British regulation of American commerce during the World War. *'In order to ship furniture, shoe polish, etc., from my own district to Norway in American boats from our own ports, I had to go to the British embassy here for a permit to ship them. The application had to indicate the character of the material, how it was to be packed, the size of it, and the cost. That information was turned over to the commercial office of Great Britain in London. The permit itself was issued in London. Do you think a powerful nation upon the seas would countenance such an insult? No; it never would have asked that permission.'*

Born in Chicago, Illinois, Britten attended Healds Business College, San Francisco, California. He was a construction worker and a business executive before his political career

Imperial Japanese Navy (IJN) dreadnought battleship *Nagato*. This vessel was laid down in 1920 The ship was formally commissioned on 25 November 1920 to begin a career that would last until the end of World War Two. *(USN)*

began. He served as a member of the Chicago, Illinois, city council from 1908 to 1912. He served as member and chairman of the city civil service committee in Chicago in 1909. Then he served as a member of the executive committee of the American group of the Interparliamentary Union from 1923 to 1934. He also served as a delegate to the Republican National Convention in 1936.

Britten was elected as a Republican to the Sixty-third and to the ten succeeding Congresses (4 March 1913–3 January 1935). On 5 April 1917, he was one of the 50 representatives who voted against declaring war on Germany. He also served as chairman of the Committee on Naval Affairs (seventieth and seventy-first Congress).

Congressman Britten stated: *'It has been argued that the American doctrine of neutral rights had very little value. It is true that neutral trade rose to unprecedented heights both before 1812 and 1917, and it is also true that when the USA began fighting, their profits were lost. But even though this is fact, yet American pride prohibited the nation from submitting to interference with their neutral trade on the part of a belligerent. Some thought that it was sad that the plans for abolishing wars went awry, for it is only through peace that commerce could be really made profitable'.*

The fundamental motive behind US naval policy was that of protectionism. This was and is the economic policy of restricting imports from other countries through methods such as tariffs on imported goods, import quotas, and a variety of other government regulations. Proponents claim that protectionist policies shield the producers, businesses, and workers of the import-competing sector in the country from foreign competitors. However, they also reduce trade and adversely affect consumers in general (by raising the cost of imported goods), and harm the producers and workers in export sectors, both in the country implementing protectionist policies and in the countries protected against.

There is a consensus among economists that protectionism has an adverse effect on economic growth and economic welfare, while free trade, deregulation, and the reduction of trade barriers has a positive impact on economic growth. Protectionism has been implicated by some scholars as the cause of some financial crises, in particular, the Great Depression. However, trade liberalisation can sometimes result in substantial and unequally distributed losses and gains, and can, in the short run, cause significant economic dislocation of workers in import-competing sectors. It is a policy that is continued today by President Donald J Trump.

Back in the day it was seen that the navy had to defend American heritage - seen as the land where 106,500,000 people lived in 1920 - the wealth that was the outgrowth of the country's enormous resources, social interests and institutions. Fortunately, it was not difficult to guard the United States against enemy attack. The geographic position gave the advantage of long distances on the east and west between the country and foreign nations and an invasion of the country along either of the shores was almost unbelievable.

Congressman Britten: *'There is no reasonable chance that a foreign goverment would be able to take the coast of the United States against the defense of our fleet. The only danger would be from enemy aircraft carriers reaching a distance from which it would be*

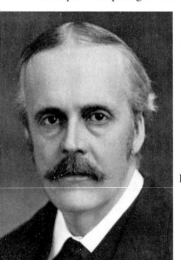

Left: Arthur James Balfour, 1st Earl of Balfour, KG, OM, PC, FRS, FBA, DL [C] (*b*. 25 July 1848, *d*. 19 March 1930) was a British statesman who served as Prime Minister of the United Kingdom from 1902 to 1905.

Right: Arthur Hamilton Lee, 1st Viscount Lee of Fareham, GCB, GCSI, GBE, PC [C] (*b*. 8 November 1868, *d*. 21 July 1947) was an English soldier, diplomat, politician, philanthropist and patron of the arts. He was also First Lord of the Admiralty 13 February 1921–31 October 1922.

Left: William Edgar Borah [R] (*b*. 29 June 1865, *d*. 19 January 1940) was an outspoken Republican US Senator, one of the best-known figures in Idaho's history.

Right: Charles Evans Hughes Sr. [R] (*b*. 11 April 1862, *d*. 27 August 1948) was an American statesman and the 11th Chief Justice of the United States. He was also the 36th Governor of New York, a presidential nominee in the 1916 presidential election, and the 44th United States Secretary of State. *(both NARA)*

possible to send out aircraft to raid coastal cities.

Next to guarding the continental United States, the safeguarding of the Panama Canal was necessary since war vessels could pass through it from ocean to ocean with great expediency. Commercially, also, the canal was and is of tremendous value and the USA could not permit its capture.

In the Pacific, the question arose as to how far the United States should extend its naval power. The imperialists within the USA advocated that the Philippine islands must be defended a defence which would require an extremely large navy since the forces would be maintained in waters far distant from their homeland. The protection of the Hawaiian Islands was carefully made. Pearl Harbor, located 2100 miles from San Francisco, was regarded as being well fortified. By 1929 it was considered a strategic point of importance by American naval officers and it had been built up to a high point of excellence and strength., as William T Stone recorded in 'Outlying Naval Stations', published in Vol. V of the journal of the Foreign Policy Association Service. 'Heavy guns defend it, and the barracks, good roads, electric lights, the modern water and sewage system, its radio station, its submarine base facilities, its oil depot, its large dry-dock and machine shop to repair battleships, all contribute to make Pearl Harbor an extremely up-to-date strong base and a protection for the United States against attack.'

By now it was expected that the US Navy

was to use 'neutral rights' to guard commerce. In the case of Great Britain and Japan, both highly industrialised, populous, maritime countries, the imports from overseas lands is an absolute necessity. To these nations protection of the sea lanes is as important as the protection of their homelands. One important aspect of modern warfare is the struggle of the warring nations for food and materials and the British are particularly vulnerable. Without their navy and air defence they could easily be blockaded.

Fortunately, the food resources of the United States were so great that there was never any fear of starvation because of a blockade.

As Lillian Ruth Nelson, of Loyola University, wrote in her dissertation: *Our wheat, fruits, meats, fish, and dairy products are sufficient. We have, of course, come to rely upon imported foods, also, such as coffee, sugar, cacao, and exotic tropical fruits and in time of war, the coffee situation could be most irritating. We are the greatest coffee users in the world, importing their entire supply and we would dislike having the importation of it cut off. However, its loss would not be disastrous.*

Regarding other raw materials, the United States is again fortunate, but we do lack some of the products necessary for modern industrial efficiency. Particularly, do we require certain minerals? Even though the United States produces about forty per cent of the world's minerals, yet we import other minerals. The Committee on Foreign and Domestic Mining Policy of the Mining and Metallurgical Society of America has listed the minerals we lack

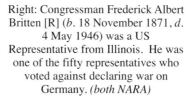

Left: Josephus Daniels [D] (*b.* 18 May 1862, *d.* 15 January 1948) was a newspaper editor and publisher from North Carolina who became active in politics.

Right: Congressman Frederick Albert Britten [R] (*b.* 18 November 1871, *d.* 4 May 1946) was a US Representative from Illinois. He was one of the fifty representatives who voted against declaring war on Germany. *(both NARA)*

entirely and those of which we have inadequate supplies nickel, cobalt, platinum, tin, diamond dust, antimony, asbestos, manganese, mica, and others.

The committee illustrated the importance of imported minerals by using manganese as an example. To the steel industry, manganese is indispensab1e. It is used as a deoxidiser, and a desulphuriser, and as an alloy to provide further resistance to steel. We do have a small supply of manganese ore, but it could be mined only at great expense and would very soon be exhausted. To illustrate how necessary steel is to modern warfare, Colonel William P. Wooten explained that during the World War, the Allies used nearly two and a half tons of steel annually for each soldier in the field. Since steel is essential to military equipment, and since manganese is crucial to the manufacture of steel, our navy must make it possible for manganese to reach us at all times.

Besides certain minerals, the United States also lacks such products as rubber, which we import from the British and Dutch East Indies, sisal from Mexico, Manila from the Philippines, and shellac from India. The task of guaranteeing that these supplies will reach the United States at all times, belongs to the navy and it is a most difficult if not impossible job. To do so would mean that the United States must maintain a navy strong enough to defend American trade everywhere in any waters of the world, against any power or combination of forces. Theoretically, this might be possible; but in practice, such an aim is impossible of realisation. If war should come, the United States must expect to worry along without

certain imports and look for new sources wherever possible. Since protection of commerce is such a hopeless charge, it seems more feasible to guarantee this by planning for peaceful and cordial relations with the world. When naval expansion became so high as to interfere with the maintenance of friendship with other countries it would do more harm than good to American commerce.

The New Naval Race.

It was in 1919 that the world realised that a new naval race was in progress with Japan, Great Britain and the United States the main participants. The Great War had ended, and the need for US products ceased. That nation's commerce was practically at a standstill, but the vast war-materials machine had to go on. It was decided to go on with the 1916 programme. The second of the 1916 battleships was laid down in 1919, and a start was made upon the other eight. In 1920, the remaining eight light cruisers were also begun as well as the first of the battlecruisers. In 1921 the USA made a start on the last five battlecruisers.

By waiting until 1919 to begin their programme, the USA had all the lessons of the war at their disposal, and as a result, the new ships were to be so much more potent than the earlier dreadnoughts as to outclass them entirely.

On 18 December 1920, the *Washington Post* made an apparently startling discovery: 'Within three years the United States will hold supremacy on the seas. After three hundred years of undisputed supremacy, the British navy will take second place, the Stars and Stripes will float over a fleet stronger than the two fleets *that fought the battle of Jutland.'*

There was only one minor problem with that; calculations like this rested on the assumption that US new building, would bring no answer from overseas, and that it could plunge into a project for supremacy without arousing other people's navalists. It was a completely unwarranted assumption, but it stirred up American pride and ambitions, especially amongst the so-called 'imperialist hawks' in the Department of the Navy.

Japan, meanwhile had seized Shantung and Tsingtan, crushing its way to dominance over China; she had occupied the former German colonies in the Pacific and planted a foothold in Siberia; she had strengthened her public finances, extended her manufacturing and commerce and in general had taken a huge step toward the goal nearest the nation's heart - that of ascendancy in the Far East. As one of the three great powers of the world, she challenged white supremacy. Her so-called 'eight and eight' naval plan was ambitious. This was designed to give the Japanese navy by 1927, two squadrons each of eight battleships and eight armoured cruisers none of which should be more than

eight years old. A third squadron was to be formed of older battleships. Also, Japan planned to build twenty-six small cruisers and to increase as well her submarines, torpedo boat destroyers and aviation flotillas. Last, of all, she proposed to erect a series of coastal defences that would give her an impregnable line of sea fortresses and naval bases from Sakhalin on the north, to the Bonin Islands, and thence to Marianne, Caroline, Marshall, and Pelew archipelagos in the central Pacific. She would thus have a line of military posts from the equator to the fiftieth degree north latitude, interrupted only by the American Philippines.

At the completion of Japan's new naval plan, she would have only two capital ships fewer than America, and her ships would have been more modern. This new development caused grave concern in the United States and Great Britain, while Australia and New Zealand watched with jealous hostility Japan's expansion southward.

Naturally, Great Britain could not stay out of this naval race. The deep feeling with which the doctrine of naval supremacy was regarded was given expression by Winston Churchill, who

The *Akagi* was laid down in 1920 as an Amagi-class battlecruiser but was converted to an aircraft carrier while still under construction to comply with the terms of the Washington Naval Treaty. It entered service in 1927. The vessel was rebuilt from 1935 to 1938 with the original three flight decks consolidated into a single enlarged flight deck and an island superstructure. *(Russell Plummer Collection)*

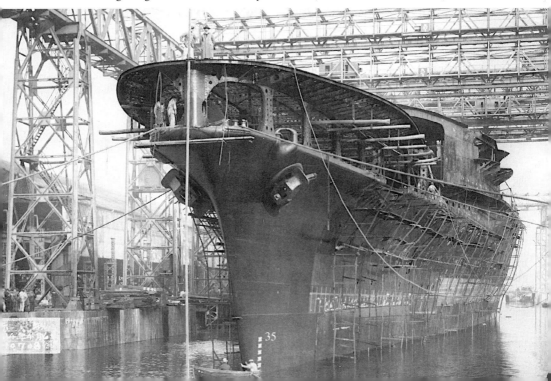

said: '...*Nothing in the world, nothing that you may think of, or dream of, or anyone may tell you, no arguments, however spacious, no appeals, however seductive, must lead you to abandon that naval supremacy on which the life of our country depends.*'

Speaking in the House of Commons on 17 March 1921, Lt Col Martin Archer-Shee explained: '*By 1925, this great nation overseas will have built a fleet which will practically make obsolete all of the battleships of our fleet with the exception of the Hood.....To meet this situation the government proposes to lay down four ships only this year.*'

But the four, it was said, would go to 50,000 tons apiece and each would mount eighteen-inch guns. The dreadnoughts the USA were constructing would be retired by these super-ships. Another new American building programme would be necessary, which would frighten the Japanese into their new building programme and so the race would go on. Neither the United States, Great Britain nor Japan would stop as long as the other nations kept on. It would avail them little to match new ship with the new ship, plane with plane, gas with gas, for their relative positions would remain the same.

Great Britain and Japan were limited by depleted treasuries. It is sometimes said that the USA had more money than Great Britain and Japan combined and could outbuild them. But would Great Britain and Japan wait for the US to finish such a massive plan? Very likely not. They would form a combination and strike before the USA were ready. The prospect of spending millions upon something so unstable that what one nation did would completely upset everything done by another could not have any popularity with the taxpayer.

It appeared that the continuance of the programme was highly undesirable and it was the height of statesmanship for the United States to invite her chief naval rivals on 11 August 1921 for a Conference on the Limitation of Armament.

When the Harding Administration assumed control of the government, there were obstacles before it. Anglo-American relations were strained. Great Britain was maintaining and increasing a vast fleet, but not only that was remaining a party to a military alliance with Japan which needed no renewal to keep it alive.

The USA feared that this alliance might be directed against it. Again, its relations with Great Britain were strained due to the fact that certain Americans had sympathised too concretely with the Irish in their hopes of becoming free.

Concerning the Far East and the Pacific, there were unsettled questions which had produced an international tension. Their adjustment was necessary before any naval limitation could be arranged. They concerned China, as well as the United States, France, Great Britain and Japan. Charles E Hughes, Secretary of State, was anxious to get these international matters settled amicably.

Besides, there was a strong current of public opinion in favour of naval disarmament. Appeals were sent to Congress; speeches were made from pulpits and platforms, articles appeared in the newspapers, all demanding that naval expenditures be reduced. It was difficult to see wherein it was practical to build battleships costing; it was said '*...nearly forty-million dollars apiece, which become obsolete and useless after fifteen years of peaceful floating about the seas?*'

There were, however, 'doves' in both the US government and the Navy. Secretary of the Navy Josephus Daniels gave a statement to the newspapers favouring naval disarmament: *With reference to the naval program of the United States, there are just two courses open. First, to secure an international agreement with all, or practically all nations, which will guarantee an end of competition in navy building, reduce the national burden and lead in the movement to secure and buttress world peace. Second, to hold aloof from agreement with the other nations as to size of armament. This will require us to build a navy strong enough and powerful enough to be able on our own to protect Americans and American shipping, defend American policies in the distant possessions as well as at home, and by the presence of sea power to comand the respect and fear of the world.*

Of the two plans I press the first. An international conference to end competitive navy construction was proposed by me in my first annual report in December 1913, and proposed in every successive report and in every hearing before the Naval Affairs Committee for nearly eight years'.

In December 1920, Senator William E

Borah introduced a joint resolution - later embodied in the Naval Supply Bill which was approved on July 12, 1921- urging the President to invite Great Britain and Japan to a conference to draw up an agreement by which the naval expenditure of the three powers should be reduced. This resolution was passed by both the Senate and the House of Representatives - in the Senate unanimously, and in the House by a vote of 230 to 4. Also, in 1920, the Republican party had been emphasizing the necessity of the USA entering into some form of association with other nations for the reduction of armaments, and in June 1920, the Republican National Committee had warned its leaders that the party stood to lose a large number of votes unless naval expenditures were reduced. The government was thus carrying out the wishes of the people in issuing the invitation to the Conference, the immediate aim of which was later described in the following terms by the American delegation to the Conference in their report to the President: *The declared object was, in its naval aspect, to stop the race of competitive building of warships which was in process and was so distressingly like the competition that immediately preceded the war of 1914. Competitive armament is, however, the result of a state of mind in which a national expectation of an attack by some country causes preparation to meet the attack. To stop competition, it is necessary to deal with the state of mind from which it results. A belief in the pacific intentions of other Powers must be substituted for suspicion and apprehension.*

The 1921 British Naval Estimates planned four battleships and four battlecruisers, with another four battleships to follow the subsequent year.

The US public was largely unwelcoming of the new arms race. The United States Congress disapproved of Wilson's 1919 naval expansion plan, and during the 1920 presidential election campaign, politics returned to the non-interventionalism of the prewar era, with little appetite for continued naval expansion.

In late 1921, the US government became aware that Britain was planning a conference to discuss the strategic situation in the Pacific and Far East. To forestall the conference and satisfy domestic pressure for a global disarmament conference, the Harding administration called the Washington Naval Conference during November 1921.

The 1921 Washington Conference
Washington, Armistice Day, 11 November 1921, a Friday. A long procession with President Harding, the ambassadors, the delegates, the troops of all arms, and poor ex-President Wilson had gone out to Arlington cemetery to take part in the ceremony of the burial of The Unknown Soldier. The whole city was drenched in tears. It seemed an appropriate introduction to the epochal naval disarmament conference which opened the following day. The delegates from

A stereoscopic photograph taken during the 1921 naval conference in the Continental Hall of the Daughters of the Revolution in Washington DC.*(NARA)*

Disarmament Conference in Session, Continen-

The conclusion of the Naval Conference of 1921/2, which resulted in the 1923 arms reduction treaty.*(NARA)*

Great Britain, Japan, France, Italy, Holland, Belgium, Portugal, China and the United States met in the classical building known as the Hall of the Daughters of the American Revolution. This was to be open diplomacy, and the place was crowded with reporters anxious to see and hear everything that took place at the rectangular table in the centre around which the delegates were seated. President Harding gave the introductory address, concluding with the sentence:

'We are met for a service to mankind. In all simplicity, in all honesty, and all honor, there may be written here the avowals of a world conscience refined by the consuming fires of war and made more sensitive by the anxious aftermath'.

Each country sent its foremost statesmen. The USA was represented by four delegates, Secretary Hughes, Elihu Root, and Senators Henry Cabot Lodge and Oscar Underwood, all of whom had established reputations.

From the beginning, the forceful and convincing personality of Secretary of state Hughes dominated the convention. He was anxious to remove causes of friction and to build up goodwill. Without a doubt, the climax of Hughes' successful career came at the opening of the Washington Conference. In a speech, delivered on the first day of the conference, he outlined in detail, practically all that was to be accomplished in the way of naval tonnage limitation. Offering to give up the American building of capital ships in return for certain concessions from Great Britain and Japan, he said: *'The first is that the core of the difficulty is to be found in the competition in naval programs, and that, in order appropriately to limit naval armaments, competition in its production must be abandoned. The competition will not be remedied by resolves concerning the method of its continuance. One program inevitably leads to another, and if competition continues, its regulation is impractical. There is only one adequate way out, and that is to end it now. It is apparent that this cannot be accomplished without serious sacrifice. Enormous sums have been expanded upon ships under construction, and building programs which are currently underway cannot be given up without substantial loss. If the present construction of capital ships goes forward, other ships will inevitably be built to rival them, and this will lead to still others. Thus the race will continue so long as the ability to maintain lasts. The effort to escape sacrifice is futile. We must face them or yield our purpose.*

He then presented an exact plan for reduction which he summarised as follows:

- That all capital shipbuilding programmes, either actual or projected should be abandoned.
- That further reduction be made through scrapping of certain of the older ships.
- That in general, regard should be had to the existing naval strength of the powers concerned.
- That the capital ship tonnage should be used as the measurement or strength for navies and a proportionate allowance of auxiliary combatant craft prescribed.

He also named the capital ships which should be scrapped by America, Great Britain and Japan and those which should be retained by each power. Charles E. Hughes' speech was a radical departure from the usual vague, meaningless statements which had been the ruin of previous disarmament conferences. The British writers Kenworthy and Young exclaimed that: *'He was sinking in a few sentences more tonnage in battleships than all the battles of the world had sunk in a century.'*

Journalist Mark Sullivan described it in his book *The Great Adventure in Washington*. He gave the reaction to what he called 'that inspired moment', of various persons in the plenary session. He declared that Admiral Beatty of the British Navy *'...came forward in his chair with the manner of a bulldog, sleeping on a sunny porch, who has been kicked in the stomach by an itinerant soap-canvasser'* and that Arthur Hamilton Lee, 1st Viscount Lee of Fareham, GCB, GCSI, GBE, PC, then the First Lord of the British Admiralty *'...reached around excitedly for pencil and paper'*.

Louis Siebold wrote: *'There was no discounting the surprise of Prince Tokugawa, Baron Kate, and Ambassador Shidehara. The Italians, Portuguese, and Belgian envoys seemed to be greatly pleased if a trifle startled'*.

These writers had great reason to be enthusiastic. They were witnesses to history in the making at one of its most exciting times.

It was a time when idealism characterised the Americans. When Secretary Hughes reached the sentences, *'There should be a naval holiday.*

11 June 1930: USS *Saratoga* CV-3 northbound in the Panama Canal. *(USN)*

The Royal Navy's HMS *Hermes*: Built in 1923, at 10,800 tons, top speed of 25 knots, carried 15 aircraft, and had a crew of 660 plus aircrew. *(Russell Plummer Collection)*

It is proposed that for not less than ten years there should be no further construction of capital ships...' he was interrupted by loud applause. The Americans present, in particular, applauded. *'But what were they applauding?'* asked Professor George H. Blakeslee of Clark University, who had served as technical adviser to the American delegation, *'A proposal to surrender the potential command of the seas within the grasp of the United States.'* It appealed to the American people to sacrifice for a just cause - *'equitable mutual reduction'*.

At the second plenary session, Arthur James Balfour, 1st Earl of Balfour, KG, OM, PC, FRS, FBA, DL arose and accepted the American proposals for the British government, not with cool approbation, but with full, loyal and complete cooperation. *'....We have considered your scheme with admiration and approval, and we agree with its spirit and purpose as making the greatest reform ever carried out by courage and statesmanship'.*

The Naval Treaty
The starting point for limitation and reduction was Mr Hughes' third point - that of existing naval strength. In ascertaining this amount, it was planned to include *'...the extent of construction already effected in the case of ships in progress',* and this definite quantity was to give the ratio between the several Powers. This was further explained in the report of the American Delegation to the Conference, which described the method thus:
'It was evident that no agreement for

limitation was possible if the three Powers were not content to take as a basis their actual existing strength. General considerations of national needs, aspirations, and expectations, policy and program, could be brought forward by each Power in justification of some possible relation of naval strength with no result but profitless and interminable discussion. The solution was to take what the Powers had, as it was manifest that neither could better its relative position unless it won in the race which it was the object of the Conference to end. It was impossible to stop competition in naval armaments if the Powers were to condition their agreement upon the advantages they hoped to gain in the competition itself. There was general agreement that the American rule for determining existing naval strength was correct, that by capital ship tonnage upon ships laid or upon which money had already been spent....that ships in the course of construction should be counted to the extent to which construction had already progressed at the time of the convening of the Conference.

The Japanese argued against the last point, saying that a ship wasn't a ship unless it was finished and ready to fight, but they were won over to the principle that a completed per cent was so much naval strength. Both the British and Japanese accepted the ratio which the American government had proposed.

This starting point being accepted, the US Government proposed to carry out points one and two, also, by scrapping six battle cruisers, seven battleships in the course of construction, and two battleships already launched - and fifteen older existing battleships. It was suggested that the British Empire and Japan reduce their navies in the same proportions according to their 'existing strength'. The ships belonging to the three Powers were considered individually and in setting them off against each other, their age as well as their tonnage was taken into account.

Concerning replacement, the proposals were as follows:

1. That it be agreed that the first replacement tonnage should not be laid down until ten years from the date of the agreement.
2. That replacement be limited by an agreed maximum of capital ships as follows: The USA and Great Britain, 500,000 tons each and for Japan, 300,000 tons.
3. That subject to the ten-year limit above fixed and the maximum standard, capital ships might be replaced when they were twenty years old, by new capital ship construction.
4. That no capital ship should be built in replacement with a tonnage displacement of more than 35,000 tons.

Neither France nor Italy was asked to scrap any existing tonnage in capital ships, since it was recognised that the relatively small size of their respective fleets would not constitute a fair basis for any scheme of reduction. There was much discussion about the inclusion or exclusion of individual warships. In particular, the Japanese delegation was keen to retain their newest battleship *Mutsu,* which had been funded with great public enthusiasm, including donations from schoolchildren. That resulted in provisions to allow the United States and Britain to construct equivalent ships.

On 6 February 1922, these five governments, USA, Great Britain, France, Italy and Japan signed a Treaty for the Limitation of Naval Armament which was ratified and entered into effect on 23 August 1923. The Treaty stated that from 1923 to 1931 when replacements could begin, the status of battleships of the five powers should be:

Country	Capital Ships	Tons
British Empire	20	558,950
USA	18	525,850
Japan	10	301,320
France	10	221,170
Italy	10	182,800

The tonnage for the British Empire was somewhat larger at first, but that was due to the fact that all her ships were older than those of the United States, where ships, also, carried more guns than the British. The ships scrapped by the three great naval Powers amounted to about forty per cent of their capital ship strength built and building.

Beginning in 1931, replacements could be made so that by 1942 the capital ships of the five naval powers could be as follows:

Country	Capital Ships	Tonnage	Ratio
United States	15	525,000	5
British Empire	15	525,000	5
Japan	9	315,000	3
France	No. not fixed	175,000	1.67
Italy	No. not fixed	175,000	1.67

The British delegation largely accepted the

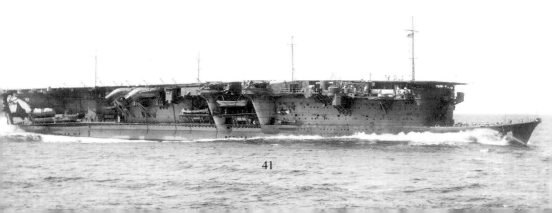

JIN aircraft carrier *Ryūjō* - meaning Prancing Dragon - was a light aircraft carrier built for the Imperial Japanese Navy (IJN) during the early 1930s. Small and lightly built in an attempt to exploit a loophole in the Washington Naval Treaty of 1922, she proved to be top-heavy and only marginally stable and was back in the shipyard for modifications to address those issues within a year of completion. *(NARA)*

USS *Arizona* was a Pennsylvania-class battleship built for and by the United States Navy in the mid-1910s. Named in honour of the 48th state's recent admission into the union, the ship was the second and last of the Pennsylvania class of 'super-dreadnought' battleships. Although commissioned in 1916, the ship remained stateside during the Great War. Shortly after the end of the conflict *Arizona* was one of some American ships that briefly escorted President Woodrow Wilson to the Paris Peace Conference. The battleship was sent to Turkey in 1919 at the beginning of the Greco-Turkish War to represent American interests for several months. Several years later, she was transferred to the Pacific Fleet and remained there for the rest of her career. *(US Navy)*

proposals regarding capital ships, but they were controversial with the British public. It would no longer be possible for Britain to have adequate fleets in the North Sea, the Mediterranean, and the Far East simultaneously. The facts provoked outrage from parts of the Royal Navy. Nevertheless, there was massive pressure on Britain to agree. Publically, the risk of war with the USA was increasingly regarded as merely theoretical, as there were very few policy differences between the two countries. Naval spending was unpopular in both Britain and its dominions. Furthermore, Britain was implementing significant decreases in its budget because of the economic crisis created by the end of the war.

The Japanese delegation was divided. Japanese naval doctrine required the maintenance of a fleet seventy per cent the size of that of the United States, which was felt to be the minimum necessary to defeat the United States in any subsequent war. The Japanese envisaged two separate engagements, first with the US Pacific Fleet and then with the US Atlantic Fleet. It calculated that a 7:5 ratio in the first battle would produce a significant enough margin of victory to be able to win the subsequent engagement so a 5:3 ratio, or sixty per cent, was unacceptable. Nevertheless, the director of the delegation, Katō Tomosaburō, preferred accepting a sixty per cent ratio to the prospect of an arms race with the United States, as the relative industrial output of the two

nations would cause Japan to lose such an arms race and an economic crisis. Going into the negotiations the Japanese had only fifty-five per cent as many capital ships as the Americans and eighteen per cent of the GDP.

His opinion was opposed strongly by Katō Kanji, the president of the Naval Staff College, who acted as his chief naval aide at the delegation and represented the influential 'big navy' school of thought. It held that in the event of war the United States would be able to build more warships indefinitely, given its vast industrial power, and Japan thus needed to prepare as thoroughly as possible for the inevitable conflict with America. Katō Tomosaburō was finally able to persuade the Japanese high command to accept the Hughes proposals, but the outcome of the treaty was a cause of controversy in the Japanese navy for years to come.

The French delegation responded angrily to the idea of reducing its capital ships tonnage to 175,000 tons and demanded 350,000, slightly above Japan. In the end, concessions regarding cruisers and submarines helped persuade the French to agree to the limit on capital ships. Another issue that was seen as critical by the French representatives was Italy's request of substantial parity, which was seen as unsubstantiated; however, pressure from the American and British delegations led them to give in. That was seen as a great success in Italy although parity would never actually be reached.

It was once common for historians to refer to the 1920s as a period of 'isolationism', thanks to the refusal of the US Senate to ratify the Versailles Treaty, and the resulting failure of the United States to join the League of Nations.

But while the efforts of American people in business to promote economic stability in Europe was no doubt important, the activities of various antiwar organisations were far more visible. In the wake of the horror produced by The Great War, pacifism was the country's - and indeed, the world's - fastest-growing political movement. Thousands of Americans, particularly women, flocked to organisations such as the National Council for the Prevention of War, and the Women's International League for Peace and Freedom. In the 1930s these groups would press for legislation that would keep the USA out of foreign wars; in the 1920s, however, the focus was still on international efforts to keep the peace - although without the sort of military commitments implied by the League of Nations.

Because most peace activists believed that the sheer size of the armed forces in the years leading up to the Great War had been an essential cause of the war's outbreak, one of the most consistent aims of the antiwar forces in the USA was the conclusion of arms control agreements. In this, they were often able to make common cause with conservative Republicans who sought to decrease government spending of all types.

Another critical domestic and international objective for the peace movement in the 1920s was to have the waging of war declared a violation of international law. Few outside the community of anti-war organisations took this

idea particularly seriously until 1927, when the French foreign minister, Aristide Briand, proposed a bilateral agreement with the United States in which both sides agreed never to go to war with one another. Frank B. Kellogg, the US Secretary of State, suspected - quite rightly, it turned out - that this was a French attempt to lure the United States into an alliance against Germany, but he feared the political consequences of turning down such a seemingly innocuous proposal. He, therefore, offered to do Briand one better; why not, he suggested, make this a multilateral agreement in which all the world's countries would be invited to renounce war 'as an instrument of national policy?' Thus the Kellogg–Briand Pact was born.

Most Americans embraced Kellogg-Briand as enthusiastically as they had welcomed the Five-Power Pact, and there was widespread support for the agreement even outside the peace movement. There were some dissenters, however. Some objected that lacking any means of enforcement, the treaty was useless; others claimed that, because the agreement included exceptions for wars of self-defence, the signatories would attempt to argue that any battle they decided to wage was being fought in the name of national self-preservation. In any case, such criticisms were quickly brushed aside, and the Senate ratified the Kellogg–Briand Pact by a vote of 85 to 1.

It is difficult to assess the long-term importance of either the Five-Power Treaty or the Kellogg-Briand Pact in contributing to international peace. However, it is clear that some of the signatories felt free to ignore or even repudiate the agreements whenever they became inconvenient. Japan announced in 1934

Left: Senator David Aiken Reed [R] (*b*. 21 December 1880, *d*. 10 February 1953) was an American lawyer and Republican party politician from Pittsburgh, Pennsylvania. He represented Pennsylvania in the United States Senate.

Right: Senator Robert Marion La Follette Sr. [R] (*b* 14 June 1855, *d*. 18 June 1925) was an American lawyer and politician. He was suceeeded by his son Robert Marion La Follette Jr. (b. 6 February 1895 d. 24 February 1953) *(both National Archives)*

that it would no longer abide by the naval disarmament clauses of the Five-Power Treaty. As for Kellogg-Briand, the promise to renounce war did not prevent Japan from invading Manchuria in 1931; nor did it stand in the way of repeated acts of aggression by Japan, Italy, and Germany later in the decade. What is clear is that the agreements demonstrated the enthusiasm of Americans for any measure that promised the prevention of war. Once the negotiations fell apart in the 1930s, however, antiwar activists turned their attention away from international cooperation to preserve peace, and toward legislation that would keep the United States out of wars that might break out anywhere else in the world.

Stirring up a hornet's nest

As previously described in the resulting Five-Power Treaty the British, U.S., Japanese, French, and Italian delegations agreed to scrap - or at least to cancel construction of - significant numbers of capital ships; that is battleships, battlecruisers, and aircraft carriers, and to limit the overall tonnage of such vessels in their navies. The US Navy and its supporters were outraged, claiming that the country had lost its best opportunity to become the world's preeminent naval power, but such views were given scant regard in the face of the overwhelming demand for peace and economy in government.

The treaty received much press comment. The Hearst newspapers, on the whole, were against everything accomplished by the Washington Conference and the *New York American* admonished the country that the peace pact was a 'war-breeder, not a peacemaker'. The governments of Great Britain, France, and Japan were called imperialistic and militaristic. *'To go into partnership with these international highwaymen is to become an insurer of their stolen goods - to pledge our military, naval, and financial help to the thieves*

SMS *Frithjof* was the third vessel of the six-member Siegfried class of coastal defense ships (Küstenpanzerschiffe) built for the German Imperial Navy. She served in the German fleet throughout the 1890s and was rebuilt in 1900–1902. *Frithjof* was demobilised in 1915 and used as a barracks ship thereafter. The vessel was scrapped in 1930. *(Russell Plummer Collection)*

whenever the rightful owners of the goods try to regain their property'.

Arthur Brisbane, also a Hearst man, described the UK, France, Japan and the United States as four *'gentlemen highwaymen trying to agree not to cut each other's throats over the spoils'*. The treaty was said to be a great British diplomatic triumph. Another Hearst writer claimed it was a step toward America's recognition of the League of Nations. He wrote: *Article eighteen of the Covenant of the League of Nations provides that 'Every treaty or international engagement entered into hereafter by any member of the League shall be forthwith registered with the Secretariat and shall as soon as possible be published by it. No such treaty or international engagement shall be binding until so registered.'*

This made it mandatory to Great Britain, France and Japan who signed the covenant, to register this new proposed agreement with the Secretariat of the League of Nations, and the United States recognised the League *ipso facto*

President John Calvin Coolidge Jr. [R] (*b.* 4 July 1872, *d.* 5 January 1933) was an American politician and the 30th President of the USA from 1923 to 1929.

when it entered into an agreement which it knew must be approved by the League of Nations before it became binding.

Senator David A Reed and Senator Robert M La Follette were against the treaty, also. Reed denounced the treaty as *'treacherous, treasonable, and damnable'*, while La Follette asserted that it had *'all the iniquities of the League of Nations, with none of the virtues claimed for that document'*.

Although there was adverse criticism of the treaty, the favourable criticisms far out-numbered them. The *Houston Chronicle* maintained that it was a good beginning, establishing a precedent for further agreements of the same kind, and summed up: *'Thus the Pacific is to be made the home of a new policy-- a policy of reduced fleets, of fewer fortifications, of less aggressiveness, of reliance and peaceful adjustments'*.

Agreeing with this, the *New York Tribune* wrote: *'Concerts of this sort need not be limited to the Pacific, but can be extended to other parts of the world where stabilisation is sought and*

HMS *Gloucester* was one of the last batch of three Town-class light cruisers built for the Royal Navy during the late 1930s. *(Russell Plummer Collection)*

where American cooperation is desirable.'

The papers of the west were optimistic. *The Los Angeles Times* reported that the Pacific agreement was *'a long step in the direction of world peace'* and the *Denver Rocky Mountain News* said that it *'brings very much closer the English-speaking peoples'*. The overseas papers likewise praised the treaty, commending the 'idealism in action' of President Harding and Secretary Hughes. The *London Daily Chronicle* seemed satisfied as it stated that it was possible to regard the Conference as having put an end for the present to the evil prospect of a Pacific armaments race and the fateful friction and jealousies in China and also as placing Pacific affairs on a most satisfactory footing of mutual consultation, recognition, and guarantee.

Japan was pleased, for in a Tokyo dispatch the world was told that Japan considered her international standing raised and anything she might have lost through the abrogation of the Japanese alliance with Great Britain, she has regained through the Four-Power treaty.

Meanwhile, the debates in the Senate were heated, long, and drawn out, centring chiefly on the Four-Power Pact, with such questions as: Did the Four-Power Treaty imply the use of force? Was it a basis for security and peace? Did it involve the United States in entangling alliances? The group favouring this pact defended it chiefly on the ground that it did not

do so. Among those holding this view were Senator Miles Poindexter of Washington and Senator Irvine Lenroot of Wisconsin. Meanwhile, Hannis Taylor, a prominent lawyer in Washington wrote articles in favour of the pact, calling its stipulations 'war-preventing agreements', which involved no entangling alliances. These were written into the Congressional Record.

In opposition were members of both parties. Senator Borah of Idaho commented that no American could have written the piece, but later read a letter from Mr Enghes in which he acknowledged the authorship.

Senator Glass of Virginia opposed the pact because there must have been some underlying meaning in it that was most satisfactory to the Japanese since they seemed to be pleased about the termination of the Anglo-Japanese alliance. Charles E. Russell, journalist, author, and a member of the Special Mission sent to Russia in 1917, wrote Senator Borah that by joining the Four-Power Pact he believed that the United States would aid Great Britain and Japan at the expense of helpless China. Senators King of Utah and La Follette of Wisconsin also argued against the pact. Finally, it was agreed that the United States would accept with the reservation that *'there is no obligation to join any defense'*. The vote was sixty-seven to twenty-seven, a margin of four over the necessary two-thirds. A

US Navy destroyers USS *Hull,* (DD-350) USS *Worden* (DD-352) and USS *Macdonaugh* (DD-351) exercising the the Fleet in 1937. *(US Navy)*

USS *Colorado* (BB-45) was a battleship of the US Navy that was in service from 1923 to 1947. It is seen here at New York in 1932. *(US Navy)*

scathing editorial followed in Mr Hearst's *New York American,* entitled *'England Recaptures Her Colony'.*

The accusation against the Senate was as follows: *The Senate voted for an alliance, not with all the nations of the earth like the League of Nations, but an exclusive alliance to guarantee the possessions and the indefinable rights of the three aggressive imperialism of the earth - Britain, France and Japan. They are the same three imperialisms for which we have just sacrificed twenty-six thousand millions of treasure.*

The Senate commits the country to an exclusive alliance designed to protect the aggressions of Japan against our friends Russia and China. It is an alliance to prop up the tottering British Empire. It is an alliance so threatening that to-day it is driving together, for self-protection the brains of Germany and the brawn of Russia, those two republics gasping for the breath of life. The Senators failed us, opened the gates, let in the foreign foe.

The British made no secret of the fact that they wished more cruisers than other nations.

Lord Birkenhead and Austen Chamberlain explained the situation to some visiting editors saying *'that as Great Britain could not put in the supply of food for longer than a seven-week period she was forced to have great cruisers in place to protect her trade lanes'.*

In the USA a bill authorising the construction of eight 10,000 ton cruisers was passed by Congress on 18 December 1924, and appropriation of five of these was made in the naval appropriations acts of 1925 and 1926. The American Navy Department pointed out that the US Navy was much inferior to other navies in cruisers and that *'...to put our fleet on a basis of equality with the UK, the construction of 22 large cruisers was necessary instead of eight'.* Congress held back from making appropriations for them in the hope that a new limitation of arms conference would be held. The desire that armaments be effectively reduced in the interest of peace and economy were shown in the naval appropriations bill of 1923 1924 and 1925.

President Coolidge was in sympathy with the efforts to reduce naval armaments, which in his estimation had two goals, that of peace and

The 'Asashio' class comprised ten destroyers designed for the Imperial Japanese navy in the mid-1930s and in service before and during World War Two. *(Russell Plummer Collection)*

thrift. In his inaugural address he called for a display of reason rather than a display of force and said *'if we expect others to rely on our fairness and justice we must show that we can rely on their fairness and justice'.*

Addressing the American Legion in Omaha on 6 October 1925 he said *'...we have been attempting to relieve ourselves and the other nations from the old theory of competitive armaments. In spite of all the arguments in favour of great military forces, no nation has ever had an army large enough to guarantee it against attack in the time of peace or to ensure its victory in time of war. No nation ever will. Peace and security are more likely to result from fair and honourable dealings and mutual agreement for a limitation of arms amongst nations, than by any attempts at competition in squadrons and battalions. I can see no merit in any necessary expenditure of money to hire men to build fleets and carry muskets when international relations in agreement permit the turning of self-resources into the making of good roads the building of better homes, the promotion of better education, and all the other parts of which pays administration to the advancement of human welfare.*

In February 1927 the United States renewed its plans for the reduction of naval disarmament. President Coolidge took the plunge and a formal proposal was delivered to the foreign offices in London, Paris, Rome and Tokyo by the American ambassadors.

The call was to attend a conference to be held in Geneva for the consideration of the separate problem of naval armaments and more particularly the limitation of those vessels which are not been covered by the Washington Treaty.

President Coolidge included this idea in his invitation and said: *'...the American government was disposed to accept in regard to cruisers and extension of the 5:5:3 ratio with reference to the USA, Great Britain and Japan and to leave the ratio of France and Italy for discussion - due consideration being given to the national requirements'.*

It was hoped that this conference would succeed where the Washington conference had failed. Both France and Italy refused the invitation to send delegates to the conference, but later they did agree to send representatives as observers. A French note dated 15 February 1927 began in the usual diplomatic manner by praising the ideals of the American proposals; then it went on in an unruffled strain to reject it. Several reasons were given. First, the authority of the League of Nations would be weakened if this work was taken from it; secondly all the nations with navies were concerned in the limitation of cruisers, not only the five invited to the conference, and thirdly the American proposal had ignored the French contention that only the changes should be limited not the classes. Italy refused on the grounds that her geographical peculiarities made it impossible for her to commit herself to naval limitation.

Japan accepted President Coolidge's proposals in an answer made public on 19 February, but stated that the ratio established at the Washington conference for capital ships would not be accepted for smaller ones. After consulting the governments of the dominions the British government also accepted the invitation; the British notes contain the following statement regarding their position: *'... the views of his Majesty's government upon the* special geographical position of the British Empire, the length of inter-imperial communications, and the necessity for the protection of its food suppliers are well-known, and together with special conditions and requirements of the other countries invited to participate in the conversations, these must be taken into account. His Majesty's government is nevertheless prepared to consider to what extent the principles adopted in Washington can be carried further, either as regards the ratio in different classes of ships between the various powers or in other important ways'.

In spite of the refusal to have all the interested powers, it was decided after further consultation to hold a three power conference in Geneva. The first session opened on 20 June 1927 and the delegates from the USA, Great Britain and Japan tried to agree upon cruisers, destroyers and submarines.

Three proposals were put on the table. The Americans proposed a programme based on parity, economy and security. It was defined by Hugh S Gibson who said in part: 'the American delegation has come to the conference with an estimate of what we consider equitable tonnage allocations in the various categories of vessels. We are prepared to discuss the question of tonnages fully and frankly in the light of our several legitimate needs. We have none of us a right or interest to maintain naval force sufficient for our legitimate requirements of national defence'.

The American proposal was that no change should be made in the prevailing limits to sizes of ships, but that the three powers should agree to limit their tonnage in each class of subsidiary ship - cruiser, destroyer and submarine to conform to a 5:5:3 ratio.

Gibson continued: '...we demand parity with Great Britain for two reasons; first to protect their foreign trade since there were some important products we could not do without, manganese, rubber and tin, and second our right as a neutral state which England had threatened to disturb in the past'.

The Japanese proposal was that the relationship between the three powers, at the

Imperial Japanese Navy battleship *Kongō* in dry dock at Yokosuka Naval Arsenal during her first reconstruction, as she was being transformed from a battlecruiser to a battleship.
(Russell Plummer Collection)

The big destroyers of the French La Fantasque class were very fast, making 35 knots in speed trials - here X101 is seen making full speed. *(Russell Plummer Collection)*

time, as indicated by the actual number of vessels built and being built, should be stabilised that henceforth none of the three powers should be allowed to obtain any new ships except for replacement. This would work out at roughly a ratio of 5:5:4, instead of 5:5:3. Japan did not want to scrap anything of value, nor did she want to begin a large and expensive naval programme. They would not agree to any limitation of eight-inch gun cruisers as a matter of principle, except to declare that they would not build any further eight-inch gun cruisers except those already authorised, provided Japan was given a total tonnage of at least 315,000 tons of cruisers and destroyers combined.

Both the American and Japanese proposal seemed simple, the Japanese having the apparent merit of no further enquiries in the scale of expenditure, but not on the other hand

involving any reduction. The American delegation objected at once to the Japanese plan because of the changing ratio.

The British proposal was complicated. It began by opposing the principle of limitation of total tonnage alone, on the grounds that the maximum size ship - a 10,000 ton eight-inch gun - would inevitably become a minimum. The delegates, instead, proposed a reduction in the size of ships and guns and that the naval strength should be rationed on the basis of reasonable needs of the three countries. First, they suggested that there be a strict limitations on the 10,000 ton eight-inch gun ship, and second, that there be established a secondary type of 6,000 tons carrying six-inch guns, and they produced definitive figures.

Great Britain, they said, required seventy cruisers and they refused to change this number throughout the conference. This was absolutely necessary, they declared, to meet its special needs. This number of vessels would run the total tonnage up to approximately 600,000 tons, and on this figures she would grant parity to the USA. This figure was twice the American figure and would mean naval increase rather than naval reduction if America tried to reach parity.

The plans were assigned to the technical committee for investigation and meanwhile the newspapers daily predicted failure. In criticism of the British proposals the *New York Herald Tribune* said on 22 June 1927: '*...to revise the agreements as to capital ships announced tonnage and armament maximum of the cruises, and to delay replacements in both classes, as the British suggest, would play havoc with naval equality.*

'*The British-backed*

Winston Churchill - First Lord of the Admiralty from 1911 until 1915.

cuts in tonnage and armaments ignore the importance to the USA of possessing both capital ships and cruisers of any steaming radius. They overlook an existing disparity in naval stations and bases'.

'*It is not conceding anything essentially valuable to Great Britain to advocate smaller battleships, smaller aeroplane carriers, smaller cruisers, destroyers, and submarines, or to recommends sweeping reductions in the calibre of guns. To allow no auxiliary to carry a gun and heavier than six inches at a stroke vastly increased Great Britain's cruiser strength. She*

has many emerging ships which can be fitted with six-inch guns and converted quickly into naval auxiliaries'.

'*The Washington treaty unwisely aggravated our poverty in naval bases and stations. Our lack of bases further east than Hawaii compels us to maintain a Navy of Washington Treaty units and requirements. It would be folly under such circumstances to listen to British pleas for unit tonnage which would further handicap us and relatively to increase British naval strength*'.

The *Chicago Daily Tribune* was equally bitter: '*... British naval action in all her later wars has been to blockade the enemy. 'Contraband' is whatever Britain wishes to declare contraband. The guarding of Imperial commerce in fact has meant interference with neutral commerce, whenever it suited British interest to interfere. This has worked a serious injury to American Commerce in the past and may do so again as long as the protection of trade routes is allowed to remain a British monopoly*'.

'*Our interest in foreign trade is increasing. America is beginning to outsell Britain in her own dominions. At the same time our dependence on the raw materials of industry which are not found in our country is becoming greater and without which our industrial system must stagnate. If not our lives, then our prosperity and our standard of living will be imperilled by cutting us off from the world*'.

The clashes of opinion was the main clash between Great Britain and the United States of America. Since both governments had been genuinely anxious to reduce overall naval expenditure and the general danger of war it was absurd that they could not agree on some means.

After weeks of anxious discussions by the experts, and after all three parties had consulted with their respective governments on more than one occasion, and after the British delegation actually suspended the conference by returning to London to consult with the cabinet, it was found it impossible to enter into a written agreement. The cause of the clash was the cruiser. With regard to the submarines and destroyers, some measurement of agreement seemed likely. In the matter of further limitation of capital ships, which had been informally suggested by the British delegates, an agreement seemed possible. On the issue of cruisers, the conference broke. Both sides wanted the advantage.

The first contention was over the question of parity and the British naval men did not want parity with the USA in cruisers. The Right Honourable E S Amery, former first Lord of the Admiralty wrote: '...we agreed at the Washington conference to what is in effect equality of battlefleet strength with the USA. But obviously, it would be impossible to arrive at any similar figure with regards to the strength of cruisers required for commerce protection.

Admiral of the Fleet John Rushworth Jellicoe, 1st Earl Jellicoe, GCB, OM, GCVO, SGM, DL (b. 5 December 1859, d. 20 November 1935). Jellicoe served as First Sea Lord from 1915 but was relieved at the end of 1917. Jellicoe was promoted to Admiral of the Fleet on 3 April 1919. He became Governor-General of New Zealand in September 1920. Following his return to Great Britain, he was created Earl Jellicoe and Viscount Brocas of Southampton in the County of Southampton on 1 July 1925.

For us, at any rate, a sufficiency of cruisers is a matter of life and death'.

Mr Bridgeman, the chief British delegate said: '... , it would be a very dangerous thing for Great Britain to allow it to be thought that we could be satisfied with the one power standard in cruisers for example. In cruisers, at any rate, we want to feel superior to other countries'.

Winston Churchill, then Chancellor of the Exchequer, agreeed with Mr Bridgeman and in no uncertain terms gave his opinion: '... therefore we are not able now - and I hope at no future time - to give everybody in a solemn international agreement any words which would bind us to the principle of mathematical parity in naval strength'.

Lord Jellicoe gave as reasons why Great Britain should have more cruisers than the USA. First Great Britain's insular position and her great need for raw materials and food, and second the great length of her trade routes and the extensive coastline of all parts of the empire which must be protected.

The United States delegates would not recognise that Great Britain's needs were any greater than their own and finally Great Britain was forced reluctantly to grant parity.

The second problem in confronting the delegates was the apportioning of the various units of tonnage. The American delegation declared that it would not agree to limit the number of 10,000 ton cruisers to less than 25 because, unlike the British Empire, the United

States did not have a large number of naval bases strategically situated with respect to its trade routes. The United States needed ships with larger cruising radiuses.

It was at this point that the British delegates returned to London and came back with a new set of proposals. The new plan provided a total tonnage for cruises destroyers and submarines of 590,000 for Britain and the United States and 385,000 tons for the Japanese. First the 10,000 ton cruisers were to be limited to twelve for the USA and Great Britain and eight for Japan. Second the total tonnage and destroyer class could be used for vessels of 1500 tons and under, but only sixteen per cent could be used for flotilla leader ships, that is, vessels above 1500 tons and limited to a maximum of 1850 tons. Third the retention of overage vessels to the extent of twenty-five per cent of the total tonnage had to be allowed.

The failure of the conference can be attributed to the inability of the United States and Great Britain to come to terms on these issues; one side or both needed to make substantial compromises to solve the problem. Far from allowing the friendship of their shared heritage to bring cooperation, it seemed that few at the conference on either side had definitively ruled out the possibility of the two nations engaging on opposite sides of a future conflict, so each hoped to maintain as much of an edge as possible in naval capacity. In the wake of the failed talks at Geneva, the United States passed a bill to build fifteen new cruisers and an aircraft carrier, and thereby joined the naval arms race. This led Japan and Britain to consider their building programs, making the result of the conference a potential new arms race, rather than limitation. The United States and Great Britain realised that without an agreement, the cruiser issue would block advancements at any future conferences, so they continued discussions in the years that followed. In 1929, the two sides agreed on a limit of fifty cruisers and 339,000 tons, with a limit to the maximum number of heavy cruisers. Both sides compromised heavily to reach this deal, but the issue of how many heavy cruisers would be

What was to come - but never really happened. The German aircraft carrier *Graf Zeppelin* was the lead ship in a class of two carriers of the same name ordered by the Kriegsmarine. She was the only aircraft carrier launched by Germany and represented part of the Kriegsmarine's attempt to create a well-balanced oceangoing fleet, capable of projecting German naval power far beyond the narrow confines of the Baltic and North Seas. The carrier would have had a complement of 42 fighters and dive bombers. The keel was laid down in December 1936 at the Deutsche Werke shipyard in Kiel. Political infighting within the Nazi party meant that the ship was never completed, but was finally captured by the Russians and eventually scuttled. *(Russell Plummer Collection)*

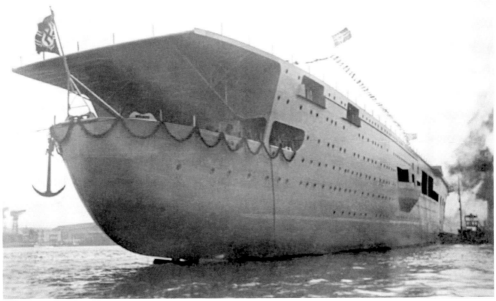

53

USS *Arizona* at anchor. *(US Navy)*

permitted was not settled.

As a result of the failure of the Geneva conference, the tension between the English-speaking nations was increased, and the most startling building programme it has ever had to consider was brought before the Congress. This programme called for 25 cruisers, nine destroyer leaders, 32 submarines, and five aircraft carriers to be built at a total cost of $725,000,000. There was too much opposition for the Congress to pass this bill, but in February 1929, a bill was passed that still called for a rather large construction programme; this new bill called for fifteen cruisers and one aircraft carrier and was to cost $274,000,000. A time limit was added requiring that all fifteen of the eight-inch gun cruisers be started by 1 July 1931 and finished by 1935. The only concession made was the authorisation to suspend the building if an international agreement for further limitation of naval armaments was concluded.

In February 1929 Congressman Fred Britten, chairman of the house committee on naval affairs and the leader of the 'Big Navy'

group in the USA wrote that the completion of fifteen American cruisers authorised in 1929 '... *will, unless Great Britain or Japan extend their naval programs. place the USA on the basis somewhere near equality with any other naval force might be called upon to meet'*.

If the 1929 programmes were completed Great Britain would have a superiority in cruisers but that would be offset by the fact that the USA would have five large eight-inch gun cruisers more than the British superiority in destroyers and submarines. It seemed as if another naval race might be looming in the near future unless something definite could be done to limit naval armaments.

Clearly this was not enough for the proponents of the 'Big Navy' concept, nor for the Imperialists within the Department of the Navy. It was time to start planning for other options. It was time to think the unthinkable; invade Canada and the Caribbean and destroy the British Empire once and for all. It was time to consider War Plan Red.

Chapter Three

The Run-Up to Red.

Colours of the rainbow coalesce into fifty shades of red.

The apparent failure of a number of Naval Conferences and the frustration of many in the American Department of the Navy created an atmosphere in which many thought actions should be taken. In late 1929 and early 1930, a set of papers were drawn up by the Joint Board of the Department of the Navy. These papers were a part risk assessment, part attack plan showing the high level of paranoia existing within the US military establishment at the time, for the US Navy were considering a possible invasion of the US mainland by the British Empire via Canada! There was also serious consideration given to the possibility that the British Empire would blockade the Panama Canal via its possessions in the Caribbean. The documents also clearly show the high level of what can only be called jealousy - in the main from the US Navy Admirals - towards the British Empire in general and the Royal Navy in particular.

The use of colour coding of nations involved may be thought of as confusing. The Americans allocated a different colour code to Great Britain and British territories that made up the Empire. The United Kingdom was 'Red', Canada 'Crimson', India 'Ruby', Australia 'Scarlet' and New Zealand 'Garnet'. Ireland, at the time a free state within the British Empire, was named 'Emerald'. The USA was, of course, 'Blue'.

As far as can be ascertained - for some of the microfilms are not the easiest to read - the documents had been initially sent to both the Secretary of the Navy, Charles Francis Adams III, and Patrick J Hurley, Secretary of War for approval over the signature of Admiral Charles F Hughes, Senior Member before distribution.

Hughes had been appointed Commander-in-Chief of the US Fleet in 1926 and 1927, before being elected to his then current post.

A large number of recently located declassified papers show the long, and somewhat convoluted 'risk assessment' part first: '*The Red or British Empire was, in both terms of territory and population the greatest in the world. It was distributed in all quarters of the globe. Its land frontiers are nowhere*

Above: Admiral Charles Frederick Hughes (*b*. 14 October 1866, *d*. 28 May 1934) who served as Chief of Naval Operations from 1927 to 1930.

Left: Patrick Jay Hurley [R] (*b*. 8 January 1883, *d*. 30 July 1963) was the United States Secretary of War from 1929 to 1933.

Right: Charles Francis 'Deacon' Adams III [R] (*b*. 2 August 1866, *d*. 10 June 1954), was the United States Secretary of the Navy.

American tanks demonstrated to the troops sometime after World War One.

contiguous to those on the active military power except in the case of Canada, described as 'Crimson'. The United Kingdom is the heart of the Red Empire and the existence of this Empire depends upon the maintenance of sea communications between the United Kingdom and the dominions, colonies, protectorates and mandates which make up the Empire. To protect such sea communications, Red has established a system of naval bases and protected harbors along almost every important trade route throughout the world. This makes it possible for Red to concentrate naval forces to threaten sea frontiers and the commerce of any probable enemy, while at the same time safeguarding its own. However, the wide distribution of the British Empire and its seaborne trade tend to demand a considerable dispersion of naval forces to protect them.

The United Kingdom is itself vulnerable to attack by aircraft based on the European continent, but, without an ally in Western Europe, this fact would be of no advantage to the USA in a war with the British Empire.

In a war between the British Empire and the USA, the Dominions of Canada are not subject to attack, and the military or naval forces of these Dominions would be available, in combination with other Empire forces, to attack the American possessions in the Pacific and any American commerce therein.

The British Empire maintains military and naval forces in India and other Empire possessions and Mandates in the Middle East. Since these portions of the Empire are secure against attacks from the USA, these forces, except such are necessary to guard frontiers and to provide internal security, would be available to undertake operations against American interests particularly those of the Philippines and Guam.

The British Empire further maintains relatively large naval forces and small military forces in Far Eastern waters and possessions. These would also be available to attack US possessions and commerce.

The British Empire dominions and possessions in Africa also are so situated as to be secure against American attack, and their forces would be available to assist other British Empire forces. On account however of their relatively small white populations, such contribution would not be of great importance.

In a war of long duration where the bulk of the American naval forces would have to be retained in the Atlantic, the Hawaiian islands might be subjected to serious attack by Australian and Indian troops or by Allied forces in case Japan (code-named Orange) should intervene in the war on the side of the British Empire.

In the Caribbean Sea and West Indian waters, the British Empire has potential advanced naval bases at Jamaica (Port Royal) Trinidad, and St Lucia. In addition the empire has outlying subsidiary naval bases at Bermuda. There are suitable harbours elsewhere within the British Empire and North American possessions, exclusive to Canada which are capable of serving as bases for small craft, particularly submarines. *Notable amongst these are the Bahamas and the British Leeward Islands. These harbours are important not only for the protection of Empire's seaborne trade but also as sally points from which to attack American commerce.*

Jamaica constitutes a serious threat to the security of the Panama Canal and to all American trade routes passing through the Caribbean Sea and is the most important West Indian submarine cable communications centre. Bermuda is well off to interfere with American seaborne trade to the West Indies and along the American South Atlantic coast. In addition, it is capable of serving as bases for aircraft carriers designated to conduct their raids against vital American areas. The Bahamas are so situated as to forward bases from which to control American trade through the Straits of Florida and to Cuba. Trinidad, St Lucia and the British Leeward Islands lie on the flank of American trade routes to the east coast of South America and constitute severe threats to the integrity of American commerce and trade therewith.

Of the British and North American possessions exclusive of Canada, only Jamaica and Bermuda are at present defended, although the defences are neither extensive nor modern, and the present garrisons are small.

Geographically Canada affords the British Empire bases for naval military and air forces close to the vital area of the USA and is so situated as to provide a comparatively short line of sea communications to the United Kingdom, which is not flanked by American

territory which can be used as a naval base. Due to the eastward projection of Canada relative to the American coast, a concentration of the British Empire fleet in Canadian waters, particularly in the Halifax, Nova Scotia area would permit the British Empire to transfer forces to Canada with such freedom as to require only small detachments to safeguard such lines of communications. This relative location of Nova Scotia, Cape Breton Island and Newfoundland would render it difficult for American naval forces to attack successfully the British line of sea communications. Ports of the Maritime Provinces of Canada form strong points from which to initiate an invasion of American territory by joint Army Navy and air force operations. Naval raids may be launched from these bases against American commerce and vital areas. The Eastwards projection of these provinces also facilitates the rapid transfer the British units to Canada even should the USA have control of the St Lawrence Valley.

The British Empire also has a sea route to Hudson Bay which is easily secured as soon as the British Empire establishes naval superiority in the western Atlantic. During the short season when this route is open to navigation, British forces would be enabled to reach central Canada with greater ease and facility, provided transportation through the railway bottleneck at Winnipeg was uninterrupted. This route would be particularly valuable for the transfer of air units from other portions of the British Empire to Canada.

There are harbors with well-developed port

British Colonial troops on exercise 'sometime in the 1930s'.

facilities on the Pacific coast of Canada noticeably at Victoria–Vancouver and at Prince Rupert. These harbors have good rail communication eastwards and would afford base facilities for naval operations against American Pacific commerce especially that passing through the Straits of Juan de Fuca and with Alaska. They would be available as ports of debarkation for Canadian forces or Japanese forces should Japan eventually intervene in the war on the side of the British Empire.

Geographically while Canada provides the British Empire as a whole with advantageous bases at such separated points as to invite an initial dispersion of American Armed Forces, Canada itself occupies an extremely weak position with respect to the USA. While its territory is of great extent, all well-developed parts thereof lie close to the American border; hence they are especially vulnerable to attack from the USA. In eastern Canada Montréal is the principal city and it is particularly susceptible to attack launched from American territory. The reinforcement of Canadian forces in this region by strong British Empire contingents require the free use of the St

Lawrence River and the rail lines having terminals in the Maritime Provinces. On account of the severe winter climate of this portion of Canada, the St Lawrence River and Gulf are closed to navigation for several months of the year. The great salient into eastern Canada formed by the state of Maine would provide the USA with a base from which to conduct operations to cut communications between the Québec–Montréal area and the Maritime provinces, or to initiate a land or air offensives against Halifax and St John New Brunswick, the ports best suited for use by major units of the British Empire fleet.

The Ontario peninsular south-west of the line Midland–Oshawa inclusive, is the principal manufacturing area of Canada and contains approximately one-third of Canada's present munitioning capacity. The denial to the Ontario peninsular of the Niagara power and the coal imported from the USA and the western provinces of Canada would produce an immediate strangulation of its manufacturing and munitioning industries. Approximately ninety per cent of Canada's present munitioning capacity is confined to

From the early 1910s until the 1930s, US armed forces took part in military occupations that are colloquially known as the Banana Wars. During this time, the US Navy and Marine Corps conducted multiple invasions and small scale counterinsurgency campaigns in Latin America under the guise of an updated Monroe Doctrine, which declared that the US had 'international police power' and therefore the right to enforce good behaviour in the Western hemisphere. While the Monroe Doctrine had been created to halt European imperial expansion into Central and South America, by the early 20th century, it was the philosophy used to justify numerous American interventions into Latin American politics *(NARA)*

On 19/20 April 1930, the US Army Air Corps held an air show that brought large numbers of people to Mills Field Municipal Airport, San Francisco. Some reports put the attendance as high as 100,000 spectators who turned out to watch 135 military aircraft performing precision manouevres. *(NARA)*

Canada's territory bordering and adjacent to Lake Ontario and the Ottawa and St Lawrence Rivers. The self-destruction of this munitioning capacity would be affected by the isolation of the Ontario peninsula from its industrial power sources and an offensive which controls the St Lawrence River Valley from Ottawa to Québec. Pending the expected development of the hydro-power in the James Bay area which progress is indicated in the near future by the present rapid growth of the metallurgical operations from Sudbury towards James Bay and its interconnection of this power with the lines from the Niagara Falls area, the Niagara Power is considerably more vital to Canada than to America. The destruction of the Niagara power facilities would have but slight effect on the USA's munitioning capacity.

For the industrial life and munitioning capacity of the USA, the Great Lakes except for Lake Ontario and the waterways connecting them are of the greatest importance as routes of transportation. In a war of long duration, possession of the Great Lakes transportation system west of the Welland Canal would now be of vital importance to America's munitioning capacity. The narrow defiles of the St. Clair River, the Detroit River, the St. Mary's River including the Salt Ste. Marie canals and the Straits of Mackinac along those routes are extremely vulnerable to attack both by air and by mobile artillery. The Welland Canal is of no industrial use to the USA, therefore, its disposition would be determined entirely from military considerations.

Winnipeg constitutes a rail bottleneck which connects eastern and western Canada. Australia or other forces landed on the Pacific coast of Canada or the southern shore of Hudson Bay would require the uninterrupted views of this railroad center to reinforce eastern Canada. Vital supply of coal from The western provinces of Canada passes through this bottleneck in reaching the Ontario and Québec provinces munitioning areas; as those also the supply of wheat and other grains raised in western Canada and required in the eastern part of that country. The Winnipeg Railroad Center is particularly vulnerable to attack from the USA.

Empire Colonial troops with British officers.

National Characteristics and Internal Conditions.

The race making up the United Kingdom is essentially a homogenous more or less phlegmatic but determined and persistent group when once committed to a policy and is noted for its ability to fight to a finish. On the other hand, the British Empire is essentially heterogeneous, being composed of peoples of nearly every colour, race and religion. Dissident factions are numerous and revolutionary groups are known to exist. Some of the coloured races, however, come of good fighting stock and, under white leadership, can be made into very efficient troops.

The government of the United Kingdom is well suited for war-making, the cabinet ruling the state in the name of the sovereign by virtue of its control of Parliament. The government is subject to change as a whole only through failing to command the support of Parliament or by defeat in a general election of the party to which it belongs. In future wars, as in the World War, it is possible that the Prime Minister will be advised on all war policies by a small group of the cabinet known as the 'War Cabinet'. It is believed that in war, there is no greater likelihood of a major change in the government than there is in the case of the United States of America. The Prime Minister and the cabinet of the United Kingdom dictate the policy of the British Empire as a whole although, in certain major foreign policies the self-governing dominions are consulted.

Based upon the fundamental understanding by all British citizens of the vital character of UK trade and the necessity for its protection and of the evident necessity for keeping the war away from UK territory, the cabinet is unlikely to find any difficulty in obtaining appropriations for making preparations for a foreign war should it be deemed vital to United Kingdom's commercial interest. Propaganda to such ends would be intensive and thorough. The solidarity of the British race in cases dealing with national interests is proverbial where a foreign government is concerned.

While there has been no act of parliament since the World War designed to produce national plans for war, it is believed that the lessons of the war have been well digested, and the Chiefs of Staff of the three fighting services may be assumed to have well-considered war plans for the conduct of any probable war ready at the time to present to the Prime Minister.

It may be taken for granted that no UK government will undertake to commit the Empire to a major war unless it is assured of the firm support of the labor elements of United Kingdom. Since the laboring class constitutes four-fifths of the population, its support is essential to success in war.

In the Irish Free State, while the irreconcilable elements are no longer in a position to interfere with a policy of the state, it is believed that Irish support of the UK in a war with USA will be far from unanimous and the internal security of this Dominion will be a matter of concern to the UK. On the other hand on account of the economic situation is believed that this Dominion will remain loyal to the Empire.

In the dominions of Australia, while feeling against the USA is not likely to be prominent, it is believed that the principle of Empire Solidarity will prevail. However in case, Japan should intervene in the war on the side of the British Empire, these dominions will probably insist upon guarantees of their paramount interest in the South Seas and their participation in any territorial readjustments that may take place after the conclusion of the war.

In the dominion of South Africa, Imperial feeling is divided; however, support of the UK in a war with the USA by this Dominion will probably be a small importance.

In India, and generally throughout British possessions, protectorates and mandates in the Near and Middle East, unrest is always prevalent, but it is believed that the UK will be able to maintain sufficient forces in these regions to suppress promptly any uprising as well as to repel attacks on the frontiers by the warlike tribesmen.

In Canada, Imperial feeling is strongest in British Columbia and quite strong in the Maritime provinces, Newfoundland and Ontario. It is weakest in the prairie provinces exclusive of Manitoba. In Québec Province, Canadian feeling rather than an imperial feeling is strong. However, it is estimated that in the event of war between the British Empire and USA, local feeling would have little effect and the Canadian provinces would take united action.

The possibility that Canada may declare neutrality, which under the rather lose Constitution of the British Empire - or rather British Commonwealth of Nations - the dominion is in a position to do, should receive careful consideration. Such action on the part of Canada would necessarily involve permanent or temporary secession from the Empire, but there are several reasons why such

British Empire Colonial troops line up for bayonet practice.

Three Fairey IIIFs of 734 Squadron Fleet Air Arm over Malta. The picture was taken from a fourth. Below the aircraft is 'battleship row' in Grand Harbour, Valletta. Six battleships can be seen along with the floating dock (far left). A cruiser and destroyer are at the bottom.

steps appear to be advantageous to Canada. Not only is this Dominion more closely bound by commercial, financial and cultural ties to the USA than any other part of the British Empire, but it appears inevitable, in case Canada does not declare neutrality that large parts of the Canadian territory will become theatres of military operations with consequent suffering to the population and widespread destruction and devastation of the country as well as almost total suppression of normal trade and industry. Such action, however, might be considered advantageous to the UK as it would relieve the Empire of the moral obligation to defend this far-flung Dominion against the full military strength of the USA and would permit concentration of British military and naval strength against American commerce and overseas possessions. On the other hand, it would deprive the UK of the best-suited base from which to conduct war against the USA and would thereby bring about a limited war, chiefly maritime in character, of prolonged duration and leading to no decisive results.

From the standpoint of the USA, it would appear to be advantageous for Canada to be allied with the UK. In this case, the USA would be free to employ her significantly superior manpower in overrunning Canada and holding that dominion to offset such losses as the USA might suffer elsewhere. Canadian neutrality would be a little military advantage to the USA since the duration of such neutrality would always be a matter of doubt and might be employed to protect Canada during the period when the dominion was weakest. In any case, large American military forces would have to be retained in readiness to advance into Canada should that country enter the war on the side of the British Empire. It appears to be almost certain that Canada would not ally with the USA unless in the highly improbable event that the British Empire failed to respect neutrality declared by Canada. Unless Canada goes as far as to declare her independence of the British Empire and to ally herself with the USA, it would appear to be advantageous not to accept such neutrality unless accompanied by guarantees. Among such guarantees, the

USA should demand and insist upon occupation until the end of the war by American military forces of the ports of Halifax, Victoria, and St John's New Brunswick, and of bridgeheads in Canadian territory, in the vicinity of Sault Ste. Marie, the St. Clair and Detroit Rivers and of the Ontario peninsula along with the line of the Welland Canal.

However, it is believed that Canada is more likely to remain loyal to the British Empire and that there will be no local differences of sufficient strength to assume importance to the USA.

Aside from the fact of having a common King–Emperor the British Empire is bound by common commercial, financial, cultural, racial and political interests and these would probably be strong enough to hold it intact in case of war with America, although such a war is not likely to be unanimously supported as in the case of the Empire in the world war.

Due to the possibility that the self-governing Dominions will be reluctant to take part in a war against the USA, especially if started by the UK without their consent, it is estimated that the decision to engage in such a war will be reached by the Empire as a whole, the view of the dominions having received full consideration.

When it becomes apparent that war with the USA is possible, it may be expected that the British Empire will begin secretly to increase her military, naval and air forces in her American possessions and in north-western Atlantic waters, although such an increase would be gradual at first. Among the first of these possessions to receive consideration will probably be Jamaica, Bermuda and Trinidad. It is likely that the garrisons in these islands will be augmented by the recruitment of local forces.

War Causes and British Empire Aims.
The most probable cause of war between the USA and the British Empire is the constantly

A US Navy Vought O2U Corsair floatplane flying over the Cavite Navy Yard, Philippines, circa 1930. The seaplane tender USS *Jason* (AV-2) is docked in the yard. Sangley Point is visible in background with the Naval Radio Station. *(USN)*

increasing American economic penetration and commercial expansion into regions formerly dominated by British Empire trade to such extent as eventually to menace British Empire standards of living and threaten economic ruin.

The war aim of the British Empire in the war with the USA is conceived to be the definite elimination of the USA as an important economic and commercial rival in international trade. This objective is to be accomplished by destruction of the US Merchant Marine and foreign trade and by the acquisition of US overseas possessions including control by the British Empire of the Panama Canal.

The British Empire may be regarded as a great economic unit represented on the one hand by the United Kingdom, highly organised industrially, importing the major portion of the foodstuffs and raw materials required, and producing a large exportable surplus of manufactured goods and refined materials, which are exchanged for those imports. On the other hand are the dominions, colonies, protectorates and mandates which are chiefly characterised as producers of exporting surpluses of foodstuffs and raw materials which they exchange for manufactured articles and refined materials.

This great politico-economic unit is tied together by great Empire banking organisations, and the most comprehensive system of cable and radio communications and by a gigantic merchant Marine which not only carries the greater portion of the products of the Empire, but also a large part of the products of the other countries of the world. To assist in this mercantile system, fuelling stations and ports of call under the British flag have been provided in almost every port of the globe.

The 'risk assessment' aspect then turned to the American perspective: 'America's national political organisation is well adapted to making war. The American nation is essentially homogenous, confident, aggressive and resourceful. It, however, shares with the British Empire a national antipathy towards making large expenditures for military and naval purposes during peace and therefore usually enters upon war in an unprepared state. On the other hand, despite racial affinity, common culture and similar political systems, the great majority of the American nation possesses an anti-British Empire tradition, and it is believed that the American government would experience little difficulty in mobilising public sentiment in favour of a vigorous prosecution of the war once hostilities began.

So far as the continental USA is concerned America's internal situation is excellent. The only significant minority group, the American Negro, has no political or racial ties with any other nation and is resistant to foreign propaganda. A large number of UK citizens residing in the USA and a small number of professional pacifist and communist groups would be the only elements with which it would be necessary to deal with internally.

So far as the outlying possessions are concerned, the situation is not so favourable,

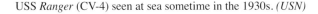

USS *Ranger* (CV-4) seen at sea sometime in the 1930s. *(USN)*

although considered much better than the analogous British Empire situation. A strong separatist groups exist in the Philippine Islands, and this group would probably receive much support from the British Empire. A separatist group exists in Puerto Rico but is not believed to have much importance. The large alien groups in Hawaii would be a matter of much concern to the USA particularly if Japan interferes in the war on the side of the British Empire.

War causes and War Aims.

The probable ultimate cause of war between America and the British Empire had previously been estimated to rise out of American competition and interference with British foreign trade although other proximate causes of the war may be alleged.

It is not believed that the USA, when relations become strained, will be likely to take the initiative in declaring war. At the same time, the British Empire, in order to preserve an appearance before the world as non-aggressor, will likely refrain from declaring war on the USA and will make every endeavour to provoke the USA into acts of hostility. For those reasons, it is considered probable that neither will issue a formal declaration of war, but, after hostilities break out, each, in accordance with its constitutional procedure will formally be recognised that the state of war exists between them.

A formation of Boeing P-26 aircraft of the 20th Pursuit Group seen in flight. (NARA)

It is believed that America's war aims in case of war with the British Empire should be the expulsion of the Empire from North and South America, including the waters adjacent thereto, and the definite elimination of the British Empire as a strong competitor in foreign-trade.

On account of the great strength of the British Empire, as well as the possibility that other nations may intervene in the war on the side of the Empire, the accomplishment of the above war aims will require the maximum effort on the part of the American Army, Navy and civil powers. Because of the proved tenacity of both America and British nations in war, it is concluded that any war will be one of prolonged duration.

The USA is one of the greatest industrial nations in the world. Its industries are capable of producing almost every essential commodity, and it produces within its own territory the bulk of the raw materials consumed. At the same time, the USA is one of the leading agricultural nations that not only feeds its own population but is a large exporter of surplus foodstuffs. American population relative to the extent of territory is comparatively small, and there is room for considerable expansion. For those reasons primarily the American national wealth is the greatest in the world, and the American people have the highest standard of living of any of the principal nations.

America enjoys probably the strongest financial position of any of the great nations and is believed to be thoroughly capable of financing a long war.

The following general plans of operation are available to American army forces:

Canadian troops parading at the reopening of Fort York, Toronto by Lord Bessborough after partial restoration on 24 May 1934.

A. Plan I. To initiate an immediate general offensive against Canada with a view to penetrating vital Canadian areas, preventing mobilisation of Canadian forces and disrupting Canadian economic life.

Advantages

1. It has all the advantages of initiative.
2. Canada may be crushed before the British Empire can reinforce her.
3. Early operations by either the British Empire or Canada will be made difficult.
4. It renders difficult for the British Empire the establishment on Canadian territory of forces suitable for the invasion of the USA.

Disadvantages.

1. Dispersion of effort without direction to a decisive objective.
2. The best American units will become involved immediately and perhaps offer such losses that the subsequent development of larger forces and more important operations will be seriously affected.
3. It will require a reduction of security measures at other points.

B. Plan II. To initiate properly operations to separate Canadian forces from the British Empire through the destruction of enemy forces in Canada and the seizure of vital Canadian areas this plan contemplates:

1. Preparation for a joint overseas expedition against Halifax Nova Scotia, which will be dispatched in case the situation at the outbreak of war indicates the practicability of the operation otherwise Halifax will be neutralised by air operations.
2. An early advance to seize the Montréal Québec area.
3. Measures to defend all sensitive points along the Great Lakes waterways including minor operations in adjacent Canadian territory.
4. An operation to cut Canadian railroad communications at Winnipeg.
5. Initially conduct an active defence on other fronts.

Advantages

1. It has all the advantages of initiative.
2. The initial concentration and direction of advance cover the American vital north-east area.
3. It strikes at the vital Canadian area.
4. It provides a plan for the quickest method of capturing the principal ice free port of Canada.

5. It may permit combined action of the army and navy.

Disadvantages.
  1. The operations must be pushed rapidly to be successful.
  2. If the joint expedition against Halifax be included, it will involve all difficulties in joint operations and forced landings on hostile shores, intensified by the menace of a powerful hostile fleet.

C. Plan III. Same as Plan II except that there will be no provision for a joint overseas operation against Halifax Nova Scotia.

Advantages
  1. It has all the advantages of initiative.
  2. The initial concentration and direction of advance cover the American vital north-east area.
  3. It strikes at the vital Canadian area.
  4. It permits the use of the stronger initial force in the advance against the Montréal Québec area than would be the case if an expedition were sent against Halifax.
  5. It is largely independent of naval action and thus frees the Navy for other operations.

Disadvantages.
  1. It leaves Halifax available to the enemy for use as a naval base and as a port for debarkation for reinforcements and supplies unless neutralised by air attacks.
  2. The neutralisation of Halifax by air attacks would require the use of so much of the American air force as to prevent sufficient attacks against other important objectives.

D. Plan IV. To assume the strategic defensive against the enemy along the Canadian frontier and to concentrate the army effort initially in co-operating with the Navy in driving the British Empire from the Caribbean area.

Advantages
  1. It would ensure a prompt and complete control of the Caribbean area.
  2. It is the best method of defending the Panama Canal.

Disadvantages.
  1. It would permit the British Empire to reinforce Canada and when ready to launch a major offensive against the USA from Canada.
  2. It would not secure for America any objective which would seriously

The US Army on parade in the Panama Canal Zone in 1928. *(NARA)*

cripple the British Empire.

    3. It would not be taking advantage of America's immense man power since operations in the Caribbean area would not require large land forces.

E. *Plan V. To assume the strategic defensive on all fronts. This plan contemplates deploying such traits as may be necessary for covering missions; reinforcing overseas garrisons, and building up in the meantime forces suitable to a major offensive. This is, in reality, the taking up of the position in readiness pending the building up of strong forces.*

Advantages

    1. It provides for the immediate protection of the American frontier.

    2. It permits the orderly organisation and training of large American forces.

    3. It permits the organisation of American war industrial effort.

    4. It assures a heavy and concentrated blow when adequate forces become available.

Disadvantages.

    1. It surrenders, initially, the advantages of the initiative.

    2. It permits the systematic strengthening of Canadian defences.

    3. It permits the uninterrupted concentration of large British Empire forces in Canada.

    4. It makes possible launching of a major offensive by the British Empire against America before America is prepared.

    5. It places no immediate pressure on the British Empire to come to the assistance of Canada with land forces.

    6. It fails to take advantage of the

An American M2A3 light tank at the Army Day Parade in a very wet Washington DC. *(NARA)*

initial superiority of the USA in the western hemisphere. It may result in a longer and more costly war.

7. *Much popular clamour would probably be raised against this lack of aggressive measures.*

The following general plans of operations are available to American naval forces:

A. *Plan I. to adopt the strategic offensive with the American Main Fleet and seek out and engage the British Empire main fleet decisively while conducting secondary operations in other theaters to weaken the British Empires economic power.*

Advantages.

1. *It retains the initiative.*
2. *It ensures a quick decision at sea.*
3. *If successful ensures immediate effective control of the sea.*

Disadvantages

1. *It risks the American fleet against the stronger British Empire fleet under conditions which may be disadvantageous to America.*
2. *If unsuccessful it gives the British Empire almost undisputed control of the sea and practically isolates America.*
3. *If unsuccessful it gives the British Empire access to the products of the world.*
4. *In the case of the American initial defeat the British Empire could thereafter for a long time exceed the USA in sea power.*

B. *Plan II. To establish the American main fleet in the western North Atlantic insufficient strength to dominate sea communications between the UK and Canada while conducting secondary operations in other theatres for the purposes of weakening the British financial ability to support the war and disperse in her naval power. The above operation is to be undertaken with a view towards attacking into force the British Empire fleet or detachments thereof whenever the favourable opportunity arises.*

Advantages.

1. *The American fleet is near home bases.*
2. *It preserves the integrity of the American fleet while awaiting favourable opportunity to strike against the British Empire fleet.*
3. *It automatically forces the British Empire to maintain a extremely expensive convoy system.*
4. *It compels the British Empire to retain assembled fleet superior to America.*
5. *The American fleet is strategically located to exercise control of the western Atlantic.*
6. *It permits an opportunity for gradual attrition of British Empire naval forces.*

Disadvantages

1. *It delays the ultimate decision on the sea.*

C. *Plan III. To assume the strategic defensive with the major units of the American fleet exercising any favourable opportunity that may arise to defeat British Empire naval forces in*

A flight of Royal Air Force Hawker Furies in formation.

69

US Navy destroyers and cruisers at anchor in Balboa Harbor, Panama Canal Zone 23 April 1934 (USN)

detail and to exert the main naval effort against the British Empire overseas commerce and seaborne trade.

Advantages.

1. It maintains the American fleet as a 'Fleet in being'.
2. It directly exerts economic pressure against the British Empire by threatening her vital sea communications.
3. It will cause widespread dispersion of the British naval forces to safeguard trade.

Disadvantages

1. It surrenders the initiative to the British Empire.

2. It risks defeat of American naval forces in detail.
3. It provides for no cooperation with the army.
4. It will probably involve diplomatic difficulties with other nations and alienate foreign support of the USA.
5. As a method of warfare, it has uniformly failed in the past.

Now that all risk assements had been completed and directly described here in italics, and all options considered, it was time for the Plan to be drawn up in detail and submitted to higher authority following the same proceedure.

70

Chapter Four

War Plan Red.

'You are beaten. It is useless to resist. Don't let yourself be destroyed...'

Seventy-five copies of the original document were issued: Numbers one and two went to the Commander in Chief United States Fleet and the remainder descended down to the Commandants, Navy Yards, with the final six being held in reserve and as library copies.

Much of the document appears repetitively boring in general terms, but must be regarded as explosive in the nuances of detail and therefore deserves reproducing here in as full a manner as possible, including the Secondary Theater of Operations. Where I have quoted directly from the Plan document I have reproduced the text in italics, complete with spelling and grammatic errors. It clearly shows that as far as the US Navy was concerned, the plan was to ensure world domination and to establish the USA as the world's only superpower.

The original 1930 document is divided into two sections: Part One, is a seventy-four-page section that goes into great detail:

Chapter I - Introduction.
The Navy Basic Plan - Red, and the Army Special Plan - Red, are founded upon and support Joint Army and Navy War Plan - Red. (Joint Report No.325, Serial No. 435), which was approved by the Secretary of the Navy on 10 May 1930, and by the Acting Secretary of War on 10 May 1930.

In this, Part I, will be be found summaries of the Joint Army and Navy Estimates of the Situation Blue-Red and certain aspects from the Army Strategical Plan - Red.

Chapters II and III contain the summaries of the Joint Estimate. On account of the length and scope of the original, it is impractical in this Navy Basic Plan Red to quote it in full. However, complete copies of the Estimate will be furnished by the Chief of Naval Operations to the Commander-in-Chief, United States Fleet, and to certain other designated Commanders of Theaters of Operations.

Chapters IV and V contain a copy of the Joint

Army and Navy Basic War Plan - Red.

Chapter IV contains certain extracts from the Army Strategical Plan Red - which will be found to be of special value to the Commanders of Naval Forces who may be required to co-operate with the Army Forces. The Chief of Naval Operations will furnish the Commander-in-Chief, United States Fleet with a complete copy of the Army Strategical Plan, when such a plan is issued.

Estimates from both sides are considered: *'In the Caribbean Sea and the West Indian waters, Red has potential advanced naval bases at Jamacia (Port Royal) Trinidad and St. Lucia. In addition, Red has an outlying subsidiary naval base at Bermuda. There are suitable harbors elsewhere within Red North American possessions (exclusive of Crimson) which are capable of serving as bases for small craft, particularly submarines. Notable among them are the Bahamas and the Red Leeward Islands. These harbors are important not only for the protection of Red seaborne trade, but as sally points from which to attack Blue commerce.*

Jamaica constitutes a serious menace to the security of the Panama Canal and to all Blue trade routes passing through the Caribbean Sea and is the most important West Indian submarine cable communications center. Bermuda is well located to interfere with Blue seaborne trade to the West Indies and along the Blue South Atlantic Coast. In addition, it is capable of serving as bases for aircraft carriers designated to conduct air raids against Blue vital areas. The Bahamas are so situated as to afford bases from which to control Blue trade through the Straits of Florida and to Cuba.

Trinidad and St Lucia, and the Red Leeward Islands lie on the flank of Blue trade routes to the East coast of South America and constitute serious threats to the integrity of Blue commerce engaged therewith.

Of the Red North American possessions, exclusive of Crimson, only Jamaica and

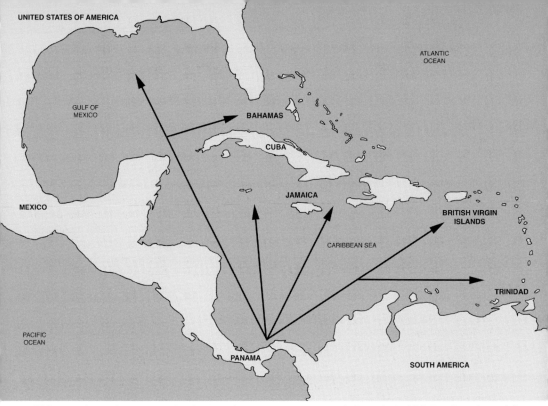

This map shows the reasons why the Americans were so concerned about the British Empire - through its possessions in the Caribbean - having ways to control access to the Pamama Canal.

Bermuda are at present defended, although the defenses are neither extensive nor modern and at present the garrisons are small.

Political matters involving the United Kingdom and also their dominions of Canada, Australia, India, South Africa and New Zealand were also studied in depth: *The possibility that Crimson may declare neutrality, which, under the rather loose constitution of the Red Empire - or rather the Red Commonwealth of Nations, the Dominion is in a position to do, should recieve careful consideration. Such action on the part of Crimson would necessarily involve permanent or temporary secession from the Empire, but there are several rerasons why such a step appears to beadvantageous to Crimson. Not only is this Dominion more closely bound by commercial financial and cultural ties to Blue than any other part of the Red Empire, but it appears inevitable in case Crimson does not declare neutrality that large parts of Crimson territory will become theaters of military operations with consequent suffering to the population and widespread destruction and devastation of the country as well as almost total suppression of normal trade and industry. Such action, moreover, might be considered advantageous to Red as it would relieve the Empire of the moral obligations to defend this far-flung Dominion against the full military strength of Blue and would permit concentration of red military and naval strength against Blue commerce and overseas possessions. On the other hand, it would deprive Red of the best-suited base from which to conduct war against Blue, and would thereby bring about a limited war, chiefly maritime in character of prolonged duration and leading to no decisive result.*

Because of the probability that the self-governing dominions will be reluctant to take part in a war against Blue, especially if initiated by Red without their consent, it is estimated that a decision to engage in such a war will be reached before the empire as a whole, views of the dominions have received full consideration.

When it becomes apparent that war with Blue is probable, it may be expected that red will begin secretly to increase her military, naval and air forces in her American possessions and in western North Atlantic waters, although such increases will be gradual at first. Among the first of these possessions to receive consideration

72

will probably be Jamaica, Bermuda and Trinidad. It is likely that the garrisons in these islands will be augmented by the recruitment of local forces.

While, during a period of strained relations, Red would be unlikely to precipitate hostilities by the open movement of considerable land, sea or air forces to North American possessions, Red light naval forces basing on Halifax will be increased. The land elements of the defences of that base will probably be provided by Crimson contingents, and while it is unlikely that will Red will send a force combat units to Crimson at this time, Crimson may be expected to provide the base troops and facilities required for their reception with a view to beginning operations immediately on landing. Crimson will probably also expand her own air forces.

It may be expected that Red, prior to undertaking a war against Blue, will make such arrangements and agreements with other powers as will provide for the security of Red's interests in Europe and will permit concentration of the bulk of Red military, naval and air forces in or about the United Kingdom, including the major portions of the naval forces now stationed in the Mediterranean.

On the other hand since a Blue-Red war is bound to involve the struggle for Maritime supremacy, and Red will be obliged to adopt and carry out measures of blockade involving severe restrictions on neutral commerce, it is probable that Red will soon be involved in diplomatic difficulties with other powers. However, on account of the financial benefits likely to recruit a neutral is through the supply of Red war requirements, and of Red propaganda which may be expected to be very effectively exhorted against Blue, it is unlikely that any stronger power will, in the early stages of the war, intervene on the side of Blue.

The Economic aspects were also studied: In the United Kingdom is almost entirely deficient in food production, being self-sustaining only in

The Panama Canal allowed the USA to exchange vessels between it's Pacific and Atlantic fleets fairly quickly without having to make the tedious, time-consuming two-week trip around South America. American strategists quickly realised that British Empire possessions in the Caribbean could, if they wish apply a high degree of blockade control over ships passing through the area. Here the USS *Ohio* (BB 12) is seen passing the Cucaracha Slide, while transiting the Panama Canal on 16 July 1915. She appears to be under tow. This event occurred about a month before the grand opening of the canal.

the fish and certain vegetables. About seventy-five per cent of the wheat and 5fifty per cent of the meat consumed, as well as a large proportion of other grains, butter, cheese, eggs, sugar and tea, are imported, the larger part of which comes from other parts of the empire although much is obtained from foreign sources. Cereals, pork and pork products are heavily imported from blue, and cereals, chilled and frozen beef, Madison and lamb are imported from the Argentine. The other parts of the Empire, especially the great self-governing dominions, are, in the main, entirely self-sustaining in the foodstuffs.

With exception of coal and a portion of the iron ore, practically all the raw materials are required by the industries of the United Kingdom must be imported. The most important deficiencies are cotton, wood, jute, copper, iron ore, nitrates, petroleum, mercury, manganese, nickel and rubber. Of these raw materials, all except cotton, petroleum, Iron ore and nitrates are produced within the empire in sufficient quantities to meet war needs. It is believed that, through production within the Empire from sources not now economically profitable, the Empire can be made self-sustaining in war, except for cotton, for which the utilisation of inferior substitutes might be forced for non-military uses.

The Red merchant marine (1929) had a gross tonnage of 23,115,147, in 10,679 ships of 100 gross tons or over. Of those totals, 22,841,369 gross tons were in 9,860 steam or motor-propelled vessels. There were a total of 3,453 steam or motor-propelled vessels of 2,000 gross tons or over. There were 427 tankers of 1,000 gross tons or over having a total tonnage of 2,393,117. Of the total tonnage of steam or motor vessels of 2,000 tons or over. 756 with a total tonnage of 4,519,121 were not over five years of age. Speed classification of steam or motor vessels of 2,000 tons and over is:

Having a speed of 20 kts or over	42
Having a speed between 17 & 20 kts	78
Having a speed between 14 & 17 kts	370
Having a speed between 12 & 14 kts	603
Total	1,393

It is estimated that, in the event of a war with Blue, shipping tonnage requirements of the Red empire would aggregate:

For Economic Requirements	10,000,000
For Red Naval Forces	3,500,000
Undergoing repairs and otherwise unavailable	1,500,000
Total	15,000,000

This leaving available for the transportation and supply of overseas expeditions, a total of slightly over 8,000,000 tons. This is considered sufficient for all probably needs.

Part One then looked at the strenth and distribution of the Empire Armed Forces, starting with the Army: The strength and distribution of the Red Empire Army Forces on 11 November 1929 were:

	At Home	Colonies	Total
Regular Army, excluding India*	110,148	24,648	134,796

It was not just naval military traffic that the American Navy were worried about - they were also concerned about interuptions to commercial traffic, either passenger if cargo. Here SS *Excalibur* of American Export Lines is seen going about her business in 1931.

74

Above: A group of British Army officers pose for a snapshot during a training exercise in India.

Below: Just as they did during the great War, the British Army relied on the railway network to move troops around. Here the 11th Hussars are seen alighting from a train at the Lydda junction on their arrival from Egypt. Lt. General R.H. Haining, Commander-in-Chief, British Forces in Palestine & Transjordan - circa 1938.

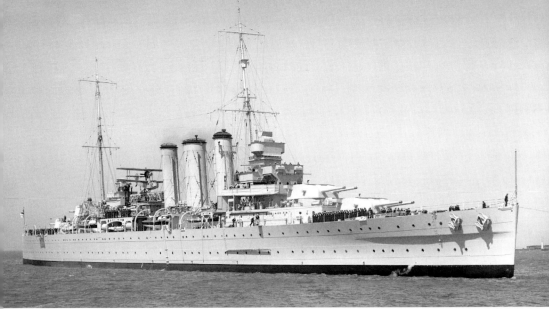

HMAS *Australia* was laid down by John Brown & Sons on Clydebank in 1925 for the Royal Australian Navy. It was commissioned in 1928. *(Royal Australian Navy)*

Colonial and Native

Indian Corps	-	*2,137*	*2,137*
Territorial Army	*138,011*	-	*138,011*
Militia	-	*2,140*	*2,140*
Reg. Army Reserve	*90,906*	-	*90,906*
Supplimentary Reserve	*14,061*	-	*14,061*
Reg Army Reserve			
of Officers	*13,983*	-	*13,983*
Totals	*367,109*	*28,925*	*396034*

* - includes 3,265 in China in excess of normal garrison. Jamaica detatchment numbers 827; Bermuda detatchment numbers 275. Red Army in India is included in Indian establishment.

Australia

Permament Force	*1,811*
Citizen Force	*46,294*
Total	*47,995*

New Zealand

Permanent Force	*514*
Territorial Force	*20,375*
Total	*20,889*

Union of South Africa

Permanent Force	*1,072*
Non-Permanent Force	*8,381*
Total	*9,453*

India

Red Army	*59,659*
Aden and elsewhere	*1,728*
Indian Army	*156,495*
Auxiliary Force	*33,181*
Territorial Force	*20,000*
Indian State Forces	*36,056*
Reservists	*29,924*
TOTAL	*347,243*

Table XXX Strength of Red Empire Naval Forces, July 1930.

	Atlantic Fleet	Mediterranian Fleet	China Station	US & W Indies	East Indies	African Station	NZ Station	Austr. Station	Canada Station	Home Fleet
Battleships	5	6	-	-	-	-	-	-	-	5
Battle Cruisers	4	-	-	-	-	-	-	-	-	-
Cruisers	5	10	6	5	3	2	3	4	-	18
Destroyer Leaders	2	5	1	-	-	-	-	1	-	8
Destroyers	18	36	8	-	-	-	-	7	2	73
Minelayers	1	-	-	-	-	-	-	-	-	-
Minesweepers	-	9	2	-	-	-	-	-	3	15
Submarines	-	7	4	-	-	-	-	2	-	39
Aircraft Carriers	1	2	-	-	-	-	-	-	-	3
Seaplane Tenders	-	-	-	-	-	-	-	1	-	1
Sloops.	1	2	4	2	3	-	-	2	-	11

Crimson
Permanent Force	3,533
Non-Permanent Force	52,105
Reserve of Officers	12,213
Reserves (estimated)	30,000
TOTAL	97,851

Irish Free State
Regular Army	6,976
Reserve	10,000
Total	16,976

This gives an aggregate Red Empire Army strength of 936,441.

The strength and disposition of the Empire Navy was considered in detail, but much of it weas shown in two charts: *The present strength and distribution (July 1930) of the Red Empire Naval Forces is shown in Table XXX: It is estimated that the Red Atlantic and Mediterranean fleets and the North American and West Indies squadrons will be concentrated, upon mobilisation, into a Grand Fleet. It is further estimated that the Australian, New Zealand, China, South African and East Indian* squadrons *will be concentrated, upon mobilisation, into an Asiatic Fleet. It is expected that the Grand Fleet will concentrate in the Channel ports and that the Asiatic Fleet will concentrate in Singapore.*

Finally, Part One studied the Empire Air Forces: *Under an agreement which now exists between the Red air force and the Red Navy, or floating based aviation is to be controlled by the Red Navy. This force is called the fleet arm and includes the complement of aircraft carriers and of the aeroplanes carried on battleships and cruisers. It can be used by the Red air force only by order of the cabinet. The Red Navy can be considered therefore to include the Fleet Air Arm. This fleet arm will be considerably augmented upon mobilisation. The extent of such augmentation may be estimated is equal to be unused aeroplane carrying capacity of the Red fleet, which at the present time, July 1930, is estimated at 277 aeroplanes. No air force is assigned to the control of the Red Army, although it is the duty of the Red air force to provide observation aeroplanes for duty with the Red army. Such units are termed Army Co-*

Table: Personnel strength, Red Empire Navy, 1 October 1929.			
Regulars			
	Officers	Enlisted	Totals
Royal Navy	7,576	80,793	88,371
Royal Marines	414	9,644	10,058
Royal Canadian Navy	77	429	506
Royal Australian Navy	492	4,546	5,038
New Zealand division, Royal Navy	75	879	954
South African Naval Service	16	130	146
Royal Indian Marine	158	1,162	1,320
Midshipman under instruction	797	-	797
Royal Air Force assigned to Royal Navy	300	3,800	3,100
Civilian crews of naval auxiliaries	253	3,912	4,165
TOTAL:	10,160	104,295	114,455
Reserves			
Special reserve of engineer officers	116	-	116
Emergency officers	155	-	155
Royal Fleet Reserve	-	20,919	20,919
Royal Naval Reserve	1,635	7,799	9,434
Royal Naval Volunteer Reserve	462	3.681	4,143
Royal Navy Auxiliary Sick Birth Reserve	-	1,375	1,375
Australian Naval Reserve	784	9,546	10,333
Canadian Naval Reserve	97	936	1,053
New Zealand Naval Reserve	72	882	954
South African Naval Reserve	47	734	781
TOTAL:	3,368	45,772	49,140
GRAND TOTAL:	13,528	150,067	163,595

Hawker Audax K3114 from an Army co-operation squadron picking up a message 'somewhere in the Middle East'. This was a common method of communication in the days pre-reliable radio.

Operation units. The strengths and distribution of the Red Empire Air Forces July 1930 is shown in the following tables.

Royal Air Force squadrons consist of ten aeroplanes each for the twin-engined type and twelve aeroplanes in the single-engine types. Naval flights consist similarly of five to six aeroplanes each. There is a reserve of approximately 620 aeroplanes in addition to training and experimental aeroplanes.

The regular air forces maintained in readiness for war and stand mobilised (although all of it is not available to services outside the Empire, including mandated territories). This force is augmented by the mobilisation of special reserve auxiliary squadrons beginning on M +30, by the organisation of the air force reserves into squadrons between M +60 and M +90 and by the organisation of new squadrons beginning on M+180. Four squadrons

TABLE: Royal Air Force Squadrons (10 to 12 aircraft each)						
Location	Bomber	Fighter	Army Co-Op	Comms	Flying Boat	Totals
Home	14	13	5	1	4	37
Meditterranean	-	-	-	-	1	1
Middle East	4	-	2	-	-	6
Aden	1	-	-	-	-	1
Iraq	4	-	-	-	1	5
India	4	-	4	-	-	8
Totals	27	13	11	1	6	58

Table: Royal Air Force Flights (5 to 6 aircraft each)
1 x VO-VS Coastal Defence Co-Operation. 1 x VP Flying Boat Development.
1 x VS Home Communications. 1 x VF Night Flying. 2 x VB Station Flights. 1 x VF Station Flight.

Table: Fleet Airt Arm Flights (5 to 6 aircraft each)

Location	VF (Fleet Fighter)	VO-VS Obs/Recon	VT Torpedo	Totals
Atlantic/Home	7	10	4	21
Mediterranean	1	1	1	3
Totals	8	11	5	24

Table: Reserve Squadrons (10 to 12 aircraft each)
Special Reserve (bombers) at home = 4 Auxiliary Air Force (bombers) at Home = 5. Total = 9.

appearing on M+15 are Crimson. A number of squadrons and flights have peacetime duties which will continue in war. These units will not, therefore, be available for combat.

Based on the assumption available aeroplane carriers may be used to transport these claims and combat personality forced to Crimson immediately after M day, the development rate in Crimson could be attained without making it necessary to remove the Fleet Air Arm from the carriers. This plan will necessitate previous arrangements on the part of Crimson to receive and service Red air force units. The remainder of the radio forces to be shipped over as cargo under the assumption that by removing all aeroplanes required by the Fleet Air Arm from aeroplane carriers and by using such carriers as aeroplane transports the entire available land-based, therefore, it could be transported to Crimson territory and be in operation by M +15 day. Such an operation, however, it Would jeopardise the carriers, and, while possible, it is extremely unlikely.

We then come to the second part of War Plan Red, which was described as 'The Strategic Plan'. This explains the general missions, theatres of operations, Commands, Forces for Tasks, Categories of Defence, Subarines, Chemical Warfare and Contraband.

General Missions
Concept: A war of long duration, involving the maximum effort of the armed forces and civil power of the United States, directed initially towards the isolation of Crimson from Red , and the defeat of Red Armed Forces in North America and the Western North Atlantic, including the Caribbean Sea and West Indian waters, and finally toward the economic exhaustion of the Red United Kingdom.

National Mission: To undertake and prosecute the measure, military, naval, political, financial and economic, required to win the war.

Mission for the Armed Forces: While protecting the United States territory and interests, to destroy Red armed forces in North America and the western North Atlantic, including the Caribbean Sea and West Indian waters; to isolate Crimson from Red; to deny to Red the use of bases in the western hemisphere; to occupy such territory in Crimson and other Red possessions as may be necessary; and to gain and exercise such control of sea

A pair of Vought O2U-2 Corsairs of Marine Corps Scouting Squadron 14 (VS-14M) fly past the USS *Saratoga* (CV-3) while preparing to land sometime in 1930. *(USN)*

A trio of US Navy Curtiss O2C-1 Helldivers assigned to Naval Reserve Air Base, New York fly in formation sometime in 1930, just as War Plan Red was being prepared. *(USN)*

communications as will contribute towards Reds economic exhaustion.

A. *Mission for the army: to provide for the defence of United States territory and industries; to destroy Red Armed Forces in North America; and, ultimately, to occupy such territory in Crimson and other Red possessions in the western hemisphere as may be necessary.*

B. *Mission for the Navy: to gain and exercise control of the sea in the western North Atlantic including the Carribean Sea and West Indian waters and in the Pacific adjacent to Crimson, preventing supply and reinforcement of Crimson; to protect essential trade routes; and, ultimately, to extend such control of sea communication areas necessary to affect economic exhaustion of Red.*

C: *Mission for the civil power: to support the Armed Forces in their operations and to take such action through financial, economic, and political agencies as will most seriously damage Red interests throughout the world, while strengthening those of the USA.*

Section 2: Theaters of Operation and Command Thereof.

The principal Theater of Operations, under the command of the Commander-in-Chief, United States fleet, will comprehend the high seas of the western North Atlantic, including the Caribbean Sea and West Indian waters, and the Gulf and River St Lawrence, as far west as Cornwall Island, inclusive.

The principal Theater of Operations, will not be interpreted to include the waters of the 1st, 3rd, 4th, 5th, 6th, 7th, 8th and 15th Naval districts, or the waters of the naval stations, St Thomas, Virgin Islands and Guantánamo Bay Cuba unless the United States fleet, or major portion thereof, are actually operating in such waters, in which case the Commander -in-Chief, United States fleet, may include the particular area within his command, after notifying the commandant concerned.

The Asiatic Theater, which is a secondary theater of operations, is under the command of the Commander -in-Chief, Asiatic Fleet, and comprehends the high seas included between the meridians 150° and 100° East longitude and the parallels of 0° and 40° North latitude.

The Asiatic theater includes the 16th Naval district and the Naval Station Guam.

The Hawaiian theater, which is a secondary theater of operations, is and the command of the Commandant, 14th Naval district, and comprehends the waters included within the circumference and the tangents connecting such circumferences, of circles drawn with Midway Island, Honolulu, Hilo and Johnson Island as centres, with the radii of 300 nautical miles.

The 14th Naval district is coterminous with the Hawaiian theater.

The Panama Canal Theater, which is a secondary theater of operations, is under the command of the Commandant, 15th Naval district, and comprehends the waters of the Panama Canal zone, the Republic of Panama, the coastal waters on the Caribbean and Pacific coast thereof, and the area of the high seas included within a distance of 200 nautical miles of the boundaries and coasts of the Republic of Panama.

The 15th Naval district is coterminous with the Panama Canal theater.

The Pacific theater which is a secondary theater of operations is under the command of the Commander, Naval Forces, Pacific (to be designated on or before M-Day), and comprehends the high seas adjacent to the Pacific Coast of the United States, Alaska and Crimson, not included in any other theater.

The Pacific Theater will not be interpreted to include the waters of the 11th, 12th, and 13th Naval districts, unless the Naval forces, Pacific, are actually operating in such waters, in which case the Commander, Naval Forces, Pacific, may include the particular area within his command, after notifying the commandant concerned.

The Naval Great Lakes theater, which is a secondary theater of operations, is under the command of the Commander, Naval Forces, Great Lakes, (to be designated on or before M-Day), and comprehends the water areas of the Great Lakes, and of the St Lawrence River, eastward to Cornwell Island, exclusive.

The Commander, Naval Forces, Great Lakes, is also the naval commandant of the Great Lakes Coastal Frontier. The Naval Great Lakes theater will include the district waters on the Great Lakes and the St Lawrence River, of the 3rd, 4th and 9th naval districts

Section 3. Forces for tasks.

The below-named forces, services, and activities, will be employed to accomplish the Navy's missions and tasks thereunder, and of such other tasks as may be assigned during the progress of war with Red.

A. Operating Forces.

1. The United States fleet, less certain units initially assigned to the Hawaiian, Panama Canal, and Pacific theaters; Plus the Naval Forces, Europe, Marine Corps expeditionary forces 'A', 'B' and 'C'; certain units of the Coast Guard assigned to the principal theater of operations; all under the command of the Commander-in-Chief, United States fleet.

2. The Asiatic Fleet, including the naval local defence forces of the 16th Naval

USS *Anderson* (DD-411) was a Sims-class destroyer in the United States Navy. She was named for Rear Admiral Edwin Alexander Anderson, Jr., a Medal of Honor recipient. *(USN)*

Part of the US Navy Pacific fleet on manoeuvres in the late 1930s, with the battleships USS *Colorado* and *Maryland* leading. Many of these ships were to be attacked at Pearl Harbor in 1941 (USN)

district and the Naval Station, Guam; all under the command of the Commander - in-Chief, Asiatic Fleet.

3. The Naval Forces, Hawaii, comprising certain units of the United States fleet assigned initially to the Hawaiian theater; and the naval local defence forces of the 14th Naval district; all under the command of the Commandant, 14th Naval district.

4. The Naval Forces Panama, comprising certain units of the United States fleet assigned initially to the Panama Canal Theater; the special service Squadron, likewise assigned initially to the Panama Canal Theater; and the Naval Local Defence Forces of the 15th Naval district; all under the command of the Commandant, 15th Naval district.

5. The Naval Forces Pacific comprising of certain units of the United States fleet assigned initially to the Pacific theater; and certain units of the Coast Guard; all under the command of the Commander,

Naval Forces, Pacific.

6. The Naval Forces, Great Lakes, comprising of the naval Local defence forces of the 9th and part of the naval local defence forces of the 3rd and 4th Naval districts; and certain units of the Coast Guard; all under the command of the Commander, Naval forces, Great Lakes.

7. The naval local defence forces, Navy and Marine Corps, together with such units of the Coast Guard as are assigned to naval districts; all under the respective commands of the commandants of the 1st, 3rd, 4th, 5th, 6th 7th, 8th, 11th 12th and 13th Naval districts, and the commandants of the naval stations St Thomas, Virgin islands, Guantánamo Bay Cuba and Samoa.

B. The Services:

1. The Naval Transportation Service, under the Chief of Naval Operations (Director, Naval Transportation Service).

2. The naval Communication Service, under the Chief of Naval Operations (Director Naval Communication Service).
3. The Naval Intelligence Service, and that the Chief of Naval Operations (Director of Naval intelligence service).

C. All activities of the shore establishment, now existing, or to be created during the war, under the Commandants of the respective naval districts, or, in the case of activities excluded from the jurisdiction of district commandants, under the bureaus and offices of the Navy department concerned.

The Marine Corps forces in Haiti and Nicaragua, will continue existing operations, but will hold themselves in readiness for expeditionary Force duty elsewhere in the principal theater of operations as may be directed.

All other forces, Navy and Marine Corps, on special duty or acting independently, are, in this Navy Basic Plan, Red, assigned to the operating forces or services above and enumerated.

The remaining part of Section 5 was filled with pages of administration details regarding responsibilities, so beloved by the military.

Section 6 - Submarines, Chemical Warfare and Contraband.
The joint decisions contained in the joint Army and Navy Basic War Plan Red, applied to all naval forces, and the commanders of all operating forces, services and activities, will be guided thereby.

To employ submarines against Red combatant vessels and against Red seaborne commerce under the same rules of international law as governed the actions of surface vessels unless and until the action of Red in this respect necessitates other action.

a. *The present position of the United States relative to the method of employment of submarines against merchant shipping is stated in article 22 of the treaty for the limitation and reduction of naval armaments signed in London on 22 April 1930.*

b. *Pending the receipt of other instructions from the Navy Department, commanders of all forces to which submarines are attached will be guided in the employment of such submarines against merchant shipping by the statement of principles set forth in the above-mentioned article of the treaty, and by the provisions of the joint decision above quoted.*

c. *It is to be particularly noted that the employment of submarines against Red combatant vessels is unrestricted and such employment is contemplated in this Navy Basic Plan, Red.*

To make necessary preparations for the effective use of chemical warfare from the outbreak of the war, but to employ toxic chemical agents only if and when Red adopts their use.

a. *The present position of the United States relative to the employment of toxic chemical agents is believed to be set forth substantially in Article V of the draft treaty relating to submarines and noxious gases, signed at Washington, 6 February 1922, but which treaty has not*

Twenty R-class submarines of US Navy Submarine Divisions 9 and 14 at Pearl Harbor, US Territory of Hawaii, 12 Dec 1930. Note the repair piers and floating crane YD-25 in the distance. *(USN)*

American troops fill mustard gas shells at the Edgewood Chemical Biological Center, Maryland in 1930. *(NARA)*

yet become effective.

b. pending the receipt of other instructions from the Navy Department, commanders of all naval forces will be guided in the employment of chemical warfare aids, by Article V of the draft treaty and by the provisions of the joint decision above quoted.

c. It is to be particularly noted that the employment of non-toxic gases and smokes, including non-toxic smokescreens, is not prohibited, but, on the other hand, full use of such means is contemplated by this Navy Basic Plan Red.

d. it will be further noted that the above joint decision assigns to Red the initiative in the matter of employment of toxic chemical agents and thereby necessitates that commanders of all naval forces be vigilant in the adoption of, and training in, anti-gas methods, including provision of means of defence against toxic chemical agents, whether employed in the gas, liquid or solid form.

To declare contraband everything that contributes in any way to success in war.

a. under the joint Army and Navy Basic War Plan Red regulations for the declaration of contraband will be prepared to be promulgated at the proper time.

b. pending the receipt of such regulations, commanders of all naval forces will be governed in their interpretation is of contraband by section II of the 'Instructions for the Navy of the United States Governing Marine Warfare, June 1917.'

Chapter III - Missions and Tasks; principal theater of operations.

Section 1. Misson of the Commander -in-Chief and joint decisions and operations required thereunder.

From a consideration of the Navy's mission and joint decisions and operations required thereunder the Commander-in-Chief, United States fleet, as commander of the principal theater of operations, is assigned the following mission:

To gain and exercise control of the seas in the principal theater of operations.

The joint decisions and operations required thereunder applying into the navy alone, or the navy jointly with the army, which are assigned to the principal theater of operations are listed in the succeeding paragraphs of this section. These tasks are analysed separately in sections 2 to 5 inclusive of this chapter 3. Additional nations and tasks may be assigned to the Commander-in-Chief by the Navy Department as the necessity therefore arises during the war with Red .

Isolation of Crimson from Red - To initiate at the earliest practicable date operations designed to separate Crimson from Red .
   A. *operations to be undertaken by the Navy: The establishment of the United States Fleet in the western North Atlantic in strength sufficient to destroy all Red Naval forces in that area and to control sea communications between Red and Crimson.*
   B. *Operations to be undertaken jointly with the army.*

Preparations for a joint overseas expedition against Halifax, Nova Scotia.
   Seizure of Red bases in the North Atlantic and West Indies: to initiate, at the earliest practicable date consistent with the execution of the operations required in the preceding paragraph, operations to seize Red bases in the western North Atlantic, the West Indies, and the Caribbean Sea
   A. *Operations to be undertaken by the Navy:*

     Operations to seize and hold Jamaica, the Bahamas and in Bermuda at the earliest practicable date.
   B. *Operations to be undertaken separately or jointly with the army: operations when the forces became available to seize and hold Trinidad, St Lucia and other Red West Indian and Central American possessions.*

Extension of operations to gain complete control of Crimson: ultimately to gain complete control of Crimson.
   A. *Operations to be undertaken by the Navy: Control of sea areas adjacent to the Atlantic coast of Crimson.*

Security of United States vital seaborne trade. To provide such security for United States vital seaborne trade as is consistent with the primary mission of the United States fleet to destroy the Red Main Fleet.
   A. *Operations to be undertaken by the Navy:*
     1. *Control of the coastwise sea lanes of the intercoastal trade routes via the Panama Canal.*
     2. *Operations to safeguard United States shipping in the Atlantic to both coasts of South America.*

Economic exhaustion of Red.
Ultimately to extend naval operations to assist

One of the reasons why Halifax, Nova Scotia featured so high in the US Navy's War Plan Red - the Imperial Oil bunkering and storage facilities that was of huge importance for the eastern side of Canada. *(NARA)*

Another reason the Americans held Halifax, Nova Scotia as such a strategic target was its deep-water port complete with freight and passenger handling facilities. *(NARA)*

in effecting economic exhaustion of Red.

A. operations to be undertaken by the Navy.

1. The attainment of naval superiority by the destruction of Red forces where and when met.
2. Operations against Red seaborne trade.

B. Operations to be undertaken jointly with the army: joint operations, when the forces become available to seize and hold Red territory necessary to carry out this decision.

Section 2. Analysis of the nation and tasks; isolation of Crimson from Red.

Task one. To establish the United States Fleet in the western North Atlantic in strength sufficient to destroy all Red naval forces in the area and to control sea communications between Crimson and Red.

A. Operations required. Under the above task it will be necessary to:

1. Concentrate in the western North Atlantic all available vessels and aircraft and augment such forces as rapidly as possible to the maximum possible extent.
2. Establish a main advance base as close to the vital enemy area as naval, military and geographic considerations allow.
3. Secure such advanced base by adequate defences, particularly against submarine, mine and air attack.
4. Maintaining the fleet in constant readiness to engage decisively the

Red Main Fleet or any portion thereof, whenever a favourable opportunity arises.

5. Organise and maintain an adequate service of security and information covering enemy naval forces and operations.
6. Capture, destroy, or effectively contain all Red, or Crimson naval forces in position to disrupt control of Crimson-Red Sea communications.
7. Deny Red reinforcement or supply of Crimson by:

   A. Capture or destruction of Red and Crimson merchant shipping.
   B. Control of neutral merchant shipping plying to Crimson Atlantic ports by means of applications of regulations covering contraband,
   C. Establishment of a working control of the Gulf of St Lawrence, particularly of Cabot and Belle Isle Straits, and of the St Lawrence River as far westward as possible.

8. cooperate as far as practicable with the Army in its operations in the Crimson territory.

b. Forces for task. For the accomplishment of the above task and of other tasks under the Navy Basic Plan Red, there will be available to the commander in chief, the force is listed in Appendix II.

c. Supply. Stipulations governing supply

of the forces are contained in part three of this Navy Basic Plan Red.

d. *Bases.* The main fleet advance base will be in the Narragansett Bay - Long Island Sound area. Distribution of units within this area will be made by the commander in chief.

d. *Date for initiation of operations.* For planning purposes it will be assumed that the above operations are to be initiated on mobilisation day. Concentration of the United States fleet at war in the vicinity of the main advance base may be directed prior to mobilisation day.

Task Two Dash One.
To undertake, jointly with the Army, an overseas expedition against Halifax, Nova Scotia. *Note.* It will be observed that the joint plan goes no further than to stipulate that preparation shall be made for joint overseas expedition against Halifax, Nova Scotia. Decision and definitely to undertake such an expedition will be made in view of the situation prevailing at the actual time of entry into war. The below analysis is based on the assumption that the expedition has been definitely determined upon.

A. *Operations required.* Under the above task, it will be necessary to:
1. Provide and assemble, including such conversion as time will permit, the necessary shipping required to transport the Army Expeditionary Force and its accompanying supplies.
2. Organise and direct the overseas movement of the Army Expeditionary Force by means of convoy and suitable escort.
3. Provide security for the overseas movement and of the operations involved in the seizure, by adequate disposition of the United States fleet.
4. Provide means for landing the Army, including prior reconnaissance of the landing area and beaches.
5. Cooperate in the establishment of the Army on the shore by means of gunfire and air support and by other assistance as may be practicable and required, in accordance with the principles contained in the

Halifax also had an airport. Although primitive by the standard of today, being just a grass field, it was adjacent to a railway line that had links to other areas. *(NARA)*

confidential pamphlet 'Joint Overseas Expeditions'.

6. Provide security for the Army's overseas line of communications.

b. Forces for task.
Army forces to be deployed are listed in Appendix II. Transports and cargo vessels for the Army Expeditionary Force are listed in Appendix II. Convoy commanders and naval liaison groups will be provided by the Bureau of Navigation.

c. Command.
Command of joint forces engaged in the joint overseas expedition against Halifax Nova Scotia will be exercised by the army under the principle of paramount interest.

d. Bases.
Army Expeditionary Force will embark at Boston. The port of embarkations will be established, maintained and operated by the Army. The Army will likewise establish, maintain and operate the port of debarkation in Crimson territory.

e. Supply.
Supplies for the Army Expedition Force will be provided by the Army. Sea transportation to such supplies will be provided by the Navy. Subsistance of troops on transport will be provided by the Navy; subsistence of animals embarked will be provided by the Army.

f. Evacuation.
Evacuation of Army';s sick and wounded personnel, including hospitalisation and treatment during the period while embarked, will be provided by the Navy. Hospital ships and suitable transport for this purpose are listed in Appendix II.

g. Date for initiation of the above operations. Transports and cargo vessels will be assembled at Boston between mobilisation day mobilisation +2. Troops will be ready to embark, in case the expedition is definitely decided upon, on M +2.

Task Two Dash Two
Jointly with the army, to deny Red a secure base at Halifax Nova Scotia. Note. The above task will be undertaken in case the join overseas expedition against Halifax is not dispatched.

a. Operations required. Under the above task it will be necessary to:

1. Provide for close observation of Halifax Nova Scotia and its approaches.

2. Attack all Red lnaval units basing on the port whenever favourable opportunity arises.

3. Conduct a sustained mining offensive against Halifax Nova Scotia with the objective of rendering ingress and egress hazardous.

4. In cooperation with the Army Air Forces, conduct air raids against the port, its facilities and the shipping therein.

b. Agencies for cooperation.
Liaison will be affected through the Officer Commanding the Headquarters Air Force, based in the New York - New England Area.

c. Date for initiation of above operations. For planning purposes it will be assumed that the above operations are initiated on mobilisation +3 day, as soon as definite decision is reached that the adroit overseas expedition against Halifax will not be undertaken.

Section 3.
Analysis of mission and tasks: seizure of Red baces in the North Atlantic and West Indies.
Task three affirm. To seize and hold Jamaica until relieved by the Army.

A. Operations required. Under the above task, it will be necessary to:

1. Concentrate at the designated ports of embarkation and Marine Corps Expeditionary Force of adequate strength to overcome all hostile resistance which will probably be offered to the operations, together with the requisites and equipment and supplies.

2. Provide and assemble, including such conversion as time will permit, the necessary transports and cargo vessels required to transport overseas the Marine Corps Expeditionary Force and its accompanying supplies.

3. Organise and direct the overseas

movement of the Expeditionary Force by means of convoy and suitable escort.

4. Provide means for landing the Expeditionary Force including prior reconnaissance of the landing area and beaches.

5. Cooperate with and assist in the establishment of the expedition on shore by means of gunfire and air support and by such other assistance as may be practicable and required, in general accordance with the principle contained in the confidential pamphlet 'Joint Overseas Expeditions'.

6. Provide security for the overseas lines of communications of the Expeditionary Force.

7. Arrange for the establishment of a military government of the occupied area or areas as soon as practicable.

8. Provide for relief by the Army of the Marine Corps Expeditionary Force when Army forces become available. Note. For planning purposes, it will be assumed that no relief is practicable before M +90.

B. forces for the task.

Marine Corps Expeditionary Force Affirm, of an approximate total strength of 12,000, to be employed in the operations is listed in Appendix II. Transports and cargo vessels for this Expeditionary Force are listed in Appendix II. Convoy commanders and naval liaison groups will be provided by the Bureau of Navigation.

C. Supply.

Stipulations covering supply of Marine Corps forces operating in the principal theater of operations are contained in part three particularly chapter 2 of this Navy Basic plan Red.

D Bases.

Marine Corps Expeditionary Force affirm that will embark at Quantico and

The US Marines Corps Expeditionary Force were to target Jamaica, that would have included the capital, Kingston, as seen in this 1930s street scene.

Hampton Roads Virginia. Details of embarkation will be arranged by the commandant, Fifth Naval district. Supplies for the Expeditionary Force will be loaded at the Navy Yard, Philadelphia, Pennsylvania. Details of loading will be arranged by the Commandant, Fourth Naval district. The advanced base for operations against Jamaica will be the Naval Station Guantánamo Bay, Cuba.

E. Date for initiation of the operations.
Transports and cargo vessels will be assembled and the Expeditionary Force will be ready to embark on M+20. Date of departure of the expedition is necessarily dependent upon availability of escort and the requisite naval and air forces for cooperation. Such units will be furnished by the Commander-in-Chief, United States fleet, as soon as this situation elsewhere in the principal theater of operations permits.

F. Priority.
Priority for furnishing transport escort and naval cooperation units for the Jamaica expedition is assigned immediately after the Halifax operation in case decision is made actually to dispatch such an expedition.

Task Three Baker.
To seize and hold the Bahamas islands until relieved by the Army.
A. operations required.
These are basically the same as above.
B. Geographical objectives.
The first objective will be Nassau, New Providence Island. After it's seizure, operations will be extended with the objective of occupying remaining ports in the islands.
C Forces for task.
Marine Corps Expeditionary Force Baker of an approximate strength of 2,200, to be employed in the operations, is listed in Appendix II. Transportation and cargo vessels for this Expeditionary Force is listed in Appendix II. Convoy commanders and naval liaison groups be provided by Bureau of Navigation.
D. Supply.
See previous section.
E. Bases.
Marine Corps Expeditionary Force Baker will embark at Quantico and the Hampton Roads, Virginia. Details of embarkation will be arranged by the Commandant, Fifth Naval district. Supplies for the Expeditionary Force will be loaded at the Navy Yard,

Bay Street, Nassau in the Bahamas - another target for the US Marine Corps Expeditionary Force.

Marine Corps Base Quantico - commonly abbreviated MCB Quantico - is a United States Marine Corps installation located near Triangle, Virginia. It from from here that much of the invasion of the Caribbean would have been initiated. *(NARA)*

Philadelphia, Pennsylvania. Details of loading will be arranged by the Commandant Fourth Naval district. The advanced base for operations against the Bahamas will be Naval Station, Key West, Florida.

F. Date for the initiation of operations.
Transport and cargo vessels will be assembled and the Expeditionary Force will be ready to embark on M +20. Date of departure of the expedition is necessarily dependent upon the availability of escort and the requisite naval and air units for cooperation. Such units will be furnished by the Commander-in-Chief, United States fleet, as soon as the situation elsewhere in the principal theater of operations permits.

G. Priority
Priority for furnishing transport, escort, and naval cooperation units for the Bahama Islands expedition is the same as for the Jamaica expedition.

Task Three Cast
To seize and hold Bermuda until relieved by the Army.

A. Operations Required.
See previous section.

B. Forces for task.
Marine Corps Expeditionary Force Cast, of an approximate strength of 8,000, to be employed in the operations, is listed in Appendix Two. Transports and cargo vessels for this Expeditionary Force are listed in Appendix II. Convoy commanders and naval liaison groups will be provided by the Bureau of Navigation.

C. Supply.
See previous section.

D. Bases.
Marine Corps Expeditionary Force Cast will embark at Quantico and Hampton Roads, Virginia. Details of embarkation will be arranged by the Commandant, the Fifth Naval District. Supplies will be

loaded at the Navy Yard Philadelphia Pennsylvania. The Commandant, Fourth Naval district, will arrange the details of loading. The advanced base for operations against the Bermuda Islands will be the Naval operating base, Hampton Roads Virginia.

E. Date for initiation of the operation.

Transport and cargo vessels will be assembled and the Army Expeditionary Force will be ready to embark on M+50. Date of departure of the expedition is necessarily dependent upon the availability of escort the requisites in naval and units for cooperation. Such units will be furnished by the Commander in Chief, United States fleet as soon as the situation elsewhere in the principal theater of operations permits.

F. Priority.

Priority for furnishing transport, escort and naval cooperation units, as well as troops and equipment for the Bermuda expedition, is assigned immediately after the Jamaica and Bahama expeditions.

Task Four.

To undertake, separately or jointly with the Army when the forces become available, overseas expeditions to seize to hold Trinidad, St Lucia, and other Red West Indian and Central American possessions.

A. Operations required.

These are in general the same as those listed previously the Navy will also provide and assemble, also including necessary conversion, the transport cargo vessels required for the overseas movements of the Army Expeditionary Force, if any for their equipment and supplies.

B. Forces for tasks

1. Army forces if any, to be made available for the above operations cannot at the present time be specified, as such availability will depend on the progress of operations in other army theaters.

2. Marine Corps forces to participate in the above operations will not become available until the liquidation of Jamaica, Bahamas and Bermuda operations and the relief therein by the Army of the Marine Corps forces engaged.

C. Command.

Command and joint forces, if any, engaged in the above the joint operations will be exercised by the army under the principle of paramount interest.

D. supply.

Supplies for Army expeditionary forces will be provided by the Army. Sea transportation for such suppliers will be provided by the Navy. For supply of Marine Corps expeditionary forces see

St George's, Bermuda, another target for US Marines.

Two pictures of USS *Relief* (AH-1) and American Hospital ship. The picture above was taken while is was 'dressed overall' at Guantanamo Bay, Cuba in 1922.

USS *Relief* was later fitted with a upward-facing 'cross' of lights to inform aircraft overhead of its purpose and that it should not be attacked. The ship served until at least 1945 *(USN)*

paragraph 3 of this Navy Basic Plan Red.

E. *Bases.*

Ports of embarkation for the Army forces will be established and maintained and operated by the Army. These ports will be designated when the operations are being planned by the Army. The Army will likewise establish and maintain and operate all ports of debarkation to be established in Red territory. Marine Corps Expeditionary Forces will in general be embarked from the locations where they then are.

F. *Evacuation.*

Evacuation of the Army sick and wounded personnel, as well as sick and wounded Naval and Marine Corps personnel, including hospitalisation and treatment when embarked, will be undertaken by the Navy. Hospital ships for this purpose are listed in Appendix II. In addition to these hospital ships, a proportion of the transports will be specially fitted to carry sick and wounded.

G. *Date for initiation of the operations.*

Dates for the initiation of the above project operations cannot be specified at present. It is obvious that such dates are dependent upon the availability of Army forces, availability of escort and requisite naval co-operation units, and availability of Marine Corps Expeditionary Forces to participate therein. When the operations are being planned, the date for initiation thereof will be determined jointly by the War and Navy departments, and the Commander in Chief United States Fleet informed thereof. It is now estimated that none of the operations can be undertaken prior to M +120.

H. *Priority.*

As between the several operations and raised in the above task priority is assigned in the order stated therein, that is Trinidad, St Lucia and other Red possessions.

Members of the British Army of Bermuda line up for inspection in 1932.

Section 4
Analysis of mission and tasks; security of United States vital seaborne trade.

Task five.
To provide such as security for United States vital seaborne trade, within the principal theater of operations, as is consistent with the primary mission of the United States fleet to destroy the Red main fleet.

A. Operations required. Under the above task it will be necessary to:

    1. Capture, destroy, or effectively contain all Red naval forces within the principal theater of operations, particularly those in the position to operate on United States trade routes.

    2. Establish a working control of the Caribbean Sea and of West Indian waters.

    3. Patrol of trade routes particularly in the vicinity of Red bases and focal points, such as the Straits of Florida, Crooked Island, Windward and Mona passages, against Red cruisers and raiders.

    4. Provide suitable escort for valuable convoys.

B. Objective of the operations.
The operations will be conducted with the view primarily of affording security
for the following trade, which is considered to be especially vital to United States interests:

    1. Coastwise and intercoastal trade via the Panama Canal.

    2. Atlantic, Gulf of Mexico and West Indies trade.

    3. Atlantic coast to west coast of South America trade via the Panama Canal.

    4. Atlantic coast to east coast of South America trade.

C. Forces for the task.
Suitable merchant vessels will be armed defensively under priorities given. In addition the certain vessels have been given the designation of cruiser transports. It is contemplated that such vessels will be armed offensively as soon as they can be released from the service as transports, and will then be employed to assist in protection of United States trade as well as a attack of Red trade.

D. Date for initiation of operations.
For planning purposes it will be assumed that the above operations are initiated on M-day.

E. Priority it will be noted that in task five the security of the United States seaborne trade is subordinate to the primary task of the United States fleet.

Coastwise and intercoastal trade via the Panama Canal - So far as practicable this trade will be directed to keep within the United States coastal waters and will thereby, for the greater part, come within the cognizance of the Commandants of the several Naval Districts. This trade will not, at least initially, be operated in convoys. Until the occupation of Bermuda and the Bahamas, United States shipping to and from the Panama Canal will be routed via the Straits of Florida and the Old Bahama and Yucatan channels.

Atlantic. Gulf of Mexico and West Indian trade - The same procedure will be followed as in the preceding class. Caribbean sea crossings will be designated by the Navy Department with a view towards keeping this trade at the maximum distance from Red territory. This trade will not initially be operated in convoys.

Atlantic coast to west coast of South America - The same procedure will be followed as in the two preceding classes. If it becomes necessary to operate this trade in convoy, arrangements will be made by the Navy Department with the Commander-in-Chief, United States fleet, to furnish suitable escort to and from the Panama Canal. For defensive arming, vessels engaged in this trade will be given priority over those of the two preceding classes.

Atlantic coast to the east of South America - Arrangements but will be made by the Navy Department at as early a date as practicable, to operate this trading convoy. Suitable escort through dangerous areas will be furnished by the Commander-in-Chief, upon directions by the Navy Department. For defensive arming, United States merchant vessels engaged in this trade will be given the highest priority.

Army reinforcement of Panama and Puerto Rico

A. In case the Army is unable to complete, prior to mobilisation day, its task of reinforcing to war strength, the garrison of the Panama Canal Zone, the Navy has responsibility for the safe transportation of the remaining troops. Vessels for this purpose will be supplied by the Director, Naval Transportation Service. Escort, so far as practicable will be furnished by the Commander, Naval Forces Panama. In case additional escort is required the Commander-in-cChief, United States fleet, will be prepared to furnish it.

B. Transportation and security for the overseas movements of Army forces to reinforce Puerto Rico is likewise

USS *Houston* (CL/CA-30), was a Northampton-class cruiser of the US Navy. She was the second Navy ship to bear the name '*Houston*' and is seen here exercising with aviation elements of the US armed forces. *(USN)*

USS *Arizona* seen here during a courtesy visit to New York sometime in the 1930s. *(USN)*

assigned to the Navy. Transportation will be furnished by the Director, Naval Transportation Service. The Commander-in-Chief will be prepared to furnish suitable escort therefore.

Escort for the Naval Transportation Service vessels.
The Commander-in-Chief, United States fleet, may further be expected to be called upon by the Navy Department, to furnish suitable escort for Naval Transportation Service vessels operating within the principal theater of operations and engaged in the supply of Naval and Army forces in the outlying possessions, including supply of Army forces in Panama and Puerto Rico.

Section 5
Analysis of mission and tasks; Ultimate complete control of Crimson; Ultimate economic exhaustion of Red.
Task six
Ultimately to establish and maintain control of all sea areas adjacent to the Atlantic coast of Crimson.
    A. operations required:

Under the above task, it will be necessary to:
    1. Continue all other operations.
    2. Occupy suitable Crimson Atlantic ports as these are captured by the Army or joint forces, and base thereupon such naval units as may be necessary for control of adjacent waters.
    3. Establish and maintain control of Crimson Atlantic waters to guard against enemy action by regular or irregular naval forces.
    4. Extended naval operations along the St Lawrence river and it's tributaries as may be necessary to assist the Army in its operations.

B. Date for the initiation of the operations. The above is an ultimate task, to be undertaken when Army operations have progressed to the point where Crimson ports become available for the use of our forces, and when all major Red naval forces have been eliminated or have withdrawn from the principal theater of operations. The date for initiation of the above operations is therefore impossible to specify at the present time.

Task 7.

Ultimately, to undertake naval operations designed to affect economic exhaustion of Red, by means of destruction of Red naval forces where and when met and capture or destruction of Red seaborne trade.

    A. Operations required.

        Under the above task it will be necessary to:

        1. *Continue other operations specified.*

        2. *Initiate and conduct operations to gain a working control of the Eastern North Atlantic.*

        3. *Initiate and maintain sustained offensive against Red seaborne trade in the South Atlantic.*

        4. *Undertake and maintain a maximum naval effort directed against Red shipping in Western European waters and if practicable in the Mediterranean.*

    B. Theater of Operations.

        It is contemplated that, when the above task is undertaken, the principal theater of operations, under command of the Commander-in-Chief, United States fleet, will be extended to include all of the North Atlantic and such portions of the South Atlantic as may be necessary for the operations projected.

    C. Date for initiation of operations.

        The above is an ultimate task, to be undertaken where operations have progressed to the stage where the United States fleet, or major portions thereof, becomes available for employment the operations listed above. The date when such forces will become available cannot obviously be determined at the present time. Such dates will be decided upon at the proper time by the Navy Department after consultation with the Commander-in-Chief, United States fleet.

    D. Red petroleum supplies.

        As a separate and independent operation under the above task as well as under task five, it is considered of the highest importance that supplies of fuel oil and petroleum products originating in Mexico, Venezuela and Columbia, be denied to Red. This includes the products of the refineries in the Dutch East Indies. Operation is designed to accomplish this objective should be initiated at the beginning of the war as soon after Mobilisation Day as forces become available.

Task eight.

Ultimately, when the forces become available, to undertake jointly with the Army, overseas expedition to seize and to hold Red territory necessary for and suitable as advanced bases for the conduct of operations designed to affect economic exhaustion of Red.

    A. Operations required. Under the above tasks it will be necessary to:

        1. *Undertake operations in general similar to previous.*

        2. *Establish securely the United States fleet, or portions thereof in the*

K-15, one of the British steam-powered submarines was on the reserve list at the time of War Plan Red.

HMS *Vanguard* exercising with other Royal Navy vessels in the South China Sea in the mid-1930s.

advanced bases seized.

3. Initiate and carry out operations in general.

B. Geographic objectives.

Geographical objectives cannot be specified in detail at this present time, as they are necessarily dependent upon the situation existing at the time it is decided to undertake the task. An operation, however, to seize and hold Red Guiana as an advanced base from which to undertake operations against Red trade in the South Atlantic is indicated as desirable.

C. Forces for Task.

See previous operation.

D. Command.

See previous operation

E. Supply.

See previous operation

F. Bases.

See previous operation

G. Evacuation.

See previous operation

H. Date for initiation of the operations.

The above is an ultimate task, to be undertaken when conditions in the principal theater of operations permit, and when other tasks previously specified have been accomplished. Dates for the initiation cannot therefore be stipulated at the present time. When the operations are being planned, the dates for initiation therefore will be determined by the War and Wavy departments and the Commander in Chief informed.

Much of the information regarding what is termed 'Secondary Theater of Operations' relates to the guarding and protection of existing US territories, mainly in the Pacific.

Chapter IV. Missions and tasks: secondary theater of operations.

Section 1. Nation and tasks and analysis thereof: Asiatic theater.

From a consideration of the Navy's mission and of the joint decisions and operations required thereunder, which are applicable to the Asiatic theater, the Commander-in-Chief,

Asiatic Fleet, as commander of the Asiatic theater, is assigned the following mission: jointly with the Army to defend the Philippine Islands, and to deny Red control of Eastern Asiatic waters.

The joint decisions and operations required thereunder, applying to the Navy alone, or to the Navy jointly with the Army, which are assigned, in whole or part, to the Asiatic theater are described elsewhere and are analysed separately. The Commander-in-Chief Asiatic Fleet will supplement these tasks with such other tasks as may become practicable and necessary during planning for, or actually executing his mission.

Task one.
To cooperate with and assist the Army in defending the Philippine Islands.
- A. *Operations required. Under the above task it will be necessary to:*
  1. Put into effect the local defence plans, Navy and joint.
  2. Decisively engage all Red naval forces whenever a favourable opportunity arrives.
  3. Co-operate closely with and furnish all practicable assistance to, the Army forces in the Philippine Islands.
  4. Deny the base facilities of Manila Bay to Red in case these cannot be held for the use of our own forces.
- B. *forces for task*
  1. For the accomplishment of the above task, and in other tasks and his mission, the Commander-in-Chief, Asiatic Fleet, will have available the forces listed in Appendix II.
  2. As the 16th Naval district is also under the Commander-in-Chief, Asiatic Fleet, there will also be available the additional forces listed in Appendix II
  3. When and if the situation in other theaters permits, the Navy Department will endeavour to send reinforcements to the Asiatic theater, but such reinforcement cannot be counted upon, and the Commander-in-Chief, Asiatic Fleet, will plan upon having available only the forces specified above.
- C. *Command of joint forces.*

Within the Asiatic theater, command of joint forces of the Army and Navy is vested in the Army, under the principle of paramount interest.
- D. *Supply*
  Stipulations covering the supply of the of the Asiatic Naval forces are contained in part three of this Navy Basic Plan Red. Attention is particularly invited to the strong probability that the Commander-in-Chief, Asiatic fleet, will be obliged largely to depend upon local sources for the necessary logistic support.
- E. *Bases*
  The Asiatic Fleet will base on the Manila Bay - Olongapo area so long as this area remains available.
- F. *Date for initiation of operations.*
  For planning purposes, it will be assumed that the above operations are initiated on mobilisation day. The concentration of the Asiatic Fleet at, or in the vicinity of Manila Bay, may be directed by the Navy Department or by the Commander-in-Chief, Asiatic Fleet before the mobilisation day.

Task two.
To afford such protection as may be practicable to the United States merchant shipping and engaged in trade with the Far East.
- A. *operations required. Under the above task, it will be necessary to:*
  1. Establish and maintain a system of intelligence designed to collect and proptly disseminate information to all United States merchant vessels of the presence and location of enemy vessels.
  2. Provide an organisation to supervise and direct the routing all United States merchant vessels.
  3. Counterattack, so far as may be practicable Red naval forces engaged in operations against United States trade.
- B. *Objectives of the operations.*
  The operations will be conducted primarily with the objective of affording security, so far as is practicable, to the following classes of trade:
  1. United States trans-Pacific trade.
     Within the limits of the Asiatic theater

The Americans expected that Australian and New Zealand troops would be used against them in the war in the Pacific. Here a group of Australian soldiers pose for the camera.

vessels engaged in this trade should be directed to keep, so far as is practicable, within neutral waters. United States merchant vessels engaged in this trade will be defensively armed, with priority immediately after that of those engaged in the Atlantic coast - East coast of South America trade. It is considered advisable that, initially, all United States merchant vessels trading to South China and Asiatic ports to the southward and westward of Amoy, should be directed immediately to proceed at maximum speed to the nearest United States port, or if such is not practicable to the nearest neutral port, other than Chinese.

2. United States internal and Chinese trade.
   Vessels engaged in this trade will be safeguarded to a certain point, by the presumed neutrality of China. In case such neutrality is in doubt or appears to be ineffective, the Commander-in-Chief will take such measures as may be necessary to guard this trade.
3. Philippine Islands coastwise trade.
   Such regulations and controls of this trade, cooperation with local authorities, will be instituted as is practicable under the circumstances.
C. The date for the initiation of

operations. The above will be initiated on mobilisation day.

Task three.
Ultimately, to undertake naval operations designed to reflect economic exhaustion of Red.
  A. operations required.
    1. Under the above task it will be necessary to initiate and maintain operations directed towards the capture or destruction of Red merchant shipping engaged in trade with the Far East primarily:
      a. Red trade with China and Japan.
      b. Red trade with the East Indies.
      c. Red trade with Australia and New Zealand.
    2. Operations directed against neutral vessels under regulations covering contraband will be conducted only to the degree specifically directed by the Navy Department at the time, and to the extent that political expediency may dictate.
  B. Dates for the initiation of the operations. This task is an ultimate task to be undertaken when the situation warrants and is subordinate to the other tasks previously specified. Operations against Red merchant shipping in the Asiatic theater should, however, be initiated whenever a favourable opportunity

offers, from the date of the declaration of war, which for planning purposes will be assumed to coincide with embarkation day.

As the Naval Station, Guam is also under the Commander-in-Chief, Asiatic Fleet, the Commander-in-Chief, will include, as a separate task under his mission the following:

Task four.
To defend Guam for use as a base for our own forces.
   A. Operations required. Under the above task it will be necessary to:
      1. Put into effect the local defence plans.
      2. Deny the base facilities of Guam to Red in case these cannot be held for use by our own forces
   B. Forces for task.
      For the accomplishment of the above task, there will be available, in addition to those previously specified the force is listed in Appendix II. Prior to mobilisation day, if applicable, the Navy Department will endeavour to increase the personnel of the Marine Corps garrison in Guam, that such reinforcement cannot be counted upon, and the local defence plans will be placed upon having available only the peacetime garrison normally stationed in Guam.
   C. Date for the initiation of the operations. The above operations will be initiated on M day.
Future operations.
In case the situation due to Red military naval or air operations against the Philippine Islands becomes such as to threaten the mobility of the Asiatic Naval forces, the Commander-in-Chief, Asiatic Fleet, will be prepared to adopt one or the other of the two following alternatives, depending upon the circumstances existing at the time:
   A. Withdrawal of all available forces to Hawaii.
   B. Dispersion of suitable forces with the mission of attacking Red trade in the Indian Ocean, such forces being directed eventually to work their way into the Atlantic.

Section Two
Missions and tasks and analysis thereof: Hawaiian theater.
   From the consideration of the Navy's mission and of the joint decisions and operations required thereunder, which are applicable to the Hawaiian theater, the Commander, Naval Forces Hawaii (Commandant, 14th Naval district), is assigned the following mission: jointly with the Army to defender Hawaii, and to maintain and exercise control of the waters of the Hawaiian theater.
   The joint decisions and operations required thereunder, applying to the Navy alone, or to the Navy jointly with the Army, which are assigned, in whole or part, to the Hawaiian theater, are previously described. The Commander, Naval Forces Hawaii, will supplement these tasks with such other tasks as may become practicable and necessary during planning for or eventually executing his mission.

USS *Black Hawk* (AD-9), with USS *Bulmer* (DD-222), *Pillsbury* (DD-227), *Pope* (DD-225), *John D. Ford* (DD-228), *Edsall* (DD-219), and *Peary* (DD-226) of the US Asiatic fleet based at Chefoo in the Philippines. *(USN)*

USS *Black Hawk* (AD-9) at Chefoo in the Philippines surrounded by local coastal traffic. *(USN)*

Task one.

To cooperate with and assist the Army in defending the Hawaiian islands.

    A. *operations required. Under the task it will be necessary to:*

        1. *Put into effect the local defence plans, Navy and Joint.*

        2. *Cooperate closely with, and furnish all practicable assistance to, the Army forces in the Hawaiian islands.*

    B. *Forces for task.*

    For the accomplishment of the above task and of all other tasks under his mission, the Commander, Naval Forces, Hawaii, will have available the forces listed in appendix 2. The Commander, Naval Forces, Hawaii, will supplement these forces to the maximum extent practicable by the utilisation of all the locally available manpower, facilities and resources.

    C. *Command of joint forces.*

    Within the Hawaiian theater, command of joint forces of the Army and Navy is vested in the Army under the principle of paramount interest.

    D. *Supply.*

    Stipulations covering supply of the Hawaiian naval forces are contained in part three of this Navy Basic Plan Red.

    E. *Bases.*

    The Naval Forces, Hawaii, will normally based on Pearl Harbor.

    F. *Date for initiation of the operations.*

    The above operations will be initiated on mobilisation day.

Task Two

To afford protection as may be practicable to the United States shipping within the Hawaiian theater.

    A. *operations equired. Under the above task it will be necessary to:*

        1. *Establish and maintain a system of intelligence designed to collect and promptly disseminate information to all United States merchant vessels of the location and presence of enemy forces.*

        2. *Provide an organisation to supervise and direct the routing of all United States merchant vessels.*

        3. *Provide measures with the security of ports and coastal waters against enemy submarine and mine attack.*

        4. *Providing escort for shipping as may be necessary.*

    B. *Objectives of the operations.*

    The operations will be conducted primarily with the objective of affording security for the following classes of trade:

1. United States trade with Hawaii. Vessels are engaged in this trade will not, at least initially, be operated in convoy. Should the known or suspected presence of enemy vessels along or in the vicinity of the usual trade routes demand, convoys will be organised. Escort within the limits of the Hawaiian theater will be furnished by the Commander, Naval Forces, Hawaii. Ocean escort will be furnished by the Commander, Naval Forces, Pacific. Especially valuable vessels engaged in this trade will be defensively armed, priority for such arming is being assigned to those engaged in Atlantic trades.

2. United States trans-Pacific trade. Within the limits of the Hawaiian theater suitable escort, if required, will be furnished these vessels by the Commander, Naval Forces, Hawaii.

3. Hawaii inter-island trade. Such regulations and controls of this trade, in cooperation with the local authorities, will be instituted as practicable under the circumstances.

4. Army reinforcement of Hawaii. Transportation and security for the overseas movement of the Army forces to reinforce Hawaii were assigned to the Navy. Ocean escort will be furnished by the Commander, Naval Forces Pacific. Transportation will be furnished by the Director, Naval Transportation Service. Escort within the Hawaiian theater will be furnished by the Naval Forces Hawaii.

5. Escort from Naval transportation vessels. The Commander, Naval forces Hawaii will furnish escort within the Hawaiian theater for vessels of the Naval Transportation Services entering or passing through the waters of the theater.

C. Dates for the initiation of the operations. The above operations will be initiated on embarkation day.

Under his mission the Commander, Naval Forces Hawaii has also the following task:

Task three.
To maintain an exercise control of the waters of the Hawaiian theater.
A. Operations required. Under the above

Pearl Harbor, Oahu, 1935. USS *Virginia* is seen under way, with USS *Langley* moored adjacent to NAS Ford Island. *(USN)*

task, it will be necessary to:

1. Establishing an effective control of the important sea areas within the Hawaiian theater.
2. Counter attack all Red naval forces entering this theater.
3. Capture or destroy all Red merchant vessels found within the theater.
4. Enforce, as regards neutral vessels, the regulations governing contraband, to the extent specifically directed by the Navy Department.

B. Date for initiation of the operations.
For planning purposes will be assumed that the above operations are initiated on Embarkation day.

Section 3.
Mission and tasks and analysis thereof; Panama Canal Theater.
From a consideration of the Navy's mission, and of the joint decisions and operations required thereunder, which are applicable to the Panama Canal Theater, the Commander, Naval Forces Panama (Commandant 15th Naval District) is assigned the following mission:

Jointly with the Army to hold inviolate the Panama Canal, and to maintain and exercise control of the waters of the Panama Canal Theater.

The joint decisions and operations required thereunder, applying to the Navy alone, or to the Navy jointly with the Army, which are assigned, in whole or in part, to the Panama Canal Theater, are described elsewhere. The Commander, Naval Forces Panama, will supplement these tasks with such other tasks as may become practicable and necessary during planning for or actually executing his mission.

Task One.
To cooperate with and assist the Army in holding inviolate the Panama Canal.

A. Operations required. Under the above task it would be necessary to:
1. Execute the local defence plans both Navy and joint.
2. Co-operate closely and furnish all practicable assistance to, the Army forces in the Panama Canal Theater.

US Naval Hospital, Puget Sound, Bremerton, Washington The hospital's nursing staff, circa July 1931. Those present are (from left to right, seated): Vanderlinden, Mins, Anderson, Chief Nurse Sue S. Dauser, Krook, Sawin and Harriet Harris. (from left to right, standing): Jones, Ballerstedt, Quinn, Harkness, Farrell, Howard. *(USN)*

Representing US Navy Alaskan operations during this time is submarine tender USS *Holland* off the US Territory of Alaska with submarines USS *Pollack* and USS *Porpoise*. *(USN)*

B. *Forces for task.*
For the accomplishment of the above task, and all other tasks in his mission, the Commander, Naval Forces Panama, will have available the forces listed in Appendix II. It will be noted that these forces include, from and after mobilisation day the Special Service Squadron.

C. *Command of joint forces.*
Within the Panama Canal Theater, Command of joint forces of the Army and Navy is vested in the Army, under the principle of paramount interest.

D. *Supply.*
Stipulations covering supply of the Naval Forces Panama are contained in part three of this Navy Basic Plan Red.

E. *Bases.*
The Naval Forces Panama will normally base at Coco Solo and Balboa Canal Zone.

F. *Date for of the operations.*
The above operations will be initiated on Mobilisation day.

Task Two.
To afford such protection as may be practicable to the US shipping within the Panama Theater

A. *Operations required, Under the above task it will be necessary to:*
1. *Continue so far as is practicable, the peacetime services afforded to United States shipping transiting the Panama Canal or entering canal waters.*
2. *Establish and maintain a system of intelligence designed to collect and promptly disseminate information to all United States merchant vessels of the location and presence of enemy forces.*
3. *Provide an organisation to supervise and direct the routing of all United States merchant vessels.*
4. *Provide measures for security of ports on coastal waters against enemy submarine and mine attack.*
5. *Provide escort for shipping as may be necessary.*

B. *Objectives of the operations.*
The operations will be conducted primarily within the objectives of affording security to the following classes of trade:
1. *Inter-coastal trade via the Panama Canal. The commander, Naval forces Panama, will be responsible for the*

security of this trade while within the waters of the Panama Canal Theater.

2. Atlantic, Gulf of Mexico, and West Indie's trade. The Commander, Naval Forces Panama, will be responsible for the security of this trade while within the waters of the Panama Canal Theater.

3. Atlantic coast to west coast of South America trade. The Commander, Naval Forces Panama, will be responsible for the security of this trade while within the waters of the Panama Canal Theater and will be called upon by the Navy Department to furnish requisite ocean escort in Pacific waters to and from the Panama Canal.

4. Army reinforcement of Panama.

Note that the Commander, ~Naval Forces Panama, will furnish escort for this reinforcement, if not completed prior to mobilisation day. The Commander Naval Forces Panama, will at all times be responsible for safeguarding the overseas lines of communication between the Canal Zone and Galveston, outside the waters of the Eighth Naval district.

5. Naval transportation service vessels. The Commander, Naval Forces Panama, will be responsible for the security of these vessels while within the waters of the Panama Canal Theater and may be called upon by the Navy Department to furnish escort along the West Coast of Central America.

Scouting Force ships at, and off, the yard, 2 February 1933. Cruisers tied up at 1010 Dock are (from left to left center) *Augusta* (CA-31), *Chicago* (CA-29) and *Chester* (CA-27). USS *Northampton* (CA-26) is alongside the dock in the centre, with USS *Kane* (DD-235) in the adjacent Marine Railway and USS *Fox* (DD-234) tied up nearby. USS *Louisville* (CA-28) is in the centre distance. Moored off her bow and at the extreme right are USS *Salt Lake City* (CA-25) and USS *Pensacola* (CA-24). *(USN)*

The US Navy made use of a number of airships. Here USS *Los Angeles* (ZR-3) is seen flying over southern Manhattan Island, New York City, circa 1924-1932. There is no mention of the use of airships in War Plan Red. (NARA)

C. *Date for the initiation of the operations.*
   The above operations will be initiated on mobilisation day.
   Under his mission, the Commander, Naval Forces Panama, has the following additional task:

Task Three.
To maintain and exercise control of the waters of the Panama Canal Theater.
   A. *Operations required. Under the above task it will be necessary to:*
      1. *Establishing effective control of the important sea areas within the Panama Canal Theater*
      2. *Counterattack all Red naval and air forces entering this theater.*
      3. *Capture or destroy all Red merchant vessels found within this theater.*
      4. *Enforce, as regards neutral vessels, the regulations governing contraband to the degree specifically*

directed by the Navy Department and to the extent dictated by political expediency.
   B. *Date for the initiation of operations.*
      For planning purposes, it will be assumed that the above operations are initiated on mobilisation day.

Section 4.
Mission and tasks and analysis thereof: Pacific theater.
   From a consideration of the Navy's mission and the joint decisions and operations required thereunder, which are applicable to the Pacific theater, the Commander Naval forces Pacific, is assigned the following mission:
   To gain andexercise control of the Seas within the Pacific theater.
   The joint decisions and operations required thereunder applying to the Navy alone, or to the Navy jointly with the Army, which are assigned in whole or part to the Pacific theater are as

previously described. The Commander Naval Forces, Pacific, will supplement these tasks with such other tasks as may become practicable and necessary during the planning for or actually executing his mission.

Task One.
To control the Strait of Juan de Fuca and blockade the Pacific coast of Crimson.
   A. operations required. Under the above task, it will be necessary to:
      1. Establish and maintain an adequate patrol of the waters of the Straits of Juan de Fuca and of Washington Sound, including Haro and Rosario Straits.
      2. Establish promptly an effective blockade of Victoria and Vancouver.
      3. Establish and maintain adequate patrol of the northerly portion of Queen Charlotte Strait.
      4. As soon as practicable extend the blockade to include Prince Rupert and other such ports as experience

shows it to be necessary to blockade.
      5. Capture destroy or effectively contain all Red or Crimson naval forces within the above areas
   B. Forces for the task. For the accomplishments of the above task and of all other tasks under his mission the Commander Naval Forces Pacific will have available initially the forces listed in Appendix II.
   C. Supply.
      Stipulations covering the supply of Naval Forces Pacific are covered in Part three.
   D. Bases.
      The main base for the Naval Forces Pacific will be initially at Port Townsend Washington. Advanced bases will be selected by the Commander Naval forces Pacific and designated in his operating plans 0–3C Red.
   E. Date for initiation of the operations.
      For planning purposes it will be assumed that the above operations are initiated on mobilisation day.

US Naval Hospital, Washington, DC. A ward scene during the 1930s, with a navy doctor, nurse and corpsman attending to a patient. (NARA)

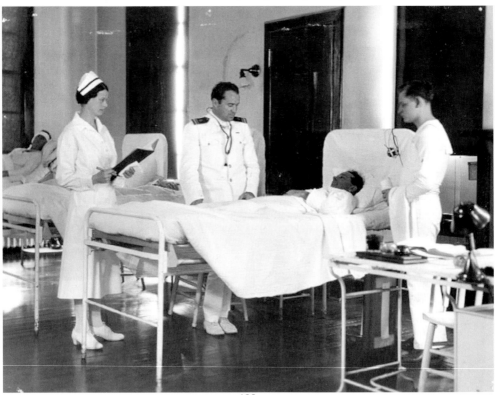

Task Two
To cooperate with and assist the Army in the defence of Alaska.
  A. Operations required.
  Under the above task it will be necessary to:
    1. Put into effect the local defence plans both Navy and joint.
        Note these plans will be prepared by the Commandant 13th Naval District, who will furnish a copy thereof to the Commander Naval Forces Pacific.
    2. Provide security for the overseas line of communications of the Army forces in Alaska.
    3. Cooperate with and furnish all assistance practicable to the Army forces in Alaska.
  B. Agencies for cooperation.
    The Commander Naval Forces Pacific will arrange for direct liaison with the senior Army commander Alaska.
  C. Date for the initiation of the operations.
    The above operations will be initiated on mobilisation day.

Task Three.
To afford such protection as may be practicable to United States shipping within the Pacific theater.
  A. Operations required. Under the above task, it will be necessary to:
    1. Capture, destroy or effectively contain all Red or Crimson naval forces particularly those in position to operate along United States trade routes.
    2. Provide suitable escort for convoys or especially valuable vessels.
  B. Objectives of the operations.
    The operations will be conducted with a view primarily of affording security for the following classes of trade:
    1. Coastwise and intercoastal trade via the Panama Canal. So far as practicable this trade will be directed to keep within United States coastal waters, where it will come under the cognisance of the several Commandants of Naval Districts, or within neutral waters. Ships engaged in this trade will not, at least initially, be operated in convoy.

    2. United States trade with Hawaii.
        Note that the Commander, Naval Forces, Pacific may be required to funish ocean escort for this ttade in case it becomes necessary to resort to the convoy system.
    3. United States trans-Pacific trade.
        The Commander Naval Forces Pacific, may be required to furnish an escort for this trade in the eastern Pacific should it become necessary to operate it in convoy.
    4. Pacific coast west to coast of South America. This trade will be routed via Panama both northward and southward bound. It will be directed to keep, so far as is possible within United States coastal or within neutral waters. Especially valuable ships will be defensively armed, with priority for arming after those engaged in the trans-Pacific trade. The Commander Naval Forces Pacific may be directed to furnish an escort for this trade along the west coast of Mexico should it become necessary to resort to the convoy system.
    5. Army reinforcement of Hawaii.
        Note that the Commander Naval Forces Pacific is to furnish ocean escort for this overseas movement.
    6. Naval Transportation Service vessels.
        The Commander Naval Forces Pacific will take measures to ensure the safety of these vessels, particularly those operating from the West Coast to Hawaii and then the intercoastal service.
  C. Date for initiation of the operations.
    For planning purposes it will be assumed that the above operations are initiated on mobilisation day.

Task Four.
Ultimately to establish and maintain control of all sea areas adjacent to the Pacific coast of Crimson.
  A. Operations required. Under the above task it will be necessary to:
    1. Continue previously specified operations.
    2. Occupy suitable Crimson Pacific

ports as these are captured by Army joined forces, and base thereupon such naval units as may be necessary for control of adjacent waters.

3. Establish and maintain control of all Crimson Pacific waters to guard against enemy action by regular or irregular naval forces.

B. Date for initiation of above operations. The above is an ultimate task, to be undertaken when all naval opposition has been overcome and Army operations have progressed to the point where Crimson ports become available for the use of our own forces. The date before the initiation of the above operations cannot therefore be specified at the present time.

Section 5.
Mission and task and analysis thereof; Naval Great Lakes theater.

From the consideration of the Navy's mission and the joint decisions and operations required thereunder, which are applicable to the Naval Great Lakes Theater the Commander Naval Forces Great Lakes is assigned the following mission:

Jointly with the Army to defend the Great Lakes coastal frontier and to gain and exercise control of the Great Lakes theater.

The joint decisions and operations required thereunder applying to the Navy alone, or to the Navy jointly with the Army, which are assigned in whole or part to the Naval Great Lakes theater, are as previously described. The Commander Naval Forces Great Lakes will supplement these tasks with such other tasks as may become practicable and necessary during planning for or actually executing his mission.

Task One.
Jointly with the Army to defend the Great Lakes coastal frontier.

A. Operations required. Under the above task, it will be necessary to:

1. Provide for the execution of the local defence plans, Navy and joint, in accordance with the categories of defence specified in part two chapter 2 of this Navy Basic Plan Red.

2. Cooperate closely with the Army and furnish all practicable assistance to Army forces engaged in defence of the Great Lakes coastal frontier in accordance with the principles contained in 'Joint Action of the Navy and the Army'.

B. Forces for the task.
For the accomplishment of the above task

USS *Tennessee* (BB-43) In harbour, circa 1938. Two SOC-3 floatplanes, of Observation Squadron Two (VO-2B), are parked on the battleship's after catapult. A third is atop gun turret number 3. *(USN)*

and of all other tasks under his mission, there will be available to the Commander Naval Forces Great Lakes, the forces listed in Appendix II. The Commander Naval Forces Great Lakes will in his operating plan 0-3D Red, provide for the rapid augmentation of these forces by requisition and conversion of suitable merchant vessels and yachts.

C. *Command.*

Within the Naval Great Lakes Theater Command of all forces is vested in the Army under the principle of unity of command. The Commander Naval Forces Great Lakes will command all naval (including the Coast Guard) and Marine Corps forces assigned to this theater. To this end, the Commandants Third and Fourth Naval Districts will place at the disposal of the Commander Naval Forces Great Lakes all forces and means available for the defence of the Great Lakes and St Lawrence frontiers within their respective districts. The Commander Naval Forces Great Lakes is also the naval commandant of the Great Lakes coastal frontier.

D. *Supply.*

Stipulations covering the supply of the Naval Forces Great Lakes are contained in part three of this Navy Basic Plan Red.

E. *Bases.*

Headquarters of the Commander Naval Forces Great Lakes will be established at Detroit on mobilisation day. Headquarters sections of the subordinate naval commanders will likewise be established on or before M-day as follows:

1. For the Sault Ste. Marie subsector of the Michigan Sector - at Sault Ste. Marie, Michigan.
2. For the Detroit sub-sector of the Michigan sector - at Detroit Michigan.
3. For the Erie sector - at Cleveland Ohio.
4. For the Buffalo sector - at Buffalo New York.

F. *Date for initiation of the operations.*

The above operations will be initiated on M day.

Task Two.

To support the Army in its operations in adjacent Crimson territory.

A. *Operations required.* Under the above task it will be necessary to:

1 Co-operate closely with and assist the Army in its operations particularly those in the following localities:
   A. Saint Mary's River and Sault Ste. Marie Canals.
   B. St Clair and Detroit Rivers.
   C. Niagara River and Welland Canals.

2. Co-operate closely with and furnish all practicable assistance to the Army in its operations in the Montréal – Québec area in so far as these come within the Naval Great Lakes theater.

B. *Date for initiation of the operations.*

For planning purposes it will be assumed that the above operations are initiated on embarkation day.

Task Three.

To gain and exercise control of the Great Lakes.

A. *Operations required.* Under the above task, it will be necessary to:

1. Mobilise, man, equip, supply, organise and concentrate the necessary forces.

2. Select, organise, man and equip, the bases required for the operations of these forces.

3. Provide security for United States shipping on the Great Lakes by patrol of the important shipping routes particularly where passing through narrow defiles and connecting waterways and escort especially valuable vessels.

4. Capture, destroy or effectively contain all Red or Crimson naval forces, regular or irregular.

5. Capture, destroy or blockade all Red and Crimson merchant shipping within the Great Lakes theater.

B. *Forces for task.*

As the forces assigned are in the main nonexistent. In peace time, selection and *designation of an adequate number of suitable merchant vessels and yachts for conversion to naval observatories should form part of operating plan 0–3D Red.*

C. *Command and organisation.*

Without contravening the supreme authority of the Commander Naval Forces Great Lakes, on account of the large area involved and the geographic conformation of the lakes, it will be necessary to subdivide the Naval Forces of Great Lakes into various task groups, each with a definite area of operations. Each task group should be under a separate commander, but with provisions for mutual support and assistance whenever such becomes necessary. The following task groups are suggested:

1. *The Lake Superior Forces, with headquarters at Sault Ste Marie, to include as its area of operations all Lake Superior, Saint Mary's River, Saint Joseph Channel and the detour passage.*

2. *The Lake Huron Forces, with headquarters at Detroit to include as its area of operations Lake Michigan, Huron and St Clair, Georgian Bay, North Channel, Straits of Mackinac, St. Clair and Detroit Rivers.*

3. *Lake Erie forces, with headquarters at Cleveland to include as its area of operations all Lake Eirie but excluding Buffalo harbor.*

4. *The Lake Ontario Forces, with headquarters at Buffalo to include as*

its area of operations all Lake Ontario, the Niagara River and St Lawrence River to Cornwall Island.

D. *Supply.*
   See previous notes

E. *Bases.*
   In addition to designating headquarters sections, the Commander Naval Forces Great Lakes, will in his operating plan 0–3D Red, slect and designate the section bases for the operating forces. The following localities are suggested:

   1. *For the Lake Superior forces: Deluth, Minnesota - Superior, Wisconsin, and Hancock Michigan.*

   2. *For the Lake Huron forces: Cheboygan, Michigan, Alpena Michigan, and Port Huron Michigan.*

   3. *For the Lake Erie forces: Toledo, Ohio and Erie Pennsylvania.*

   4. *For the Lake Ontario forces: Charlotte (Rochester), New York, Oswego, New York and Ogdensburg, New York.*

F. *Date for initiation of the operations.*
   For planning purposes it will be assumed that the above operations are initiated on embarkation day.

As can be seen, the langauge was dreary, repetitive and tedious but the Joint Plan was put in place. No records have been located to suggest that it went any further up the chain of command to either Congress or the President.

Chapter Five

How to Win Friends and Influence People

Where America is swamped by the views of the extreme right,
is brainwashed by the views of the Radio Priest
and big business jumps on the Nazi bandwagon.

The War Plan Red set of documents as promulgated by Admiral Charles F Hughes in May 1930 clearly demonstrates that there was a strong vein of belief existing within the American military establishment and also within the wider USA that promoted the concept of American imperialism, and the desire to become what was later called a 'superpower'. This belief clearly ran deep and wide and had links with other socio-political concepts.

When the plan became at least partially known of by the public, many would have it believed that there were very few with Far-Right leanings in the USA, that the Imperialists, Isolationalists and American Nazis were few in number and had even less influence. That was far from the case, as we are about to see.

American Imperialism was, and still is a policy aimed at extending the political, economic, and cultural control of the United States government over areas beyond its boundaries. It could be accomplished in any number of ways: by military conquest, by treaty, by subsidisation, by economic penetration through private companies followed by intervention when those interests were threatened, or by regime change.

Thomas Jefferson, in the 1790s, awaited the fall of the Spanish Empire '...until our population can be sufficiently advanced to gain it from them piece by piece'. Detailing George Washington's description of the early United States as an 'infant empire', Benjamin Franklin's writing that '...the Prince that acquires new Territory ... removes the Natives to give his own People Room ... may be properly called [Father] of [his] Nation', and Thomas Jefferson's statement that the United States 'must be viewed as the nest from which all America, North and South is to be peopled', further strengthened the concept.

President James Monroe presented his famous doctrine for the western hemisphere in 1823. Historians have observed that while the Monroe Doctrine contained a commitment to resist colonialism from Europe, it had some aggressive implications for American policy since there were no limitations on the US's actions mentioned within it. Scholars have noted that the tactics used to implement the doctrine were '...modeled after those employed by British imperialists' in their national competition with Spain and France and that the Monroe Doctrine was little more than 'imperial anti-colonialism.'.

The concept of expanding territorial control was popularised in the 19th century as the doctrine of Manifest Destiny and was realised through conquests such as the Mexican – American War of 1846, which resulted in the annexation of 525,000 square miles of Mexican territory. While the US government does not refer to itself as an empire, the continuing phenomenon has been acknowledged.

The Indian Wars against the indigenous population began in the British era. Their escalation under the federal republic allowed the US to dominate North America and carve out the 48 continental states. This is now understood to be an explicitly colonial process, as the Native American nations were usually recognised as sovereign entities before annexation. Their sovereignty was systematically undermined by US state policy that usually involved enforced the application of unequal or broken treaties and white settler-colonialism. The climax was the California genocide where in the mid-to-late 19th century actions by the United States federal, state, and local governments resulted in the decimation of the indigenous population of California following the US occupation of California in 1848. Actions included encouragement of volunteers and militias to kill unarmed men, women and children.

War Plan Red of 1930 was just two more

stages of this imperialist expansion - to annexe Canada and the whole of the Caribbean - the added bonus was that it would destroy the British Empire and thus allow America to take up the mantle of being the world's only superpower!

A variety of factors converged during the so-called 'New Imperialism' of the late 19th century when the USA and the other great powers rapidly expanded their overseas territorial possessions.

The prevalence of overt racism, notably John Fiske's conception of Anglo-Saxon racial superiority, and Josiah Strong's call to 'civilise and Christianise' were manifestations of a growing Social Darwinism and racism in some schools of American political thought.

Early in his career, as Assistant Secretary of the Navy, Theodore Roosevelt was instrumental in preparing the navy for the Spanish-American War and was an enthusiastic proponent of testing the US military in battle, at one point stating *'I should welcome almost any war, for I think this country needs one'*.

Roosevelt claimed he rejected imperialism, but he embraced the near-identical doctrine of expansionism. When Rudyard Kipling wrote the imperialist poem *'The White Man's Burden'* for Roosevelt, the politician told colleagues that it was *'...rather poor poetry, but good sense from the expansion point of view.'* Roosevelt was so committed to dominating Spain's former colonies that he proclaimed his corollary to the Monroe Doctrine as justification, although his ambitions extended even further, into the Far East. There was definitely resemblance and collaboration between US and British military activities in the Pacific at this time.

Industry and trade are two of the most common motivations of imperialism. American intervention in both Latin America and Hawaii resulted in multiple industrial investments, including the popular industry of Dole bananas. Big business and corporate America were prepared to use any means to achieve this, even if it meant going to war, or to turn a blind eye on atrocities. If the United States was able to annex territory, in turn, they were granted access to the trade and capital of those territories. In 1898, Senator Albert Beveridge proclaimed that an expansion of markets was necessary, *'American factories are making more than the American people can use; American soil is producing more than they can consume. Fate has written our policy for us; the trade of the world must and shall be ours.'*

American sailors with a Gatling gun on Haiti as part of a conflict known as the 'banana wars' of the early 20th century, when the American military sent their troops south into Central America to keep their business interests there intact, despite the locals fighting for their freedom from corporate oppression. For the American government, all this fighting for freedom was bad for business. Companies like the United Fruit Co. had a vested interest in keeping their Central American plantations stable and so they called in the American Army to crack down on those who were disrupting the system. *(NARA)*

American rule of ceded Spanish territory was not uncontested. The Philippine Revolution had begun in August 1896 against Spain, and after the defeat of Spain in the Battle of Manila Bay, started again in earnest, culminating in the Philippine Declaration of Independence and the establishment of the First Philippine Republic. The Philippine-American War ensued, with extensive damage and death, ultimately resulting in the defeat of the Philippine Republic.

Parallel to the idea of American Imperialism is that of the far more nebulous, but equally real idea of American exceptionalism; an ideology holding the United States as unique among nations in positive or negative connotations, concerning its ideas of democracy and personal freedom.

Though the concept has no formal definition, there are some themes common to various conceptions of the idea. One is that the history of the United States is different from other nations. In this view, American exceptionalism stems from the American Revolution, becoming what political scientist Seymour Martin Lipset called 'the first new nation' and developing the American ideology of 'Americanism', based on liberty, egalitarianism, individualism, republicanism, democracy, and laissez-faire economics. Another theme is the idea that the USA has a unique mission to transform the world. Abraham Lincoln stated in the Gettysburg address of 1863, Americans must ensure *government of the people, by the people, for the people, shall not perish from the earth*. Another theme is the sense that the United States' history and mission gives a superiority over other nations.

The theory of the exceptionalism of the USA has developed over time and can be traced to many sources. French political scientist and historian Alexis de Tocqueville was the first writer to describe the country as 'exceptional' in 1831 and 1840. The phrase 'American Exceptionalism' was also used by Soviet leader Joseph Stalin as a critique of a revisionist faction of American Communists who argued that the American political climate was unique, making it an 'exception' to some aspects of Marxist theory.

As has already been demonstrated in the previous two chapters, War Plan Red was not only a concept with roots that were strongly based in American Imperialism, there were also strong connections with the American Isolationalists.

Isolationalism.

The term 'Isolationism' is government policy or doctrine of taking no role in the affairs of other nations. A government's policy of isolationism, which that government may or may not officially acknowledge, is characterised by a reluctance or refusal to enter into treaties, alliances, trade commitments, or other international agreements.

Supporters of isolationism, known as 'isolationists', argue that it allows the nation to devote all of its resources and efforts to its advancement by remaining at peace and avoiding binding responsibilities to other countries.

While it has been practised to some degree in US foreign policy since before the War for Independence, isolationism in the United States has never been about total avoidance of the rest of the world. Only a handful of American isolationists advocated the complete removal of the nation from the world stage. Instead, most American isolationists have pushed for the avoidance of the nation's involvement in what Thomas Jefferson called 'entangling alliances'. Instead, American isolationists have held that the USA could and should use its wide-ranging influence and economic strength to encourage the ideals of freedom and democracy - as determined by the USA of course - in other nations by means of negotiation rather than warfare.

In the main, isolationism refers to America's longstanding reluctance to become involved in European alliances and wars. Isolationists held the view that America's perspective on the world was different from that of European societies and that America could advance the cause of freedom and democracy by means other than war.

Isolationist feelings in America dates back to the colonial period. The last thing many American colonists wanted was any continued involvement with the European governments that had denied them religious and economic freedom and kept them entangled in wars. Indeed, they took comfort in the fact that they were now effectively 'isolated' from Europe by the vastness of the Atlantic Ocean.

Despite an eventual alliance with France during the War for Independence, the basis of American isolationism is found in Thomas Paine's paper *Common Sense,* published in 1776. Paine's passionate arguments against foreign alliances drove the delegates to the Continental Congress to oppose the alliance with France until it became apparent that the American revolution would be lost without it.

Twenty years and an independent nation later, President George Washington spelt out the intent of American isolationism in his Farewell Address: *'The great rule of conduct for us, in regard to foreign nations, is in extending our commercial relations, to have with them as little political connection as possible. Europe has a set of primary interests, which to us have none or a very remote relation. Hence she must be engaged in frequent controversies the causes of which are essentially foreign to our concerns. Hence, therefore, it must be unwise of us to implicate ourselves, by artificial ties, in the ordinary vicissitudes of her politics, or the ordinary combinations and collisions of her friendships or enmities'.*

Washington's opinions of isolationism were widely accepted. As a result of his Neutrality Proclamation of 1793, the US dissolved its alliance with France. And in 1801, the nation's third President, Thomas Jefferson, in his inaugural address, summed up American isolationism as a doctrine of *'...peace, commerce, and honest friendship with all nations, entangling alliances with none...'*

Somewhat interestingly, around 150 years later the German American Bund used iconic images of George Washington at their rallies, claiming that he was 'the first Fascist', and that Washington 'knew democracy could not work.'

Through the first half of the 19th century, America managed to maintain its political isolation despite its rapid industrial and economic growth and potential status as a world power. Without abandoning its policy of limited isolationism, the United States expanded its own borders from coast-to-coast and began creating territorial empires in the Pacific and the Caribbean during the 1800s. Without forming binding alliances with Europe or any of the nations involved, the US fought three wars: the War of 1812, the Mexican War, and the Spanish-American War.

In 1823, the Monroe Doctrine boldly declared that the United States would consider the colonisation of an independent nation in North or South America by a European country to be an act of war. In delivering the historic decree, President James Monroe voiced the isolationist view, stating, *'In the wars of the European powers, in matters relating to themselves, we have never taken part, nor does it comport with our policy so to do'.*

But by the mid-nineteenth century, a combination of world events began to test the resolve of American isolationists. The expansion of the German and Japanese military industrial empires that would eventually immerse the United States in two world wars had begun.

Though short-lived, the occupation of the Philippines by the United States during the Spanish-American war had inserted American interests into the Western Pacific islands - an area considered to be part of Japan's sphere of influence. Steamships, undersea communications cables, and radio enhanced America's stature in world trade, but at the same time, brought her closer to her potential enemies. Within the United States itself, as industrialised mega-cities grew, while small-town rural America - long the source of isolationist feelings - shrank.

Though actual battle never touched her shores, America's participation in World War One marked the nation's first departure from its historical isolationist policy. During the conflict, the USA entered into binding alliances with the United Kingdom, France, Russia, Italy, Belgium, and Serbia to oppose the Central Powers of Austria-Hungary, Germany, Bulgaria, and the Ottoman Empire.

However, after the war, the United States returned to its isolationist roots by immediately ending all of its war-related European commitments. Against the recommendation of President Woodrow Wilson, the US Senate rejected the war-ending Treaty of Versailles, because it would have required the US to join the League of Nations. Some members of Congress opposed membership in the League out of concern that it would draw the United States into European conflicts, although ultimately the collective security clause sank the possibility of US participation. During the 1930s, the League proved ineffectual in the face of growing militarism, partly due to the US decision not to participate.

World War One brought an end to America's open attitude toward immigration. Between the pre-war years of 1900 and 1920, the nation had admitted over 14.5 million immigrants. After the passage of the Immigration Act of 1917, fewer than 150,000 new immigrants had been allowed to enter the US by 1929. The law restricted the immigration of what was termed 'undesirables' from other countries, including *'...idiots,*

Ellis Island, in Upper New York Bay, was the gateway for over 12 million immigrants to the USA Ellis Island was opened 1 January 1892. The island was greatly expanded with land reclamation between 1892 and 1934. Before that, the much smaller original island was the site of Fort Gibson and later a naval magazine. Generally, those immigrants who were approved spent from two to five hours at Ellis Island. Arrivals were asked 29 questions including name, occupation, and the amount of money carried. It was important to the American government the new arrivals could support themselves and have money to get started. The average the government wanted the immigrants to have was between 18 and 25 dollars . Those with visible health problems or diseases were sent home or held in the island's hospital facilities for long periods of time.

imbeciles, epileptics, alcoholics, poor, criminals, beggars, any person suffering attacks of insanity…'. Although not exactly the same idiology as the Nazi 'Aryan Master Race' concept, that Immigration Act certainly has echoes and tones of similarity.

During the 1930s, the combination of the Great Depression and the memory of tragic losses in World War One contributed to pushing American public opinion and policy toward isolationism. Isolationists advocated non-involvement in European and Asian conflicts and non-entanglement in international politics. Although the USA took measures to avoid political and military conflicts across the oceans, it continued to expand economically and protect its interests in Latin America. The leaders of the isolationist movement called upon history to bolster their position drawing upon the farewell address, of President George Washington who had advocated non-involvement in European wars and politics. For much of the nineteenth century, the expanse of the Atlantic and Pacific Oceans had made it possible for the United States

to enjoy a kind of 'free security' to remain detached from Old World conflicts. During World War One, however, President Woodrow Wilson made a case for US intervention in the battle and a US interest in maintaining peaceful world order. Nevertheless, the American experience in that war served to bolster the arguments of isolationists; they argued that marginal US interests in that conflict did not justify the number of US casualties.

In the wake of the World War One, a report by Senator Gerald P. Nye, a Republican from North Dakota, fed this belief by claiming that American bankers and arms manufacturers had pushed for US involvement for their profit. The 1934 publication of the book Merchants of Death by H.C. Engelbrecht and F. C. Hanighen, followed by the 1935 tract 'War Is a Racket' by decorated Marine Corps General Smedley D. Butler both served to increase popular suspicions of wartime profiteering and influence public opinion in the direction of neutrality. Many Americans became determined not to be tricked by banks and industries into making such great sacrifices again. The reality of worldwide economic depression and the need for increased attention to domestic problems only served to bolster the idea that the USA should isolate itself from troubling events in Europe. During the interwar period, the US Government repeatedly chose non-entanglement over participation or intervention as the appropriate response to international questions.

The Japanese invasion of Manchuria and subsequent push to gain control over larger expanses of northeast China in 1931 led President Herbert Hoover and his Secretary of State, Henry Stimson, to establish the Stimson Doctrine, which stated that the USA would not recognise the territory gained by aggression and in violation of international agreements. With the Stimson Doctrine, the United States expressed concern over the aggressive action without committing itself to any direct involvement or intervention. Intreguingly, all this was happening in public while War Plan Red was being put in place. Other conflicts, including the Italian invasion of Ethiopia and the Spanish Civil War, also resulted in virtually no official commitment or action from the United States Government. Upon taking office, President Franklin Delano Roosevelt tended to see a necessity for the United States to participate more actively in international affairs, but his ability to apply his personal outlook to foreign policy was limited by the strength of isolationist sentiment in the US Congress. In 1933, Roosevelt proposed a congressional measure that would have granted him the right to consult with other nations to place pressure on aggressors in international conflicts. The bill ran into stiff opposition from the leading isolationists in Congress, including progressive politicians such as senators Hiram Johnson of California, William Borah of Idaho, and Robert La Follette of Wisconsin. In 1935, the controversy over US participation in the World Court elicited similar

opposition. As tensions rose in Europe over Nazi Germany's aggressive manoeuvres, Congress pushed through a series of Neutrality Acts, which served to prevent American ships and citizens from becoming entangled in external conflicts. Roosevelt lamented the restrictive nature of these, but because he still required congressional support for his domestic New Deal policies, he reluctantly complied.

The isolationists were a diverse group, including progressives and conservatives, business owners and peace activists, but because they faced no consistent, organised opposition from internationalists, their ideology triumphed time and again. Roosevelt appeared to accept the strength of the isolationist elements in Congress until 1937. In that year, as the situation in Europe continued to grow worse and the Second Sino-Japanese War began in Asia, the President gave a speech in which he likened international aggression to a disease that other nations must work to 'quarantine'. At that time, however, Americans were still not prepared to risk their lives and livelihoods for peace abroad. Even the outbreak of war in Europe in 1939 did not suddenly diffuse popular desire to avoid international entanglements. Instead, public opinion shifted from favouring complete neutrality to supporting limited US aid to the Allies short of actual intervention in the war. The surprise Japanese attack on the US Navy at Pearl Harbor in December 1941 served to convince the majority of Americans that the United States should enter the war on the side of the Allies.

Will no one rid me of this meddlesome priest?
In the 1920s and 30s America may have been riven by disparate groups following the nebulous ideology of different '-isms' but there were also other individuals and groups pushing their own agendas. One such person was Charles Edward Coughlin (*b*. October 25, 1891, *d*. October 27,

Left: Herbert Clark Hoover (*b*. 10 August 1874, *d*. 20 October 1964) was America's 31st President. He was a Republican when he took office in 1929, the year the US economy plummeted into the Great Depression.

Right: Henry Lewis Stimson (*b*. 21 September 1867, *d*. 20 October 1950) was an American statesman, lawyer and Republican Party politician.

118

1979), a Canadian - American Roman Catholic priest based in the USA near Detroit. He was the founding priest at the National Shrine of the Little Flower church.

Commonly known as Father Coughlin, and broadcasting under the grandiose phrase of 'The Radio Priest', Coughlin was one of the pioneers of the US mass communications industry, and built up one of the first multimedia empires. In 1926, Coughlin began broadcasting on Detroit radio station WJR and

The 'Radio Priest' Father Charles Edward Coughlin in full broadcasting flow.

created the model of the angry, belligerent no-holds-barred talk-show host that became so popular in the early 21st century. Political pundits such as Ann Coulter, Sean Hannity and Alex Jones clearly could have used 'The Radio Priest' as a role model and Glenn Becks' rants on Fox News were straight out of Coughlin's playbook.

Surviving recordings of Coughlin's broadcasts show that he had something of a pompous, evangelical 'fire and brimstone' style so typical of the day. This was complemented and contrasted by the station's continuity announcer who introduced the priest by saying in somewhat hushed, reverent tones that *'Father Coughlin is about to address you...'* as if the listener was about to be granted the undoubted honour of hearing sparkling pearls of wisdom brought down to earth from on high by God's own personal representative.

When radio station group Goodwill Stations acquired WJR in 1929, owner George A. Richards encouraged Coughlin to focus on politics instead of religious topics. Becoming increasingly fierce, the broadcasts attacked the banking system and Jews. Coughlin's programme was picked up by CBS in 1930 for national broadcast. That same year Coughlin began a series of attacks against socialism and Soviet Communism, which was strongly opposed by the Catholic Church. He criticised capitalists in America whose greed had made communist

ideology attractive, warning: *'Let not the working man be able to say that he is driven into the ranks of socialism by the inordinate and grasping greed of the manufacturer'.* Having gained a reputation as an outspoken anti-communist, in July 1930 Coughlin was given star billing as a witness before the House Un-American Activities Committee.

In 1931, the CBS radio network dropped Coughlin's programme when he refused to accept network demands to review his scripts before broadcast. He raised independent money to fund his national network, which soon reached millions of listeners through a 36-station syndicate originating from flagship station WJR, for the *Golden Hour of the Shrine of the Little Flower,* as the programme was called.

Against the deepening crisis of the Great Depression, Coughlin strongly endorsed Franklin D Roosevelt during the 1932 presidential election. He was an early supporter of Roosevelt's New Deal reforms and coined the phrase 'Roosevelt or Ruin', which entered common usage during the early days of the first FDR administration. Another phrase for which Coughlin became known for was 'The New Deal is Christ's Deal'. In January 1934, Coughlin testified before Congress in support of FDR's policies, saying, *'If Congress fails to back up the President in his monetary program, I predict a revolution in this country which will make the French Revolution look silly!'* He also said to the congressional hearing, *'God is directing President Roosevelt'.*

Coughlin's support for Roosevelt and his New Deal faded in 1934 when he founded the National Union for Social Justice (NUSJ), a nationalistic workers' rights organisation. Its platform called for monetary reforms, nationalisation of major industries and railroads, and protection of labour rights. The membership ran into the millions, but it was not well-organised locally, and its leaders grew impatient with what they considered the President's unconstitutional and pseudo-capitalistic monetary policies. Coughlin preached increasingly about the negative influence of the 'money changers' and 'permitting a group of private citizens to create money' at the expense of the general welfare. He spoke of the need for monetary reform based on 'free silver'. Coughlin claimed that the Great Depression in the United States was a cash famine and proposed monetary reforms, including the nationalisation of the Federal Reserve System as the solution.

By 1934, Coughlin was perhaps the most prominent Roman Catholic speaker on political and financial issues, with a radio audience that reached tens of millions of people every week. He foreshadowed modern talk radio and televangelism. The Radio Priest expressed isolationist, and conspiratorial views, concepts that resonated with many listeners.

In 1934, when Coughlin began criticising the New Deal, Roosevelt sent Joseph Kennedy, Sr. and Frank Murphy, both prominent Irish Catholics, to try to influence him. Kennedy was reported to be a friend of Coughlin. Coughlin periodically visited Roosevelt while accompanied by Kennedy.

Increasingly opposed to Roosevelt, Coughlin began denouncing the President as a tool of Wall Street. The priest supported populist Huey Pierce Long Jr. as Governor of Louisiana until Long was assassinated on 10 September 1935. He assisted William Lemke's Union Party in 1936. Coughlin opposed the New Deal with a growing vehemence. His radio talks attacked Roosevelt, capitalists, and alleged the existence of Jewish conspirators. Another nationally known priest, Monsignor John A. Ryan, initially supported Coughlin but opposed him after Coughlin turned on Roosevelt. Joseph Kennedy, who strongly supported the New Deal, warned as early as 1933 that Coughlin was *'becoming a perilous proposition'* as an opponent of Roosevelt and *'an out and out demagogue'*. Kennedy worked with Roosevelt, Bishop Francis Spellman, and Cardinal Eugenio Pacelli (the future Pope Pius XII) in a successful effort to get the Vatican to silence Coughlin in 1936.

In 1935, Coughlin proclaimed, *'I have dedicated my life to fight against the heinous rottenness of modern capitalism because it robs the labourer of this world's goods. But blow for blow I shall strike against Communism because it robs us of the next world's happiness'*.

Coughlin's NUSJ gained a strong following among nativists and opponents of the Federal Reserve, especially in the Midwest. Michael Kazin has written that Coughlinites saw Wall Street and Communism as twin faces of a secular Satan. They believed that they were defending those people who were joined more by piety, economic frustration, and a common dread of powerful, modernising enemies than through any class identity. Coughlin called for the US Government to be replaced by one of his own design, the analogies with Hitler being obvious. One of Coughlin's campaign slogans was: *'Less care for internationalism and more concern for national prosperity'*, which appealed to the 1930s isolationists in the United States. Coughlin's organisation especially appealed to Irish Catholics.

In March 1935 General Hugh S Johnson made the Hitler – Coughlin comparison clear on national radio: *'Someone sent me a parallel of what you and Adolf Hitler proposed and preached and they were alike as peas in a pod. As a foreign-born, you could not become President'* Johnson told Coughlin *'...but you could become Reichfürer - just as Austrian Adolf became a dictator in Germany'*.

A December 1938 Gallup Poll found that twenty-two per cent of Americans listened to Coughlin's programmes the previous month that translated into a 29 million audience. It has been estimated that his audience was the largest in the world far surpassing any other radio star of the time.

Coughlin began to use his radio programme to broadcast an anti-semitic commentary. In the late 1930s, he supported some of the fascist policies of Adolf Hitler, Benito Mussolini, and Emperor Hirohito of Japan. According to Coughlin, Jewish bankers were behind the Russian Revolution and he strongly backed the Jewish Bolshevism conspiracy theory. The broadcasts have been described as 'a variation of the Fascist agenda applied to American culture'. His chief topics were political and economic rather than religious, using the slogan 'Social Justice'. Many American bishops, as well as the Vatican, wanted him silenced.

Coughlin also promoted his controversial beliefs employing his weekly rotogravure magazine, *Social Justice*, which began publication in March 1936. During the last half of 1938, *Social Justice* reprinted in weekly instalments the fraudulent, anti-semitic text *The Protocols of the Elders of Zion*. The Protocols were proved to be a Russian forgery that purported to expose a Jewish conspiracy to seize control of the world.

On 20 November 1938, just two weeks after Kristallnacht, the Nazi-orchestrated attack on German and Austrian Jews, their synagogues, and businesses, Coughlin, referring to the millions of Christians killed by the Communists in Russia, said: *'Jewish persecution only followed after Christians first were persecuted'*. After this speech, some radio stations, including those in New York City and Chicago, began refusing to air Coughlin's speeches without subjecting his scripts to prior review and approval. In New York City, his programmes were cancelled by WINS and WMCA, and Coughlin broadcast only on the Newark part-time station WHBI. On 18 December 1938, thousands of Coughlin's followers picketed the studios of station WMCA in New York City to protest the station's refusal to carry the priest's broadcasts. Many protesters yelled anti-semitic statements, such as *'Send Jews back where they came from in leaky boats!'* and *'Wait until Hitler comes over here!'* The protests continued for several months. According to some authors, who have made use of the archives of the FBI and German government there is supposedly documentary evidence that Coughlin received indirect funding from Nazi Germany during this time.

In March 1940, The Radio League of the Little Flower, creators of *Social Justice* magazine, self-published a book titled *An Answer to Father Coughlin's Critics*. Written by *'Father Coughlin's Friends'*, the book was an attempt to *'...deal with those matters which relate directly to the main charges registered against Father Coughlin ... to his being a pro-Nazi, anti-Semite, a falsifier of documents, etc'*.

After the outbreak of World War Two in Europe in 1939, the Roosevelt administration finally forced the cancellation of his radio programme and forbade distribution by mail of his newspaper, *Social Justice*.

When Coughlin's broadcasting permit was denied, he was temporarily silenced. Coughlin worked around the restriction by purchasing air-time and playing his speeches via transcription.

Senators, Congressmen and other assorted politicians.

Adolf Hitler's rise to power started in September 1930 when his party gained a victory in the Reichstag, obtaining 107 seats. The Nazis became the second largest party in Germany. In America, Franklin Delano Roosevelt won the thirty-seventh quadrennial presidential election, held on Tuesday, 8 November 1932. by a landslide in both the electoral and popular vote, carrying every state outside of the northeast and receiving the highest percentage of the popular vote of any Democratic nominee up to that time.

In the federal election of July 1932, Hitler's NSDAP won just over thirty-seven per cent of the popular vote, an upswing by nineteen points, becoming the largest party in the Reichstag, holding 230 out of 608 seats.

By now the Germans had a number of simple objectives: encourage apathy and confusion by sowing discord, discredit the British nation and turn the Americans against each other.

Nazi propaganda hoped to sow enough discord to make sure the US stayed out of world events. The Nazis and their supporters set about their task with a will. The cities were soon full of Nazi propaganda planted by those in academic circles, isolationist quarters and political precincts. There were four aims.

1. Blame the war on Great Britain. Make a war of Empire profit and trade. Scoff that the war was about democracy.
2. Smear the British empire.
3. Cast doubt on the newspapers and newspapermen who favoured the Allied cause.
4. If the administration claimed national defence call the American president a warmonger. Start attacks along religious and racial lines. Keep the US fighting amongst itself.

This was a classic disinformation campaign full of 'fake news' that had echoes in a certain campaign two generations later. Business leaders were courted by German envoys, who promised huge profits if they could convince Roosevelt to stay out of the war.

The politicians and their staff were easy targets for the Germans - a number of senators and congressmen were clearly anti-Roosevelt. One such example was Senator Ernest Lundeen who had been elected to the United States Senate in 1936 as a member of the Farmer-Labor Party.

Left: Senator Ernest Lundeen (*b*. 4 August 1878, *d*. 31 August 1940) was an American lawyer and politician.

Right: George Sylvester Viereck (b. 31 December 1884, d. 18 March 1962) was a German-American poet, writer, and pro-Nazi propagandist

He consistently claimed that he did not want to live in America that would sacrifice it sons for the self-interest of the European powers especially the British Empire.

From the early 1930s onwards, the German embassy in Washington DC operated an ingenious propaganda scheme that used more than twenty-four US senators and congressmen to spread pro-German and anti-British invective to millions of Americans using the American Political Mail system operated by the US Postal Service. A Congressional office in a House office building became the centre of the plot. Stacks of printed material and pre-printed envelopes arrived during the day and sat waiting for distribution around the country. Many of the elected officials were fully aware of what was happening. This was physical 'spamming' long before the electronic version surfaced in time for the elections of the early 21st century. At the centre of the scheme was George Sylvester Viereck - referred to by some as Hitler's number one Benedict Arnold.

Viereck became the Third Reich's most effective weapon for recruiting Americans in Washington DC and made regular political intelligence reports back to Berlin. The Nazis based their strategy around Viereck's operation and their consulates around the country began persuading the senators, congressman and other officials - including those in the military - with three major aims:

1. Convincing the US that the Allies, especially the UK, were doomed in the event of war; this was mainly done by spreading rumours and disinformation in the media.
2. Ensuring the American public remained opposed to the notion of entering the war in Europe under any circumstances. This was done by pressing public officials to support neutrality and disparaging the Roosevelt administration.
3. Ensure continuing trade between the USA and Germany.

Viereck founded two publications, *The International* (of which the notorious poet Aleister Crowley was a contributing editor for a time) and *The Fatherland,* which argued the German cause during World War One. Viereck became a well-known supporter of National Socialism. In 1933, Viereck again met with Hitler - he first met him in 1923 - but was now Germany's leader, in Berlin. In 1934, Viereck gave a speech to 20,000 'Friends of the New Germany' at New York's Madison Square Garden, in which he compared Hitler to Franklin Delano Roosevelt and told his audience to sympathise with National Socialism without being anti-semites. His Jewish friends denounced him as 'George Swastika Viereck', but he continued to promote National Socialism.

Viereck visited Berlin in late 1938 and was given the task of running a large-scale anti-British operation in the USA. To complete the arrangement, Viereck was hired by the German Library of Information - a propaganda organisation based in Manhattan - with instructions to place favourable articles in the US press, ostensibly as a writer doing 'special editorial work'.

His key contact and paymaster was Heribert von Stempel, first secretary of the German Embassy in Washington. The political climate could hardly have been any more conducive. Isolationist and non-interventionist sentiments were running high.

Corporate America

The dog-eat-dog world of American corporate executives cared little about who they did business with. The deal was everything, and the art with which it was done had just one importance - the bottom line of the balance sheet.

In the 1930s they showed little reluctance about doing business with the Third Reich - many American corporations were already heavily invested in Germany and showed little hesitation about continuing to do so; they knew the alternative was to suffer heavy losses. The 1920s had been an era of rapid globalisation, particularly by those American companies who used their prosperity to acquire European rivals. Until the 1929 stock market crash this certainly looked like a winning strategy particularly for American companies who were looking to gain access into an undeveloped German market.

Some figures suggest American corporations had an estimated at $300 million invested in German corporate branches and manufacturing facilities when Hitler rose to power. This was simply too much capital for the American corporate bosses to walk away from when the political circumstances changed. It was a clear incentive for American corporate leaders to behave as if they were Hitler's friends whether they agreed with his policies or not.

This was particularly noticeable in the auto industry. A 1929 newspaper report estimated there were only 1.2 million cars on the road in Germany while 23 million were operating in the USA. German carmaker Mercedes produced excellent luxury cars, but no company provided an excellent serviceable cheap vehicle for the average man. The article went on to say that 'the German market scene is one of the most promising in the world' a comment that would soon entice both General Motors and Ford.

Other American companies had seen similar opportunities. International Business Machines — known as IBM — created the European division as did the Coca-Cola Corporation. In 1929 Standard Oil, one of the world's most potent corporations entered a business relationship with the German company I G Farben that allowed Standard to take a twenty-five per cent share in Farben's gasoline business. The two companies also entered a patent-sharing agreement that gave Farben the ability to boost its octane levels and therefore supplied the German Luftwaffe with more efficient fuel. A subsidiary of I G Farben, Degesch (Deutsche Gesellschaft für Schädlingsbekämpfung MbH, or German Company for Pest Control) produced a cyanide-based pesticide, Zyklon B, that was used to kill over one million people, mostly Jews, in gas chambers in Europe, including in the Auschwitz II and Majdanek extermination camps in occupied Poland.

In March 1929 both GM and Ford made attempts to purchase Opel, the largest carmaker outside the USA. GM's Alfred P Sloan outmanoeuvred Ford by gaining eighty per cent of Opel's stock for $33.3 million making the German company GM's largest foreign holding. The prospect is using Opel's manufacturing facilities to produce a new low-cost car seemed an incredible business deal, but by the early years of the depression, GM was losing money in Germany. The obvious solution was to make a swift exit from the German market, but in 1931 the government imposed capital controls to prevent companies from taking money out of the country. GM was trapped.

Nazi policies offered some opportunities as well. Hitler's tax cuts on cars were followed by a speech in 1934 in which he announced a national effort to produce a small and affordable vehicle that could be purchased by five million Germans making average incomes. The idea of owning a people's automobile - or Volkswagen - became incredibly popular among the German public.

This was exactly the opportunity GM was looking for when it purchased Opel. The company was already offering the cheapest car on the German market so it made sense for Hitler to choose the company to produce his peoples automobile. GM executives began making plans to convince the government to give Opel exclusive rights to the Volkswagen. However, it was not to be - they were outmanoeuvred by engineer Ferdinand Porsche, who successfully networked his way through the Nazi bureaucracy and into the Fuhrer's affections. Opel then switched production to Germany's favourite form of mechanised transportation - trucks. Their profit margins soared.

Meanwhile, Ford opened a subsidiary in the German city of Cologne - Ford Werke AG - which soon became the only overseas Ford plant allowed to produce the V-8 engine.

In 1929 an American expatriate Ray Rivington Powers started bottling Coca-Cola in Germany and quickly found the market for more

Above: Ford Werke AG's factory at Cologne on the banks of the river Rhine.

Right: a Ford truck in the service of the German Luftwaffe, somewhere in the Italian Alps.

Left: On 30 July 1938, Henry Ford (centre) celebrated his 75th birthday by receiving the Grand Cross of the German Eagle. He received the award in his office, joined by the German consuls from Cleveland and Detroit.

A longtime admirer of Ford's, Adolf Hitler sent a personal note of gratitude to be delivered at the ceremony. Signed on 7 July, the parchment scroll warmly thanked Ford for his 'humanitarian ideals' and his devotion, along with the German Chancellor, to 'the cause of peace'.

than 100,000 cases of the soft drink. By 1936 more than one million cases of Coca-Cola were being sold in the Third Reich making it one of the country's favourite beverages.

It was not just profit motives and business opportunities that drove American corporate bosses into the arms of the Nazis. They were somewhat motivated by genuine affinities for Nazism. Possibly the most potent example of this was Henry Ford one of America's most famous businessmen. Ford's engineering and business acumen were beyond doubt, but there had always been indications that his personal views were somewhat suspect. During World War One he adopted the view that the conflict had been the product of an international plot by Jewish bankers anti-Semitic slurs soon became a common aspect of his vocabulary. In the early 1930s he owned a newspaper called the *Dearborn Independent* that transformed into a viciously anti-Semitic mouthpiece.

Like so many of Hitler's American friends by the mid-1930s, Henry Ford was blaming financiers and moneylenders for both the new deal and the prospect of another world war. Rumours began to circulate that Ford was secretly funding the German-American Bund, although these claims were never conclusively proven. One of his many admirers was Adolf Hitler himself, who once indicated his desire to help 'Heinrich' Ford become the leader of a growing fascist movement in America.

By 1938 Ford's Dearborn office was making arrangements to secretly supply truck parts to its Cologne plant to fulfil the German government's demand for military vehicles. These had to be officially built in Germany so Ford simply provided kits of parts that could be quickly combined to produce working vehicles. In June 1938 the German military requested more than 3100 trucks from Ford for use in the future occupation of Czechoslovakia. The vehicles were assembled in the dead of night at the cologne factory after being shipped in pieces from the USA. On 30 July, the German Consul in Cleveland pinned the Grand Cross of the German eagle on Ford's chest in honour of his 75th birthday and his services to the automotive industry, though his specific contributions to the German truck industry went unmentioned.

The company's founder Henry Ford remained personally infatuated with Nazism throughout the war. More than one account states that he continued to make personal gifts to the Führer until it was no longer possible to do so. His son, Edsel, continued operations in France after that country fell to German occupation. One Ford plant near Paris began turning out aircraft engines, military trucks and other vehicles for the German military just as it had done in Cologne. The profits continued to mount up, even more so when they gained the benefits of slave labour.

The American Dream was open to all comers, although the American Reality was firmly in the hands of a small group of rich white businessmen who viewed their success as proof that rich white people were genetically superior. Thus, the cream of the American business community – including du Pont, Rockefeller, Henry Ford, Andrew Carnegie, JP Morgan, Andrew Mellon, Averell Harriman and Prescott Bush – all viewed the presence of Chinese, Jews, Italians, as an alarming dilution of the white gene pool.

Prescott Sheldon Bush (*b*. 15 May 1895, *d*. 8 October 1972) was a founding member and one of seven directors of the Union Banking Corporation, an investment bank that operated as a clearing house for many assets

Friedrich 'Fritz' Thyssen (*b*. 9 November 1873, *d*. 8 February 1951), German steel magnate and financier of Adolf Hitler. Thyssen used the Union Banking Corporation in the USA, one director of which was Prescott Bush. (NARA)

and enterprises held by German steel magnate Fritz Thyssen. In July 1942, the bank was suspected of holding gold on behalf of Nazi leaders. A subsequent government investigation disproved those allegations but confirmed the Thyssens' control, and in October 1942 the United States seized the bank under the Trading with the Enemy Act and held the assets for the duration of World War Two. Journalist Duncan Campbell pointed out documents showing that Prescott Bush was a director and shareholder of some companies involved with Thyssen.

Friedrich 'Fritz' Thyssen was a German businessman, born into one of Germany's leading industrial families. In 1923, Thyssen met former General Erich Ludendorff, who advised him to attend a speech given by Adolf Hitler, leader of the Nazi Party. Thyssen was impressed by Hitler and his bitter opposition to the Treaty of Versailles and began to make large donations to the party, including 100,000 gold marks in 1923 to Ludendorff. In this, he was unusual among German business leaders, as most were traditional conservatives who regarded the Nazis with suspicion. Thyssen's principal motive in supporting the National Socialists was his great fear of communism; he had little confidence that the various German anti-communist factions would prevent a Soviet-style revolution in Germany unless the popular appeal of communism among the lower classes were co-opted by an anti-communist alternative. Postwar investigators found that he had donated 650,000 Reichsmarks to right-wing parties, mostly to the Nazis, although Thyssen himself claimed to have donated 1 million marks to the Nazi Party. Thyssen remained a member of the German National People's Party until 1932 and did not join the National Socialist German Workers' Party until 1933.

In November 1932, Thyssen and Hjalmar Schacht were the main organisers of a letter to President Paul von Hindenburg urging him to appoint Hitler as Chancellor. Thyssen also persuaded the Association of German Industrialists to donate 3 million Reichsmarks to the National Socialist German Workers' Party for the March 1933 Reichstag election. As a reward, he was elected a Nazi member of the Reichstag and appointed to the Council of State of Prussia, the largest German state. Thyssen welcomed the suppression of the Communist Party, the Social Democrats and the trade unions. In 1934 he was one of the business leaders who persuaded Hitler to suppress the SA, leading to the 'Night of the Long Knives'. Thyssen accepted the exclusion of Jews from German business and professional life by the Nazis and dismissed his Jewish employees.

The breaking point for Thyssen was the violent pogrom against the Jews in November 1938, known as Kristallnacht, which caused him to resign from the Council of State.

However, according to John Loftus, a former prosecutor in the Justice Department's Nazi War Crimes Unit, for the Bush family, the Nazi connection via Thyssen was a skeleton that rattled around in the family closet for decades to come. From 1945 until 1949, one of the lengthiest and, it now appears, most futile interrogations of Nazi war crimes suspects began in the American Zone of Occupied Germany. Fritz Thyssen talked and talked and talked to a joint US-UK interrogation team. For four long years, successive groups of inquisitors tried to break Thyssen's simple claim that he possessed neither foreign bank accounts nor interests in foreign corporations, and no assets that might lead to the missing billions in assets of the Third Reich. The inquisitors failed because what Thyssen deposed was true. The Allied investigators never asked Thyssen the right question. Thyssen did not need any foreign bank accounts because his family secretly owned an entire chain of banks. He did not have to transfer his Nazi assets, all he had to do was move the ownership documents - stocks, bonds, deeds and trusts - from his bank in Berlin through his bank in Holland to his American friends in New York City: Prescott Bush and Herbert Walker. Thyssen's partners in

Prescott Bush and his son George H W Bush.

crime were the father and father-in-law of President George Herbert Walker Bush and the paternal grandfather of President George W. Bush and Governor Jeb Bush.

US Government investigators concluded that: '...*huge sections of Prescott Bush's empire had been operated on behalf of Nazi Germany and had greatly assisted the German war effort.*'

Then there is the story of William Rhodes Davis (*b.* 10 February 1889, *d.* 1 August 1941). Davis was a United States businessman whose oil interests involved him in furthering the strategic interests of Nazi Germany.

His career in the oil industry began in 1913 when he organised a small company in Muskogee, Oklahoma, and became a wildcatter. He volunteered for the US Army during World War One and was discharged as a second lieutenant in 1920. He saw action in France and later claimed to have been wounded, though the only injuries he received occurred when he jumped from a moving train. He worked as an oil broker in Tulsa, Oklahoma, and late in the 1920s was party to a complicated conflict between several independent oilmen and Standard Oil that revolved around settling thousands of colonists on land in Peru.

In 1933 he built an oil refinery called Eurotank in Hamburg, Germany, and developed business interests for a short time in Great Britain and somewhat longer in Germany. He served as the principal negotiator of the arrangement that allowed Germany and Italy to build up their oil reserves in the years before World War Two using expropriated Mexican oil until the British blockade put an end to the enterprise. 'He is said', according to the *New York Times*, to have won the arrangement thanks to an introduction to Vicente Lombardo Toledano, a 'powerful Mexican labour leader', provided by his longtime friend John L. Lewis, head of the Committee for Industrial Organization (CIO).

He was involved in many legal battles in the course of his career. In one instance, a British judge called him '*an unscrupulous and ruthless financier*' and said, '*I do not accept him as a witness of truth*'.

During the 1940 US elections, Davis used funds provided by the German government to contribute approximately $160,000 to a Pennsylvania Democratic organization to help defeat Senator Joseph Guffey, a Democrat and a prominent critic of Germany, and to bribe the Pennsylvania delegation to the 1940 Democratic National Convention to vote against Roosevelt, moves which both failed.

For all the credit Roosevelt has been given for the success (or otherwise) of the New Deal, there was opposition in America to both what he was doing with regards to his economic policies to combat unemployment and to the beliefs he was perceived to have held.

The New Deal, was to transform America's economy which had been shattered by the Great Depression. The economic downturn that followed the Wall Street Crash also had a significant psychological impact on America and that Roosevelt was doing something did a great deal to boost America's self-esteem.

In Roosevelt's first Hundred Days many acts were introduced which were to form the basis of the New Deal. The New Deal was to cover as many issues as could be imagined, be they social, economic, financial... The wave of popularity that had swept Roosevelt into power meant that parts of the New Deal were passed without too much scrutiny. In later years many acts in the New Deal were deemed unconstitutional by the Supreme Court of America.

The New Deal introduced acts that became part of the law and numerous agencies that worked with the Federal government in ensuring that the acts were enacted. On 15 March 1933, Roosevelt asked Congress to pass the Economy Act. This cut the pay of everybody who worked for the government and the armed forces by fifteen per cent Government departmental spending was also cut by twenty-five per cent. The saved money, about $1 billion, was to go towards financing his New Deal.

Roosevelt also introduced higher taxes for the rich. They felt that he had betrayed his class and he was expelled from his social club for letting down 'his people'. Roosevelt's social class was horrified by the actions of the President, who had been born in to a privileged family who lived a rich lifestyle on the east-coast of America – Roosevelt had been born at Hyde Park in New York State and spent his summer holidays at Campobello Island where the family had a summer holiday home.

It is not surprising that he made many enemies, so corporate opposition to the Roosevelt administration was nothing new. The president's efforts to pull the country out of the Great Depression was greeted by observations from

Major-General Smedley Darlington Butler (*b*. 30 July 1881 *d*. 21 July 1940). The picture on the right is of him testifying before the House of Representatives *(both NARA)*

Wall Street that he was alternatively borrowing from the latest Communist playbooks despite those same critics being less vocal when Roosevelt had dramatically intervened to save the American banking system in the first weeks in his presidency.

In late 1934, Smedley Darlington Butler was called to testify before Congress. Butler was a United States Marine Corps Major General, the highest rank authorized at that time, and at the time of his death the most decorated Marine in US history.

A special committee of the House of Representatives headed by Representatives John W. McCormack of Massachusetts and Samuel

Dickstein of New York, who was later alleged to have been a paid agent of the NKVD, heard his testimony in secret. The McCormack–Dickstein committee was a precursor to the House Committee on Un-American Activities.

In November 1934, Butler told the committee that one Gerald P. MacGuire told him that a group of businessmen, supposedly backed by a private army of half a million ex-soldiers and others, intended to overthrow Roosevelt and establish a fascist dictatorship. Butler had been asked to lead it, he said, by MacGuire, who was a bond salesman with Grayson M-P Murphy & Co. The *New York Times* reported that Butler had told friends that General Hugh S Johnson, former

The second page of the distribution list of Navy Basic Plan - Red, showing the three Marine Corps copies that went out, the first of which must have gone to General Butler. *(NARA)*

NAVY BASIC PLAN - RED

CONFIDENTI

SECRET

DISTRIBUTION LIST (CONTINUED) (W.P.L. 22)

OFFICIAL TO WHOM ISSUED

REGISTERED NUMBERS

Major General Commandant, U. S. Marine Corps	40
Commanding General, Headquarters, Department of the Pacific, U.S.M.C., San Francisco, Calif.	41
Commanding General, Marine Barracks, Quantico, Virginia	42
Judge Advocate General, U. S. Navy	43
The Assistant Secretary of the Navy (Navy Yard Division)	44
President, General Board	45
War Plans Division, General Staff, War Department	46
President, Naval War College (Issue withheld)	47
Senior Naval Officer, Staff, Army War College (Issue withheld)	48
Commandant, First Naval District	49,50
Commandant, Third Naval District	51

head of the National Recovery Administration, was to be installed as dictator, and that the J P Morgan banking firm was behind the plot. Butler told Congress that MacGuire had told him the attempted coup was backed by three million dollars, and that the 500,000 men were probably to be assembled in Washington, DC the following year.

Butler claimed to be appalled by the scheme, and and decided to play the plotters for time while he contacted FBI Director, J Edgar Hoover. The news media dismissed the plot, with a *New York Times* editorial characterizing it as a 'gigantic hoax'. When the committee's final report was released, the *Times* said the committee *'purported to report that a two-month investigation had convinced it that General Butler's story of a Fascist march on Washington was alarmingly true'* and *'... also alleged that definite proof had been found that the much publicized Fascist march on Washington, which was to have been led by Major Gen. Smedley D. Butler, retired, according to testimony at a hearing, was actually contemplated'*. The individuals involved all denied the existence of a plot, despite evidence to the contrary. Though the media ridiculed the allegations, a final report by a special House of Representatives Committee confirmed some of Butler's statements.

In the end there were no prosecutions and Roosevelt himself appear to wanted the matter to simply go away. Given what has since surfaced about War Plan Red, one has to wonder if this was just another evolving avenue of the same plan. This is especially intriguing, for copy No.40 of Plan Red was allocated the 'Major General, Commandant US Marine Corps'. Butler was not named in the distribution list - however, as he took over this post upon the death of Maj. Gen. Wendell C Neville on 8 July 1930, He was to remain in post until requesting retirement and left active duty on 1 October 1931, so Butler must have known about it.

American Nazis.
Friends of New Germany was an organisation founded in the USA by German immigrants to support the concept of National Socialism - in German, *Nationalsozialismus*, more commonly known as Nazism. This is the ideology and practices associated with the Nazi Party - officially the National Socialist German Workers' Party (*Nationalsozialistische Deutsche Arbeiterpartei* or NSDAP) – and of other far-

Nearly 1,000 uniformed men wearing swastika arm bands and carrying Nazi banners, parade past a reviewing stand in New Jersey on 18 July 1937. The New Jersey division of the German-American Bund opened its 100-acre Camp Nordland at Sussex Hills. Dr. Salvatore Caridi of Union City, spokesman for a group of Italian-American fascists attending as guests, addressed the bund members as 'Nazi Friends'. *(NARA)*

German American Bund parade in New York City on East 86th St. on 30 October 1939. *(NARA)*

right groups with similar aims that came to prominence during the 1920s.

Nazism is a form of fascism and showed that ideology's disdain for liberal democracy and the parliamentary system, but also incorporated fervent anti-semitism, scientific racism, and eugenics into its creed. Its extreme nationalism came from Pan-Germanism and the Völkisch movement prominent in the Germanic nationalism of the time, and it was strongly influenced by the anti-Communist *Freikorps* paramilitary groups that emerged after Germany's defeat in World War One.

Followers subscribed to theories of racial hierarchy and Social Darwinism, identifying the Germans as a part of what the Nazis regarded as an Aryan or Nordic master race. It aimed to overcome social divisions and create a homogeneous German society based on racial purity which represented a people's community, termed Volksgemeinschaft. The Nazis sought to unite all Germans living in historically German territory, as well as gain additional lands for German expansion under the doctrine of Lebensraum and to exclude those who they deemed either community aliens or inferior races.

The term National Socialism arose out of attempts to create a nationalist redefinition of socialism, as an alternative to both international socialism and free market capitalism. Nazism rejected the Marxist concept of class conflict, opposed cosmopolitan internationalism, and sought to convince all parts of the new German society to subordinate their interests to that of the common good, accepting political interests as the main priority of the economic organisation.

The Nazi Party's precursor, the Pan-German nationalist and anti-semitic German Workers' Party, was founded on 5 January 1919. By the early 1920s, the party was renamed the National Socialist German Workers' Party – to attract workers away from left-wing parties such as the Social Democrats (SPD) and the Communists (KPD) – and a former Geman Army Corporal called Adolf Hitler assumed control of the organisation. The National Socialist Program or '25 Points' was adopted in 1920 and called for a united Greater Germany that would deny citizenship to Jews or those of Jewish descent, while also supporting land reform and the nationalisation of some industries. *Mein Kampf* (*'My Struggle'*), an autobiographical book by Nazi Party leader Adolf Hitler, describes the process by which Hitler became anti-semitic and outlines his political ideology and plans for Germany. Volume 1 of *Mein Kampf* was published in 1925 and Volume 2 in 1926. Hitler's deputy Rudolf Hess edited the book.

Hitler began *Mein Kampf* while imprisoned in Landsberg gaol for what he considered to be 'political crimes' following his failed Putsch in Munich in November 1923. Although Hitler received many visitors initially, he soon devoted himself entirely to the book. The governor of Landsberg noted at the time that *'he* [Hitler] *hopes the book will run into many editions, thus enabling him to fulfil his financial obligations and to defray the expenses incurred at the time of his trial'*.

Hitler outlined the anti-Semitism and anti-Communism at the heart of his political philosophy, as well as his disdain for representative democracy and his belief in Germany's right to territorial expansion. Despite slow initial sales, the book was a bestseller in Germany after Hitler's rise to power in 1933.

The rise of National Socialism in the USA.
Nazis outside of Germany made considerable efforts to establish an American counterpart organisation. Recruiting began as early as 1924 with the formation of the Free Society of Teutonia, which was formed in 1924 by four German immigrants, including Nazi Party members Fritz and Peter Gissibl and their brother Andrew. The organisation was initially led by German immigrant and non-citizen Fritz Gissibl, who made his headquarters in Chicago, from where it set about recruiting ethnic Germans who supported German nationalist aims. The Teutonia Society initially functioned as a club, but soon raised a group of militants based on the Sturmabteilung or SA, literally meaning Storm Detachment, which was the Nazi Party's original paramilitary arm.

With membership increasing, the society became vocal critics of Jews, communism and the Treaty of Versailles. Alongside this, however, it retained a social function, with meetings frequently ending up in heavy beer drinking sessions.

The group changed its name to the Nationalistic Society of Teutonia in 1926, at which point Peter Gissibil was advising members also to seek Nazi Party membership. The group gained a strong, if relatively small following, and was able to establish units in Milwaukee, St. Louis, Missouri, Detroit, New York City, Cincinnati and Newark, New Jersey. The group's treasurer was Fritz Gissibil, who was also the chief Nazi Party representative in the United States and who regularly collected money for the

Members of the German-American Bund form a guard of honour before the speaker's stand as Fritz Kuhn, leader of the Bund, addresses a crowd at Hindenberg Park, La Crescenta, near Los Angeles, California, on 30 April 1939. *(NARA)*

Thousands of people attended the American Bund Rally near Yaphank, New York, in the summer of 1937. *(NARA)*

Nazis through the Society.

The group accepted Hitler as its titular leader, and members adopted the Nazi salute. The Society changed its name again in October 1932 to become the Friends of the Hitler Movement.

Under orders of German immigrant and German Nazi Party member Heinz Spanknöbel, the Society was dissolved in March 1933. Two months later, Nazi Deputy Führer Rudolf Hess gave Heinz Spanknöbel authority to form an American Nazi organisation. Shortly after that, with help from the German consul in New York City, Spanknöbel created the Friends of New Germany by merging two older organisations in the United States, Gau-USA and the Free Society of Teutonia. The Friends of New Germany, in turn, formed the basis of the German American Bund in 1936, the latter name being chosen to emphasise the group's American credentials after press criticism that the Society was unpatriotic.

One of the leaders of the Teutonia Society was Walter Kappe, who arrived in the United States in 1925 and worked in a farm implement factory in Kankakee, Illinois. Later he moved to Chicago and began to write for German language newspapers. Kappe was fluent in English and later became the press secretary for the German American Bund. He founded their paper *Deutscher Weckruf und Beobachter* and its predecessor *Deutsche Zeitung*. In 1936, when the German American Bund was established, Kappe organised the AV Publishing Company and five other Bund corporations. Fritz Kuhn ousted Kappe from his position in the Bund, seeing him as a dangerous rival. In 1937, Kappe returned to Germany, where he was attached to Abwehr II (the sabotage branch of German intelligence) when he obtained a Naval commission with the rank of lieutenant. He was designated by Adolf Hitler to launch a sabotage operation against America shortly after the attack on Pearl Harbor.

The Friends of New Germany was openly pro-Nazi and engaged in activities such as storming the German language newspaper *New Yorker Staats-Zeitung* with the demand that Nazi-sympathetic articles be published. Members wore a uniform, a white shirt and black trousers for men with a black hat festooned with a red symbol. Women members wore a white blouse and a black skirt.

In an internal battle for control of the Friends, Spanknöbel was soon ousted as leader, and in October 1933 he was deported because he had failed to register as a foreign agent.

At the same time, Congressman Samuel Dickstein (D-NY) was Chairman of the Committee on Naturalization and Immigration, when he became aware of the substantial number

132

of foreigners legally and illegally entering and residing in the country, and the growing anti-Semitism along with vast amounts of anti-Semitic literature being distributed. This led him to investigate the activities of Nazi and other fascist groups independently and led to the formation of the Special Committee on Un-American Activities authorized to investigate Nazi propaganda and certain other propaganda activities. Throughout the rest of 1934, the Committee conducted hearings, bringing before it most of the significant figures in the US fascist movement. Dickstein's investigation concluded that the Friends represented a branch of German dictator Adolf Hitler's Nazi Party in America.

The organisation existed into the mid-1930s with a membership of between 5,000 to 10,000, consisting mostly of German citizens living in America and German emigrants who only recently had become citizens. In December 1935, Rudolf Hess recalled the group's leaders to Germany and ordered all German citizens to leave the Friends of New Germany. By March 1936, Friends of New Germany was dissolved and its membership transferred to a newly formed German American Bund, the new name was chosen to emphasise the group's American credentials after press criticism that the organisation was unpatriotic. The Bund was to consist only of American citizens of German descent.

In March 1936, the German American Bund was established as a follow-up organisation for the Friends of New Germany in Buffalo, New York. The Bund elected a German-born American citizen, Fritz Julius Kuhn, as its leader (Bundesführer). Kuhn was a veteran of the Bavarian infantry during World War One and an Alter Kämpfer (old fighter) of the Nazi Party who, in 1934, was granted American citizenship. He was initially effective as a leader and was able to unite the organisation and expand its membership but came to be seen simply as an incompetent swindler and liar.

The administrative structure of the Bund mimicked the regional administrative subdivision of the Nazi Party. The German American Bund divided the United States into three Gaue: Gau Ost (East), Gau West and Gau Midwest. Together the three Gaue comprised 69

Pro-Nazi members of various singing and gymnastic societies salute a procession of flags at White Plains Hall in New York in the 1930s. They were gathered for a German Day celebration. *(NARA)*

A crowd of approximately 20,000 attended a German American Bund Rally at New York's Madison Square Garden on 20 February 1939. At centre is a large portrait of George Washington, claimed as an icon by the Bund, who called him 'the first Fascist', claiming Washington 'knew democracy could not work.' *(NARA)*

Ortsgruppen (local groups): 40 in Gau Ost (17 in New York), 10 in Gau West and 19 in Gau Midwest. Each Gau had its own Gauleiter and staff to direct the Bund operations in the region in accordance with the Führerprinzip. The Bund's national headquarters was located at 178 East 85th Street in the New York City borough of Manhattan.

The Bund established a number of training camps, including Camp Nordland in Sussex County New Jersey, Camp Siegfried in Yaphank, New York, Camp Hindenburg in Grafton, Wisconsin, Deutschhorst Country Club in Sellersville Pennsylvania, Camp Bergwald in Bloomingdale New Jersey, and Camp Highland in New York State. The Bund held rallies with Nazi insignia and procedures such as the Hitler salute and attacked the administration of President Franklin D. Roosevelt, Jewish-American groups, Communism, so-called Moscow-directed' trade unions and American boycotts of German goods. The organisation claimed to show its loyalty to America by displaying the flag of the United States alongside the flag of Nazi Germany at Bund meetings, and declared that George Washington was 'the first Fascist' who did not believe democracy would work.

Kuhn and a few other Bundsmen travelled to Berlin to attend the 1936 summer Olympics. During the trip, he visited the Reich Chancellery, where his picture was taken with Hitler. This act did not constitute an official Nazi approval for Kuhn's organisation: German ambassador to the United States Hans-Heinrich Dieckhoff expressed his disapproval and concern over the group visit to Berlin, causing distrust between the Bund and the Nazi regime. The organisation received no financial or verbal support from Germany. In response to the outrage of Jewish war veterans, congress in 1938 passed the Foreign Agents Registration Act requiring foreign agents to register with the State Department. On 1 March 1938, the Nazi government decreed that no *Reichsdeutsche*

[German nationals] could be a member of the Bund, and that no Nazi emblems were to be used by the organisation. This was done both to appease the US and to distance Germany from the Bund, which was increasingly a cause of embarrassment with its rhetoric and actions.

Arguably, the zenith of the Bund's activities was the rally at Madison Square Garden in New York City on 20 February 1939. Some 20,000 people attended and heard Kuhn supposedly criticise President Roosevelt by repeatedly referring to him as 'Frank D. Rosenfeld', calling his New Deal the 'Jew Deal' and denouncing what he believed to be Bolshevik-Jewish American leadership. Most shocking to American sensibilities was the outbreak of violence between protesters and Bund stormtroopers.

In 1939, a New York tax investigation determined that Kuhn had embezzled $14,000 from the Bund. The Bund did not seek to have Kuhn prosecuted, operating on the principle (Führerprinzip) that the leader had absolute power. However, New York City's district attorney indicted him in an attempt to cripple the Bund. On 5 December 1939, Kuhn was sentenced to two and a half to five years in prison for tax evasion and embezzlement.

A number of new Bund leaders replaced Kuhn, most notably Gerhard Kunze, but only for brief periods. A year after the outbreak of World War Two, Congress enacted a peacetime military draft in September 1940. The Bund counselled members of draft age to evade conscription, a criminal offence punishable by up to five years in jail and a $10,000 fine. Gerhard Kunze fled to Mexico in November 1941.

The Silver Shirts

The Silver Legion of America, commonly known as the Silver Shirts, was an underground American fascist, para-military league founded by William Dudley Pelley that was headquartered in Asheville, North Carolina and announced publicly on 30 January 1933.

William Dudley Pelley was an American writer, spiritualist and fascist political activist. He came to prominence as a writer, winning two O. Henry Awards and penning screenplays for Hollywood films. His 1929 essay *Seven Minutes in Eternity* marked a turning point in Pelley's career, earning a significant response in the *American Magazine* where it was published as a popular example of what would later be called a near-death experience. His experiences with mysticism and occultism drifted towards the political. He ran for president of the US in 1936 as the candidate for the Christian Party.

A white-supremacist, anti-semitic group, modelled after Hitler's Brownshirts, the paramilitary Silver Legion wore a silver shirt with a blue tie, along with a campaign hat and blue corduroy trousers with leggings. The uniform shirts bore a scarlet letter L over the heart: an emblem meant to symbolise Loyalty to the United States, Liberation from materialism, and the Silver Legion itself.

By 1934, the Silver Shirts claimed to have about 15,000 members. In 1935, a Nazi agent working with the Silver Shirts befriended mining fortune heiress Jessie Murphy, convincing her to contribute cash, and the use of her ranch, recently purchased from screen cowboy Will Rogers, to the fascist movement. The Silver Shirts began construction of the Murphy Ranch, situated on a secluded, 55-acre site in the Los Angeles hills, meant to serve as a fortified world headquarters after the expected fascist global conquest.

Pelley travelled nationwide, holding rallies, lectures, and public speeches. He founded Silver Legion chapters in almost every state in the country. Membership peaked at 15,000 in 1935, dropping to below 5,000 by 1938. His political ideology consisted of anti-Communism, anti-semitism, racism, patriotism, isolationism and British Israelism, themes which were the primary focus of his numerous magazines and newspapers, which included *Liberation*, *Pelley's Silvershirt Weekly*, *The Galilean* and *The New Liberator*.

Pelley and the Silver Shirts were adept at making alliances with similarly minded groups at the local level even if

Silver Shirts leader William Dudley Pelley
(*b*. 12 March 1890, *d*. 30 June 1965)

their leaders vehemently clashed over money and personal differences. Perry was an angry and controlling influence - and, in the minds of many a complete madman but his local organisers proved far more capable and managed to strike meaningful alliances with several local German American Bund and Ku Klux Klan chapters

Pelley called for a 'Christian Commonwealth' that would combine the principles of racism, nationalism, and theocracy while excluding Jews and non-whites. He claimed he would save America from Jewish communists just as *'Mussolini and his Black Shirts saved Italy and as Hitler and his Brown Shirts saved Germany'*. Pelley ran for president of the USA in the 1936 election on a third-party ticket. Pelley hoped to seize power in a what he called 'a silver revolution' and set himself as dictator of the United States. He would be called 'the chief' just like other fascist world leaders who had similar titles. However, the presidency remained in the hands of Franklin D Roosevelt.

After the Japanese attack on Pearl Harbor on 7 December 1941, local police occupied the 'world headquarters' bunker compound and detained members of the 50-man caretaker force. The declaration of war on the United States by Nazi Germany and Italy led to the rapid decline of the Silver Legion.

America First!

The America First Committee (AFC) was the foremost US non-interventionist pressure group against the American entry into World War Two. Started on 4 September 1940, it experienced mixed messaging with anti-semitic rhetoric from leading members, and it was dissolved on 10 December 1941, three days after the attack on Pearl Harbor had brought the war to America. Membership peaked at 800,000 paying members in 450 chapters. It was one of the largest anti-war organisations in American history.

When the war began in September 1939, most Americans, including politicians, demanded neutrality regarding Europe. Although most Americans supported strong measures against Japan, Europe was the focus of the America First Committee. The public mood was changing, however, especially after the fall of France in the spring of 1940.

The America First Committee launched a petition aimed at enforcing the 1939 Neutrality Act and forcing President Franklin D. Roosevelt to keep his pledge to keep America out of the war. They profoundly distrusted Roosevelt and argued that he was lying to the American people.

On the day after Roosevelt's lend-lease bill was submitted to the United States Congress, Wood promised AFC opposition *'with all the vigour it can exert'*. America First staunchly opposed the convoying of ships, the Atlantic Charter, and the placing of economic pressure on Japan. In order to achieve the defeat of lend-lease and the perpetuation of American neutrality, the AFC advocated four basic principles:

* The United States must build an impregnable defence for America.
* No foreign power, nor group of powers, can successfully attack a prepared America.
* American democracy can be preserved only by keeping out of the European war.
* 'Aid short of war' weakens national defence at home and threatens to involve America in war abroad.

'America First' made much of its celebrity endorsements. Charles Augustus Lindbergh was an American aviator, military officer, author, inventor, explorer, and environmental activist. At age 25 in 1927, he went from obscurity as a US Air Mail pilot to instantaneous world fame by winning the Orteig Prize: making a nonstop flight from Roosevelt Field, Long Island, New York, to

Charles Augustus Lindbergh
(*b*. 4 February 1902, *d*. 26 August 1974)

Paris, France. Lindbergh covered the 33 1/2-hour, 3,600-statute-mile flight alone in a single-engine purpose-built Ryan monoplane, the *Spirit of St. Louis*. This was not the first flight between the two continents, but he did achieve the first solo transatlantic flight and the first non-stop flight between North America and the European mainland. Lindbergh was an officer in the US Army Air Corps Reserve, and he received the United States' highest military decoration, the Medal of Honor, for the feat.

Lindbergh's achievements made him a national and international celebrity. Barely two months after Lindbergh arrived in Paris, G P Putnam's Sons published his 318-page autobiography *WE*, which was the first of fifteen books he eventually wrote or to which he made significant contributions.

At the request of the United States military, Lindbergh travelled to Germany several times between 1936 and 1938 to evaluate German aviation. Hanna Reitsch, the famous female test pilot, demonstrated the Focke-Wulf Fw.61 helicopter to Lindbergh in 1937, and he was the first American to examine Germany's newest

bomber, the Junkers Ju.88, and Germany's front-line fighter aircraft, the Messerschmitt Bf.109, which he was allowed to pilot. He said of the Bf 109 that he knew of *'no other pursuit plane which combines simplicity of construction with such excellent performance characteristics'*. There is disagreement on how accurate Lindbergh's reports were, but Cole asserts that the consensus among British and American officials was that they were slightly exaggerated but badly needed. Lindbergh also undertook a survey of aviation in the Soviet Union in 1938.

In 1938, Hugh Wilson, the American ambassador to Germany, hosted a dinner for Lindbergh with Germany's air chief, Hermann Göring and three central figures in German aviation, Ernst Heinkel, Adolf Baeumker, and Willy Messerschmitt. At this dinner, Göring presented Lindbergh with the Commander Cross of the Order of the German Eagle. Lindbergh's acceptance proved controversial after Kristallnacht, an anti-Jewish pogrom in Germany a few weeks later. Lindbergh declined to return the medal, then writing: *'It seems to me that the returning of decorations, which were given in*

American aviator Charles Lindbergh receives a sword of honor of the German Air Force presented by Hermann Goering in Karinhall during his visit to Germany in 1936. On the far left is Lindbergh's wife Anne Morrow Lindbergh. *(NARA)*

Crowds gather around Charles Lindbergh at an America First rally. It is interesting to note that this organisation also used the image of George Washington, just as the American Bund did. *(NARA)*

times of peace and as a gesture of friendship, can have no constructive effect. If I were to return the German medal, it seems to me that it would be an unnecessary insult. Even if war develops between us, I can see no gain in indulging in a spitting contest before that war begins'.

At the urging of US Ambassador Joseph P Kennedy, who will be investigated in the next chapter, Lindbergh wrote a secret memo to the British warning that a military response by Britain and France to Hitler's violation of the Munich Agreement would be disastrous; he claimed that France was militarily weak and Britain over-reliant on its navy. He urgently recommended that they strengthen their air power to force Hitler to redirect his aggression against 'Asiatic Communism'. In a controversial 1939 *Reader's Digest* article he wrote, *'Our civilisation depends on peace among Western nations ... and therefore on united strength, for Peace is a virgin who dare not show her face without Strength, her father, for protection'*. Lindbergh deplored the rivalry between Germany and Britain but favoured a war between Germany and Russia.

His first radio speech was broadcast on 15 September 1939, on all three of the major radio networks. He urged listeners to look beyond the speeches and propaganda that they were being fed and instead look at who was writing the speeches and reports, who owned the papers and who influenced the speakers.

Following Hitler's invasion of Czechoslovakia and Poland, Lindbergh decried suggestions that the United States should send aid to countries under threat, writing *'I do not believe that repealing the arms embargo would assist democracy in Europe'* and *'If we repeal the arms embargo with the idea of assisting one of the warring sides in overcoming the other, then why mislead ourselves by talk of neutrality?'* He equated assistance with war profiteering: *'To those who argue that we could make a profit and build up our industry by selling munitions abroad, I reply that we in America have not yet reached a point where we wish to capitalise on the destruction and death of war'*.

In late 1940 Lindbergh became the spokesman of the non-interventionist America First Committee, soon speaking to overflowing crowds at Madison Square Garden and Chicago's Soldier Field, with millions listening by radio. He argued that America had no business attacking Germany; in writings published posthumously he justified this stance: In his 1941 testimony before the House Committee on Foreign Affairs opposing the Lend-Lease bill, Lindbergh proposed that the United States negotiate a neutrality pact with Germany. President Roosevelt publicly decried Lindbergh's views as those of a 'defeatist and appeaser', comparing him to US Representative Clement L Vallandigham, who had led the 'Copperhead' movement that had opposed the American Civil War. Lindbergh promptly resigned his commission as a colonel in the US Army Air Corps, writing that he saw 'no honourable alternative' given that Roosevelt had publicly questioned his loyalty.

At an America First rally in September, Lindbergh accused three groups of *'pressing this country toward war: the British, the Jewish, and the Roosevelt Administration'*. He was deeply concerned that the potentially gigantic power of America, guided by uninformed and impractical idealism, might crusade into Europe to destroy Hitler without realising that Hitler's destruction would lay Europe open to the rape, loot and barbarism of Soviet Russia's forces, causing possibly the fatal wounding of western civilisation.

'Instead of agitating for war, the Jewish groups in this country should be opposing it in every possible way for they will be among the first to feel its consequences. Tolerance is a virtue that depends upon peace and strength. History shows that it cannot survive war and devastation' he said.

He went on to warn of *'large* [Jewish] *ownership and influence in our motion pictures, our press, our radio, and our government'*, though he condemned Germany's anti-semitism: *'No person with a sense of the dignity of mankind can condone the persecution of the Jewish race*

in Germany.' He continued, *'... I am not attacking either the Jewish or the British people. Both races, I admire. But I am saying that the leaders of both the British and the Jewish races, for reasons which are as understandable from their viewpoint as they are inadvisable from ours, for reasons which are not American, wish to involve us in the war. We cannot blame them for looking out for what they believe to be their interests, but we also must look out for ours. We cannot allow the natural passions and prejudices of other peoples to lead our country to destruction'*.

Responding to criticism of his speech, Lindbergh denied he was anti-Semitic but did not back away from his positions. Anne Lindbergh felt that the speech might tarnish Lindbergh's reputation unjustly; she wrote in her diary: *'I have the greatest faith in him as a person - in his integrity, his courage, and his essential goodness, fairness, and kindness - his nobility... How then can I explain my profound feeling of grief about what he is doing? If what he said is the truth (and I am inclined to think it is), why was it wrong to state it? He was naming the groups that were pro-war. No one minds his naming the British or the Administration. But to name 'Jew' is un-American - even if it is done without hate or even criticism. Why?'*

Interventionists created pamphlets pointing out his efforts were praised in Nazi Germany and included quotations such as *'Racial strength is*

For someone who claimed to be a shy and retiring person, Charles Lindbergh was not exactly backward in coming forward to preach to the assembled masses at America First rallies. *(NARA)*

vital; politics, a luxury'. They included pictures of him and other America Firsters using the stiff-armed Bellamy salute (a hand gesture described by Francis Bellamy to accompany his Pledge of Allegiance to the American flag); the photos were taken from an angle not showing the flag, so to observers, it was indistinguishable from the Hitler salute.

Roosevelt disliked Lindbergh's outspoken opposition to his administration's interventionist policies, telling Treasury Secretary Henry Morgenthau, *'If I should die tomorrow, I want you to know this, I am convinced Lindbergh is a Nazi.'* In 1941 he wrote to Secretary of War Henry Stimson: *'When I read Lindbergh's speech I felt that it could not have been better put if it had been written by Goebbels himself. What a pity that this youngster has completely abandoned his belief in our form of government and has accepted Nazi methods because apparently, they are efficient.'*

On 20 June 1941, Lindbergh spoke to 30,000 people in Los Angeles and billed it as a *'Peace and Preparedness Mass Meeting'*. He criticised those movements which he perceived were leading America into the war, and proclaimed that the USA was in a position that made it virtually impregnable. He claimed that the interventionists and the British who called for *'...the defence of England really means the defeat of Germany'*.

Nothing did more to escalate the tensions than the speech that Lindbergh delivered to a rally in Des Moines, Iowa on 11 September 1941. In that speech, he identified the forces pulling America into the war as the British, the American Jews and the Roosevelt administration, and American Jews. While he expressed sympathy for the plight of the Jews in Germany, he argued that America's entry into the war would serve them little better. He said in part: *'It is not difficult to understand why Jewish people desire the overthrow of Nazi Germany. The persecution they suffered in Germany* would be sufficient to make bitter enemies of any race. No person with a sense of the dignity of mankind can condone the persecution the Jewish race suffered in Germany. But no person of honesty and vision can look on their pro-war policy here today without seeing the dangers involved in such a policy, both for them and for us.

Instead of agitating for war the Jewish groups in this country should be opposing it in every possible way, for they will be among the first to feel its consequences. Tolerance is a virtue that depends upon peace and strength. History shows that it cannot survive war and devastation. A few far-sighted Jewish people realise this and stand opposed to intervention. But the majority still do not. Their greatest danger to this country lies in their large ownership and influence in our motion pictures, our press, our radio, and our government'.

So, as has been seen, far from the United States of America having just a few on the extreme right and having a few firebrands who supported the German *Nationalsozialistische Deutsche Arbeiterpartei* there were clearly many thousands who actively supported the concept and many hundreds of thousands more - possibly millions - who at least gave the spokespersons a sympathetic ear. They also seemed to be *de facto* anti-British.

Charles G Grey, founder editor of *The Aeroplane*. (*b*. 13 November 1875, *d*. 9 December 1953). Grey was a prolific purveyor of propaganda for Hitler and Mussolini.

It was a time well before the internet, tweets and social media. The only way the American public - and if the truth be known, ninety-nine per cent of the politico - military establishment - could get information was through the narrow lens of the written word in the press.

Words that came from the specialist press, like *The Aeroplane*. Charles Grey Grey, or C G as he was known, was the founding editor of that aviation weekly and the second editor of *Jane's All the World's Aircraft*. Among many honours, he was an honorary Companion of the Royal

Aeronautical Society.

Grey's first job was as a staff writer for *The Autocar.* His secondary role as the magazine's aviation specialist resulted in a commission from Iliffe and Sons, Ltd. to edit a penny weekly aviation paper called *The Aero.* In 1911, in partnership with Sir Victor Sassoon, Grey founded *The Aeroplane,* remaining as editor of the influential weekly until November 1939. He was a man of decided opinions, as evidenced in his editorials for the magazine over three decades. Unfortunately for him, these included strong support for the fascist dictators of Italy and Germany, which played no small part in his leaving the magazine.

Great Britain had other fascists, notably Oswald Mosley. Sir Oswald Ernald Mosley of Ancoats, 6th Baronet was a British politician who rose to fame in the 1920s as a Member of Parliament and later in the 1930s became the leader of the British Union of Fascists (BUF). Mosley was never knighted, inheriting the title 'Sir' as the sixth Baronet of a title that was in his family for centuries.

The BUF claimed 50,000 members at one point, and the *Daily Mail,* running the headline

The charismatic, if odiously arrogant Oswald Mosley (*b.*16 November 1896, *d.* 3 December 1980). He ran the British Union of Fascists.

'Hurrah for the Blackshirts!', was an early supporter. The first Director of Propaganda, Wilfred Risdon, was appointed in February 1933, and was responsible for organising all of Mosley's public meetings. Despite strong resistance from the anti-fascists, including the local Jewish community, the Labour Party, the Independent Labour Party, and the Communist Party of Great Britain, the BUF found a following in the East End of London, where in the London County Council elections of March 1937, it obtained reasonably successful results in Bethnal Green Shoreditch, although none of its candidates was elected.

Possibly the greatest fascist sympathiser was Edward VIII (Edward Albert Christian George Andrew Patrick David; 23 June 1894 – 28 May 1972) King of the United Kingdom and the Dominions of the British Empire, and Emperor of India, from 20 January 1936 until his abdication on 11 December the same year, after which he became the Duke of Windsor and married American divorcee Wallis Simpson. In October 1937, the Duke and Duchess visited Nazi Germany, against the advice of the British

The Duke of Windsor inspects stormtroopers during his visit to Germany in October 1937.

The Duke and Dutchess of Windsor, the former Mrs Wallace Simpson were personally welcomed to the Berghof in Bavaria by Adolf Hitler himself. *(Simon Peters Collection)*

government, and met Adolf Hitler at his Berghof retreat in Bavaria. The visit was much publicised by the German media. During the visit the Duke gave full Nazi salutes. In Germany, '*...they were treated like royalty ... members of the aristocracy would bow and curtsy towards her, and she was treated with all the dignity and status that the Duke always wanted*'.

Much of this was faithfully reported by the American newspapers.

War Plan Red had been shelved, but not scrapped, for as each day passed it was becoming clearer that the British Empire was poorly equipped for the conflict that was seemingly bound to happen. Public opinion was against America being dragged into the war, as demonstrated by numerous Gallup Polls. Accounts suggest that within 'the establishment' of the USA there was the growing thought that there was no need to go to war with the British Empire - the potential for war with Germany may have been increasing, but Hitler had never expressed any interest in the geopolitical importance of the USA and was

downright dismissive of the country on racial grounds. He predicted that the country's downfall would be brought about by its racial diversity, not its purity. It seems that many in the military began to think that it might well be a good strategy to let the two protagonists slug it out, and then move in to pick up the pieces!

After Roosevelt's election in 1933, he offered the ambassadorship to Ireland to Bostonian Joseph Patrick Kennedy, who turned it down. The next July, FDR appointed Kennedy to head the newly created Securities and Exchange Commission, a body that would oversee Wall Street and stop illegal trading among its members- this was akin to the poacher turning gamekeeper!

In 1938, President Roosevelt appointed Joseph Kennedy as the US ambassador to Great Britain, an extraordinary post that put him in the spotlight of international affairs. For Joe, the appointment was the fulfillment of a lifetime of work in the political realm, a chance to put to rest all the slights he felt as a Catholic outsider in Boston society.

Chapter Six

The Ambassador, His Son, and a Spy.

Where 'Jittery Joe' runs scared, is advised by his son and a spy runs amok in Grosvenor Square

In early December 1937, President Franklin Delano Roosevelt, the 32nd President of the United States, announced a new ambassador to the Court of St. James in London, the United States' representative to Great Britain replacing Robert Worth Bingham (b. 8 November 1871 – d. 18 December 1937) a politician, judge, newspaper publisher who was ambassador from 1933 to 1937. Roosevelt had chosen Bostonian Joseph Patrick 'Joe' Kennedy. It was to be a stormy appointment.

The American military was well aware of the need to gain intelligence - on both 'friend' and 'foe' alike from wherever and by whatever means possible. The obvious method was to attempt to gain permission to base 'observers' in the relevant Embassies. In the case of Great Britain, it was done under the auspices of the War Department with the knowledge and acquiescence of Ambassador Joe Kennedy and with the full permission and knowledge of British Foreign Secretary Edward Frederick Lindley Wood, 1st Earl of Halifax and Prime Minister Neville Chamberlain. This aspect is covered in detail in a later chapter.

Joe Kennedy was what could be called a 'character' - a serial philanderer, an opportunist who was rabidly anti-British, a manipulator for whom no level to sink was too low, and inside-trader and a possible bootlegger who was involved with the Cosa Nostra. The list of the man's charms and abilities

Joseph Patrick Kennedy (b. September 1888, d. 18 November 1969) seen at age 25 in 1914, when he claimed to be America's youngest bank president.

were almost endless, and they deserve investigation for they play a large part in this story over many years.

Born in Boston, Massachusetts, on 6 September 1888, Joseph Patrick Kennedy was the son of Mary Hickey and Patrick Joseph Kennedy, an important figure in the Irish community of Boston. Known as 'PJ', Patrick J Kennedy had risen from common labourer to highly successful businessman, and was eventually instrumental in the organisation of two different Boston financial institutions, the Columbia Trust Company and the Sumner Savings Bank. Early on, Patrick J Kennedy had also entered politics, and Joseph, his first child, was born during PJ's third term in the Massachusetts House of Representatives. Patrick J. Kennedy also served in the Massachusetts Senate, but his enduring political power was in the unofficial capacity of a 'ward boss' who held sway in the East Boston Ward 2 for more than thirty years.

Young Joseph grew up in East Boston and attended Catholic schools until the eighth grade when his family enrolled him in Boston Latin School, a college preparatory academy. Despite an aptitude for mathematics, Joseph P Kennedy's academic record at Boston Latin was mediocre at best. Nonetheless, he found favour with teachers and was popular with fellow students, who elected him class president during his senior year. Upon graduating from Boston

Latin in 1908, he entered Harvard University, where he earned his BA in 1912. That fall, Kennedy procured the position of Assistant State Bank Examiner for Massachusetts, the first step in a career in finance that would bring him great wealth.

In his last years at Harvard and as he embarked upon his career, Joseph P Kennedy began to court Rose Fitzgerald, daughter of Boston Mayor John F 'Honey Fitz' Fitzgerald. The two had grown up in the same circles and had even spent a summer vacation together when they were children.

Joseph Kennedy after his marriage to Rose Fitzgerald on 7 October 1914.

In their adolescent years, Joseph Kennedy started accompanying Rose to dances and parties; he would later say that he was *'never seriously interested in anyone else'*. With Rose Fitzgerald's debut in society and Kennedy's graduation the courtship became firmly established. The couple were married on 7 October 1914, and after a two-week honeymoon, they settled in the Boston suburb of Brookline. Their first son, Joseph P Kennedy Jr., was born on 28 July 1915, while Rose Kennedy was staying at a summer cottage in Hull, Massachusetts.

Meanwhile, Joseph Kennedy had taken a significant business step. Columbia Trust, the bank his father had helped start, was ailing and its stockholders were on the verge of selling out. Sensing an opportunity, the younger Kennedy borrowed $45,000 - well over $1 million today - from family and friends and bought back control, becoming, according to the press, the youngest bank president in the country, at twenty-five. As head of Columbia Trust, Kennedy worked hard to cultivate connections both high and low, maintaining good relations with his working-class client base but always seeking new links to Boston's business elite. His election confirmed his entry into that circle to the Board of Trustees of the Massachusetts Electric Company, New England's leading public utility at the time. He was named to the Board on 29 May 1917, the

same day his second child, John Fitzgerald, was born.

Even apart from his election to the Board, however, Kennedy's connections were beginning to pay off. In 1917, fellow Board member Guy Currier, a prominent Boston lawyer and counsel for Bethlehem Steel, recommended Kennedy to Bethlehem chief executive Charles M Schwab for the position of assistant general manager at the company's Fore River Shipyard in Quincy, Massachusetts. Already one of the largest shipyards in the country, Fore River was booming with orders as a result of the United States' entry into World War One, and a companion yard was being built at nearby Squantum. Kennedy's close supervision would keep this work under control. It was during his tenure at Fore River that Kennedy would first meet – and sometimes clash – with Franklin D Roosevelt, then Assistant Secretary of the Navy.

By the time the War entered its final months, the weight of work at Fore River had pushed Kennedy to exhaustion, which was compounded by worry over Rose who was expecting a child in the midst of the deadly Spanish flu epidemic that was was just starting to surface and was proving a particular threat to pregnant women. Rose safely gave birth to her first daughter Rosemary on 13 September 1918. Observing the inevitable peacetime slackening of pace at the Bethlehem Shipbuilding Corporation, Kennedy realised that there would not be the same challenges and, more importantly, prospects with the company. He determined to return to finance and cast about for the best option.

In 1919, Kennedy joined the prominent stock brokerage firm of Hayden, Stone & Co where he became an expert dealing in the unregulated stock market of the day, engaging in tactics that were later considered to be insider trading and market manipulation.

His mentor was Galen Stone, an associate from the Massachusetts Electric Company Board.

Joseph Kennedy on the right, at the Fore River Shipyard. *(Library of Congress)*

Joseph Kennedy absorbed the precepts and practicalities of the stock market, increasingly investing his capital.

He happened to be on the corner of Wall and Broad Streets at the moment of the Wall Street bombing on 16 September 1920 and was thrown to the ground by the force of the blast.

When Stone retired at the beginning of 1923, Kennedy decided to move on. He left the firm of Hayden, Stone – though not the physical address – and established himself in his own right as 'Joseph P Kennedy, Banker', offering a range of financial services based on the knowledge and skills he had developed working with Galen Stone. For the next three years, on his behalf and that of others, Kennedy would undertake a series of business ventures that would make him a wealthy man, with a net worth of two million dollars.

He formed alliances with several other Irish-Catholic investors, including Charles E. Mitchell, Michael J. Meehan, and Bernard Smith. He helped establish a 'stock pool' to control trading in the stock of glassmaker Libby-Owens-Ford. The arrangement drove up the value of the pool operators' holdings in the stock by using insider information and the public's lack of knowledge. Pool operators would bribe journalists to present information most advantageously. They tried to corner a stock and drive the price up, or drive the price down with a 'bear raid'. So it was when Kennedy got into a bidding war for control of Yellow Cab Company.

Kennedy later claimed he understood that the rampant stock speculation of the late 1920s would lead to a market crash. Supposedly, he said that he knew it was time to get out of the market when he received stock tips from a shoe-shine boy. Kennedy survived the crash because he possessed a passion for facts, a complete lack of sentiment and a marvellous sense of timing.

During the Great Depression, Kennedy vastly increased his fortune by investing most of his money in real estate. In 1929, Kennedy's fortune was estimated to be $4 million (equivalent to $57.1 million today). By 1935, his wealth had increased to $180 million (equivalent to $3.22 billion today)

Kennedy's next career step appears to be a radical departure. In 1926, engineering a deal to buy the company Film Booking Offices of America (FBO) which specialized in Westerns produced cheaply, he stepped fully into the still-new and burgeoning movie industry. But as with most of Kennedy's business moves, the decision had long roots and was the result of careful observation. As early as 1919, Kennedy had purchased the Maine and New Hampshire Theaters Company, a small chain of New England movie houses. His experience with the chain showed him the promise of the movie business but also that the real money was being made in production rather than distribution. His first connection with FBO was through Hayden, Stone, which had been approached by a British firm that held a controlling interest in the Robertson-Cole Company, the parent organisation for FBO. Dissatisfied with the money-losing habits of Robertson-Cole/FBO, its British owners looked to Stone for help in finding a buyer in the United States. Because of his interest in the film industry, the project was assigned to Joseph Kennedy, who was also retained as a financial advisor to Robertson-Cole. Although he was unsuccessful in finding a buyer, his position with Robertson-Cole/FBO gave Kennedy further insight into the movie business and fueled in him the ambition to purchase the company himself. But it was not until the summer of 1925 that Kennedy could put together an offer, in a consortium that included Guy Currier, Louis Kirstein, head of the Boston chain of Filene's department stores, and even his father-in-law, 'Honey Fitz' Fitzgerald. The million-dollar offer was turned down flatly as insufficient; yet a little more than six months later, the British owners, perhaps finally discouraged by the many ways FBO found to lose money, suddenly chose to accept the bid.

So Joseph Kennedy represented a new and coming thing for Hollywood. Movie making had always been a business, and often a cut-throat one at that, but its newness had worked against it, encouraging lax business practices and deterring stable investment. When he took over FBO, Kennedy brought both the stability and the expertise of an established businessman. With the creation of a finance company, Cinema Credits Corporation, Kennedy could tap into his many contacts in the financial world. At the same time, he enforced a fiscal discipline on FBO that was new to the company and, indeed, Hollywood in general.

Marking his new position as a movie mogul, Kennedy made a significant move personally,

taking his family from Boston to the New York suburb of Riverdale. The family had doubled in size. Three more girls had followed Rosemary – Kathleen (*b*. 20 February 1920), Eunice (*b*. 10 July 1921), and Patricia (*b*. 6 May 1924) – before a third boy, Robert, was born on 20 November 1925. Another girl, Jean (*b*. 20 February 1928) would be born not long after the family settled in New York. In later years, Kennedy would state that the social constraints on his Irish Catholic family in Yankee-dominated Boston had motivated the move, but at least as much of a factor was Kennedy's need to enter a broader, more varied business arena now that his interests had widened and enlarged.

Kennedy spent a lot of time getting FBO on a sound business footing. He did undertake a profitable side venture, arranging for a series of lectures at Harvard, subsequently turned into a book, on the history of film, to be given by some of the most notable names in Hollywood. These men, many of whom had little-organised education beyond elementary school, were

A FBO poster for the 1927 movie *Cyclone of the Range* that had Joseph Kennedy well to the fore.

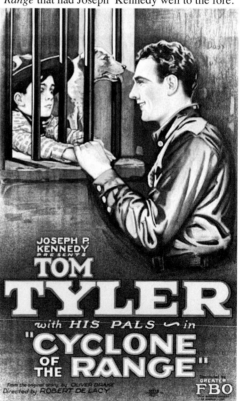

Another FBO 1927 movie *Bulldog Pluck* was also presented by Joseph Kennedy.

That autumn, Kennedy began in earnest his efforts to advance his position in Hollywood by approaching David Sarnoff, head of Radio Corporation of America who were developing Photophone, a sound system for the new talkies. RCA needed to forge a connection with Hollywood to sell its product. Kennedy knew that he needed to compete in the new market of sound films and to do so he would have to have access to a technology that was not proprietary, which was the case with Warner Brothers' Vitaphone, the most successful sound process to date. The corporate alliance between FBO and RCA was cemented with the purchase by FBO of the Keith-Albee-Orpheum theatre chain, which would provide the venues for Photophone process pictures. In the meantime, Kennedy's success with FBO had been noticed, and he was invited in to perform the same kind of corporate turnaround, first for Pathé-DeMille, a production company that already had an uneasy affiliation with KAO, though Kennedy's role was independent, and then with First National. As a condition of his work, Kennedy demanded absolute power in the companies, and wound up in control of Pathé, but the requirement did not sit well with the board of First National, which ultimately dispensed with his services. Still, for a brief period in 1928, Joseph P. Kennedy was the de facto head of four different companies.

The degree of vertical integration represented by the FBO-KAO combination suggested to observers an imminent merger, especially because of the connection KAO already had with the production company Pathé-DeMille. The deal that eventually developed involved the purchase by RCA of a major stakeholding in KAO to complement the majority holding it already had in FBO. Pathé for the moment remained outside of the compact, and Kennedy continued to run that company.

In August 1928, he unsuccessfully tried to run First National Pictures. In October 1928, he formally merged his film companies FBO and KAO to form Radio-Keith-Orpheum (RKO) and made a large amount of money in the process. Then, keen to buy the Pantages Theater chain, which had 63 profitable theatres, Kennedy made an offer of $8 million ($114 million today). It was declined. He then stopped distributing his movies to Pantages. Still, Alexander Pantages refused to sell. However, when Pantages was later charged and tried for rape, his reputation took a battering,

immensely flattered by invitation to speak at one of the great universities of the country. Despite Harvardites who complained at a connection with anything so disreputable as the movies, the university also benefited, not least from a sizable donation by Kennedy to help set up a film library. As the recipient of gratitude from all sides, Kennedy profited most of all, gaining an introduction to and the confidence of some of the most powerful men in the film industry.

In March 1926, Kennedy moved to Hollywood to focus on running film studios. At that time, film studios were permitted to own exhibition companies, which were necessary to get their films on local screens. With that in mind, in a hostile buyout, he acquired the Keith-Albee-Orpheum Theaters Corporation (KAO), which had more than 700 vaudeville theatres across the United States that had begun showing movies. He later purchased another production studio called Pathe Exchange and merged those two entities with Cecil B. DeMille's Producers Distributing Corporation in March 1927.

and he accepted Kennedy's revised offer of $3.5 million ($50 million today). Pantages, who claimed that Kennedy had set him up, was later found not guilty at a second trial. The girl who had accused Pantages of rape, Eunice Pringle, confessed on her deathbed that Joseph Kennedy was the mastermind of the plot to frame Pantages.

Despite these abundant and complex business interests, Kennedy did not ignore opportunities to engage in independent production. As early as 1923 he had arranged a personal corporation to manage the film career of FBO cowboy star Fred Thomson. Many estimate that Kennedy made over $5 million ($71.4 million today) from his investments in Hollywood.

But his most important independent work was with Gloria Swanson, one of the biggest stars of the silent era. Kennedy met Swanson in late 1927 when the actress was in considerable financial difficulties because of a disastrous attempt at self-production under the aegis of United Artists Corporation, problems she aggravated with her extravagant lifestyle. Kennedy embarked on a three-year affair with the actress, at the same time taking over Swanson's

personal and professional finances, creating Gloria Productions to oversee her filmmaking opportunities. In early 1928, Kennedy hired director Erich von Stroheim to direct Swanson in a lavish film designed to restore her somewhat dimmed star power.

He arranged the financing for her films *The Love of Sunya* (1927) and the ill-fated and unfinished *Queen Kelly* (1928). Although *Queen Kelly,* was never completed, Kennedy and Swanson produced other films, including Swanson's first talking feature, *The Trespasser.* The duo also used Hollywood's famous 'body sculptor', masseuse Sylvia Ulback, known as Sylvia of Hollywood, she was an early Hollywood fitness guru. Their relationship ended when Swanson discovered that an expensive gift from Joseph had been charged to her account.

1930 also saw Joseph P. Kennedy extricating himself from his other Hollywood commitments. From a personal sense of foreboding and on the advice of trusted associates, Kennedy divested himself of virtually all of his stock holdings, including the stock he held in Pathé, before the October 1929 crash. He would spend the next

Joe Kennedy became film star Gloria Swanson's business partner and and lover for a number of years even taking her on a vacation to Europe along with his wife Rose. Their relationship was an open secret in Hollywood. Kennedy was supposed to make Swanson millions. Unfortunately, Kennedy left her after the disastrous *Queen Kelly* and her finances were in worse shape than when he came into her life. (NARA)

The Kennedy family at their home in Hyannis Port, Massachusetts. sometime in the summer of 1931. Rosemary Kennedy is seated on the far right in front of Joseph Jnr. while John is kneeling on the left.

year sounding out potential buyers for the company, culminating in a sale to RKO, which already had business connections to Pathé that it had inherited from KAO.

A recurring rumour alleges that he made money in bootlegging illegal liquor during Prohibition. Doris Kearns, the only historian to have access to Kennedy's papers, found scant evidence to support the claims made by amongst others gangsters Meyer Lansky and Frank Costello of large underworld deals. Certainly, there is abundant evidence that as the end of prohibition loomed in 1933, Kennedy invested heavily in Scottish distilleries. As soon as it became legal, he imported large shipments of expensive Scotch and made a substantial profit. Numerous criminals spread various contradictory bootlegging stories, such as Canadian distiller Samuel Bronfman and to New England bootlegger Danny Walsh and his crime syndicate. They did illegally smuggle spirits across the Canada - US border. After Prohibition ended, Bronfman had a bitter rivalry with Kennedy in acquiring North American liquor distribution rights. It was the work of a man who knew well where the subterranean rivers of illicit booze had run during the prohibition that he kept the knowledge close. His papers guard the secrets still. At the start of the Franklin Roosevelt administration in March 1933, Kennedy and

Congressman James Roosevelt II founded Somerset Importers, an entity that acted as the exclusive American agent for a number of drinks importers. Kennedy kept his Somerset company for years. Kennedy himself drank little alcohol. He so disapproved of what he considered a stereotypical Irish vice that he offered his sons $1,000 to not drink until they turned 21.

Kennedy invested his profits from alcohol into residential and commercial real estate in New York, the Le Pavillon restaurant, and the Hialeah Park Race Track in Hialeah, Florida. His most important purchase was the largest office building in the country, Chicago's Merchandise Mart, which gave his family a grounding in that city and an alliance with the city's Irish-American political leadership.

Kennedy's foray into Hollywood brought him a vast and significantly liquid fortune that allowed him to continue his investments in real estate, notably his homes in Hyannis Port and Palm Beach, even as he was scaling back his activities in Hollywood and the stock market. But at the beginning of the 1930s, the real focus of Kennedy's energies became politics. As a successful businessman, Kennedy's expected allegiance would have been to Hoover and the Republicans in the 1932 election, but the breadth and depth of the Depression had shaken Kennedy's faith in Republican solutions.

Believing that a change to the system was necessary to preserve the system, and willing to accept the toll on his wealth that might be involved, Kennedy threw his personal and financial support behind Franklin D Roosevelt's presidential campaign. He rode on Roosevelt's campaign train, and by some accounts, his intercession brought about the support of powerful newspaper magnate William Randolph Hearst.

In 1933, with the election won, and Roosevelt inaugurated, Joe and Rose Kennedy took a ship for Europe in September with Jimmy and Betsy Roosevelt, on a trip combining pleasure and profit. By midsummer, enough States had ratified the repeal amendment to ensure the end of prohibition in 1933. Joe exploited public expectations of repeal, and he wanted to be in on the liquor boom when it came. Although representatives of British distillers were already in the US lining up distributors, Kennedy went to the top in London. He was appointed the US agent for Haig & Haig, Ltd., John Dewar & Sons, Ltd., and Gordon's Dry Gin Co., Ltd., which meant millions of Americans thirsting for good

Scotch and honest gin would get it through Kennedy. Copying a gambit used by others, he arranged for his newly organised Somerset Importers to import and stockpile thousands of cases of liquor, the stuff coming into the legally dry US under 'medicinal' licences.

In 1934, Congress established the independent Securities and Exchange Commission to end irresponsible market manipulations and dissemination of false information about securities. Roosevelt named Kennedy to head the SEC clean up of Wall Street. The New Deal attracted many of the nation's most talented young lawyers. Roosevelt's brain trust drew up a list of recommended candidates for the SEC chairmanship. Kennedy headed the list, which stated he was the best bet for Chairman because of his *'executive ability, knowledge of habits and customs of business to be regulated and ability to moderate different points of view on Commission'*. It was something akin to putting a wolf in charge of a flock of sheep.

Kennedy sought out the best lawyers available giving him a hard-driving team with a mission for reform. They included William O.

Joe Kennedy knew the value of having the media on his side, and is seen here not long after being apppointed the head of the Securities and Exchange Commission cultivating 'the gentlemen of the press' in Washington DC. (NARA)

President Franklin D. Roosevelt (seated) congratulates Joe Kennedy on becoming the new ambassador to Great Britain. Associate Justice Stanley Reed, centre, administered Kennedy's oath. (NARA)

Douglas, and Abe Fortas, both of whom were later named to the Supreme Court. The SEC had four missions. First and foremost was to restore investor confidence in the securities market which had collapsed on account of its questionability, and the external threats supposedly posed by anti-business elements in the Roosevelt administration. Second, the SEC had to get rid of the penny-ante swindles based on false information, fraudulent devices, and get-rich-quick schemes. Thirdly, and much more critical than the frauds, the SEC had to end the million-dollar manoeuvres in significant corporations, whereby insiders with access to much better information about the company knew when to buy or sell their securities. A crackdown on insider trading was essential. Finally, the SEC had to set up a complex system of registration for all securities traded in America, with a clear set of rules, deadlines and guidelines that all companies had to follow. The challenge faced by the young lawyers was drafting precise rules. The SEC succeeded in its four missions, as Kennedy reassured the American business community that they would no longer be deceived and taken advantage of by Wall Street.

He trumpeted for ordinary investors to return to the market and enable the economy to grow again. Kennedy's reforming work as SEC chairman was widely praised on all sides, as investors realised the SEC was protecting their interests. He left the SEC in 1935 to take over the Maritime Commission, which built on his wartime experience in running a major shipyard.

From the end of 1935 through 1936, Kennedy acted as a consultant in business and government. After a six-week tour of Europe in the fall of 1935, he reported to Roosevelt on the European economic situation. He followed up that work with a more formalised stint as a paid advisor to David Sarnoff of RCA, which had suffered severe setbacks in the early Depression years. Kennedy also returned briefly to the movie industry, preparing a business review at the request of Paramount Pictures.

The 1936 presidential campaign brought Kennedy back into politics. Roosevelt sought his help on the drive, and Kennedy responded with his book *I'm for Roosevelt,* which he had published and made sure was widely distributed. Written with the help of his friend, *New York Times* columnist Arthur Krock, the book

Three of the Kennedy men. Left to right: Joseph Jnr, Joseph Snr, John. (NARA)

presented arguments for why businesspeople should support Roosevelt and the New Deal, told from the perspective of Kennedy's endorsement. The book had a significant impact in the business community, and after his re-election, Roosevelt appointed Kennedy chair of the United States Maritime Commission. Created by the Merchant Marine Act of 1936, the Commission was expected to rejuvenate America's merchant shipping industry, which was crippled by an outdated fleet and a difficult labour situation. Kennedy spent only ten months at the Commission. In early December 1937, Roosevelt named Kennedy the new ambassador to the Court of St. James, the US' representative to Great Britain. Kennedy officially resigned from the Maritime Commission in February 1938. Kennedy hugely enjoyed his leadership position in London high society, which stood in stark contrast to his relative outsider status in Boston. Kennedy began brilliantly in London, being dubbed 'Jolly Joe, the Nine-Child Envoy' by one tabloid and displacing George Washington as 'the father of his country' in a music-hall routine, but he did not make many friends.

His views were becoming inconsistent and increasingly isolationist; British MP Josiah Wedgwood, 1st Baron Wedgwood, who had himself opposed the British Government's earlier appeasement policy, said of Kennedy: *'We have a rich man, untrained in diplomacy, unlearned in history and politics, who is a great publicity seeker and who apparently is ambitious to be the first Catholic president of the US'.*

As a result of these 'weaknesses', it seems that Joseph Kennedy made use of having his Harvard-educated sons around, especially John. As we shall see later, John soon developed a habit of reporting everything back to his father, at the same time providing him with advice and 'bullet-points' on items he was to discuss.

While in Great Britain twenty-one year old John set about researching a thesis that he somewhat pretentiously called *'WHY ENGLAND SLEPT - an answer to Winston Churchill's WHILE ENGLAND SLEPT'*.

Clearly he used both his father's name and connections to gain access to and interview important people in the UK political establishment.

The preface to the thesis explained that it was a document devoted to the Munich Agreement of 29-30 September 1938. which was a settlement reached by Germany, Great Britain, France, and Italy that permitted German annexation of the Sudetenland, in western Czechoslovakia. After his success in absorbing Austria into Germany proper in March 1938, Hitler looked covetously at Czechoslovakia, where about three million people in the Sudeten area were of German origin. It became known in May 1938 that Hitler and his generals were drawing up a plan for the occupation of Czechoslovakia. The Czechs were relying on military assistance from France, with which they had an alliance. The Soviet Union also had a treaty with Czechoslovakia, and it indicated willingness to cooperate with France and Great Britain if they decided to come to Czechoslovakia's defence, but the Soviet Union and its potential services were ignored throughout the crisis.

'The Munich Pact itself...' John wrote, *'... should not be the object of criticism but rather the underlying factors, such as the state of British opinion and the condition of Britain's armaments, which made 'surrender' inevitable.*

To blame one man, such as Baldwin, for the unpreparedness of British armaments is illogical and unfair, given the conditions of democratic government'.

Although in Britain as in the US he moved with ease in all sorts of company, Kennedy naturally drew closest to men who manipulated money in the City and to those who gave that interest political voice. As war approached, he

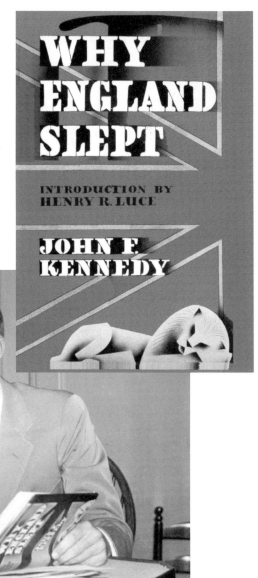

John F Kennedy poses for this publicity photograph for his book *'Why England Slept'*, taken from his university thesis of the same name. It later came to light that his father Joeseph Kennedy bought thousands of copies to shoot it high up the bookseller lists. (NARA)

was drawn, therefore, to the appeasement-minded Neville Chamberlain. Early in his ambassadorship he publicly urged coexistence between the Western democracies and Hitler's Germany. At the time of Munich, he took up the cause of the appeasers and used his influence at the office of Will Hays in Hollywood to have a Paramount newsreel censored. The scenes deleted showed two British newsmen talking sympathetically with heartsick Czechs in Prague. His cables grew increasingly pessimistic and private notes to favourite reporters - which invariably leaked into print - were more bluntly candid.

Kennedy rejected the belief of Winston Churchill that any compromise with Nazi Germany was impossible. Instead, he supported Prime Minister Neville Chamberlain's policy of appeasement. Throughout 1938, while the Nazi persecution of the Jews in Germany intensified, Kennedy attempted to arrange a meeting with Adolf Hitler. Shortly before the Nazi bombing of British cities began in September 1940, Kennedy once again sought a personal meeting with Hitler without the approval of the US Department of State, to '...*bring about a better understanding between the United States and Germany'*.

What neither Joe Kennedy nor anyone else could predict, as he and his large (nine children) and gregarious family arrived in Britain on 1 March 1938, was that one year later all of Europe would be embroiled in another full-scale war.

At 49 years of age, he was now pulled directly into a line of fire that few US ambassadors ever had to endure; much of it was of his own making. For example, he made his first public speech in Great Britain at London's Pilgrim Club, whose attendees were the leading figures in British politics and business. He startled the audience with his comments in which he said that it was in America's best interests to stay neutral in any coming conflict with Germany and that the US would not see eye to eye with Britain as it had done in the past. Those were strong words for an ambassador to say to the citizens of the country in which he was residing.

Naturally, Joe's remarks caused quite a stir in the British press as well as in Washington. In a letter to his friend Bernard Baruch, Kennedy said that he wanted to '*reassure my friends and critics alike that I have not yet been taken into the British camp'*. In time, Kennedy's actions would cause more consternation and irritation across both sides of the Atlantic.

Joseph Kennedy had a number of meetings with the German ambassador in London, and after the war, transcripts and reports of their conversations surfaced: '*Anti-Semitic views claimed to have been expressed by Joseph P Kennedy - during the time when he was US ambassador in London - in his conversations with the German ambassador there in 1938, were*

Ambassador Kennedy said that, in case of war between Britain and Germany, America might remain neutral - words that angered Britain to say the least. Here he meets with German Foreign Minister Joachim von Ribbentrop at a London reception in 1938. *(NARA)*

later revealed in captured German diplomatic documents made public by the State Department.

The documents, which claim that Kennedy approved of the Nazi treatment of Jews in Germany, were discovered in the secret archives of the German Foreign Ministry. One of them is a letter from the German ambassador to Great Britain, Dr Herbert von Dirksen, to Baron Ernst von Weizsaecker, State Secretary of the German Foreign Ministry who had been convicted on war crimes charges. In this report, von Dirksen wrote of Kennedy as follows:

'The Ambassador then touched upon the Jewish question and stated that it was naturally of great importance to German-American relations. In this connection it was not so much the fact that we wanted to get rid of the Jews that was so harmful to us, but rather the loud clamour with which we accompanied the purpose. He himself understood our Jewish policy completely; he was from Boston and there, in one golf club, and in other clubs, no Jews had been admitted in the past fifty years. In the USA, therefore, such pronounced attitudes were quite common, but people avoided making so much

Joseph P Kennedy, Kathleen Kennedy, and John F Kennedy, arrive at the House of Parliament in London to hear Prime Minister Chamberlain's announcement that a state of war existed between Great Britain and Germany. 3rd September 1939.

outward fuss about it.

'Although he did not know Germany, he (Kennedy) had learned from the most varied sources that the present government had done great things for Germany and that the Germans were satisfied and enjoyed good living conditions. The report by the well-known flier, Lindbergh, who had spoken very favourably of Germany, made a strong impression upon Ambassador Kennedy, as I know from an earlier conversation with him.

'As an illustration of how wrong impressions regarding Germany were being spread, Ambassador Kennedy related that recently 'Johnnie' Rockefeller, (John D Rockefeller Jr) a very influential and sensible man, had told him that according to a report by one of the leading professors of the Rockefeller Institute, the limited amount of food available in Germany was being reserved mainly for the army, with the result that the rest of the population had to suffer want. As far as knew, the professor who made the report was a Jew. He - Kennedy - had set Rockefeller right.'

Emphasising in his report that when Kennedy

The entire Kennedy family in their London residence. *(NARA)*

From left to right: Lord Halifax, American undersecretary-of-state Sumner Welles, British Prime Minister Neville Chamberlain, American Ambassador Joseph P. Kennedy, London, 1940. Clearly, given that the Americans were wearing Morning Dress, it was a formal event. (NARA)

spoke favourably of Germany, people had confidence in his statements because he was a Catholic, the German envoy added that he had 'repeatedly and emphatically' welcomed Kennedy's intention to enlighten President Roosevelt about Germany. He then quoted Kennedy as stating: 'The President was not anti-German, but desired friendly relations with Germany. However, there was no one who had come from Europe and had spoken a friendly word to him regarding present-day Germany and her government.

'When I remarked that I feared he was right in this, Kennedy added that he knew he was right. Most of them were afraid of the Jews and did not dare to say anything good about Germany; others did not know any better, because they were not informed about Germany,' von Dirksen reported.

He added that when he brought up the question of the anti-Nazi attitude of the American press, Kennedy did not have much to say to these statements *'and merely mentioned that the press on the East Coast was unfortunately predominant in the formation of public opinion in America and that it was strongly influenced by the Jews'*.

Believing that his effectiveness as ambassador was coming to an end, Kennedy, on 6 October 1940, wrote a letter to FDR asking that he be relieved of his duties in London and demanded that he be brought home. If his request was denied, he would come home anyway. The Roosevelt administration accepted Kennedy's wishes, and he arrived in New York on 27 October, arriving at La Guardia Airport. FDR had asked Joe and Rose to come to see him at the White House when they arrived, and they took the train to Washington immediately. After dinner, Joe gave the president a piece of his mind. He told FDR that he did not like the way he was treated in London, saying candidly that he was kept out of the loop as far as policy formulation was concerned. He took a direct swipe at the State Department, saying it was directly responsible for his being shut out of policymaking.

Joe arrived home one month before the 1940 presidential election in which FDR was running for an unprecedented third term. The press was aware of the growing rift between FDR and Kennedy, and speculation was the order of the day when it came to what trouble Kennedy might inflict on the campaign. Joe agreed to make a radio speech endorsing the president, which he paid for himself. It cost $20,000 for a nationwide hookup. He endorsed FDR but said that he still believed it wise for the US to stay out of the European war.

Joseph Kennedy resigned as US ambassador the day after the American election in 5 November 1940, but the resignation was not officially instigated until February 1941, one month into FDR's third term. His final remarks were, '*Having finished a rather busy political career this week, I find myself much more interested in what young Joe is going to do than what I am going to do with the rest of my life.*'

Kennedy also argued strongly against providing military and economic aid to the United Kingdom. As the Roosevelt administration was debating whether or not to grant military aid to Britain - a March 1941 Lend-Lease deal would eventually send 50 obsolete destroyers to Great Britain in exchange for leases from the British of a number of bases in the Caribbean - Kennedy publicly spoke out against any such US action. He chilled both Washington and London with his comments, '*Democracy is finished in England. It may be here*', he stated in the *Boston Sunday Globe* of 10 November 1940. While German troops had overrun Poland, Denmark, Norway, Belgium, the Netherlands, Luxembourg, and France, and with daily bombings of Great Britain, Kennedy unambiguously and repeatedly stated that the war was not about saving democracy from National Socialism (Nazism) or Fascism. In an interview with two newspaper journalists, Louis M. Lyons, published on 9 November 1940 in the *The Boston Globe,* and Ralph Coghlan, of the *St. Louis Post-Dispatch*, Kennedy said:

By now Great Britain was directly involved in the war, and under attack. Barrage balloons were being trundled out of their hangars by solicitious crews like so many nannies with their prams. Every aircraft seen in the skies was studied with great intensity.

From left to right: American Undersecretary-of-State Sumner Welles, British Prime Winston Churchill and , American ambassador Joseph P Kennedy, London, 1940. *(NARA)*

'It's all a question of what we do with the next six months. The whole reason for aiding England is to give us time ... As long as she is in there, we have time to prepare. It isn't that [Britain is] *fighting for democracy. That's the bunk. She's fighting for self-preservation, just as we will if it comes to us. ... I know more about the European situation than anybody else, and it's up to me to see that the country gets it.*

Kennedy did not endear himself to the British population during German air raids on London. As the Blitz attacks grew stronger, the Ambassador moved his family out of London to escape the raids. After touring the destruction in London, he remarked at how much he admired the local citizens for their bravery and fortitude in the face of such horrific German attacks. In time, the papers began calling Kennedy, 'Jittery Joe.'

JFK has JPK's back...

There is something of an interesting follow-on to the Kennedy ambassadorship in London. On 6 December 1940 John F Kennedy wrote a letter to his father Joe that in retrospect was a prime example of political 'spin' to rehabilitate his

father in the eyes of the American public; *'I am sending you a rough outline of some points that I feel it would be well for you to cover'.*

The words that JFK hoped his father would say are thus: *'On November 6, the day after the election, I resigned from the post I had held for nearly three years, that as American Ambassador the Court of King James. In the statement which I gave when the resignation was made public, I said that I will now devote my future to aiding the President in keeping out the war. And this I propose to do.*

For this reason, I have decided to set down for the people of America what I really believe and feel about the great problems that faced this country. The problems facing America today are not academic. They demand concrete answers, and rightly or wrongly they must be answered soon. As the decisions to be made in the next few years will have a far-reaching effect on our lives and the lives of our children, I feel that the American people, from whom the ultimate decision must come, should have and must have all the facts before them. All viewpoints must be considered. Colonel Lindbergh and William Allen White must both

158

be given fair and impartial hearings if the American people are to have a fair voice in determining what sort of country they are to live in.

For my own part, I have always felt that the art of diplomacy was far too shrouded in mystery. This tendency to treat diplomacy as a sort of Machiavellian poker game in which only experts could sit in on has been in a great measure responsible I think for the fatal inertia of the democracy during the last tragic years.

Joseph Kennedy just before he left London for the safety of the USA.

How foolish it is to expect the people from whom the ultimate decisions must come to take the vigorous and forceful action necessary to match the dictators when they have been lulled into a false sense of security and complacency until the last hysterical moment.

The views that I now set down are not new to me. I have held them since the tragic days in Munich. The war has only cemented them. And I have emphasised them in every conversation I have had since then with both American and British leaders. Now that I am a private citizen I feel that the American people should hear them. Since returning home especially, I have repeatedly emphasised these views to newspapermen all through the country. I have spoken to them on every possible occasion. Of necessity the conversations have been off the record. My official position forbade any direct interviews.

Throughout my public career during the last seven years I do not recall ever having refused to talk to newspapermen on any subject. This has not been a one-sided bargain however by any means. The best informed that I have met in twenty-five years of a varied career are not statesmen, diplomats or college professors, but American newspapermen.

During the last two years, however, I have tried especially to give newspapermen all the background that circumstances and my job permitted. I felt that their responsibility is great, as it is upon them that the American people depend for their knowledge on the problems facing them. The manner in which the settlement of Munich was treated in this country demonstrated to me powerfully the danger that lack of adequate information could bring.

JFK then directly explained the reasoning

28 September 1939: Joseph P Kennedy walking beside a pile of sandbags at upon leaving the Treasury building in London.

Great Britain during the blitz.

Above: the raiders may come with regularity, but so does the milkman!

Below: the gas pressure may have been low, and the kitchen was in the back alley - but lunch was served!

behind his views in this sub-text paragraph. *Dad: you might work in here some of your own ideas of Munich and the background to it. That is, what you thought; how you felt it would be serious danger to America if there was a war at that time; that America's own defences were completely down as well as England's; that England might have been bombed into submission overnight due to her complete lack of defenses and America would have been in an exposed and dangerous position. You might put in here that it was worth any risk for America to have a Europe at peace, and therefore you supported Chamberlain. You feel about Munich was misunderstood in America and that the bitterness of the attacks on England for not fighting has given America a great moral responsibility in this present war, which she should not have undertaken. You cannot blame many Englishmen for feeling that they have been let down, that we were continually urging them to fight as we did in October 1938. This I think, of course, was a mistake. We should not have taken such a critical viewpoint without any more knowledge.*

The main narrative continued: *Through the last months, it has been more and more evident that Munich was inevitable due to the complete lack of preparedness. But in this country at the time the settlement was attacked with a bitterness seldom equalled. It was attacked as a failure of*

Left: Joseph Wright Alsop V (*b*. 10 October 1910, *d*. 28 August 1989) was an American journalist and syndicated newspaper columnist.

Right: Robert E. Kintner (*b. 12* September 1909, *d. 20* December 1980) was an American journalist and later a television executive, who served as president of both the National Broadcasting Company (NBC) and the American Broadcasting Company (ABC).

British diplomacy to provide security where it should have been attacked as a failure of British democracy to provide adequate arms. It might have been a trumpet call to America to awaken, but it wasted its energy in a bitter attack on the individuals involved. That taught me a vital lesson, and since then I have always tried to give as thoroughly as circumstances would permit any information that I could that would help newsmen get nearer the truth.

I have had many such talks since returning home. From several of these rumours have sprung that I am defeatist, that I am an appeaser. Joseph Alsopp [sic] and Robert Kintner in their column said I hold views unacceptable to ninety per cent of the American people. I do not think that I do, but I am setting my views down here sincerely and with complete frankness. I think that the American people can decide whether or not my views agree with theirs much more accurately than Mr Alsop and Mister Kintner.

I must confess at that the outset that my views are not pleasant. I am gloomy, and I have had been gloomy since September 1938. It may be unpleasant for America to hear my views but let me note that Winston Churchill was considered distinctly unpleasant to have around during the years from 1935 to 1939. It was felt he was a gloom-monger. In the days of the blitzkrieg, the optimist does not always do his country the best service. It is only by facing the reality that we can hope to meet it successfully.

It is not easy for me to discuss what should be our attitude towards England without emotion - purely from the point of view of what is best for America. I have lived in England for many months. My wife and I have many friends there. My children have gone to school there. I have seen the English stand with their backs to the wall and not whimper. I have seen the grim

determination with which the man in the street meet the news of the disasters of May and June. I have seen the soldiers coming back from the hell that was Dunkirk with their thumbs still up. I have heard this story as the fight of the Grenadier Guards. (Here you might tell the story you were telling me about the guards singing and driving the Germans out of the town losing so many men). I have seen the boys who were friends of my children die in the air. I have seen the spirit of the Londoners through 244 air raids. I repeat therefore, it is not easy for me to discuss the situation from purely an American point of view but I feel I must, I feel that the situation today is so fraught with peril and disaster for us we must take the course, for many it may be the hardest, of looking at the situation completely from the point of view of what is best for America.

Kennedy then inserted another explanatory sub-text section: *Dad: Here's a sort of general introduction. You will probably want to approach some of the points I have brought out in it in a different way, but the points themselves may be of interest. In regards to Alsop and Kintner, you may not want to take direct issue with them as they had 365 days a year to strike back. If you do hit at them I think it would be well to do it not in the form of attacking them for personal reasons, but rather because they have by their malicious and untrue attacks misinterpreted the truth and have their standards of service to the people of the USA, who need the truth so badly. Here is a paragraph on them.*

I must confess also another reason for wishing to set down what I really think and this is more a personal one. I have lately noted several bitter attacks on me in a gossip column taking me to account for being an appeaser and defeatist. I give these columnists who attacked me credit for complete sincerity. I believe that when

A solitary soldier forms the congregation of this bombed out church in Southampton on the south coast of Great Britain. *(W/O Paddy Porter Collection)*

Joseph Alsop and Robert Kintner devoted a whole column to discuss in a newspaper interview they felt they were giving the truth. I cannot understand it quite so clearly when they fail to even mention it when the invasion was denied and repudiated by me. I believe also that when Joseph Alsop and Robert Kintner attacked me in their column of August (I am not too sure of the date of this, or of its accuracy, but it can be checked on) complaining about a wire I had sent to the State Department of the previous week, that they felt that I was doing real public service. That the wire in question was confidential to the President and Secretary of State is not the important matter, or that they were able to gain access to a confidential wire and felt free to make a public news story of it, is also not really the important matter. The important point is that they completely misquoted it, I trust unintentionally and thus gave the American people and a completely untrue version of what the American Ambassador to England, who was supposedly in the best position to observe what was happening in England really felt.

I believe in this that their disservice was great and theirs is a severe responsibility. To misinform the American people for the benefit of the story is, I believe, in these times, a grave offence. Now

that they have seen fit to release the wire and place a completely false implication on its contents, I will show where they were wrong and what effect this might have. (Here if you have it, you might see fit to compare what Alsop and Kintner said about the wire and what the wire really said and show the danger that this misinformation might cause. I am rather vague about this as you just mentioned it briefly in the plane but you might be able to work something out from these lines).

The wrong, I believe, has not been down so much to me as it has been done to the people of the United States when they are desperately trying to learn the truth of the situation. It is puzzling even to those who have a great many more of the facts before them.

To me, it is of a grave and serious concern this matter should have been handled with such a complete disregard for the actual truth. In the same way and for the same reason I take serious issue with some of the later stories which brand me as an appeaser and a defeatist on the basis of the newspaper interview which I later denied.

The original story was given an entire column, the denial not a single line. It is thus also to nail these particular stories for the lie that they are that I set down what I really think the

162

American people have the right to know.

Point #2: In order to show why it necessary for you to write an article on why America should not enter the war, it might be well to bring in Hiram Johnson's statement in San Francisco, December 4, that America is definitely headed for entry into the war; that it is inevitable. This will answer any of those who claim that there is no need to write such an article that both candidates promised to keep us out and none of the American people wish to go in. You might bring in that during the next few months the pull towards war is going to become stronger and stronger and that the American people must have the arguments of those who think we should go in and those who think we should not go in right out on the table before them.

Point #3: In giving your reasons why America should not go into war, I would not state that Britain does not want it as you did in your speech because I imagine that they will be asking for more direct aid in the near future.

Point #4: It is well to remember also that while many people, the more vociferous ones, might be sore because you are not pro-British enough, there are others such as the Father Coughlin group who are sore because you are too pro-British and that you feel we should give them money as a form of insurance. While they may not be nearly as important, I believe that these people also are also entitled to an explanation as to why you feel Britain should get this money. There is still a considerable group of complete isolationists. You should explain to them how and why you differ.

Point #5: I imagine that you'll have to explain your views on the Johnson Act and about the advisability of loaning money. It would seem to me that the British undoubtedly should be forced to pay as well as they can but it should also be brought out exactly how much money we are spending and will spend throughout the long years to come on defense, which we will save if Britain wins the war or achieves a deadlock, and secondly how important it is that Britain goes on fighting in order to give us time to prepare ourselves both economically and defensively for the future.

Point #6: It might also be worthwhile to mention your views on whether you feel that the British are liable to say to hell with it if they see we are completely selfish or if they see we are definitely not coming in. This might be a reason for giving more aid.

Point #7: Of course, it will have to be

Dover may have been within range of the German long-range gun batteries, but the seagulls still needed to be fed. *(W/O Paddy Porter Collection)*

mentioned whether you feel that England can hold out and if so how long. You can avoid a direct prophecy as you have before by stating that you cannot judge this unless you know Germany's strength. You can put in a boost by saying you know the bombing won't make them quit.

Point #8: You might bring out how important it is that we start immediately to organise our economy for the post-war world and how thoroughly we must become adjusted to the change, not just a few experts in Washington, but the whole country. This is worth quite a bit of space.

Point #9: It must be remembered continually that you wish to shake off the word 'appeaser'. It seems to me that if this label is tied to you it may nullify your immediate effectiveness, even though in the long run you may be proved correct. Lindbergh may prove a good example of this. I don't mean that you should change your ideas or be all things to all men, but I do mean that you should express your views in such a way that it is difficult to indict you as appeaser unless they indict themselves as warmongers.

Point #10: You might bring out the point that you have always told the British frankly where you stood, that you have never given any Englishman the slightest hope that America would ever come into the war. You have done this for two reasons - because you believed it would be disastrous for America to come into the war and that Americans were firmly against it, and secondly, because you felt that you would be doing the British just as great a disservice. It would have been much easier during the trying days of the summer to have held out some hope - but you thought it would have been a disservice to both the country to which you were accredited as well as the country from which you came. You might also make some mention that the diplomatic wires when released will bear you out.

Point #11:

I have not a copy of Bevan's speech, but of course you will want to bring it in. The impression that people should have if possible, after reading your article is how right you have been from the beginning. This will make them more anxious to hear from you in the future. Of course, this will have to be subtly expressed, as otherwise, it will open you too wide to cracks from those wise-apple columnists that you're more interested telling you how are you have been than in helping the American people.

If you ever think that perhaps you are giving the impression that you feel you know it all, you can always imply that it is not that you are so smart, but merely that after all, you have been closer to the situation than anyone else in this country for three years. In showing how you always looked out for America's interest in you

Manchester also received the attention of the Luftwaffe. *(W/O Paddy Porter Collection)*

To Horse! It was not just the towns and cities that were bombed. Country life so beloved by the gentry that Joseph Kennedy so wished to become part of was also under threat. *(W/O Paddy Porter Collection)*

might show that at Munich you agreed closely with British policy, and were very popular, yet during this last winter you became quite unpopular because of your firm stand against America's entry and your statements that America would never come in and couldn't if she wanted to. You felt that while it hurt you temporarily, in the long run, you feel and felt before you left that the British appreciated that you had played fairly with them by telling them the truth as you saw it. In the same way, you think that in the long run this country will be glad you are telling them the truth.

Point #12: Another approach to Alsop and Kintner etc, you might just mention them, treating what they say as insignificant, that you don't care what they say, in the long run, you have confidence in the people: that you will continue to tell the truth - that you will submit to the judgement of your country - if not received favourably now, then in the future. You answer Alsop and Kintner merely because the situation is now so acute that you feel what you think you should be on the record. But you don't give a damn what they say about you personally.

Point #13: In reading Alsop and Kintner's latest remarks and their continual use of the word appeasement without amplifying its meaning, I received the impression that they, like so many other Americans, are guilty of throwing around the term when they never have stopped to think exactly what it meant. It might be a good idea to try and get a definition of what they mean. This is necessary because no one - be they isolationist, pacifist, etc., - no one likes to be called an appeaser. Is Hiram Johnson an appeaser? They would probably answer no - well, is Lindbergh an appeaser? - Yes. But where does the difference in their beliefs lie - Johnson must express himself better because he has avoided the label - yet in essence, they both stand for the same thing. The word appeasement, of course, started at Munich; the background of it seems to be the idea of believing that you can obtain a satisfactory solution of the points in dispute by making concessions to the dictators. But you do not believe this - you predicate your views on other grounds. Where I think Lindbergh has run afoul

At night, much of London moved underground to escape the Luftwaffe bombs. The Underground railway system such as the station at Piccadilly Circus became temporary air raid shelters.
(W/O Paddy Porter Collection)

is in his declarations that we do not care what happens over there - that we can live at peace with a world controlled by the dictators - or at least that is the impression he has given.

I would think that your best angle would be that of course, you do not believe this, you with your background cannot stand the idea personally of dictatorships - you hate them - you have achieved the abundant life under a democratic capitalistic system - you wish to preserve it. But you believe that you can only preserve it by keeping out of Europe's wars etc. It's not that you hate dictatorship less - but that you love America more.

The point that I am trying to get at is that it is important that you stress how much you dislike the idea of dealing with with the dictatorships, how you would'nt trust their word a minute - how are you have no confidence in them - but that you feel that they can be fought off, internally as well as externally, if we build ourselves up strong economically and defensively, and we can only do that by following the procedure you advocate.

In that way, you can prevent their fastening the word appeaser on you. You could take the word appeasement apart and question what it

means. Does it mean fighting for the Dutch East Indies etc? Stress the danger of speaking in such broad terms, try to give a fair definition of what Alsop and Kintner mean by appeasement and then show how you could not possibly believe in it. If, however, it means getting us into the present war - you must plead guilty - it would be great if you could get from some others who hold what they do - a definition of what exactly they mean, and then answer it.

Point #14: You might bring out that many of the people who want to get us into war - argue that Hitler has piece-meal gobbled up Europe's democracies and that we should avoid their mistake and get in and help while we still have England. It would seem to me that the fallacy in that argument lies in the difference between Norway's or Belgium's position and ours. We must not always identify ourselves too closely with other's experiences and try too vigorously to make them apply to ourselves.

Point #15: In talking about the gloom charge - it might be well to mention that you don't enjoy being gloomy. It's much easier to talk about how pleasant things are. The only advantage of doing so, is that you hope that it may prove of some

Despite the threat of Luftwaffe air attack, King George VI and Queen Elizabeth remained in London to bolster the morale of the public - unlike American Ambassador Kennedy who literally 'ran away' as soon as he was able.
(W/O Paddy Porter Collection)

value to the country. You believe that the optimists in England and France did their countries a profound disservice. It is not that you believe that come hell or high water - everything is going to be bad. I think you have to show some hope for the future - otherwise people will say 'oh well - no matter what we do - he says we are all doomed'. Rather than you think that by preparing for the worst - you may be able to meet it. You might bring it home by saying that you have seen plenty of optimists cleaned out in the stock market before you went into the diplomatic service - and you have seen plenty of optimistic statesmen cleaned out since then.

It seems to me that you've got a wonderful point here, provided you make it appear you are not gloomy for gloom's sake. You can bring out those French optimists who believed in the Maginot line etc. You might bring out that it is necessary for politicians to stress the bright side of things - they are in politics and must get the people's vote - you don't care what people think - you are interested only in the long run point of view of what is best for this country.

Point #16: I noticed in Alsop and Kintner's latest article that they said you odayed (?) Lyon's story twice. I should think it would be easy to disprove this. The Globe [thought to be the *Boston Globe* newspaper] itself might help you out.

Point #17: It is well to remember that businessman are always distrusted as being the

prime appeasers, due to the fact that this was the group that is promoted it in England. This is why I emphasise that you will have to disclaim any similar beliefs 'having confidence in the dictatorships' etc. This, of course, will not interfere or in any way change what your views really are. It is merely just a point that you should emphasise.

Clearly from the previous the young JFK was providing his father Joe with some serious advice as to how to handle media attacks on him.

The Feds are watching...
The FBI, under the leadership of J. Edgar Hoover, opened a file on Joseph Kennedy, just as it did with many other prominent people. Joe

Kennedy's FBI files are now available to the public and show the extent of the interest the FBI had in him. One unidentified person wrote the following on Ambassador Kennedy:

'(Blank) described Mr Kennedy as a man with a very dynamic personality who was brilliant and that he feels there is not a more patriotic man in the United States than Mr Kennedy.

'He said that Mr Kennedy is a man whose temperament is such that he easily becomes angry and that during the time he is angry, he does not care what he says. He stated, however, that he does not believe that even during a period of anger, Mr Kennedy is the type of man who would reveal any information which would be detrimental to the interests of the United States'.

An FBI memo from Director Hoover to his aide, D M Ladd, gives more information on the Bureau's relationship with Ambassador Kennedy: 'In June 1938, Special Agent (Blank) advised that he had received very cordial treatment from Ambassador Kennedy in London, while (Blank) was there visiting Scotland Yard. Kennedy's Ambassadorship to Britain is widely regarded in the United States as demonstrating that Kennedy was an appeaser and believed that Britain would lose the war. His appointment during this period is thought to be important only as it throws light on his present views about Russia as reported by Mr Arthur Krock.

'Arthur Krock, of the New York Times … described Kennedy as spokesman for a group of industrialists and financiers, who believe that Russia should not be opposed at any point. All energies should be devoted to keeping America prosperous'.

The FBI was interested in using Joe Kennedy as a source of information, and the memos from that time spell out what they hoped to gain from his knowledge of world affairs. On 18 October 1943, well after Kennedy ended his role as

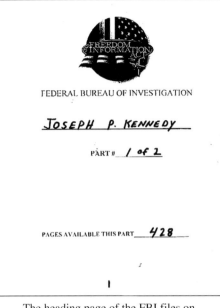

FEDERAL BUREAU OF INVESTIGATION

JOSEPH P. KENNEDY

PART # 1 of 2

PAGES AVAILABLE THIS PART 428

The heading page of the FBI files on Joseph P Kennedy

ambassador to Great Britain, Hoover wrote the following memo to the special agent in charge in the FBI's Boston office:

'In the event, you feel that Mr Kennedy is in a position to offer active assistance to the Bureau such as is expected of Special Service Contacts, there is no objection to utilizing him in this capacity. If he can be made use of like a Special Service Contact, the Bureau should be advised as to the nature of the information he is able to provide, or the facilities he can offer for the Bureau's use. Every effort should be made to provide him with investigative assignments in keeping with his particular ability, and the Bureau should be advised the nature of these assignments, together with the results obtained.'

Despite the work that Ambassador Kennedy did for the Bureau (and the records do not reflect exactly what he did), Director Hoover 'recommended that the meritorious service award not be awarded to Mr Joseph P. Kennedy for the reason that he has not affirmatively actually done anything of special value to the Bureau despite his willingness to perform such services.'

A nest of spies?

The FBI file on Kennedy is well over 400 pages thick. Twenty four pages relate to the affair of a cypher clerk who was spying out of the American Embassy while Joseph Kennedy was ambassador.

Tyler Gatewood Kent (b. 24 March 1911 d. 20 November 1988) was born in Newchwang, Manchuria where his father was the US Consul. Kent went to the prestigious Kent School in Connecticut, then to St. Albans, with other sons of upper-echelon journalists, diplomats, politicians, and high-ranking civil servants. He starred in soccer and football and won St. Albans' top prize for languages. At Princeton, it was the same: top marks in languages, with a summer studying Russian at the Sorbonne, then Spanish at the University of Madrid. At five-feet nine inches tall, with wavy brown hair, and fluent in a range of languages that included Icelandic, Kent had the perfect pedigree to be a leader in America's foreign service. In later life, he admitted that he had anti-Semitic tendencies for many years. He also believed that '.. *all wars are inspired, fermented and promoted by the great international bankers and banking combines which are largely controlled by the Jews.*'

Through his father's connections, he joined the State Department and was posted to Moscow under William C Bullitt, the first American ambassador to the Soviet Union. Kent was chosen for his knowledge of Russian, but he had other advantages: a glowing letter of recommendation from Democratic Virginia Senator Harry F Byrd topped a stack of endorsements from publishers, bank presidents, and a Princeton Assistant Dean. Kent was hired on 12 February 1934, for a salary of $2,500, plus housing and food allowances. There he was promoted to the trusted post of cipher clerk encrypting and decrypting information that ranged from 'Confidential' right up to 'Top Secret'.

Kent soon became bored - he spent time denouncing Jews, claiming they were driving humanity to a new war. He took to heavy drinking and equally heavy womanising, pursuing actresses and ballet dancers – some of them planted at the Metropole Hotel and a rented dacha by The People's Commissariat for Internal Affairs (Народный комиссариат внутренних дел, Narodnyi Komissariat Vnutrennikh Del), abbreviated NKVD. Soon Kent was sharing his bed with Tatiana (Tanya) Alexandrovnaya Ilovaiskaya, a blond, green-eyed part-time translator for International News Service's Moscow bureau, and full-time operative of the NKVD.

It did not take long for Kent to discover that his girlfriend was an NKVD agent –she made no effort to conceal it or her privileges – and just as quickly, he was passing secrets to her from the Embassy, stealing copies of classified signals from the embassy code room, and giving them to Tanya and the NKVD. It wasn't hard – all the safes were left open, and the codebooks lay on the tables, and morale among the poorly paid

Tyler Gatewood Kent's 'mugshot' taken on 27 May 1940.

code clerks was low.

In late 1938, Kent returned to the USA on leave and took the oral examination to become a Foreign Service officer. He failed and returned to his Moscow Embassy post, and decided to celebrate by giving away the State Department's Gray Code - named by the colour of the code book binding - to the NKVD.

Kent wasn't the only one in the Embassy that the Soviets could exploit. Ambassador Bullitt was a bisexual, having an affair with his confidential clerk and Embassy Third Secretary, Carmel Offie. Charge d'Affaires Alexander Kirk was homosexual and a drug addict. And Chief Code Clerk Henry W. Antheil, Jr., was also giving secrets to the Soviets. When the FBI suspected Antheil, his new appointment as Chief Code Clerk at the US Embassy in London was put on hold during the investigation.

With Antheil unavailable for the London post, the United States ambassador to the Court of St. James needed a new code clerk and quickly. Kent was available, had good reports from his superiors, and was eager to get out of Moscow.

Kent left the Soviet Union on 23 September 1939, travelling through Finland, Sweden, and Norway to reach Great Britain. In Sweden, he journeyed with Ludwig Matthias, a German native but naturalized Swedish citizen, who was managing director of the Ultramare Trading Company of Stockholm. Matthias was a suspected double agent, working for the Germans and the Russians, now allies of convenience under the Nazi-Soviet Non-Aggression Pact. Matthias gave Kent a cigar box to carry to Great Britain as a favour, to avoid British customs search, and Kent agreed. Matthias said he would pick it up in London.

Tyler Kent reported to the American Embassy at Grosvenor Square in Mayfair on Thursday, 5 October, and at first stayed

Anna Nikolayevna Wolkova (b. 1902, d 2 August 1973), sometimes known as Anna de Wolkoff is seen in her wartime Auxilliary Fire Service uniform

at the Cumberland Hotel. There, Matthias came to collect his package. This meeting was noted by two detectives from Scotland Yard's Special Branch, who were following Matthias, believing him to be a German spy. While it seems more likely that Matthias was, in fact, working for the Soviets, the British were clearly concerned that this suspicious man was socialising with a code clerk from the US Embassy, and began to watch both.

Kent moved from his hotel into a two-room flat at 47 Gloucester Place, Marylebone paying £5 a week rent. From all accounts, Kent disliked Great Britain, seeing it as run by the Jews he hated - that fury was heightened by his inability to gain the status, perks, and higher pay of a Foreign Service Officer.

In the US Embassy codes which Kent worked, vast amounts of traffic went between London and Washington, including personal messages between Roosevelt and First Lord of the Admiralty Winston Churchill were sent in the familiar Grey code.

Kent immediately started stealing signal traffic, but he had no one to sell or give them to. But from reading the correspondence between Churchill and Roosevelt, Kent decided that the President and the First Lord of the Admiralty were working to remove Chamberlain and put Churchill in power.

To keep up his conversational Russian, he connected with London's White Russian community, which was centered on the Russian Tea Room, a café-restaurant at 50 Harrington Gardens, opposite the South Kensington Underground Station.

The boss was Admiral Nikolai Wolkova, a formidably-bearded man who had been Tsar Nicholas II's naval attaché in London at the time of the October Revolution of 1917. Trapped in London by the collapse of his

The Military Attachés and others operating out of the American Embassy in London never knew when they were going to be in danger - the Luftwaffe bombed indiscriminately, including the playing fields of Eton.
(W/O Paddy Porter Collection)

empire, Wolkova, his wife Vera and their four children stayed in London, broke and homeless. Well-to-do British friends set the Wolkovas up in the café business.

By 1940, Admiral Wolkova's three daughters and one son had all become naturalised British citizens; the family star was 36-year-old daughter Anna Nikolayevna Wolkova, sometimes known as Anna de Wolkoff.

Anna ran the tea room with her cooking skills, and a successful dress design salon as well, but her main business was her absolute hatred of Bolshevism as a Jewish plot. She was furious that her Admiral father was rewarded for a lifetime of service to Mother Russia by having to own a restaurant in London. Her hatred of Jews pre-

dated the October Revolution. *'I was brought up on that, ever since I was a child...'* she testified at her trial. *'Every Russian, especially of my standing, hates Jews. I was literally suckled on it.'*

When Britain entered the war, Anna and her father both regarded it as a mistake, saying the decision was engineered by Jews. They called upon Prime Minister Chamberlain to make peace. Anna had access to some high society through her dress design business - her clientele included the Duchess of Gloucester and Wallis Simpson, the Duchess of Windsor.

Sharing a mutual hatred of Jews, Anna and Kent became friends, and possibly lovers, sharing weekends together. Kent transferred her car to his name, so he could use Embassy fuel coupons.

Kent found a mistress via Anna, one Irene Danischewsky, the redheaded wife of Alexander Danischewsky, another White Russian émigré and business figure. Oddly enough, Irene and her husband were Jewish. Irene and her husband were already under surveillance by MI5 as possible Soviet spies due to their regular visits to the USSR.

Irene wasn't Kent's only girlfriend – he had several. Irene was the elder sister of Basil Mirionoff, whose daughter, Helen, would later change her name to Mirren, and go on as an actress to win an Oscar for playing Queen Elizabeth II in the 2006 movie *The Queen*.

Through Anna, Kent also met another leading British anti-Semite, Captain Archibald Henry Maule Ramsay, (*b.* 4 May 1894, *d.* 11 March 1955). Ramsay had an impressive pedigree: Eton, Sandhurst, Coldstream Guards in World War One, where he had been wounded and earned a Military Cross.

Ramsay had been one of Britain's loudest anti-Semites, speaking at Rotary Clubs about the evils of Communism and Jews, with a standard 'Red Wings Over Europe' speech, which stressed the Jewish aspects of Bolshevism. This rhetoric played well with voters in the Scottish district of Peebles and Southern Midlothian in the 1931 General Election, gaining him the seat amid the despair of the Great Depression. Once in the House of Commons, Ramsay was no great success, introducing the Aliens Restriction (Blasphemy) Bill, which would have prevented aliens residing in Britain from attending international communist congresses. He was also a rabid supporter of Francisco Franco when the Spanish Civil War broke out.

When not denouncing Communists on the House floor, he did so for the National Citizens Union, the Order of the Child, and the British Israel World Federation, which claimed that the British - not the Jews - were God's 'Chosen People'.

Ramsay was also a supporter of the Anglo-German Fellowship, a respectable enough organisation in peacetime, which sought better

Ambassador Kennedy, centre, talks with volunteer drivers of the American Ambulance Unit of Great Britain in London, July 1940. Kennedy donated the money to purchase one of the vehicles.
(W/O Paddy Porter Collection)

The bombs may have fallen, the street may be full of rubble, but life goes on, and there is still work to be done. *(W/O Paddy Porter Collection)*

relations between Britain and Germany. Two of its members were Communist infiltrators reporting to their masters in Moscow, Kim Philby and Guy Burgess.

More worrisome to Special Branch was Ramsay's membership in an group called 'The Link', an extreme pro-German organisation, whose branches numbered 35 and membership 4,329. Through its official organ, the *Anglo-German Review*, it spouted Joseph Goebbels' lies almost verbatim. Even that wasn't enough for the angry Ramsay. He formed his group in May 1938, the 'Right Club', which was a secret society, in best schoolboy style, with emblem (an eagle crushing a viper), ranks (based on how much members paid), and pro-Nazi rhetoric. Its members included a bizarre array of characters: William Joyce, the future Lord Haw-Haw, was number eight on the list, but other members included such names as four of the five Mitford girls, twelve Members of Parliament, and the current Duke of Wellington, who coordinated the Right Club's pro-German, anti-Communist, and anti-Semitic activities.

Ramsay, describing the Right Club, boasted that '*...The main objective was to oppose and expose the activities of organised Jewry*'.

Even though Anna Wolkova was under surveillance by the British and the Americans knew that she could not be stealing secret correspondence from the US Embassy in London – there had to be a leak in Grosvenor Square.

She was also bragging to her friends that Kent was telling her about confidential exchanges between Kennedy and the British foreign secretary, Lord Halifax and that '*...Tyler Kent was using the American diplomatic bag on behalf of the Right Club for communicating with contacts in the United States.*' Allegedly Ramsay even turned over his locked red leather-bound ledger to Kent for safekeeping, hoping that Kent's diplomatic immunity would prevent it from being found in a police raid.

On 18 May Guy Liddell, director of B Division at MI5, head of Britain's counterespionage service contacted US Embassy official Herschel Johnson, who phoned Ambassador Kennedy at his residence in Windsor he was dining with Clare Boothe Luce, the playwright, future ambassador to Italy, and wife of *Time-Life* magnate Henry Luce. Johnson could only give bare details over the unsecured phone line. Kennedy was shocked.

Next day, Johnson drove to Windsor to give Kennedy a full report, along with the British request to arrest Kent and put him on trial. Kennedy had no choice but to agree to the British request and to waive diplomatic immunity.

That night Kent stole what would be his last document – a message from Churchill to Roosevelt begging the Americans for their new P-40 fighter aircraft to replace aircraft shot down over France. The letter further warned that while his administration would fight to the end, a replacement government, appointed in despair or defeat, might surrender, turning over to Hitler the immensely powerful Royal Navy.

On 20 May Knight, joined by Detective Inspector Pearson of Special Branch, two detective constables, and the US Embassy's Second Secretary, Franklin C. Gowen, knocked on the back door of 47 Gloucester Street in Marylebone. Pearson rang the bell and told the maid that he wanted to see Tyler Kent.

The maid went to find the landlady, Edith Welby, and Constable Scott followed her down, while the rest of the team headed up to the second floor, where they found Mrs. Welby. The police showed her a warrant, and she pointed out Kent's door. Detective Inspector Pearson tried it, found it locked, and rapped on it. Supposedly a man's voice yelled out, *'Don't come in!'*

Pearson put his shoulder to the door and smashed open a panel, and the lock and the Britons faced Kent, standing beside the bed in his pyjamas. The security servicemen introduced themselves, cautioned Kent and then asked if he had any property of the United States government, and more specifically that of the American embassy in London in his possession.

Kent denied having anything, but a search quickly revealed that he was lying. They found around 2,000 documents, plus glass photographic negatives of Churchill's telegrams, and Ramsay's record book.

Kent was not taken initially to a police station, but the US Embassy, where First Secretary and Consul General John G Erhardt and Herschel Johnson were waiting with Ambassador Kennedy himself in the boss's sparsely-furnished second-floor office. Kent was

kept outside Kennedy's office while the ambassador was shown the evidence. There were hundreds of papers, thirty file folders, and Kent's ledger, all ranging in classification from confidential to secret. In all, there were 1,929 separate documents, and it took British and American clerks until 4 June to list them all.

It was clear that this was espionage of the highest order: messages from Churchill to Roosevelt, including Churchill's desperate pleas for destroyers and aircraft, along with Kennedy's covering note saying that he believed Britain was doomed and the weapons should not be sent.

That message alone was unnerving for Joseph Kennedy – if it was made public, it would reveal to both the British and American publics his defeatist, anti-British stance.

The British police and American diplomats opened a tin box which contained Kent's name cards and his address book. Many of the names on the list were under surveillance by MI5 and Scotland Yard, and several would be convicted of violating the Official Secrets Act – including suspected Gestapo agent Ludwig Matthias. There were also Kent's illegally-made duplicate keys and his photographic negatives.

Records of the day show that Ambassador Kennedy was infuriated by the revelations, as he was learning the full scale of the treason for the first time, while Kent, on the other hand, remained icily calm under questioning.

The British moved – with reluctant Kennedy's approval – to have all of Kent's calls at work answered by a Special Branch detective. Despite being held, Kent continued to get plenty: from his other girlfriends, the president of the Russian Refugee Committee, and his tailor, demanding payment for an overdue £10.9.0. Kent's solicitor paid the bill later.

But the most important call came from a woman named Enid Riddell, who was wondering why Kent cancelled dinner with her after his arrest. Special Branch raided Ms Riddell's home, to find nothing incriminating. But Enid had a story to tell. The dinner that Kent was supposed to attend was to be with her and Duke Del Monte. There was the linchpin to the case – Kent was clearly giving the messages to Del Monte, who was passing them by diplomatic routes to Rome, who passed them to the German Embassy there, who in turn sent them to Berlin.

Churchill's son, Randolph was to provide an insight into what has been going on behind the scenes - and on the American ambassador's defeatism: *'We had reached the point of bugging potential traitors and enemies. Joe Kennedy, the American ambassador, came under surveillance.'* Ironically, during that 20 May encounter between Tyler Kent and Kennedy, an American ambassador who himself did not believe in the war, who ridiculed Britain's chances of survival, and who practised his own brand of anti-Semitism berated a lowly code clerk who shared both his politics and his prejudices. Kennedy treated the matter as he always did when his principles collided with his survival. He pulled the rug on Kent. Two days after his talk with the ambassador, Kent was fired by the State Department, Kennedy denied him diplomatic immunity and the code clerk remained in the custody of the British.

The British had their man. The Americans were furious. With Secretary of State Cordell

The Old Bailey Court in London where Tyler Kent and Anna de Wolkoff were placed on trial. The building itself was severely damaged by German bombing. *(W/O Paddy Porter Collection)*

Hull laid low by illness, UnderSecretary of State Sumner Welles was in charge. He exploded at the department's number three, Breckinridge Long, both over the espionage and the potential damage the exposure could do for American foreign relations with Britain, invaded neutrals like Belgium and The Netherlands, and nations still on the war's sidelines. And what else could Kent have stolen?

The State Department ordered a full investigation of its London Embassy and found that at least no code or cypher books were missing. But Long scrutinised the list of recovered documents and found it *'appalling. Hundreds of copies – true readings – of dispatches, cables, messages . . . It is a terrible blow – almost a major catastrophe'*.

Kent was taken to a cell at New Scotland Yard. Knight presented Kent with a letter from Kennedy saying that he had been dismissed from the US Foreign Service, which Kent had to sign. With Kent in jail came a new issue for the British – he had to be charged with something. So far, Kent was being held under the Emergency Powers (Defence) Act, passed through Parliament on 24 August 1939, when a war was likely. It gave the government the right to impose a wide range of restrictions on the public, but it had been amended several times. It could not be used to arrest people simply on suspicion that they were about to commit an offense.

The arrest of Kent and Anna Wolkoff forced a new regulation, 18B(1A), which became law, permitting the detention of members of hostile organisations on the suspicion that they were likely to endanger public safety, the prosecution of the war, and the defence of the realm.

On 22 May Churchill asked the Lord President of the Council, Neville Chamberlain, his predecessor as Prime Minister, to chair a meeting of the War Cabinet to approve special new regulations for imprisoning British Fascists as well as enemy aliens. He told Chamberlain *'I will agree to whatever the Cabinet thinks best. If any doubt existed, the persons in question should be detained without delay.'*

On 23 May Kent was given a deportation order under the Alien Restriction Acts of 1914 and 1919, never to be allowed to return to the United Kingdom. Kent was delighted. He

HE TOLD HITLER ALL OUR WAR SECRETS

GERMANY, in the early days of the war, knew the exact strength of our fighting forces, their dispositions, our inventory of war materials, our prospective war production and our strategic plans—through TYLER KENT, a code clerk at the United States Embassy in London.

Last night, for the first time the full story of the activities of this traitor—now serving seven years' penal servitude in a British jail—was revealed by MR. JOSEPH KENNEDY, American Ambassador at the time.

Mr. Kennedy said: "In the period after Britain had declared war Mr. Churchill was very complete in revealing to me, and through me to Mr. Roosevelt, Britain's unpreparedness.

"Mr. Churchill and other high British officials gave me the whole picture—figures on Britain's land, sea and air forces, the disposition of British units everywhere, Britain's home inventory of war materials, her prospective war production, and the fundamentals of Britain's strategic plans.

Terrible Damage

"Week by week these were forwarded to Mr. Roosevelt in an 'unbreakable' code.

"We had to assume that week by week this same data went to Berlin via Kent.

"As a code clerk Kent had the unbreakable code book at his elbow and that is what did terrible damage."

Mr. Kennedy disclosed that because of Kent's arrest America's diplomatic communications throughout the world were blacked out in the weeks before the fall of France.

The black-out lasted from two to six weeks, until couriers had reached the embassies with new codes.

Kent transmitted his information via Italy and Mr. Kennedy said that Italy might have been ordered to stay out of the war for 14 months because of her usefulness to Germany as a transmission channel for information.

Beans Spilled

He emphasised that Italy did not go to war until after Kent's arrest.

Scotland Yard found copies of 1,500 documents locked in a strong box in Kent's rooms.

"The beans were spilled" when the Italian Embassy telephoned Kent's rooms while Scotland Yard men and United States Embassy officials were there.

If America had been at war, Mr. Kennedy added, he would have recommended that Kent be sent back to America to be shot.

Mr. Kennedy waived diplomatic immunity with the approval of the State Department and turned Kent over to the British authorities.—Reuter.

OFFICE OF THE LEGAL ATTACHE AMERICAN EMBASSY LONDON, ENGLAND

165-27850-A

INDEXED 87 SEP 15 1944

A newspaper cutting, apparently from 1944 about the activities of Tyler Kent. The article, one of a number collected by the American Embassy in London is in the FBI files on Joespeh Kennedy.

thought it would get him home immediately, without trial or further embarrassment. But the order allowed the Crown to hold him in jail pending the pleasure of the Home Office. Kent was moved from Scotland Yard to His Majesty's Prison in Pentonville, London's central prison.

There Knight resumed interrogating Kent. The American began to cave in. Under Knight's pressure, Kent suggested in a written statement that he had photographically copied the key documents because Anna was interested in them.

That, at least, fitted in with Knight's assessment of the case, that Anna was the brain of the organisation. Now Knight believed he could easily convict Kent, Ramsay, Anna, Riddell, and a Right Club member who had been arrested, Christabel Nicholson. Del Monte, of course, enjoyed diplomatic immunity, and the Italians were unlikely to waive it.

Next was the question of what had become of the prints made from the glass negatives. The answer came in the decrypt of a German message from their ambassador in Rome to Berlin, which contained information from the Churchill-Roosevelt letters.

Kent still hoped to be deported to America, convinced his revelations would embarrass the Roosevelt administration and make him a hero to the right. However, the administration was not going to give Kent a forum in a Senate subcommittee hearing to voice his political views and justify his espionage. Sumner Welles cabled London on 22 May that Washington had no objection to the British prosecuting Kent, saying *'Publicity in connection with such charges might not be helpful under the circumstances'*. Embassy employees were ordered not to discuss Kent's disappearance.

On the British side, Kent's arrest was covered by wartime censorship regulations. When the *New York Herald Tribune* carried a brief item on 25 May that the British authorities were holding an unnamed employee, Secretary of State Hull, back at work, denied any knowledge of such an incident.

On 1 June, the British Home Office issued a statement approved by Hull that said, *'In consequence of action taken by the American Ambassador (Mr Joseph P. Kennedy) in cooperation with the British authorities, Tyler Kent, a clerk who had been dismissed from the employment of the American government, has been detained by order of the Home Secretary'*. The story hit the British papers, their American counterparts picked it up, and the US State Department gave a terse, *'No comment'*.

Now the legal battle started. At the end of May, Kent was moved to Brixton Prison in south London, a facility for persons awaiting trial and detainees under Section 18B. Since all were under remand and not sentence, conditions were quite good: no labour, decent food, books, laundry facilities, and civilian clothes instead of prison-issue uniforms.

Kent still believed he would get off because of the importance of his papers and himself, and ignored the warden's suggestion that he hire a good solicitor to handle the case and a barrister to represent him in court, under Britain's double-edged legal system. Kent was expecting a public trial, where he could denounce the British, Americans, Jews, and the whole set-up.

He was wrong. The British prosecutors had an advantage – they could conduct the trial 'in camera', meaning that the whole proceedings could be behind locked doors, with the press excluded and the lawyers and jurors sworn to secrecy. They had already done so with captured German spies who had refused to turn and become double-agents for the British.

Given that environment, Kent could not make grandiose statements from the witness box that would be taken down by the press. Ironically, if Kent had not given his papers and glass plates to Anna Wolkoff, but instead taken them home to America, he could have shown them to isolationist American senators, congressmen, and press barons, who would have trumpeted his views.

Instead the British sent a memorandum to Kennedy giving a list of the documents: they could not be shown in public, but they would be used as evidence against Kent. *'Investigators feel that in the interests of Great Britain all the defendants should be prosecuted with rigour,'* it read. But it would still take months for the trial to commence.

On 1 August 1940, Tyler Kent was driven to Bow Street Police Station, to finally be charged. There he saw Anna Wolkoff for the first time since 18 May. Both were charged with several violations of the Official Secrets Act, Kent with larceny, Anna with violations of the Defense Regulations.They were remanded in custody and returned to their cells. The press was not allowed into the courtroom and only given the general charges and none of the specific allegations.

At last Kent began to take his position seriously. He asked for legal counsel. The Embassy was in a tight spot – he was spying against them, but Kent was still an American citizen, a former State Department employee, and entitled to US protection. Hull ordered Kennedy to get Kent competent counsel, to ensure that the trial would be fair. The State Department found a reputable London solicitor, F Graham Maw, to represent Kent. Kennedy cabled Hull to note that the magistrates court appearance fees alone were $400 to $500, and further defence costs as much as $1,500 to $2,000. Kent had $2,000 in his Riggs National Bank account in Washington, but not much more than that. His spying had been ideology-based, not for profit. Kennedy urged the lawyers to work for minimal fees.

Now the legal machinery could grind into action. On 27 August Kent and Anna appeared at Bow Street again and were committed for trial at the Central Criminal Court, the Old Bailey, to start on 23 October.

Kent arrived at the courtroom on 23 October just after 9 am, in a prison van that entered an inner courtyard. Anna arrived after that, and both were placed in separate, white-tiled cells, until 11 am, when they faced Justice Sir Frederick Tucker, who wore red robes, white facings, and white wig. Brown paper was pasted on the windows and glass door panels.

Kent's barrister was Maurice Healy, and Anna was represented by Mr C G L Du Cann, part of a distinguished legal family. Representing the Crown in both cases was Solicitor General Sir William Jowitt (later Earl Jowitt), who was also a Labour MP in Churchill's coalition government.

Kent was explicitly charged with obtaining documents that *'might be directly or indirectly useful to an enemy'* and letting Wolkoff have them in her possession. He was also accused of stealing documents that were the property of Ambassador Kennedy. The only spectators allowed at the trial were official observers, including Malcolm Muggeridge, representing MI6. Two of the witnesses against Kent were Maxwell Knight and Archibald Ramsay, who

was interned on the Isle of Man under Defence Regulation 18B because he had seen the documents. British officials who were knowledgeable of the documents believed that if they had come to light at that time, it would have severely damaged Anglo-American relations, for they showed that Roosevelt was looking at ways to evade the Neutrality Acts, to help Britain survive a German onslaught. It would also have damaged Roosevelt's re-election bid for the presidency that year.

In his trial, Kent also admitted that he had taken documents from the US Embassy in Moscow, with the vague notion of someday showing them to US senators who shared his isolationist, anti-semitic views. He said that he burned the Moscow documents before being assigned to London. It was learned later that he had fallen in love with an interpreter who worked for the NKVD, thus fueling speculations that he had Soviet contacts.

On 7 November 1940, he was convicted and sentenced to seven years imprisonment. Isolationist groups in the United States claimed that he had been framed and that the trial was an attempted cover-up of an attempt to get the US to join the war.

Kent appealed, and a hearing was held on 4-5 February 1941, also in camera. The appeal was dismissed.

The fact that Tyler Kent was running a spying operation in an attempt to defeat the Americans and the British out of the American Embassy in London while working under an ambassador who himself was being defeatist in attitude is somewhat ironic. It was even more ironic that at the very same time Kent was up to his nefarious activities the Embassy was being used far more extensively by the American state for very similar reasons with full permission of the British government to gather intelligence on almost a global scale. The Military Attachés begat the SPOBS, who begat the USAFBI, who begat the ETO...

Chapter Seven

SPOBS - USAFBI.

Where the Americans establish a huge intelligence gathering organisation in the American Embassy in London, 'invaded' Iceland, tried to work with Russia, learned to deal with the IRA and created an Eighth Air Force.

The American Embassy in London had been located at 4, Grosvenor Gardens from 1912, but in 1936, the three former residential buildings at numbers 1 through 3 Grosvenor Square were demolished as part of a redevelopment scheme led by the Duke of Westminster. A new neo-classical building was erected on the eastern side of the square and the American Embassy took occupancy in 1938. During the Second World War, when the US Embassy was on one side and US General Dwight D Eisenhower's headquarters on another, Grosvenor Square became popularly known as 'Little America', or 'Eisenhower Platz'. This last, Germanic, form was a joke about Eisenhower's German-origin name.

America entered World War Two two years into the war on 8 December 1941, when all but one member of Congress passed the motion one day after the attack on Pearl Harbor in Hawaii. Although America formally maintained neutrality up until that moment, the US had long been involved in the war, providing support to the Allies.

The American Embassy in Grosvenor Square. This picture was taken after the Americans moved out and it became part of the Canadian High Commission. The building has since been demolished.

In the first two years of the war, America remained politically neutral, but President Roosevelt was working hard to prepare the Americans for what he regarded to be an inevitable conflict. He felt that the war was threatening US security and tried to find ways to help the European Allies without being formally involved in the war. He persuaded Congress in November 1939 to repeal the arms embargos that were part of the neutrality law and pass the Fourth Neutrality Act, which allowed him to trade arms with countries whose defence would seem vital to the security of the United States. The US would also provide its air force and navy to escort British convoys that transported supplies leased from America to protect them from enemy U-Boats. The US military was also deployed to replace British forces in Iceland after the British invasion there.

At least, that is how history has recorded it - until now.

Even before Great Britain went to war with Germany, the Americans were aware of the need to gain information. The files of the Historical Section, European Theater of Operations, provide fascinating insights via a set of records under the umbrella title of the Special Observer Group, or SPOBS. It seems that they were in London with the full permission and knowledge of British Foreign Secretary Edward Frederick Lindley Wood, 1st Earl of Halifax and Prime Minister Neville Chamberlain.

Whether or not the 'Special Observers' were in fact spies is a matter of debate. According to most sources a spy is a person employed by a country or organisation to gather and report information about another country or organisation secretly. Certainly, the Special Observers were in Great Britain with the knowledge and permission of the British government - but whether that same government was aware of the scope and depth of the information gathering being undertaken by the Americans is by no means clear. The scale and scope of work being undertaken by the Americans out of the American Embassy in Grosvenor Square were remarkable. Its tentacles stretched back to Iceland and the very north of Canada, westwards to the Middle East and as far as Moscow.

Almost all of the 'work' done initially was conducted by Military or Air Attachés. A military attaché is a military expert who is attached to a diplomatic mission (an attaché). This post is typically filled by a military officer who retains the commission while serving in an embassy. Opportunities sometimes arise for service in the field with military forces of another state.

An air attaché typically represents the chief of his home air force in the foreign country where he serves. The day-to-day responsibilities include maintaining contacts between the host nation and the attaché's air force. This includes arranging official visits, exchange postings and exercises. Other duties of an air attaché include travelling around the host country to determine the extent of air force infrastructure and then filing intelligence reports with the home air force. Many of the travels are disguised as other types of trips, such as vacations or family trips, otherwise, the air attaché could be expelled for spying if caught doing so.

On a smaller diplomatic mission which does not have its own air attaché, the role of the air attaché is carried out by the defence attaché who also deals with army and navy matters. Sizable diplomatic missions may be served by both an air attaché and an assistant air attaché.

The key document used here is a 204-page report called 'SPOBS. *The Special Observer Group Prior To The Activation Of The European Theater Of Operations*' drawn up in October 1944.

Even though the war was still nowhere near over and American forces were still very much in the UK, the difficulties of obtaining primary source documentation was very much to the fore, as the preface to the document explained: '*The aim of this work is to give authenticated facts clearly and simply. A secondary aim is to preserve the gist of significant and vital documents available in the theater. Many important ones to which references are made are now moldering in storage depots, forgotten warehouses and individuals' 201 files*'.

'*The history of the Indigo (Iceland) Force suffers from many gaps. This inadequacy arises because direct correspondence between headquarters, Indigo Force, the War Department was authorised. The letter in which Major General Chaney received his instructions before he came to England has not been located in the theater. Only such quotations as were read to the British officials were available. These and many other gaps await further research in repositories outside this theater. However, it is our hope that*

The Air Raid Warden (right) could be anyone - plain Mrs Smith, or a well-known art dealer. If the night was quiet, they could catch some sleep at the post. If it was not so quiet, they might get none.

Whistles mean fire-bombs, rattles mean gas It was all in a night's work.

There was no doubt that 'London could take it'.

this groundwork will obviate trouble for historians later'.

The Report gave a synopsis of the period January 1939 up to around June 1942.

'*On the eve of World War Two, few people thought that the United States would eventually be drawn into the conflict. As the war progressed, it became the duty of four military experts* [as quoted in the original primary source documents] *to profit from the costly experience of the combatants. The battlegrounds were proving grounds, and gradually the United States profited from the technical findings of several warring nations, especially from Great Britain.*

Because the United States maintained her neutrality, at least theoretically until December 8, 1941, it was necessary for her to proceed with her wartime preparations with a special caution. Nevertheless, as circumstances developed it became increasingly obvious that the United

States could not retain her neutrality. To await an actual declaration of war before making preparations would have been foolhardy.

While manpower was being drafted and men were being trained within the boundaries of the United States, reconnaissance along the lines of proposed operational plans was taking place in Great Britain.

The first representations of the War Department in Great Britain worked through the American Embassy. The offices of the Military Attaché for Air were used to advantage. During the early 1939 Colonel R F Lee, Col. Martin Scanlon, Lt Col. Bradford G Chyoweth, Maj. Stadler, and Brigadier General Sherman Miles were all assigned to the American Embassy in Great Britain and functioned as Military Attachés.

The amount of activity and the emphasis placed upon the office of the Military Attaché for Air during the years 1939 and 1940 was both sizeable and significant.

During that period thirty-six officers had visited London as Military Attachés, or Assistant Military Attachés of the Army and Air Corps or as observers. On October 24, 1940 General Frank Scowden and Colonel Raymond Bliss were assigned to the London Embassy as Military

Observers - the first usage of that term in the American Group in London.

It was not until 19 May 1941 that the Special Observers or SPOBs were officially organised as a Headquarters Detachment. General order #1 dated 19 May 1941 placed Major General James E Chaney in command. Prior to this date, according to personnel orders #235, 5 October 1940, Chaney had been ordered to investigate the efficiency of foreign aircraft, power plants, instruments, equipment, methods of operation of foreign aircraft, investigate the operation of commercial and military airlines and the performance of their aircraft and equipment. He had been rated technical observer.

Part of Chaney's task it seems involved working with the Royal Aircraft Establishment at Farnborough, who were investigating equipment removed from shot down enemy aircraft and with the Royal Air Force's 1426 (Enemy Aircraft) Flight - the so-called RAFwaffe. (see *Operation Lusty The Race For Hitler's Secret Technology* Pen & Sword 2016 by the same author). Chaney and his subordinates observed the German air drive against the British for more than a month, before returning to New York and submitting a report to the War Department from his base at Mitchell Field on 15 December1940.

On Saturday 7 September 1940, the sirens wailed again - this time in earnest. The German Blitzkrieg, so loudly promised and philosophically awaited began with the bombing of the docks in London. But Great Britain was ready.

Since the early 1800s the Burlington Arcade Piccadilly was a symbol of luxury and frivolity, Bombed, it achieved a kind of Piranesian grandeur.

This and other assorted Teutonic modifications pockmarked the London landscape during the blitz.

Below, Park Crescent marks the point where John Nash's superb Regent Street design finally flows into Regents Park; that is, until the Nazis decided upon some urban landscape changes.

The Chaney Report

This report is of great importance since it is one of the chief sources on this battle over Great Britain in the autumn of 1940. It includes the following topics: the air war over England; reasons for the success of the British; German aviation equipment; air raid precautions services; pilot training coordination and cooperation between Army, Navy and Air Force; German air strength and the possibility of an invasion of England. The immediate importance of this document nevertheless is that what it very definitely pointed the way to the solution of some of the defence problems of the United States. The report is scientific and based upon data obtained by observing the repair and maintenance of planes both day and night.

After pointing out that both in numbers and efficiency German aircraft had been greatly overrated, and describing the failure of the German air blitz, Maj. Gen Chaney discounted the danger of invasion, declaring: *'Before an invasion attempt, the Germans must get superiority in the air for an extended time over southern England and the Channel.*

Based upon their daylight operations to date,

it will be difficult for them to do so unless they have some effective surprise plan of action known only to them or a tremendous number of excellent fighter aeroplanes and pilots which they have not used so far.

Chaney expressed doubt that the Germans possessed any formidable secret weapons, and declared that the device of which they had boasted was probably the magnetic mine. He added that the British had already become familiar with this invention. He went even farther and was willing to predict that Britain would not lose the war. The significant paragraph read as follows: *'I do not believe that the Germans can invade England successfully, and with Britain maintaining control of the sea, I do not believe that England will lose the war. I believe that she is better able than Germany or Italy, in spite of being subjected to a severe air and the submarine blockade and to heavy night bombing attacks, neither of which will be decisive in my opinion, to endure a long war, and that by continuing to build her bombing strength, and tighten her blockade, over a long period of time a combination of circumstances is much more likely to develop in her favour toward winning the war than for the Axis powers'.*

The closing paragraphs of the report concerned recommendations as to which British methods the United States could best adopt to expedite its own defence programme. He advised the acquisition of much aircraft equipment as well as modern night fighters and high altitude day

fighters. Significant also were his definite recommendations for a federal system of alarms supervised by a federal agency and a well-planned civilian defence organisation. Having observed the valuable services of the women's auxiliary Corps in Great Britain he recommended that similar organisations be formed in the USA.

This was in direct contradiction to what many citizens, military and civil officials in the United States thought during the autumn of 1940. They harboured two fears: firstly that the British would be able to withstand the axis air blitz and invasion efforts, and secondly that the American defence programme could not make sufficient progress to uphold the National honour. Their views had been strengthened by the published views of Ambassador Kennedy, who after all, 'was there'. One must surmise that those few who had access to the Chaney Report were both favourably impressed and reassured.

Above: The *Times* building gave concrete evidence of the Nazi dislike of humanities and free speech.

Left: Bomb damage to this Methodist chapel created a surreal image something akin to a ruined Greek temple. *(both W/O Paddy Porter Collection).*

Chaney based report not only on observations and interviews with RAF officers but also upon the statistical reports on the raids which were published regularly by the British government. These statements revealed, for example, that even though one objective of the 1940s blitz was to destroy British airfields, at no one time during the 1940 raids was more than one airfield inoperative. They also revealed that no one airfield was unable to function for a period longer than three days.

Major General James E Chaney (*b.* 16 March 1885, *d.* 21 August 1967) (left) makes a visit to Bradley Field. Colonel George E. Lovell Jr., base commander, is on the extreme right and Colonel Ivor Massey has his back to the camera. *(NARA)*

the State Department to Joseph P Kennedy, Washington 16 October 1940 in File 121.)

On 13 August 1940, two high-ranking officers, Major General Delos Emmons and Brigadier General George V Strong, were designated as special military observers attached to the American Embassy in London. This was advised by a John C Erhardt to the Right Honourable Viscount Halifax, the British Foreign Secretary, on 5 August 1940.

The devil is in the detail
When looking at the details of the SPOBS document - recorded here in italics - there are a myriad of facinating revelations that seem to have been previously lost to history.

'The concern of the War Department over the European situation is reflected by the appointment of two officers to attaché posts in London on 14 May 1940. Colonel Carl A Spaatz, Air Corps, and Captain Benjamin S Kelsey, Air Corps, being named Assistant Military Attachés and Assistant Military Attachés for Air as recorded in File 121 (1940) Military Attaché Office, London by Instructions #1393, State Department to the American Embassy London of the same date. These officers reported for duty on 4 June 1940 and remained until 16 October of the same year when the War Department ordered their return to the United States (as recorded by

What was to prove the most significant of the scores of appointments to special military Attaché and Special Observer posts in Great Britain during 1940 however, was the one made after the start of the blitz of the Germans against Great Britain on 8 August.

'Major General Eugene Chaney and Capt James Gordon P Saville, Air Corps, were ordered on 1 October to go to observe developments in this great air battle. Other Air Corps officers in this group were Major General Barton Young, Major Alfred Marringer AC, Major James Taylor AC, Major Reuben Moffat AC, Major I S Tyler AC, Major Robert Douglas AC, Major Kerrner Hertford AC, Major Robert Williams AC Capt. Frank Armstrong AC and Capt Reginald Vance AC. Brig. Gen. Frank Snowden and Col. Raymond Bliss reached London on the same day to be military observers.

These movements were recorded in a

Left: Carl Andrew 'Tooey' Spaatz (*b.* 28 June 1891, *d.* 14 July 1974), was an American Air Force General, and one of the early air attachés in the American Embassy in London.

Right: Frank Alton Armstrong Jr. (*b.* 24 May 1902, *d.* 20 August 1969) was a lieutenant general of the United States Air Force. In 1940 he was just a captain in the USAAC when he was a Special Observer in London.

Memorandum from G Bryan Conrad, SD 1869, American Embassy, London. Incidentally, the ' Capt. Frank Armstrong' noted therein was Frank Alton Armstrong Jr. was the inspiration for the main character in the novel and subsequent film, *Twelve O'Clock High*.

The synopsis continued: '*On June 11 1941 a memo to Brigadier General Joseph T McNarny defined the SBOB function as follows: 'the SBOB will constitute the normal channel for the collection and transmission of military information pertaining to joint operations and the allocation of military equipment for projected operations both joint and unilateral'*.

Colonel Oliver Stanley in a War Cabinet meeting on American Liaison, on 27 May 1941 mentioned the main object in establishing nucleus sub-missions in London and Washington was 'to ensure that the machinery would be ready so that the change over from peace to war could be effected rapidly and smoothly if the United States decided to come into the war'.

Specifically the functions of the Special Observers in London included the following:

1. *Coordinating all details in connection with transportation, reception, location and accommodation of United States troops and Air Corps personnel in Great Britain under the joint United States-Great Britain war plan.*
2. *To assist in the coordination of the allocation of equipment from United States production and advise the United States*

Chiefs of Staff on how these requests could best be met in general interests.

3. *General Chaney was directed to inform the United States Chiefs of Staff on the manner in which US Army and Air Corps forces should be employed in the United Kingdom.*
4. *Deal with problems arising in connection with the joint basic war plan agreed upon in the Washington conversations.*

In London SPOBS functions were, from the army side organised in the following manner:

Colonel John E Dahl Dahlquist GSC was G-1 coordinator. His duties included coordination with the British for accommodation, recreation discipline etc. of American forces in Britain.

Colonel Homer Case, SSC was responsible for the G-2 functions, with emphasis on obtaining enemy information, especially in its bearing on possible operations of US forces.

Colonel Harold H McClelland GSC was assigned G-3 activities which included operations and training and the exchange of information regarding the general war situation.

Colonel G W Griner was responsible for matters concerning supply, evacuation and transportation, known as G-4.

Colonel Charles L Bolte, GSC was the Plans officer whose duties were in relation to joint planning.

In 1941 one War Department operations plan known as the Rainbow #5 stated: that initially the tasks of the USA forces in the decisive theater will

Clearly posed for the camera, but the bulldog spirit of the blitz, was very real. It was a mood that the 'Special Observers' caught - but not 'Jittery Joe' Kennedy - he wanted out. *(P H T Green Collection)*

Number 67 Any Avenue, Suburbia - the morning after the night before. It was not just London that came under Luftwaffe attack. Suburbia and many of the towns and cities in the south of the country received bomb damage. (*W/O Paddy Porter Collection*).

be restricted to the defence of those areas in which bases used primarily by US forces are located, and to offensive operations from bases in the British Isles directed primarily against German military power at its source.

It further provided for a token force for the defence of the British Isles and the relief as soon as practicable of the British garrison in Iceland.

As late as 1939, Iceland and its adjacent waters were regarded as neutral, but that island suddenly assumed tremendous strategic importance, not only as a potential depot for lend-lease material but because of the assumption by American officials that it was part of the western hemisphere for defence purposes.

The likelihood of the adoption of a land lease measure gave considerable importance to the United States-British conversations in discussions termed ABC-1 in relationship to Rainbow #5 when they opened on 27 January 1941 in Washington DC.

At these meetings were members of the United States staff committee, which represented the Chief of Naval Operations and the Chief of Staff of the Army, and representatives from the Chiefs of Staff of the United Kingdom.

The American participants were Maj. Gen. Embick, Brig. Gen. Sheman Miles, Col Joseph T McNarney, Rear Admiral R L Ghormley, Rear Admiral R K Turner, Capt A G Kirk US Navy, Capt De Witt Ramsey, US Navy, and Lt. Col O T Pheiffer, Marine Corps.

Those of the United Kingdom were Rear Admiral R M Bellairs, Rear Admiral V H Danokwerts, Maj Gen. E L Morris, Capt. A W Clarke, RN, Air-Vice Marshal J C Slessor.

Representatives of three of the members of the British Commonwealth of Nations, the Dominion of Canada, the Commonwealth of Australia, and the Dominion of New Zealand were associated with the United Kingdom delegation throughout the sessions but did not participate in the joint meetings.

The agreements were introduced by the statement that the two powers would '*collaborate continuously in planning and executing operations*'. Sections 15 and 16 ABC-1 provided an outline of duties both for the British mission established in Washington and the Special Observer Group. The exact text of these sections is the following:

15. *To affect the collaboration outlined in*

paragraph 6, and to ensure the coordination of administrative action and command between the United States and British military services, the United States and the United Kingdom will exchange military missions. The function of these Missions will be as follows:

a. To represent jointly as a corporate body, their own Chief of Staff (Chief of Naval Operations considered as such) vis-a-vis the group of the Chief of Staff of the power to which they are accredited for purposes of collaboration in the formulation of military policies and plans governing the conduct of the war in areas which that power assumes responsibility for strategic direction.

On the night of 14/15 November 1940, the Luftwaffe attacked Coventry, which included the destruction of the city's historical cathedral. The bombing of Coventry was seen as the biggest test of British resolve up to this stage of the Blitz. Known as 'Operation Moonlight Sonata', over 400 bombers attacked Coventry that night. (*W/O Paddy Porter Collection*).

b. In their individual capacity to represent their own individual military services of the power to which they are accredited in matters of mutual concern in the areas in which that power assumes responsibility for strategic direction.

16. Personnel of either nation shall not become a member of any regularly constituted body of the government of the power to which they are accredited. Their staff will, however, work in direct cooperation with the appropriate branches of the committees of the staff of the power to which they are accredited.

When the United States enters the war it will provide:

A. One reinforced division to relieve British forces now charged with the defence of Ireland.

B. Troops for ground and anti-aircraft defences for such naval and air bases used primarily by the United States forces as may be agreed at the time.

C. Approximately one reinforced regiment (Brigade Group) in the United Kingdom. Note: none of the above will be available before 1 September 1941.

Tasks:

A. In conjunction with land and naval forces, defend the British Isles against air attack and invasion.

B. in conjunction with naval forces, protect shipping against surface, submarine and air attack.

C. Conduct a sustained air offensive against German military powers in all areas within range of the United Kingdom.

United States Air Forces of the order of thirty-two squadrons (bombardment and pursuit) with appropriate command echelons will be available for dispatch to the United Kingdom during 1941. Additional units will become available, the number and positions being determined by the military situations from time to time. In addition, the United States will provide one pursuit and one bombardment Squadron for the defence of Iceland.

It was obvious that ABC-1 would necessitate the establishment of a permanent US mission in London as well as the equivalent British mission in Washington. The USA was still a neutral country however and hence would not send a group called a 'Mission', without committing a serious breach of neutrality; therefore the US Army officers sent to London with the duties resembling somewhat those of the military mission were called 'Special Observers'.

Creation of the Special Observers Group.

When Major General Chaney was named head of the above group he received a set of instructions which outlined duties in accord with section 6 of ABC-1, as well as this statement: *'...your appointment as a Special Army Observer in London is preliminary to your possible appointment at a later date as army member of the United States Military Mission'.* This was detailed to the British Chiefs of Staffs committee on 21 May 1941.

The duties of Major General Chaney and his subordinate officers were to be far more varied than those of the traditional 'Missions' which powers exchange when they become allies in war. As a rule also, such missions do not develop into military commands. The Special Observer Group was to become the official core of the United States Army forces in the British Isles which in turn came to be called the European Theater of Operations.

The personnel of the Special Observer group was not made up of elderly officers, expected to report generalities upon their return from a rather brief visit to the country of a potential ally. On the contrary, the majority of the membership consisted of men in their 'forties' who were expected to submit scientific reports or were charged with specific staff responsibilities and the solution of supplying logistical problems.

The initial roster of Major General Chaney's staffs described in General Order #2, Special Observer Group London on 21 May 1941 consisted of sixteen officers and one warrant officer:

Chief of staff:	Brig Gen Joseph T McNarney.
Personnel (G-1):	Lt Col John E Dahlquist.
Intelligence (G-2):	Lt Col Homer Case .
Operations and training (G-3):	
	Col Harold M McCelland.
Supply (G-4):	Lt Col George W Griner.
War plans (G-5):	Lt Col Charles L Bolte.
Aide:	Maj Townsend Griffies.
Air Officer:	Col Alfred Jefferson Lyon.
Asst Air Officer:	Maj Ralph A Snavely .
Anti-Aircraft Officer:	Lt Col Dale Hinman.
Engineer:	Lt Col Donald A Davison.

Ordinance Officer:	Lt Col John W Coffey.
Signals Officer:	Lt Col Jerry W Matejka.
Surgeon:	Maj Arthur B Welsh.
Adjutant General:	Lt Col Iverson B Summers.
Quartermaster:	Lt Col William H Middleswart.
Warrant Officer:	Frank A Louprette.

The first enlisted men to serve with the Special Observer group were Master Sergeants Emmett Fulford, Leland Bristol, and William C Long; Technical Sergeants Ludwig A Schwaiger, Frank E Leland and Alfred J. Rapetti; and Staff Sergeants Jack P Paisley, Anthony D Christian; while, Robert E Miller and Charles W. Sole. Technical Sergeant Arthur W Could were added later.

The group formally established their London headquarters on 19 May 1941 in the American Embassy building on Grosvenor Square. The first important step of Major General Chaney was to arrange for his official call at the headquarters of the British Chief of Staff committee in the offices of the War Cabinet, Great Georges Street, London in accordance with his letter of instructions dated 26 April 1941. This occurred on 20 May.

There he met Admiral Sir Dudley Pound, First Sea Lord and Chief of Naval Staff; Field Marshall Sir John Dale, Chief of the Imperial General Staff; Air Marshal Sir Charles Portal, Chief of the Air Staff; and Major-General H L Ismay, Chief Staff Officer to the Ministry of Defence.

Payment is Required

The problem of finance had been considered before the Major General left the USA. With the end of the current fiscal year approaching on 30 June 1941 the task of obtaining necessary funds for the activities of the proposed observer group was not a simple one. At General Chaney's suggestion, a sum of $25,000 was made available from special field exercise funds for the remainder of the fiscal year. The sum mentioned was placed at the disposal of the finance officer, US Embassy London and Major General Chaney was held responsible for the efficient disbursement of Special Observer funds. This distribution of a presumed allowance of $8,493.33 per month was as follows:

Rent of office building	$3,333.33
Travel	$ 500.00
Per Diem officers	$3,060.00
Commutation of rations	$900.00
Civilian employees	$500.00
Miscellaneous	$200.00

It was therefore with definite plans in hand that the SPOBS worked in the UK. The problems which confronted the SPOBS were many and varied. G-4 functions, which later were almost wholly centred on the successful completion of the plan BOLERO, included consideration of practically every proposed activity.

On 29 May 1941 a large group of SPOBS - Major General Chaney, Brig Gen McNarney, Lt. Col Bolte and Lt Col Case, along with the United States military attaché Brig Gen Raymond E Lee attended a meeting of the Operational Planning Section, British Joint Planning Staff. The British officers present were Col The Honourable Oliver Stanley, Director of Operational Planning Section, Capt C E Lambe, representing the Admiralty; Gp Capt V E Groom, Air Ministry and Col E A F Gueterbock, and Maj H O S Harden from the War Office.

The subject of this meeting was a question from the USA regarding the equipment strength and disposition of British posts in the Near East and India. Major General Chaney declared that the information was required in Washington as a background to its policy of aid to Great Britain. Brig Gen Lee declared that the War Department had raised an important point of policy, namely the extent to which the British were prepared to release such information to the USA.

Col. Stanley replied that it was not the intention of his government to withhold the information requested, but that there was a problem as to the form in which it might be presented without being misleading. He added that the Chiefs of Staff had authorised him to be frank with the Special Observers and to reveal all facts except those relating to operations which could not be revealed to a neutral nation for security reasons. The raising of the question of security resulted in a discussion of the best means of protecting the channels between London and Washington.

The SPOBS were told that the Russians had stated as requirements 3,000 modern fighter aircraft, 3,000 modern bombers, 20,000 anti-aircraft guns and as many 'latest big bombs' as could be spared by the British. Since the reply had been that such material could not possibly be spared, then lend-lease help would be needed. As a result, there was speculation as to whether or not the recent German advance in Russia would interfere with the routes to the Soviet Union by way of the near East.

'...in general British equipment seems heavier and possibly sturdier but ours seems more compact and modern'. British munitions and weapons were often made by women, the factories slowly making the change from toys of peace to engines of war. *(both W/O Paddy Porter Collection)*

A matter of Security...

On 11 June, Lt. Col. Bolte (G-5) reported concerning channels of communication between London and Washington. He recommended that in cases when the Special Observer Group of the British Mission was not used as a channel to transmit important information between the two capitals, the proper steps being taken so that the non-channel group would become acquainted with the facts. He also recommended that the Special Observer group in London and the British military mission in Washington constitutes the normal channels for the collection and transmission of military information about joint operations and the allocation of military equipment for projected activities both joint and unilateral. All other material was to be requested collected and transmitted through the existing military attaché system.

A further joint session was held on 11th July. The chief subject for discussion was a review of the general situation. Following this the need for secrecy was reiterated and the British members requested the Special Observers Group to *'limit to the essential minimum the number of persons to whom secret material would be available'*.

It seems that the British had not forgotten the Tyler Kent episode and did not trust the American lines of communication!

Guns, Bombs and Bullets

The Anti-Aircraft and Coast Defence Committee activities started on 5 June 1941, when the Special Observer anti-aircraft officer, Lt. Col. Dale D Hinman met General Locke who explained the organisation of the British AA battery and its relationship to other branches of the army and RAF. He also disclosed to the American office some of the problems of anti-aircraft defence of Iceland, Northern Ireland and Scotland.

Special Observers Lt Col Jerry V Matejka

Below: British Home Guard soldiers load a single launcher on a static 'Z' Battery on Merseyside, July 1942.

Right: Royal Artillerymen load a mobile multiple launcher, June 1941. It was a device such as this that Col.Hinman inspected and reported on. *(both W/O Paddy Porter Collection)*.

and Lt Col John W Coffey spent 5 June at the Ordnance Depot at Greenford. In his report to Gen Joseph T McNarney of the inspection. Col. Matejka said, '...*in general British equipment seems heavier and possibly sturdier but ours seems more compact and modern*'.

Four days later on 9 June Lt. Col Hinman reported '...*on his observations at Weymouth Camp near Norfolk England*' [sic] This is actually, Weybourne Camp in the county of Norfolk and if fairly typical of errors found in the early documents, when the Americans were not conversant with the British geographic regions. Hinman's primary interest was the newly developed rocket projector, models 9 and 11. He declared '...*the nine rocket carriage is built from the English anti-aircraft gun. They are planning on building one hundred of these immediately*'.

What Hinman reported back to General McNarney was a developed version of the Z Battery, a short range anti-aircraft weapon system, which launched 3-inch diameter rockets from ground-based single and multiple launchers. The first Z Batteries were equipped with a single-rocket launcher, the Projector, 3-inch, Mark 1. It

was soon found that the rockets did not perform as accurately as the trials had suggested and that the proximity fuses were rarely effective. Therefore, the technique of firing the rockets in large salvos was introduced, and projectors capable of firing an ever-larger number of rockets were developed. The Projector, 3-inch, No 2, Mk 1 was a twin launcher and the No 4 Mk 1 and Mk 2 fired 36 rockets in a 'ripple' firing sequence.

On 13 June 1941, Lt Cols Bolte (Plans) and Case (Intelligence) visited the airfield defence network in the county of Huntington - and area which was described as being '...*about 50 miles in diameter*'. It must be remembered that this conference took place prior to the German attack upon Russia, hence there was still considerable apprehension over a possible German invasion of Great Britain. It was pointed out to the American officers that the best manner of protecting airfields was to have one infantry battalion stationed not further than 1 mile from each as well as small mobile units which could more rapidly relieve unexpected enemy pressure.

Iceland

The first meeting between the British Air Ministry and the Special Observers took place on 6 June. At this meeting is the subject of the American occupation of Iceland was discussed. The conferees decided to joint Admiralty - War Office - Air Ministry Committee should plan for the relief of the British forces in Iceland in collaboration with the Special Observers. The Air Ministry agreed to produce a memorandum on the strength of the fighter forces essential for the defence of areas in which the United States was to defend under ABC-1.

Section 7 of the minutes of the meeting on 6

The British base at Reykjavik, Iceland. Living conditions in Nissen huts during the winter were harsh. *(both P H T Green Collection)*

June provided that the British Air Ministry would prepare a paper on the air defence of Iceland, which was submitted to the Special Observers on 15 June. The document declared that the occupation of the island was necessary for these reasons:

1. The possession of the naval and air base on the flank of the convoy routes from North America was essential.
2. It provided a staging post on the transatlantic air route from North America.
3. It was possible to use as a transit shipment point for personnel from US ships to Britain.
4. To deny its use by the enemy.

The same paper declared that the Germans might desire to occupy the islands in order to use it as a base for large-scale operations against the United Kingdom. It stated also that the Germans might launch a diversionary attack against the island while making their main invasion attack against the United Kingdom. The nature of the attack was predicted to be a seaborne invasion of three or four divisions together with a bombardment from air and sea.

In view of the desire of the British to be relieved of the task of maintaining garrisons on the island and the imperativeness of keeping it from Axis control it is not surprising that plans for the occupation of Iceland by units of the United States Army would progress rapidly.

Next day Lt Col Griner reported the probable route of the Special Observers going to Iceland would be by rail to northern Scotland and from there to Iceland by flying boat. He added that the members of the group were familiarising themselves with the details of ABC-1 and Rainbow 5 preparatory to the reconnaissance of Iceland.

Seven Special Observers undertook a inspection of Iceland; they reached the island on 11 June. At the conclusion of the reconnaissance Col Griner returned to the United States by the way of Canada for a conference with all War Department officials on Iceland. That same day he sent a message to Washington advising the steps needed to be urgently taken to secretly locate officers and enlisted men that were able to read and speak the Icelandic language as well as anyone who could speak Faroese.

On 19 June Major General Chaney sent to Washington a comprehensive report on the situation in Iceland as it would likely affect the American Armed Forces to be stationed there. He prefaced the document by stressing the importance of completing the relief of Iceland by 1 October 1941.

He also warned that the harbour facilities at Reykjavik were extremely limited because of the lack of small boats, lighters and pier cranes, and because the length of the pier and the depth of the water limited the cargo ships which might dock at it to those with a maximum draft of 20 feet and to a length of 470 feet. In view of these facts, he advised that the first convoy should include a great variety of freight handling equipment for ports.

Chaney also suggested minor revisions in the list of detachments and units which had been scheduled tentatively to arrive for the first Iceland contingent of the United States Army. Regarding hospital facilities, this change was recommended: *'Delete two 1000 and two 500-bed hospitals. Add one 150-bed one 300-bed one 250-bed four 75-bed, two 100-bed and two 400-bed hospitals'*.

This report strongly recommended that an advance party of G-2 personnel reach the island about two weeks before the arrival of the first contingent. The presence of security personnel was deemed essential because of the complex condition requiring planning. Extreme secrecy was needed for the American preparations for the relief of Iceland since the USA was still neutral.

Chaney also pointed out that in order to meet the British deficiency in fighter aircraft, an American pursuit squadron should arrive in Iceland about 20 July to provide cover for the debarkation activities. He added that if the War Department did not regard this suggestion as feasible, carrier-based aviation should be provided for the landing of troops.

The report also included the recommendation that the War Department reach an agreement with the United States Navy in regard to the supervision of the craft operating in the harbour of Reykjavik and the small vessels engaged in coastwise shipping. The statement was included however that the British would continue such supervision until the relief of Iceland by the United States had been consummated.

The next subject considered in this report of Gen Chaney was included because of the Icelandic climate. Personnel ordered to Iceland should receive cold climate clothing similar to that provided to the troops sent to Newfoundland. It pointed out also that all the heating was done with the fuel mixture composed of two parts coke and one part soft coal, and since the British fuels stocks on the island were low, the shipments of large quantities would be necessary. There was an absence of natural or artificial gas on the island

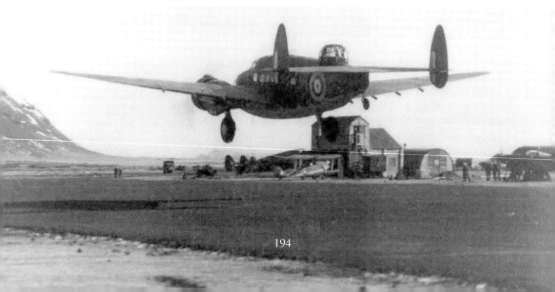

An RAF Lockheed Hudson of 269 Squuadron overflies the strip at RAF Kaldadarnes, Iceland, sometime in 1941. In the background by the control tower is a RAF DH82 Tiger Moth, and on the extreme right, what appears to be an USAAC Bell P-39 Aircobra. *(NARA)*

A trio of Hawker Hurricanes on the runway about to depart RAF Reykjavik. *(P H T Green Collection)*

and so gasoline driven motors of 220 volts 50 cycles were necessary.

The last subject considered was the tentative agreement with the British for the taking over by the United States of certain equipment. This pact provided that the United States would take over the harbour defence guns, the anti-aircraft guns together with ammunition, available gasoline and oil trucks, existing coal stocks a field bakery, class one supplies and engineer and signal supplies.

In addition to the above, the British were in a position to furnish Nissen (Quansett) hut material for the units of the United States Army sent to Iceland. It was the recommendation of Gen Chaney also that the fifteen mines in Icelandic waters which were controlled by the British Navy should remain under their control.

Other recommendations were to emanate from the Special Observers headquarters before the actual arrival of the first contingent of the forces which were to provide relief for the British in Iceland.

The Nissen hut situation was discussed in great detail on 25 June. Chaney stated that the British had erected huts for a force of 24,000 men, twelve being quartered in each 36 foot hut. Since the American Icelandic force for billeting purposes had been declared at 30,000 and since 1,000 British troops were to remain on the island during the coming winter, the total number of Nissen huts required was 7,000.

In July the War Department devised a new plan for the relief of Iceland called Indigo 2, which provided for sending only about 7000 men to the island. About a month later Indigo 2 had been amended to provide for a force of approximately 10,000 men to include the Marines already on the island.

On 6 September, the Special Observer group in London were notified that Indigo 3 Force

under the command of Maj Gen Charles H Bonesteel had sailed on the day before and had been given instructions concerning the possible approach of axis forces to Iceland: ' *in carrying out the joint task, approach of any hostile forces of the axis powers to within 50 miles of Iceland will be deemed conclusive evidence of hostile intent and will require attack on such axis forces, unless an attack under the existing circumstances would be tactically unsound'*.

Just prior to the arrival of the force it was also apparent that Maj Gen Bonesteel and his staff would be obliged to display great tact in dealing with local representatives of the United States Navy and with the officers of the British Armed Forces; therefore these instructions were issued for Maj Gen Bonesteel to follow:

'The CG United States Army forces in Iceland will exercise these functions as described in this directive which details his relations with the British and the United States Navy. In matters of mutual interest he will cooperate with the local representatives of the United States Navy. He will then take up these affairs with the British authorities. The principles of mutual cooperation will govern his solution.

The British aided the preparations for the landing of the first units of the United States Army by setting up rather flexible rules to govern the transfer of British releases on the island to the United States. In a message of 9 September 1941 Maj Gen Chaney informed the War Department of instructions of the British War Office to the General Officer Commanding Iceland regarding the transfer of part of the British installations on the island to the US Army these instructions were:

1. *Assignments to the US of agreements for hirings should be made in agreement with US authorities when necessary.*

2. *Pending decision that US forces will remain in occupation, no claim should be*

made against US authorities in respect of rents already paid from British Army funds, irrespective of whether or not the agreements has been assigned or where rates are still being paid from British Army funds.

3. Where actual liability is transferred and excepted by US forces the responsibility for further payments of rent will rest upon US authorities.

Six days later advanced units of the Fifth Infantry Division landed at Reykjavik. They were been preceded, however, by elements of the US Marine Corps and the US Navy.

On 7 July President Roosevelt announced that US forces had landed in Iceland. Although the fact was not disclosed, the detachment which began the relief of Iceland were from the First Provisional Marine Corps Brigade.

The Special Observer group was given security responsibilities in connection with the Iceland base command early in October. An order from the War Department stated that Lt Col Homer Case, in conjunction with the British War Office, should censor all still photographs and newsreels from Iceland which might reach Great Britain. The purpose of this order appears to come from its last three sentences: *'this is done in order to affect the closest coordination between American and English forces and news agencies. Delete all shots of unit designations, heavy weapons, and tactical equipment. The British mission in Washington concurs in all this'*.

Soon after learning that the 33rd Pursuit Squadron of the US Navy had been ordered to Iceland for duty, Maj Gen Chaney sent the following to the War Department: *'In order to ensure a safe arrival pursuit unit referred to* in your number 21 and immediate readiness for combat after landing, believe essential qualified officer 33rd Squadron sent to London and then to Iceland for familiarisation all details such as radio frequencies call signs, recognition signals, refuelling, dispersal and aerodrome arrangements, weather information, housing, storage and technical building his unit must fit into, then its return at earliest practicable for purpose of readying squadron of difficult duty both coming ashore and ensuring winter. Estimate one week required between his arrival here and departure the US. Admin concurs in the necessity of this.*

Five days later another communication containing data and signals for use by the crews of the 33rd Pursuit Squadron was passed to the United States Navy Department and the British Delegation in Washington. This message dated the aircraft of the 33rd Pursuit Squadron flying from the carrier to Reykjavik was to be provided with an escort from the RAF. The call sign of Reykjavik was 'Igloo', the 33rd Pursuit Squadron was 'Cockbill' while the British escort aircraft was to be 'Caretaker'.

The SPOBS also assisted in keeping the War Department informed of other British devices which had been made available for aircraft of the 33rd.

1. Availability of British recognition lights and the feasibility of installing them in Iceland is under investigation. Will advise later.

2. Regarding pyrotechnic equipment for your information, our Special Naval Observer has sent via air this week a sample with drawings of new British project which appears promising to meet special problems presented by high-speed pursuit.

In this photograph, dated 17 October 17 1941, a P-40C is unloaded at a dock in Iceland, destined for the 33rd Pursuit Squadron. This machine had previously been operated by the 57th Pursuit Group. *(USN)*

To Russia from London.

The German attack on Russia had almost two immediate effects on the mission of the Special Observers. Operation Barbarossa was the code name for the Axis invasion of the Soviet Union, which started on Sunday, 22 June 1941. The operation stemmed from Nazi Germany's ideological aims to conquer the western Soviet Union so that it could be repopulated by Germans, to use Slavs, especially Poles, as a slave-labour force for the Axis war effort, and to seize the oil reserves of the Caucasus and the agricultural resources of Soviet territories.

Both Maj Gen Chaney and members of the joint planning staff believed that this Berlin - Moscow break rendered improbable an attempted invasion of Great Britain in 1941.

Harry Lloyd Hopkins [D] (*b.* 17 August 1890, *d* 29 January 1946) was an American social worker, the 8th Secretary of Commerce, and one of President Franklin Delano Roosevelt's closest advisors. He was one of the architects of the New Deal, especially the relief programmes of the Works Progress Administration (WPA), which he directed and built into the largest employer in the country. In World War Two, he was Roosevelt's chief diplomatic adviser and troubleshooter. He is seen here boarding a flying boat for Great Britain in 1941. *(NARA)*

This warfare in Eastern Europe, moreover, was to result in both Maj Gen Chaney and his chief of staff Brig Gen Joseph T McNarney, enlarging in their duties temporarily by becoming members of special missions to the Soviet Union.

Russian requests for specific equipment and ammunition was revealed to Special Observers by the British at a meeting of the latter with the Joint Planning Staff on 4 July 1941.

President Roosevelt sent Lend-Lease Administrator Harry Hopkins to the Soviet Union for preliminary talks with its high officials. Brig Gen McNarney left London on a special train on the night of 27 July reaching Invergordon at Scotland at 12:45 pm the same day. From that point to Moscow and the journey was by aircraft, flying to Archangel, Russia, where the party spent the night of 29/30 July prior to their departure for Moscow early in the morning. Upon reaching the Russian capital Mr Hopkins lost no time in obtaining an interview with Premier at Joseph Stalin for 6:30 pm on 30 July.

Later that evening the meeting was joined by McNarney and General Yakovlev of the Russian Field Artillery. McNarney later wrote that '*...the meeting lasted over two hours and was most unsatisfactory*'.

One reason was that Mr Hopkins felt that the Soviet Union should manufacture firearms to fit the 30 calibre ammunition which the United States might furnish, while the Russian general desired that the Lend-Lease ammunition be manufactured in sizes to fit rifles and guns of the Soviet Union. Excerpts from the account of the interview by Brig Gen McNarney reveal other reasons why the conference was not regarded as satisfactory:

'*He asked* [the Russian General] *the organisation of the anti-aircraft regiment and he replies that organisation and anti-aircraft units was different depending upon the situation, whether in cities, on marches, or with the troops. He was asked if Russia manufactured 37mm guns and he replied yes. When asked the monthly output he did not know.*

He was asked if either of the generals on the Russian mission to the United States were ordinance experts. He did not know. He was asked if Russia could send their own ordinance experts with Russian equipment to the United States to test the relationship of Russian calibres to United States calibres to see whether ammunition was interchangeable. General Yakovlev said he would speak to his chief.

General Yakovlev was asked what

instruments of war did the Soviets need most. He replied that they needed aluminum, that they needed fighters and they needed modern bombers.

He was asked what speed the Russians wanted for fighters. He did not answer this question and then was asked what was the speed of the newest Russian fighter. He answered 650 kilometres per hour. He was asked what was the speed with full military load. He answered *'I am an artilleryman'*.

Mr Hopkins stated that he was surprised that General Yakovlev did not mention tanks and anti-tank guns. General Yakovlev replied *I think we have enough'*.

Mr Hopkins arranged for a second meeting with Premier Stalin at 6 pm next day.

Meanwhile, McNarney toured the Soviet capital, and closely scrutinised the activities. As a result of his observations he wrote; *'All military military attachés in Moscow are severely handicapped by the restrictions imposed upon them and the almost complete lack of official information. As a result estimates of the situation, organisation and equipment must be based almost entirely on personal observation supplemented by rumor and newspaper articles'*.

The return journey was by way of Archangel and Scapa Flow. There Mr Hopkins left for the United States while McNarney returned to London. He made these general comments on the journey: *'My general impression is based upon insufficient evidence are:*

A. *Mr Stalin is the only man in Russia who is cognizant of the entire situation.*

B. *That all available equipment and aeroplanes are in organised units, with no reserves to replace battle losses except current production.*

C. *That the ammunition the situation is good.*

D. *That the Russian armies will not disintegrate this year.*

E. *That there is no intention to undertake a counter-offensive. Counter attacks are purely local and strategic defensive will*

William Averell Harriman [D] (*b*. 15 November 1891, *d*. 26 July 1986), better known as Averell Harriman, was an American politician, businessman, and diplomat. *(NARA)*

be maintained.

F. *That the Russian air force is larger, better equipped and better trained than given credit for.*

G. *That the German armies will continue to advance at a somewhat slower rate than the average to date.*

H. *That the Russians expect to hold Moscow and Petrograd this winter providing the bad weather sets in by 15 September. That if these two cities, with their industries, are lost, Russia cannot maintain a war effort on a scale is sufficient to cope with the German army'*.

A second Mission to Russia to be led by William Averell Harriman as the chairman was planned, with Maj Gen Chaney as one of its members. Chaney left London on 21 September taking roughly the same route as Gen McNarney did two months earlier, arriving in Moscow by air on 28 September.

Even before his trip with Harriman to Moscow, Chaney had been preparing for expansion of the duties by the Special Observer Group. He provided Harriman with details of allocation of lend-lease Aircraft for the Soviet air force:

Heavy bombers	3 per month.
Light bombers	97 per month.
Pursuit fighters	300 per month.
Total	400 per month.

General Chaney did not return to London directly, but went back to Washington to report, returning to London via the Azores and Lisbon, reaching the American Embassy in London on 18 November. He brought with him news that the duties of the Special Observers in London were to be expanded significantly.

There was at the same time however, grave apprehension over the success of another duty assigned to the SPBS - the gathering of data on the best aircraft routes across eastern Asia, this task was assigned to Lt Col Townsend Griffiss.

While Maj Gen Chaney was still on temporary duties in Washington, General Arnold wrote to Brig Gen McNarney that *'plans for the movement of aeroplanes to Russia must be formulated without delay. The information from Gen. Chaney is incomplete. The routes in which the aircraft should fly are:*

1. *Nome - Vladivostok - Kuibyshev.*
2. *Basra - Aakhabad - Kuibyshev.*
3. *Nome - Markova - Yakutsk - Kuibyshev.*

Gen. McNarney was instructed in the same message to send an officer to Russia to obtain information on the above routes. The so-called 'courier' received permission from the War Department to ask Russian officials to state definitely what steps they would take to provide essential facilities for the movement of P-40, A-20 and B-25 aircraft on these routes. He also received authority to point out to the Soviet officials whom he met, that the rapid movement of aircraft to Russia might depend on using the above routes, especially the one across Siberia.

The SPOBS sent an unamed officer to a conference with Colonel Ploughachev, the Vice-Chief in Charge of Air of the Russia Mission on London on 1 November.

The attitude of the latter certainly did not indicate that the mission of Lt Col Griffiss would it be successful. Colonel Ploughachev declared that neither of the two Nome - Siberian routes were practicable during the winter months for any type of aircraft and that both were impossible for pursuit aircraft.

He added that the Moscow - Vladivostok route ferried some Russian aircraft, but that it was not well organised. Finally he stated that the route between Nome and Vladivostok was totally without ferry organisation. Finally, he expressed the belief that the Basra - Kuibyshev route was the only practicable winter one, and declared that the delivery of badly needed aircraft would not be delayed by the search for another route.

In spite of this most unsanguine interview, Col Griffiss left London on the

Lt. Colonel Townsend E. Griffiss (*b.* 4 April 1900, *d.*15 February 1942), aide to Major General James E Chaney, was killed when the aircraft in which he was a passenger was mistakenly shot down. He was the first US airman to die in the line of duty in Europe after the USA entered the war. *(NARA)*

mission. He was held up at Teheran for twelve days awaiting the permission of the Soviet government to enter Russia. He was ordered by the War Department to study the airport and radio installation as well as the logistics supply in the Teheran area during his wait.

Col Griffiss was finally granted permission to enter Soviet territory and reached Kuibyshev on board a Russian aircraft on 20 November. The initial attempt to gain information was described by Col Griffiss as follows: *'Desired information was requested of Russian officials on 2 December 1941. On a second visit on 8 December this request was followed up. To date, no information has been received. Russian officials stated that they have turned over the request to proper authorities and that they cannot press further for it. Under my present instructions, I can take no further action. When I contacted the officials, they received me cordially and it seems unlikely that they will refuse outright to furnish the information. There is only a slight hope, however, that I will be furnished with the information requested at this time.*

The attitude of the Russians is that it is impracticable to deliver aeroplanes across Siberia and that delivery can be accomplished at Archangel or at the frontier in the Near East (or if preferred, in the Near East outside the Soviet frontier).

Our insistence on getting the information leads the Russians to believe that we want it for use in relation to questions of strategy as well as in regard to aircraft deliveries. The Russians furthermore have so far been reluctant to take action which might precipitate hostilities with the Japanese.

The unpromising status of the Mission as described by Lt Col Griffiss was related to the War Department, together with the recommendation that Col Griffiss should be ordered to return to London - which was refused.

Griffiss replied with a certain amount of frustration: *'Regarding my cable of 16 December. The oral answer of the embassies was confirmed on 19 December by the written refusal of the air route information. It is improbable that this policy will be modified in the near future due to the recent Russian military successes. My presence here any longer seems unwarranted. Authority is therefore urgently requested to return to London so that action can be taken immediately to obtain a regular placements on the overcrowded transportation to Teheran. Request this to be expedited. I will obtain additional RAF information on the oilfields while I am en route to Cairo'.*

Lt Col Griffiss was obliged to stay in Russia for some additional days, however, before he was finally granted permission to return to London. He used the same route on his return journey that is by way of Teheran and Cairo.

On 15 February 1942, when the Cairo to Great Britain Liberator of the British Overseas Airways Corporation, in which he was returning to the United Kingdom was just five miles southwest of the Eddystone Lighthouse near Plymouth, it was shot down by two Polish pilots serving in the RAF who had mistaken it for an enemy aircraft. The crew and all passengers on board were drowned. Their bodies were not recovered, but the wreckage of the aircraft and the briefcase of the Lt Col Griffiss was found.

Interest in other parts the world

In September 1941 the War Department began to direct the Special Observer Group in London to furnish data on strategic areas in various parts of the world. On 11 September, for example, they were requested to obtain from the British information which would be helpful in the establishment and maintenance and supply depots in the Middle East, depots which would have facilities for the assembly, repair, overhaul and storage of American aircraft, quartermaster ordinance and signal equipment.

Next day the War Department directed Maj Gen Chaney to obtain an interview with Mr Ashley-Cooper, Director General of Finance in the British Ministry of Supply who was president of the Hudsons Bay Company. The reason for this order was that the Lt Cmdr Charles J Hubburd of the United States Naval Reserve was scheduled to take some parties undertaking research in weather conditions to Northern North America and nearby islands; hence Washington required the help of certain posts of the Hudson's Bay Company, Leaf River, Okkah, Fort Chimo,

A pair of Lockheed Hudsons are prepared at Gander, Newfoundland for the long ocean crossing to Great Britain. *(NARA)*

Two RAF Lockheed Hudsons make landfall in Scotland. *(NARA)*

Hebron, Naia and Port Burwell in Labrador, and River Clyde, Ponds Inlet, Wards Inlet, Frobisher Bay, Pangnirtung, Resolution Island, and Bake Harbor on Baffin Island.

Clearly the meeting was a success, for a week later Gen. Chaney sent to Washingtron the following: *'Further to your message 50, Ashley-Cooper advises Hudson Bay Company will do all in its power to facilitate the project. To inform company request information as to the size of weather parties and approximate dates and visit to posts, and assurance that parties will be self-contained and self-supporting, and that necessary arrangements are being made with Canadian and Newfoundland authorities. Posts are small and isolated and facilities limited'.*

The ETG and 'Operation Trigger'.
On 25 September the Special Observers received even more responsibilities - the supervision of the what was to be called the Electronics Training Group (ETG). This organisation was created to train Air Corps and Anti-Aircraft personnel to operate the latest devices used in aerial warfare.

The Special Observers also received duties relative to the functioning of a Technical Committee and the Eastern Terminus, Atlantic Division, Air Corps Ferry Command, the plans for a repair base in Northern Ireland, as well as certain obligations incident to the formation of plans for an Anglo-American operation known as 'Trigger'.

To accomplish this the SPOBS was expanded in size, with four Assistant Special Observers assigned in General Order 4, and with the rapid

recuitment of thirteen more staff assigned on temporary duties.

One of the new immediate functions of the technical committee was to advise the Special Observers on all matters pertaining to the exchange between Great Britain and the USA of experimental equipment, research information, and new designs in manufacturing methods for development purposes.

The committee was also to note for the Special Observer tests and observations of American equipment in campaigns, concerning Lend-Lease affairs concerned with production, experimentation, testing, maintenance and supply. In the interest of coordination also the secretary of the technical committee was to distribute periodically to all staff sections a digest of completed projects which included the title of the paper, a 'synopsis' of the contents and action taken.

One of them was the result of the practice of ferrying aircraft allocated to Great Britain and Lend-Lease agreements across the Atlantic by pilots of the Army Air Corps. As of 1 November 1941 under Special Observers Group General Order 6, the Eastern Terminus, Atlantic Division, Air Corps Ferry Command was transferred to the Special Observers Group.

A provisional headquarters was established on 1 December 1941 at the terminus of Air Corps Ferry Command at Prestwick airport, Scotland and an Headquarters Detachment formed in London for the administration and supervision of the group, with fifteen enlisted men assigned.

This ferry organisation was not just restricted

to the North Atlantic, but also included a route in the South Atlantic. Plans for the ferry were made as early as September 1941 when Major General Henry H Arnold sent in care of the Special Observers a message for Major General George H Brecht, who had been sent to Great Britain on a special Air Corps mission.

The message disclosed the type of aircraft to be ferried and the fact that Pan American Airways was cooperating in carrying out the project. Part of the communication read as follows:

No definite information has been received by this office even at this late date, as to the number of the following types of planes which the British wish to be flown across the South Atlantic Ocean:

B-25 [North American Mitchell]
Lockheed Hudson]
Martin 187 [Baltimore]
DB-7 [Douglas A-20 Havoc]

The necessary plans for this ferry service cannot be made until this information is received by this office and for a number of pilots needed for this service still to be determined by Pan American Airways.

In November Brig Gen McNarney requested the War Department to keep the SPOBS informed as to the cypher system used on the southern ferry route. He said: *'it might be desirable for the PAA (Pan-American Airways) and Army Ferry using southern routes to use procedures and systems of equivalent security to those used on the Newfoundland to Prestwick route by the British. Understand that Army Ferry is conversant with the British systems'.*

Another development in the autumn of 1941 with which the SPOBS were associated - as already mentioned - was the plan for using modern British equipment and personnel for training pilots in the United States. This system was sometimes referred to as 'Operation Trigger'.

The plan evolved as a result of investigations made in September 1941 by Colonel Ira C Eaker, Air Corps and members of the SPOBS. It envisioned the creation in the USA of a 'typical fighter sector' where a minimum of one day and one night fighter squadron could receive training. In a message to the War Department, Maj. Gen. Chaney stated that Colonel Eaker was bringing a full report, but that to save time he had already asked the British if personnel and equipment could be made available for this operation by

the end of the year.

The Eaker-SPOBS plan won the approval of the War Department. Maj Gen Chaney was informed on 29 October that Maj Gordon P Saville, who had accompanied him on his 1940 trip of observation to Great Britain was returning for the purposes of familiarising himself with the latest developments in fighter control procedure and equipment. Major Saville was also to conclude the arrangements for the assembly and shipment of equipment and personnel for the establishment in the USA of a fighter operational unit at the earliest possible date.

Almost a month later Maj. Savile informed the War Department that only a limited number of trained personnel could be spared for 'Trigger' and hence majors and captains with flying experience and twelve signal corps non-commissioned officers of the first three grades should be sent to the United Kingdom for necessary training for 'Operation Trigger'. His last recommendation was *'that R/OA-I maintenance men (that is, personnel trained for the use and maintenance of the British Airborne Interception Radar) who have graduated from Canada's radio school at Clinton be available at 'Trigger' not later than 1 January 1942 for installation and maintenance of British A-I Equipment now being shipped'.*

The message indicates that by the end of November 1941, the preparation for 'Operation Trigger' were virtually complete. However, this scheme failed to materialise as planned, due to the non-appearance of personnel from the USA.

Maj Gen Chaney wrote to the War Department in message #725, dated 9 March 1942. *'When Maj Gordon Saville finished his temporary duty here last fall certain tentative plans were worked out with the British. These plans included two projects which were called 82 Group SHADOW and TRIGGER. When will the personnel, both officers and enlisted, please send for reception, housing and training of some of our people who would be involved in these projects.*

As far as TRIGGER is concerned, the British have held open vacancies in some of the schools as they expected our personnel at any time.

In Northern Ireland, the British have requisitioned private homes to accommodate the personnel in the SHADOW scheme. Are these accommodations are vacant being held for us? Request any information on this project'.

Northern Ireland and dealing with the IRA.
In addition to supervising the work for the inauguration of the Atlantic Ferry, the SPOBS was given significant responsibilities in connection with plans for the construction of a base for maintenance, repair, and supply of American built aircraft which were being operated by the RAF. A survey of available sites for the latter was one reason why Maj Gen Henry H Arnold of the Army Air Force sent Maj Gen George H Brecht to the United Kingdom in the autumn of 1941. The report of the latter officer was an endorsement of the recommendations made by Maj Gen Chaney in his report on Northern Ireland of 3 September 1941. The following is a portion of that Brett Report: *'It is recommended that immediate steps be taken to establish at Langford Lodge, Northern Ireland for third echelon repair, maintenance, and supply of spare parts for American built aircraft. Facilities to be manned by American civilian personnel and centralised American control.*

It is recommended that the organisation and equipment at the depot at Langford Lodge incorporate the recommendations of Gen. Chaney to the Chief of staff in Annex #3 to Report of the Special Observer Group, London dated 3 September 1941, that liaison and key personnel for stations and Langford Lodge Depot recommended by Chaney being dispatched to Northern Ireland at the earliest possible moment to work with the headquarters staff RAF Northern Ireland on detailed requirements for an American controlled and operated supply system for all aircraft, whether RAF or US Army operated from bases in Northern Ireland'.

Since the report of Maj Gen Chaney on 3 September 1941, mentioned the suitability of the US Army constructing in Northern Ireland facilities for the maintenance of aircraft and the housing of ground forces, it is not surprising that other members of the SPOBS should visit the latter area for the study of special problems.

Three outstanding assistant Special Observers made trips to Ireland during late September and early October 1941. Lt Col Dale D Hinman inspected the anti-aircraft facilities in Northern Ireland. He visited installations at four important centres: Belfast, Londonderry, Lough Erne, and Ballyhalbert. He reported that the RAF was removing all searchlights under its control, that was installing mobile radio units all over Northern Ireland to report the movements of enemy aircraft. He declared that these units are to be operated by RAF personnel and not that of the anti-aircraft artillery.

After a survey of British installations in northern Ireland, Lt Col George W Griner made the following recommendations:

a. *Any new facilities and quarters constructed by the British to be entirely on their responsibility.*

b. *Any agreement, formal or informal, concerning the use thereof, is subject to the decision that troops will be sent to Northern Ireland.*

c. *Construction required in addition to that which may be undertaken by the British be authorised for accomplishment by the United States under the land lease act be applied as soon as practicable.*

Lt Col Homer Case, SPOBS G-2 spent 2 and 3 October 1941 in Dublin to familiarise himself with *'the military and political situation in that country (Eire) having a bearing upon the general mission of this group (Special Observers)'.* It will be remembered that the US was still a neutral and hence its military personnel could travel in neutral Eire. At this time there existed still in official circles in Washington hope that Eire would grant the United States the use of certain valuable bases on her western coast, even if the British were still denied such access. This sanguine view, according to Lt Col Case, was founded on a statement to that effect

Éamon de Valera (*b.* 14 October 1882, *d.* 29 August 1975) was a prominent political leader in Eire.

made during the winter of 1940-41 by the American minister to Eire, Mr David Gray.

By the arrival of Lt Col Case, however, Mr Gray had changed his views following several; conferences with Prime Minister Eamon de Valera. Said Lt Col Case: *'It is now Mr Gray's opinion that our entry into the war would not change the Irish policy of absolute neutrality and that the Irish government would not invite American military forces to operate from Irish bases. He states that Mr de Valera is a hard-headed, obstinate man, obsessed with a hatred of the British and that he will do nothing to aid them in this war'.*

Since many British and American military and naval officers believed in the autumn of 1941 that the Germans might launch their attack upon Great Britain by seizing Eire, Lt Col Case observed the defence network of the country. His report was just as dismal as was his analysis of the prospects of the country granting the USA access to its valuable bases.

He declared that the nation's regular army of approximately 50,000 men was 'well uniformed and made a fine appearance' that was not as yet well-trained. Also, there were 'Local Defence Forces' of 100,000 men, apparently similar to the British Home Guard or the American State Militia. Lt Col Case pronounced them as being poorly trained and equipped but 'could be of value in conducting gorilla warfare'. Finally, there were the local security forces, composed of approximately 80,000 men who performed general local police duties. 'These have little military value' said Lt Col Case.

The report served to emphasise the problem of defending Ireland in the event of an attack by the air, land and naval forces of the Axis powers.

Late in 1940 the island seem to be in grave danger of falling before an attack by the Germans for three principal reasons: firstly, the island was regarded as an ideal point of vantage for an attack upon Great Britain after the Russian armies had been knocked out as a major fighting force; Lt Cols Hinman and Case pointed out the inadequacy of the island's defences, calling attention to the fact that Britain had already removed some anti-aircraft equipment from Northern Ireland. The second reason was the description by Lt Col Case of the impotency of the fighting forces in Eire. The British action in Northern Ireland was explained by the need for sending all possible British equipment and military personnel to posts in the Far East to meet the Japanese threat.

The third reason for the danger of happenings in Ireland of a nature unfavourable to the cause of the United States was the existence of a fanatical anti-British and hence pro-German group in Eire known as the Irish Republican

Londonderry was commissioned as a naval operating base on 5 February 1942, the first outpost of the navy's shore establishment in the European theatre. Here is seen the General Headquarters area.

The warehouse area at Londonderry - lines and lines of long-span buildings were quickly erected there. *(NARA)*

Army (IRA). Its leaders possessed the intention of resorting to violence to effect the union of Northern and Southern Ireland under a republican form of government. British installations in the north were therefore in danger of sabotage. The border was most challenging to guard since it ran through the streets of towns in several places and the citizens of Eire came to Northern Ireland to work in defence projects

Given this dangerous situation, it is not surprising that the British were anxious for the United States to carry out the provisions of ARC-1 as far as Northern Ireland was concerned, for on 19 December 1941, a group of Special Observers were addressed by an unnamed British officer who declared that he had been given the choice of topics by the G-1 officer of the US Army who invited him, and he selected the possibility of the invasion of all Ireland by the German forces. He pointed out that the possession of Ireland would not only aid them in their attempts to land upon Great Britain but would also give them a most valuable submarine base. The text of this address was recorded in AG 31, BTNI (1942).

This speculation as to when the invasion forces would appear and which day they would first attempt to seize became of no importance as events overtook them. Maj Gen Chaney's dispatch in Washington two days before the address was delivered saw yet another plan surface that reiterated recommendations concerning the selection of campsites and the bringing in of troops to both Northern Ireland and Great Britain.

US War Plan Rainbow 5 called for an initial US force in Northern Ireland of 26,300 men, later increased to 36,800 men. The Plan also called for forces to protect the proposed American installations in Scotland, a 'Bomber Command' to operate from England and for a 'token force' to be stationed in Great Britain.

In regards to housing the token force, Maj Gen Chaney mentioned that in the south-east of London in the county of Kent near the town of Wrotham, the British were close to completing a camp for 5000 men using Nissen huts; thus 5,000 troops from the total of 7,677 in the token force will have housing prepared for them wrote Maj Gen Chaney.

The situation in Northern Ireland was far less reassuring. The then current plan called for sending a force of 33,421 to Northern Ireland. Maj Gen Chaney pointed out that on five airfields in the area accommodations had already been built for 7,480 and his comments on the balance are as follows: *'In addition to this (quarters for 7,480), the British have provided accommodation for 2,783 anti-aircraft personnel. The War Department has requested the US Navy to undertake construction for a total of 13,535 men by extending their existing contracts. This out of housing required for 33,421, accommodations for the additional 13,535 are constructed as has been recommended, it will still require the US Army to undertake construction for personnel totalling*

Creevagh Hospital Base, Londonderry. Here, for some unknown reason the Nissen huts were partially sunk into the earth. (NARA)

9,703. I recommend that:

   a. A program of construction designed to meet the needs of US troops in Great Britain and Northern Ireland be planned at once.

   b. Construction be commenced as soon as practicable after plans are approved.

   c. Col. D A Davison, CE, Engineer member of the Special Staff of the SPOBS be ordered to Washington on temporary duties for consultation regarding plans for construction in Great Britain and Northern Ireland.

It was recognised, in a letter dated 17 December 1941, that the British could not furnish all the materials for the construction of housing, nor for the labour required by the contemplated Rainbow 5. Factual data was considered and studies were made of logistical and technical matters arising from possible employment of US forces in the UK.

Creation of the Eighth Air Force - and the move to Northern Ireland.

January 1942 saw two significant events. The first was when General 'Hap' Arnold replied to a letter from Maj Gen Chaney, the second was when Col. Davison went to Washington with detailed data on the construction problems of the

United States Army in Great Britain and Northern Ireland. Before Col Davison even reached the capital the War Department took steps to provide a service maintenance base in Northern Ireland for American built aircraft.

Previously the Lockheed Corporation had made a start on operating a reassembly division in Liverpool, Great Britain. That month it received a request from the War Department to install the service maintenance base at Langford Lodge, west of Belfast. The Lockheed Corporation ordered one of the firm's representatives in Liverpool a Mr Henry Ogden to consult Maj Gen Chaney regarding assistance in surveying the site and its facilities. The instructions added *'upon completion of this survey, cable for information and send all details that we will need that would permit the establishment of a self-styled sustained community of about 2,500 people.'*

Although the project had been supported by both Maj Gen Brecht and Chaney, it was not to materialise before the signing of an agreement between Great Britain and the USA for the sending of US Army units to Northern Ireland. This plan, known as 'MAGNET', was the first which resulted in the landing of US troops on European soil in the Second World War. But first, that letter.

War Department
Office of the Chief of Army Air Forces
Washington
January 26 1942

Maj. Gen. James H. Chaney
Theater Commander
American Forces in Great Britain
American Embassy
London, Great Britain

Dear Chaney

I have given careful consideration to your letter of December 5, 1941, in reply to my suggestions on organisation of the United Kingdom Theater, from an air point of view. The reasons you advanced for not desiring to create an American Air Force at that time seemed quite valid to me, and I did not intend to explore the matter further at this time. However, our entrance into the war has changed circumstances quite materially. The decision by the War Department to send a Corps of three infantry divisions and one armoured division with an air support command to Northern Ireland introduces a large ground force into your theater. Obviously, this change makes it impossible to carry out in detail the plan which you had earlier proposed. For instance, it is no longer possible to make the Interceptor Commander in Northern Ireland the Force Commander there.

Our discussions with the British here have brought out certain salient features for future planning. We have concluded that it will be possible to base in the United Kingdom ultimately twenty Groups of B-17s and B-24s, twelve groups of B-29s and twenty-two Groups of B-29s or other types of heavy bombers, making a total of fifty-four Groups, which at fifty-two operational airplanes each, gives a total of 2,808 operating heavy bombardment airplanes.

In addition, there will be ten Groups of mediums, at fifty-two, making a grand total of 3,328 bombardment airplanes. It is estimated that ten Groups of pursuit will be based in England (United Kingdom). Probably seven of these Pursuit Groups will be based in England and Scotland. It is also planned to send ten squadrons of Turbinlite aircraft for night-fighter operations (240 airplanes) and ten squadrons of Photo-Reconnaissance planes (180 planes). Thus there will be a total of 4,748 operational aeroplanes in your Theater. This does not include Headquarters airplanes or reserves, nor does this list includes

the Air Support Force for 'MAGNET'. Obviously, a force of this size must have command echelons. It will be necessary to set up a Bomber Command, an Interceptor Command, and heading up this large force, it is felt that there should be an Air Force Commander and his Air Staff. This Air Staff should be capable of establishing and maintaining the lateral coordination with the Air Ministry and RAF Air Staff that will be necessary in order that two large Air Forces may work in harmony together in a small base area.

It is hoped to introduce this force into the UK in the near future. It is planned for heavy groups of bombers and two squadrons of photographic aircraft (P-38s) will be introduced into the theaters this spring and early summer. In addition there will be two groups of pursuits introduced this spring, going into Northern Ireland and one squadron of Turbinlite aircraft. We hope to have 16 to 20 groups of heavy bombers established in the UK by next January. We expect to have all five pursuit groups in the theater by next January, and ten mobile air depots to sustain this force. These forces are definitely in the planning stage now, and this movement may be seriously curtailed by lack of adequate shipping.

As for the disposition of the large force, we have had some tentative discussions with the British. Although no agreement was reached with Sir Charles Portal, our discussions indicated that it might be possible to establish an American air force sector. At this stage of the discussion, it appears that the northern half of England might be turned over to the American air force as its base. If there is any possibility of carrying out such a project, then it seems desirable to establish the initial bomber force in that area also, preferably in the vicinity of York. This will have the added advantage that the lines of communication from Liverpool to the air force area will not have to cross the heavy lines of traffic from the Midlands to London and from Liverpool to London.

I am enclosing a schematic chart of the organisation of the air force proposed for your theater. This chart has been tentatively approved by Gen McNair and has been approved in principle by Gen Marshall.

It is hoped that arrangements can be made to accept the Commanding General of the US Army Air Force in Great Britain as the 'opposite number' of the Chief of the Air RAF [sic] in such Combined

Two hastily snatched snapshots of Lockheed Hudson aircraft at Speke, sometime from April 1939 onwards. The Lockheed Aircraft Corporation won a contract to supply 250 of these aircraft to the RAF, and selected Liverpool to assemble the aircraft, following import by sea, at a time before crossing the Atlantic by air was routine. The Hudsons here lack a gun turret, which was built and fitted in the UK. They were the first of many thousands of American aircraft to arrive by sea through Liverpool Docks to be readied for flight at Speke during the wartime years. *(P H T Green Collection)*

Chiefs of Staff meetings as are agreed upon. Likewise, the Chiefs of the Plans Division should be a member of the Joint Planning meetings.

The units for this air force are now being assembled equipped and organised preparatory of movement to England. They are being organised along the general lines indicated in this chart. I will greatly appreciate your consideration of this chart, and any suggestions that you may wish to offer at this time regarding the preparation of the units for operations in the UK.

I am enclosing copies of the plans upon which we are now assembling equipping and organising the units for the army force in the British Isles. They are for your information they are for your information and any such suggestions you may wish to make.

Gen H H Arnold

As far as can be ascertained, this letter is the first description located of what was to become the 8th Air Force. Also of interest was the multiple mentions of the B-29 Superfortress: the first flight of the XB-29, 41-002 - the very first aircraft - did not occur until 21 September 1942 in the hands of Boeing test pilot Edmund T 'Eddie' Allen, with Al Reed as copilot.

The accompanying notes that went with this letter - General Order 5, HQ USAFBI, ,22 February 1942 - revealed that the War Department decided to establish a bomber command in Great Britain - the goal was to achieve 16 to 20 groups of bombers established in the UK by January 1943. The choice of the headquarters for this was to be in York, England and Brig Gen Ira C Eaker was appointed as Commanding General of the 'advanced detachment' of the Eighth Bomber Command.

The letter stated that Brigadier General Eaker was to assist in the formation of a headquarters for the American Air Forces in Great Britain. He was also to assist in the preparation of both fields and installations to garrison the first units to arrive. Eaker was also, together with his staff, to understudy the methods of the bomber command of the RAF. Finally, he was to prepare training schedules for the personnel of units that would be shortly sent to Great Britain from the USA to ensure that adequate preparation for combat in the shortest possible time.

Maj Gen. Chaney was notified by War Department Cable #399, to which he set forth a number of objections, of which the following are outstanding:

'Under conditions existing in this theater, can I say of the Army air forces in the British Isles what is described in your 399 is quite undesirable and hence I do not concur in adopting this plan. The difficulty appears to be that the organisation you propose apparently it is intended for a virgin American theater of operations, but since this is essentially a British theatre, we require an organisation which will achieve effective results under special circumstances and the conditions realistically confronting us. Viewed in this light, paralleling the British organisation with one of our own in this theater of operations would constitute a mistake of a serious nature.

Officers of rather senior in age and rank who have had experience in bombardment operations should be selected for key organisational personnel of bomber command headquarters'.

Maj Gen Chaney's belief that the US Army Air Forces in Great Britain should co-operate closely with the RAF was reiterated when he discussed the air defences for the MAGNET installations. The British agreed to furnish the initial defences for the latter, but with the formation of plans to bring American units to the British Isles, the ultimate air protection of for MAGNET was discussed. 'All pursuit and anti-aircraft artillery organisations utilised for a defence in this theater which is geographically very small, must be controlled by British Fighter Command. It is agreed that these units in Northern Ireland should be under the commander, Northern Ireland forces. however, the air defence of the British Isles is an desirable entity and the British fighter command must of necessity be responsible for the defence of the British Isles'.

In communications sent to the War Department almost a month later, Maj Gen Chaney stated that he was 'considerably disturbed' over the types of officers sent to the United Kingdom for the staff of Brig Gen Eaker.

General Ira Clarence Eaker (b. 13 April 1896, d. 6 August 1987) was a general of the United States Army Air Forces during World War Two. Eaker, as second-in-command of the prospective Eighth Air Force, was sent to Great Britain to form and organise its bomber command. (NARA)

'I have gone over personally the backgrounds of the nineteen staff officers supplied by Eaker, and find that in general they only have pursuit training. Moreover, a large number have come directly from civil life without a military background of any kind. Three served with bombardment units some years ago, their performing experience must, therefore, be regarded as virtually negligible.

Maj Gen Chaney explained that he needed experienced officers because in the preceding year the German fighter and anti-aircraft defences had been highly developed both technically and otherwise. He stated further that before the start of actual bombardment operations, more experienced officers should be supplied to the headquarters of the Eighth Bomber Command.

Clearly, at this time the American War Department were thinking of operating in a similar manner to the RAF, who had a 'Bomber Command', 'Fighter Command' and 'Coastal Command' - hence the use of the term 'Eighth Bomber Command'. However, the organisational plan, whilst still pyramidic, could not be molded into exactly the same structure, so the overall title was eventually changed to the more conventional - for the Americans - US 'Eighth Air Force'.

In the event, nearly six months were to pass before the first all-American bombing mission over German-held territory occurred. Hence the officers of the staff of Gen Eaker had ample time to 'understudy' the bomber methods of the RAF. While the officers were studying the bomber tactics of the British, the officers of the SPOBS were supervising the construction projects which were initiated to provide the US Army Air Force the structures it most urgently required.

Activation of USAFBI and USAFNI

The scope of the 'MAGNET' plan was limited to Northern Ireland, as in this summary contained in a cablegram #265 of 2 January 1942 from the War Department illustrates:

1. The dispatch of forces and material to be made through the British mission in Washington.
2. All matters pertaining to reception, distribution, accommodation, command and maintenance to be made through General Chaney and his mission.
3. 14,000 men to comprise a first increment. This force to consist of two combat teams and service troops. Maj Gen Hartle commanding, and will sail 18 January.
4. The advance party will proceed, details to be furnished later.
5. After this movement, additional movements will be governed by shipping.
6. Our forces will be fully equipped except light artillery weapons and ammunition for three square infantry divisions, that will include ammunition, transport vehicles and medium artillery.
7. Request British authority deliver to US in Northern Ireland. 144 British 25 pounders with accessories and stores; also 1500 rounds per gun. First echelon will require 24 pieces immediately.
8. British force to continue anti-aircraft protection initially of our establishments and facilities in Northern Ireland. However, it is planned to take over eventually the British equipment.
9. British will initially provide supporting and reconnaissance aircraft for US operations and training eventually to be taken over by US.
10. 'MAGNET' has been designated as codename and this concludes agreements reached with Britain.

As a step to provide Maj Gen Chaney with the headquarters necessary for the command of the MAGNET force, the War Department authorised the activation of the United States Army Forces in the British Isles (USAFBI) on 6 January 1942. The cable read:

'By the direction of the President, Maj Gen Chaney, is designated Commander United States Army Forces in British Isles, and Army Member United States Military Mission. With exception of personnel belonging to the office of the Military Attaché, which will continue to perform its function under direction of Assistant Chief of Staff, Commander of United States Army Forces in British Isles will exercise command over all United States Army Forces and personnel now within the British Isles and upon their arrival in the British Isles, over such additional United States Army Forces and personnel as are sent to the British Isles, including Northern Ireland. As Commander of United States Army Forces in British Isles, he will function under the immediate command of Commanding General Field Forces and under the strategic direction of the British Government. As a member of the United States Military Mission, including execution of duties which are delegated to his Special Army Observer, Gen Chaney will function under the immediate direction of the War Department and will report directly thereto'.

Plans were rapidly put in hand to get troops moved to Northern Ireland. General Chaney: 'As a security measure, recommend all members of advanced parties going to Northern Ireland wear civilian clothing, carry baggage that gives no indication of identity, and omit rank from hotel registers etc. This procedure is being carried out by reconnaissance officers from this unit'.

It was expanded upon by General Marshall, who said that the advance party would be in uniform, but that the SPOBS should arrange for civilian clothing for the group; supposedly the civilian apparel would be delivered to the eighteen officers and eighteen enlisted men before their arrival in Belfast.

Ths advance party left Halifax, Nova Scotia on 9 January 1942 on the Canadian troopship *Barensfjord*, which dropped anchor in the Clyde, Scotland on 19 January. Late that afternoon they left for Gourock and then by train to Glasgow. The men were taken the next day to the Glasgow branch of the well-known clothier, Austin-Reed, for civilian clothing following the orders of Chief-of-Staff Marshall.

Security was also an issue in other ways especially over the border with Eire. The British War Office advised the Americans that they thought it best to tell Eamon de Valera, the Irish Premier of their arrival in two stages. When it was certain that de Valera knew of the arrivals of the first Americans anyway, or when this force was in no danger of being attacked in Belfast, whichever was the earliest. De Valera would be told orally that US Army units were in Northern Ireland to augment defences of the UK and that more information would be furnished to him later.

When the American Commander assumed responsibility, he was to be told that a combined force of US and UK troops, predominantly American, were to defend Northern Ireland. In a message to Washington, Maj. Gen. Chaney relayed the British request that their High Commissioner in Dublin handle the matter for both Great Britain and the USA.

With the arrival of the first contingent of the MAGNET force drew near, Col Robert A McClure of SPOBS G-3 outlined the duties of G-1, G-2, G-3 and G-4 (SPOBS) in affecting the landing of personnel and in acquiring their first accommodation. G-1 was to procure needed office space and staff, make provisions for religious, recreational and welfare work, prepare needed statistics, provide for the inspection of the area and detail of military police before the arrival of the troops and to assume responsibility for burials and grave registrations.

G-2 was to be responsible for security, press relationships, censorship, issuance of codes, providing needed maps, and training radio intercept units. Given the threat from Nazi agents working from the German legation in Dublin and the risk of the IRA, this staff section had rather formidable responsibilities.

G-3, on the other hand, was to co-operate with G-1, G-2 and G-4 in determining areas to be taken over, and to prepare training directives, select and allocate training sites and firing ranges

and to orientate military personnel to the use of British weapons and training literature. Given the planning for large-scale exercises and operations, the responsibilities of the staff section were also substantial.

The duties of G-4 were also numerous - they included arranging for British guides and books to assist the first contingent in getting settled, preparing lists of material and labour available, arranging the movement of troops from ship's side to housing areas and the securing of housing facilities for each class of supply.

According to the initial plans of 8 January, the first contingent was to be comprised of about 1,000 officers and 16,000 enlisted men, but because of the reallocation of shipping facilities, the SPOBS was told a week later that the first contingent of MAGNET would only be 215 officers and 4,094 enlisted men.

Two days before the arrival of this United States Armed Forces Northern Ireland -known as USAFNI - a group from SPOBS left London on 24 January. Then, at 12:15 pm on 26 January, Maj Gen Hartle came ashore at Belfast to be met by several high officers and Mr John W Andrews, the Governor General. Accorded considerably publicity also was Private Melburn H Henke of Hutchinson, Nebraska, the first US soldier to enter the European Theater in World War Two.

Left: RMS *Queen Mary* at anchor in Gourock Bay on the the River Clyde at in 1942. Due to the ship's wartime camouflage, it was nick-named *'The Grey Ghost'*.

Above:the luxury interior of the *Queen Mary* was stripped out and racks of bunks installed, in some places up to twenty high. At the time the US military was segregated, this picture showing a group from a ordinance battalion aboard the *Queen Mary*.

The eventual size of the first contingent was 3,765 enlisted men, 230 officers, one warrant officer, forty-two US Army nurses and four civilians. The second contingent reached Belfast on 2 March and the third on 12 May. The fourth, arrived at the River Clyde aboard RMS *Queen Mary* on 18 May. According to the records, the *Queen Mary* was too large for the port of Belfast, so the troops were trans-shipped to Northern Ireland aboard lighters. This brought US strength in Northern Ireland up to 36,993 officers and men when the European Theater of Operations was established on 8 June.

PFC Milburn H. Henke from Minnesota, was officially the first American GI to set foot in the European Theatre on 26 January 1942 when he stepped ashore at Dufferin Dock Belfast. This was strictly for publicity, as several hundred GIs had already come ashore a few minutes earlier.

The problem of security became a pressing one. Maj Gen Chaney submitted the following recommendations to the War Department regarding security instructions to be issued to personnel of future increments to the MAGNET force: *'It is recommended, based on the recommendations of Gen Hartle, that all MAGNET personnel be given security instructions, in addition to the card now issued before they arrive at the port of debarkation. Their instructions should include prohibitions against sending cablegrams before the news of the arrival of the convoy is made public, against mailing letters except in an APO or on the transport, and against writing for the press or making any statement therefor. Personnel should been warned against making comments on the Irish question or Mr De Valera, of the expected activities of Axis spies, the IRA and against discussing politics and religion. they should be warned and that they must safeguard their weapons very carefully. It is suggested that these points be carefully explained to the troops by their officers'.*

The menace of the IRA caused both American and British officers in Northern Ireland grave concern. The methods which this group employed to hamper the cause of the United Nations varied; hence the officers and men of the US forces in Northern Ireland needed special security instructions. Some IRA detachments would endeavour to steal as large quantities of ordnance supplies as possible, therefore weakening the American and British forces in Northern Ireland and enhancing the supplies in their secret arsenals.

Other apparent objectives of the IRA were the destruction of British and American installations, the acquisition of secret information which would be valuable to the Axis nations, and the incitation of dislike and suspicions between the British and American forces and between the American forces and the civilian population of Northern Ireland. It was against the latter that the officers of the USAFNI especially warned their men.

Maj Gen Chaney made this summary of the security situation in Northern Ireland: *'The known presence of German spies in Ulster, the easy passage of the Irish border, and the presence in Dublin of the German Legation with shortwave wireless makes the sending of information from Northern Ireland fast and accurate'.*

The security problem in Northern Ireland during these months was further complicated, unfortunately, by the views of Lt Col Theodore B Arter, the Public Relations Officer on Gen Hartle's Special Staff. In less than two weeks after the arrival of the first increment MAGNET, that officer had so widely publicised his views on the political and religious issues in Ireland that officers of the headquarters of Maj. Gen. Chaney in London and the British Ministry of Information became alarmed. Hence the following message was sent to Northern Ireland for Gen Hartle personally: *'The following comments on the situation are for your information and should be regarded in no means as a directive.*

While favourable press in Ulster is important, it is possible Col Arter is overly concerned with minor issues. *A point of importance which Col Arter raised has to do with relations between Eire and USA and discussions by USA personnel of politics and religion. Freedom of the press is carefully cherished in the United Kingdom as in the USA, and direct or indirect pressure restricting this freedom from newcomers probably will be resented. Therefore any comments which Col Arter makes at Tuesday lunch or elsewhere should be extremely general'.*

The message gave no hint as to the exact nature of Lt Col Arter's prejudicial views.

Initial construction for the Army Air Force

The fact that Lockheed Corporation had been asked to construct an aircraft maintenance plant at Langford Lodge was sent to SPOBS by the War Department on 28 December 1941. Just a few days later, on 2 January 1942, Maj Gen Chaney reported the plans for the erection and operation of the Langford Lodge Depot after negotiations with the British ministry. He wrote:

'British to provide facilities, buildings, utilities and housing for a 1200 man Depot. Air Corps (US Army) to furnish the equipment and management and take over operation by contract with Lockheed or some other manufacturer. Equipment and facilities to provide for repair of British operated Hudsons and Liberators in addition to American operated planes'.

On 20 April 1942 Maj Gen. Chaney reported that the Lockheed workers would complete the 'technical area' of Langford Lodge about 1 June, and that entire project would be finished by 1 September. He added that hard standings and utilities such as the water and electricity supplies would be furnished either by the Army Air Force or the Lockheed Corporation. In another cable sent on the same day, Chaney stated that 50,000 square feet of the hangar area would be ready by 1 May 1942.

Langford Lodge was by no means the only Air Depot. In January 1942, the headquarters of the USAFBI arranged with the British Ministry

A chapter section page from the Lockheed Overseas Corporation Report on Langford Lodge. *(NARA)*

of Aircraft Production for the construction of a signal and aircraft maintenance depot at Warton, in Lancashire. This project was to be larger than Langford Lodge, since it was planned for 3,800 persons. An idea as to the scale of the facility can be gained by the size of the so-called 'technical area' alone.

Armoury	35,000 ft.^{2}
Engine accessories	22,000 ft.^{2}
Ferry command and Meteorology...	11,000 ft.^{2}
Parachutes and aircraft stores	34,000 ft.^{2}
Decontamination	500 ft.^{2}
Flight sheds	57,000 ft.^{2}
Airframe repair	304,000 ft.^{2}
Propeller repair	16,000 ft.^{2}
Observation tower	5000 ft.^{2}
MT Garage	20,000 ft.^{2}
Engine and Carburettor	66,000 ft.^{2}
Army signals	35,000 ft.^{2}
Guardhouse	500 ft.^{2}
Fire station	2000 ft.^{2}
Oil and paint stores	10,000 ft.^{2}
Army headquarters	15,000 ft.^{2}
Salvage hangars	20,000 ft.^{2}
Blacksmith and field services	3000 ft.^{2}
Carpenter's shop	5000 ft.^{2}
TOTAL	696,000 ft.^{2}

Because of the apparent need for a repair depot in Great Britain, before either of the previously mentioned facilities could be completed, the facilities of the Burtonwood Depot appeared necessary for the Anglo-American air programme.

Prior to its acquisition by the USA, it was British Government owned, but operated under a civilian management and afforded employment for approximately 4,000 people, as recorded by Maj Gen Chaney, who briefed SPOBS - Supply in cable Message #1312 sent on 28 April 1942, giving not only employment figures, but also that it was being operated by Fairey Aircraft and the Bristol Aeroplane Company. The transfer was confirmed on 23 May. During that transfer time, the War Department was already making plans for Burtonwood to become the initial permanent Base Depot for the Army Air Forces in the United Kingdom. At the same time Gen. Marshall announced in message #616 issued 7 May 1942 that the first depot was to have its headquarters at Warton the second at Molesworth in Cambridgeshire.

A further example of the scale of operations planned for Northern Ireland was when on 30 March 1942 a memo was sent to the Commanding General USAFNI by Maj Gen Chaney and signed Charles L Bolte, Brigadier General, General Staff Corps, Chief of Staff on the subject of US Air Support Command Northern Ireland. In it the General gave the recommended strength and composition of the command and the allocation of units to aerodromes:

1. *Long Kesh - one light bomber group headquarters, one light bomber squadron, one observation Squadron - 80 officers, 1,888 men.*
2. *Maghaberry - Two observation squadrons*

One corner of the 'Mod & Tech' drawing office at Langford Lodge. The men present at their drawing boards are a mix of American military and American and Irish civilians. (NARA)

Just one of the dining rooms at Langford Lodge - here civilian and military men ate. (NARA)

- 28 officers, 451 men.

3. St Angelo - One pursuit group headquarters. Two pursuit squadrons - 92 officers, 1480 men.

4. Mullaghmore - To go to Coastal Command in exchange for Nutts Corner.

5. Toome - One transport group headquarters. Three transport squadrons - 156 officers, 1662 men.

6. Greencastle - Two pursuit squadrons. One pursuit group headquarters - 60 officers 1200 men.

7. Maydown - Two pursuit squadrons - 100

officers, 1100 men.

8. Nutts Corner - one medium bomb group headquarters. Two medium bomb squadrons - 148 officers, 1645 men

9. Cluntoe - Two medium bomb squadrons - 61 officers, 850 men.

10. Bishop's Court - is to be built and will be ready in about one year. Two light bomber squadrons from US when completed.

11. Bally Herbert* [sic] - One pursuit group headquarters. Two pursuit squadrons - 102 officers, 1363 men

12. Kirkiston* - Two pursuit squadrons - 24

Not the best of images, but one that nevertheless shows ten Lockheed P-38 Lightnings at Langford Lodge. *(NARA)*

officers, 598 men.

13.Eglinton* - One pursuit group headquarters. Two pursuit squadrons - 130 officers, 1513 men.

14 Langford Lodge - Mobile depot group, one transport squadron. One repair centre - 200 officers, 500 civilians. 2100 men

*Airfields marked * will be retained by the British for use of 82 Group (fighter).*

Support Command Headquarters will be located near USAFNI Headquarters with an approximate strength of 30 officers and 150 men. Interceptor Command Headquarters will be located near Dundonald with the strength of 32 officers and 169 men

The preparation in Great Britain for the Eighth Bomber Command involved not only the use of considerable repair and maintenance depots such as Burtonwood, Langford Lodge and Warton. The preparations also involve such steps as acquisition or erection of billets for headquarters personnel and the construction of airfields.

In March and April 1942 the headquarters of the United States Armed Forces in the British Isles was to receive a number of tentative schedules for the arrival of aircraft for the Eighth Air Force. One such example was the schedule received in the middle of April gave a breakdown of categories of aircraft that were to leave for Great Britain about 15 May 1942. There were to be three bombardment squadrons, one reconnaissance squadron, with eight B-17s in each squadron, a group headquarters with three B-17s squadrons for each group the total to be thirty-five aircraft. There was also to be two pursuit groups, to be made up of three squadrons of twenty-five aircraft with five additional for

group headquarters. There was to be a total of eighty pursuit aircraft per group or one hundred and thirty aircraft in the two pursuit groups, although no mention was made of what types were to be used.

However, when Maj Gen Chaney heard of the plans from Brig Gen Davison it became clear that at least two groups would be made up of Lockheed P-38E twin-engined fighters. Chaney raised objections with the War Department stating that the plan to use P-38Es was unsatisfactory for use by the Eighth because:

1. *The reported speed limit of three hundred miles per hour.*
2. *The objectional handling qualities caused by compressibility stalls which affects the planes maneuvrability.*
3. *The report that the tail assembly would have to be redesigned to eliminate buffeting.*
4. *The fact that the P-38 was an Interceptor Fighter and not suitable for fighter escort or bombardment.*
5. *The understanding that the assignment of the first two pursuit groups to reach the theater were to act as support for the bombardment missions of the Eighth Air Force rendered the Spitfire as the best fighter in the theater.*

The message included arguments why the British Supermarine Spitfire should be the fighter of the Eighth Air Force. *'The Spitfire...'* stated Chaney *'... had better fire-power and maneuvrability than the P-38, a factor of great importance in furnishing protection for bomber operations'*. His other argument for the Spitfire was a virtual reiteration of his arguments for operational integration with the RAF. He declared *'...By using*

Spitfire VB of the 107th Tactical Reconnaissance Squadron (code AX), 67th TRG *(NARA)*

Gassed up and ready to go! Three P-38s at Langford Lodge *(NARA)*

the Spitfire, the tonnage saved in the initial aircraft establishment of replacements in ammunition, ground equipment, spare parts and tools would be an important factor in relieving the strain on shipping. The principal of simplicity favours the employment of one type of Air Corps fighter in this theater'.

This message, #1284 in the SPOBS - Air Force file dated 25 April 1942 appears to be over the signature of Gen Chaney, but bears the notation *'Originated by Lt Col Snavely'*.

The spare parts problem continued to arise - during April more than eighty-one operational aircraft were unserviceable due to a shortage of spares and that of the British P-51B Mustangs at least fifty per cent were unserviceable. Chaney therefore insisted that at least ninety days worth of spare parts were shipped to Great Britain before the arrival of operational units.

The War Department pondered for several weeks over this problem before apparently deciding that the views of a general officer of the USAFBI were needed to supply further information on the issues of the Eighth Air Force. To this end it summoned Brig. Gen. Eaker to Washington - an action that caused Maj. Gen. Chaney to send the following message to Washington for the personal attention of General Marshall: *'In your cable 389 you stated that Gen Eaker is desired in Washington before a conference. In cable 1208 reply was made that Gen Eaker was not available at this time and it was suggested that the conference be held in the United Kingdom with a representative from Washington in attendance. Today's statement is made to cable 446 that Gen Eaker will be returned to Washington to confirm on supplies shipping etc. Because of the illness of Col McClelland and because of the shortage of experienced air officers the staff is greatly handicapped at the present time. In addition Gen Eaker's attention should not be diverted to supply matters, not only because he has an important tactical job in the United Kingdom but also* because he must assist in conferences now starting with the British'.

Since the War Department had already told the SPOBS that the first aircraft for the Eighth Bomber Command/Air Force would arrive about the middle of May 1942, the formation of the Headquarters appeared to Maj Gen Chaney as a step that must be taken immediately.

As it transpired, none of the May and June delivery schedules for the Eighth Bomber Command materialised. A message to the War Department dated 13 June 1942 did, however set forth a comprehensive plan which was to be followed.

It defined the general area where the bulk of the units of the United States Army Air Force coming to the United Kingdom would be located. This region was south of the line from The Wash to Leicester and north and north-east of London. The plan provided for this location of the first bomber units just west of Cambridge, those arriving later were to be placed in East Anglia. No aircraft from Eighth Bomber Command reached Great Britain in what is sometimes called the Chaney period of the history of the ETO. A portion of the headquarters staff requested by Maj Gen Chaney for the Eighth Bomber Command reached 'Pinetree' near High Wycombe on 12 May 1942. The Commander of the group was Capt O'Dilliand Turner.

Although there were no aircraft assigned to any unit of the USAFBI for offensive or tactical purposes during the Chaney period nevertheless some officers of the USAFBI headquarters were confronted with problems that were to be a huge part of aircraft operation namely those responsible for the functioning of the Air Corps Ferry Command.

Air Technical Services.
The function and duties of the Air Technical Section emerged gradually from the pressing need for the exchange of technical information concerning   design   requirements   and

Spitfire VBs of the 67th Tactical Reconnaissance Group. Two squadrons are represented here: 'ZM' coded machines are assigned to the 12th Tactical Reconnaissance Squadron; 'VX' coded aircraft belong to the 109th, an activated National Guard squadron from Minnesota. *(NARA)*

developments in building and perfecting military aeronautical equipment. There were a number of agencies within the US government who were desperately interested in information for technical reasons. In the early period of the war, this information was necessary for the formulation of the total war policy, allocation of equipment and evaluation of both the enemy power and Allied defence.

While the USA was supposedly a neutral nation, these matters were investigated and transmitted by the Military Attaché for Air to the interested parties in the War Department especially the Army Air Forces. However, the activities of the Military Attachés were limited by small staffs and the fact that the British government could not be expected to release classified technical information - no matter how obtained - except by special arrangement to neutral nation.

Capt Benjamin S Kelsey, Air Corps, was the Military Attaché for Air from 4 June to 16 October 1940. After the air attacks on Great Britain during August and September, the concern of the War Department in gathering more complete information was shown in the appointment of a number of special Military Attachés and Special Observers as has already been detailed.

The Air Technical Section was organised with departments for research and development, production requirements, special projects, statistics and administration. As a liaison agency, the Technical Section had no authority to order modification or changes of equipment. Their activity was in determining operational requirements and investigating new developments for transmittal to the interested parties. The Technical Section through the specialised knowledge and interest in Gen

Chaney and Gen Alfred Jefferson Lyon, had been in close touch with all developments in military aircraft since the beginning of the war, and there was a file of information on experimental British and American aircraft, equipment, statistical data on production operations and equipment. In addition the personnel established extremely close contact with the Air Ministry and the Ministry of Aircraft Production which greatly facilitated the exchange of information between the Materiel Command, Wright Field, Dayton Ohio, and the Assistant Chief of the Air Staff, Material, Maintenance and Distribution, Washington, and their counterparts in the Ministry of Aircraft Production in London.

The activities of Air Technical Services was broken down into the following items:

a. Transmitting of reports on modification and developments of aeronautical equipment between the RAF and Material Command, USAAF.

b. Compiling statistics on operations and maintenance of aircraft.

c. Procuring information on enemy aircraft equipment methods and their developments in conjunction with Air Corps intelligence.

d. Forming committees for the joint study of developments and modifications.

e. Visiting British agencies and companies and the maintenance of offices within these firms to keep in touch with technical developments.

f Transmitting unsatisfactory reports on equipment from the Eighth Air Force to the Materiel Command.

g. Facilitating the visits of civilian technical representatives from the US in the UK.

Brig Gen Lyon was the Chief of the Section until his death in November 1942, when Col.

Harold Fowler was acting head untl Col H C Bunker was appointed Chief.

Even in the early days, the size and scope of the section were enormous. Apart from more general sections, there were offices covering Engine and Propeller Projects, Armaments, Fighter Aircraft, Radar and Electronics Projects Office, Radio and Electrical Equipment office, Air technical Intelligence Office, Bomber Aircraft Office, Chemical Office, Air/Sea Rescue office... the list was almost endless,

The Air Technical Services also had representatives on a number of committees: Mission for Economic Affairs, London Munitions Assignment Board, Airframe Modifications Committee, Engines, Propellers and Accessories Committee, Ministry of Aircraft Production and Admiralty...

From located microfilms, it appears that Air Technical Services had involvement with Power Jets Limited, as they did with other aircraft engine manufacturers and establishments.

Founded on 27 January 1936, Power Jets consisted of Frank (later Sir Frank) Whittle, Rolf Dudley-Williams, James Collingwood Tinling, and Lancelot Law Whyte of investment bankers O T Falk & Partners.

Initial premises were rented from steam-turbine manufacturer British Thomson-Houston (BTH) at Rugby, Warwickshire. In addition to the founder members, the company initially 'borrowed' some fitters from BTH to assist in the project and later Power Jets was able to get 'one or two' people on loan from the RAF. By the beginning of 1940, the company had a total workforce of about twenty-five. In 1938 Power Jets had moved from Rugby to BTH's works in Lutterworth.

A significant breakthrough for the company came in 1940 when at the prompting of Stanley Hooker, Ernest Hives, chairman of Rolls-Royce, visited Lutterworth and offered to make any parts Whittle required at Rolls-Royce's Derby experimental shop.

The Power Jets W.1 design was the first turbojet to run, being first tested on 12 April 1937, and powered the Gloster E.28/39, the first jet aircraft to fly in the United Kingdom. The W.1 was also the first jet engine built in the United States where, as the General Electric I-A, it was the first US-built jet engine to run, and as the production General Electric J.31 it powered the Bell P-59A Airacomet.

This came about after a visit to Great Britain mid-1941 by General Arnold who was so impressed by flight demonstrations of the Gloster E.28/39 jet aircraft he had witnessed that he arranged for the Power Jets W.1X turbojet engine to be shipped by air to the US, along with drawings for the more powerful W.2B/23 engine, so that the US could develop its own jet engine.

General Electric's extensive experience in turbocharger production made them the natural choice for producing such an engine. The initial prototype, the General Electric I-A, was essentially based on the W.2B/23. It first ran on 18 April 1942 and developed a static thrust of 1,250 pounds.

The I-A air intake consisted of two peripheral slots which led to a double-sided, centrifugal

Air Commodore Sir Frank Whittle, OM, KBE, CB, FRS, FRAeS (*b.* 1 June 1907, *d.* 9 August 1996) at his desk, with a model of the Gloster E.28/39 on it with another model of his W-1 engine behind, and on the extreme left, a Gloster Meteor. Through the efforts of Air Technical Services, the Americans quickly 'caught up' on jet engine development.

Gloster test pilot Gerry Sayer takes Whittle's work aloft for the first time on 15 May 1941.

compressor. A series of vanes guided the air into the impeller eyes. After radial compression, the air was diffused and turned 90 degrees rearwards, before entering a set of ten reverse-flow combustion chambers. A relatively short shaft connected the compression system to the single stage axial turbine. After expansion through the turbine, the combustion products exhausted the engine through the simple conical propelling nozzle, via the jet-pipe. For the turbine section, GE used a proprietary metal developed for their turbochargers, Hastelloy B. Problems were uncovered with overheating bearings and solved by fitting the turbine with larger cooling blades and changing the air diffuser, as well as switching to a ram air cooling air inlet.

Using their turbocharger expertise, General Electric was able, in a short space of time, develop a 1,400 pounds thrust thrust version, known as the I-14. Later they increased the thrust to 1,600 pounds thrust . This version was referred to internally as the I-16 However, the USAAF later decided to standardise all their jet engine naming, at which point the I-16 became the J31.

In 1941 experiments with boosting the W.1's thrust by introducing a liquid coolant were initiated, the first fluid tried being liquid ammonia which proved to be too effective, resulting in the engine over-speeding and pushing the thrust and rpm indicators off the scales, before later trials changed to using water, and then water-methanol. A system to test the technique in the E.28/39 was devised but never fitted.

The Power Jets W.2 was intended to be produced by Rover, but because of delays was later transferred to Rolls-Royce where it entered

production as the Welland, powering early versions of the Gloster Meteor. The W.2B/500 design, modified by Rover as the B.26, after transfer to Rolls-Royce and further redesign, entered service as the Derwent, which replaced the Welland in the Meteor.

After initial suggestions in 1939 by the Engine Department of the Royal Aircraft Establishment (RAE), the latter's Pyestock Section experimented with the technique of injecting fuel into the engine's exhaust nozzle, later known as reheat, and this technique was further refined after Power Jets, and the personnel from Pyestock had been amalgamated. Reheat was then flight trialled in the W.2/700 engines in a Meteor I. The technique increased the Meteor's speed by 30-40 mph.

On 28 March 1944, after discussions with the Air Ministry, Whittle reluctantly agreed to the nationalisation of Power Jets Ltd for £135,000, and the company became Power Jets (Research and Development) Ltd.

After the Second World War, the company was merged with the Turbine Division of the Royal Aircraft Establishment (RAE) at Farnborough, to form the National Gas Turbine Establishment (NGTE Pyestock).

In 1951 Power Jets received $4,000,000 (£1,428,600) from the US Government in advance payment for American use of some 200 Power Jets Whittle gas turbine patents for the next 20 years. Previously, patent fees payable by the US had been waived by Power Jets for the duration of the war.

There was also Air Technical Services contact with Major Frank Halford who was an English aircraft engine designer. He is best known for the series of De Havilland Gipsy engines, widely used by light aircraft in the 1920s and 30s but also work on turbines. During the war, he became interested in jet engines and designed a simplified version of Frank Whittle's centrifugal-flow designs with the air intake on the front and 'straight-through' combustion chambers. Known initially as the Halford H.1, the project was undertaken for De Havilland, who produced it as the De Havilland Goblin.

Major Frank Bernard Halford CBE FRAeS MSAE,(b.7 March 1894, d.16 April 1955) the Technical Director of the De Havilland Aircraft Company. *(DH Aircraft Co.)*

The Halford H.1 was on paper in April 1941, drawing went to the manufacturing shops at Stonegrove and Stag Lane in August, and the first engine ran the following April, reaching 3,010 pounds thrust two months later. No airframe existed for it, but eventually, two were cleared for flight in a Gloster F.9/40 and was first flown 5 March 1943.

The Bell Aircomet was not the only American jet aircraft under development that suffered from lack of American expertise in jet engines. After receiving documents and blueprints comprising years of British jet aircraft research arranged by the Military Attachés in London, General Arnold believed that American machines could benefit from the British-made jet engines, and the Materiel Command's Wright Field research and development division tasked Lockheed to design such an aircraft. With the Germans and British clearly far ahead in development, Lockheed was pressed to develop a comparable jet in as short a time as possible and the legendary Clarence 'Kelly' Johnson submitted a design proposal in mid-June and promised that the prototype would be ready for testing in 180 days. The Lockheed team, beginning 26 June 1943, produced the airframe designated the XP-80 in 143 days, delivering it to Muroc Army Airfield on 16 November.

The project was so secret that only five of the more than 130 people working on it knew that they were developing a jet aircraft, and the British engineer who delivered the Goblin engine was detained by the police because Lockheed officials could not vouch for him. After the engine had

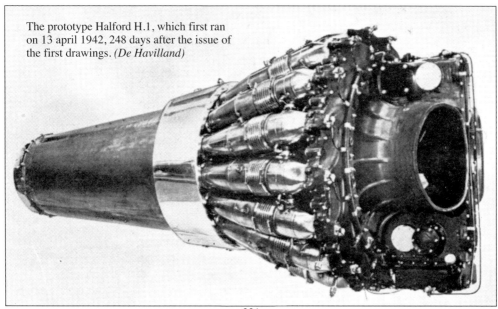

The prototype Halford H.1, which first ran on 13 april 1942, 248 days after the issue of the first drawings. *(De Havilland)*

been mated to the airframe, foreign object damage during the first run-up destroyed the engine, which delayed the first flight until a second engine (the only other existing and robbed from the prototype De Havilland Vampire) could be delivered from Britain.

The first prototype (44-83020) was nicknamed *'Lulu-Belle'* (also called *'Green Hornet'* because of its paint scheme). Powered by the replacement Halford H.1 taken from the prototype de Havilland Vampire jet fighter, it first flew on 8 January 1944, with Lockheed test pilot Milo Burcham at the controls. Following this flight, Johnson said, *'It was a magnificent demonstration, our plane was a success – such a complete success that it had overcome the temporary advantage the Germans had gained from years of preliminary development on jet planes'.*

The British jet engine data obtained by Air Technical Services had proved invaluable. In test flights, the XP-80 eventually reached a top speed of 502 mph at 20,480 feet, making it the first turbojet-powered USAAF aircraft to exceed 500 mph in level flight.

Air Technical Services also provided a myriad of technical data and actual examples of hundreds of British inventions or developments. Once such case was the cavity magnetron - a high-powered vacuum tube that generates microwaves using the interaction of a stream of electrons with a magnetic field while moving past a series of open metal cavities called cavity resonators. Electrons pass by the openings to these cavities and cause radio waves to oscillate within, similar to the way a whistle produces a tone when excited by an air stream blown past its opening. The frequency of the microwaves produced, the resonant frequency, is determined by the cavities' physical dimensions. H. Gerdien invented an early form of the magnetron in 1910, and other forms were invented and developed in the 1920s and 30s.

John Randall and Harry Boot radically improved the cavity magnetron in 1940 at the University of Birmingham, England. They invented a valve that could produce multi-kilowatt pulses at 10 centimetre wavelength, an unprecedented discovery. The high power of pulses from their device made centimetre-band radar practical for the Allies of World War Two, with shorter wavelength radars allowing detection of smaller objects from smaller antennas. The small cavity magnetron tube drastically reduced the size of radar sets so that they could be more easily installed in night-fighter aircraft, anti-submarine aircraft and escort ships.

In the post-war era, the magnetron became less widely used in the radar role. This was because the magnetron's output changes from pulse to pulse, both in frequency and phase. This makes the signal unsuitable for pulse-to-pulse comparisons, which is widely used for detecting and removing 'clutter' from the radar display. The magnetron remains in use in some radars but has become much more common as a low-cost microwave source for microwave ovens. In this form, approximately one billion magnetrons are in use today.

Ferry them Across!
The SPOBS had assumed responsibility for the Eastern Terminus Atlantic Division Air Corps Ferry Command on 1 November 1941. The operations in the North Atlantic ceased to function for some time during the early spring of 1942, but the War Department ordered that they

'Lulu-Belle' the Lockheed XP-80, serialled 44-83020. *(Simon Peters Collection)*

The library and crew rest area of the Atlantic Ferry Command at Prestwick. *(NARA)*

be resumed on 1 April 1942. Resumption was made in order to permit a B-24 Ferry Command aircraft to return to the United States. Due to spares shortages, four fuel booster pumps were borrowed from RAF operational aircraft so the flight could take place. The basis of this loan was that the USAAF would replace the pumps borrowed as soon as possible. Maj Gen Chaney stated that prompt action be necessary *'in order to obtain the cooperation of the RAF in the future'*.

When Major General Arnold made his inspection of the British Isles in May 1942, he was not satisfied with the operation of the Army Air Corps Ferry Command on the North Atlantic route. He criticised especially the weather communications and operational control. The message of Maj Gen Chaney which reported the criticisms of the commanding general for the Army Air Force seems to be sufficiently important to be quoted: *'Conference with Gen Arnold this date. He is not satisfied with weather communications and operational control of ferry*

route. He directs that if these services are not functioning perfectly on return flight, I am to personally advise Gen Spaaz that Gen. Arnold direct movements to be held until services are adequate. This is for a AAFFC. Gen. Arnold insists on united control points by senior operations officer for the entire route. This setup would not conflict with a plan of the tactical organisation to be responsible for actual clearance. Whether communications control officers will answer directly to senior operations officer for any deficiencies of which may occur. I have recommended Presque Isle as control point. Gen. Arnold desires control board to be constructive as control station, board to be similar to RAF Ferrying Command Boards at Prestwick and Montréal. Gen. Arnold is not interested in proposed plans or reasons why route is not functioning. He was told route would be functioning for movement. Route was not functioning on May 24'.

The criticism of the Ferry Command summarised in the cable from Chaney resulted in definite steps for its improvement. Presque Isle became a control point, and Brigadier General Frank O'Driscoll Hunter became the 'Movement Operational Control Officer'. Brigadier General Benjamin F Giles was placed in charge of communications and weather staff, its headquarters also being at Presque Isle. Still another step was taken to avoid communication difficulties in the future, namely coordination of such facilities with those of the Canadians. On 1 July 1942 however, the Ferry Command was taken over by the European wing, Air Transport Command.

Steps were also taken to improve the communication system on the eastern end of the route. On 6 June 1942 Maj Gen Chaney requested the War Department provide four SCR277 Mobile Radio Range Beacons for use on the Eastern Terminus of the Atlantic Division Air Corps Ferry Command. He stated that the IFF to be carried were not known. He added if it would be possible to switch from narrow to broad pulse bands on the IFF, since the latter would be required in case of forced landings or emergencies. IFF, of course, stands for Identification Friend or Foe .

Another step to improve the facilities of the Eastern Terminus of the Atlantic Division Air Corps Ferry Command in June 1942 was an investigation conducted by Air Corps officers on the staff of Maj Gen Chaney to determine how many Ferry Command personnel should be billeted at Prestwick and Stornoway. At that time Prestwick was a town of approximately 8,500 populations about 38 miles south-west of Glasgow Stornoway was on the island of Lewis which had a population at that time of around 3,700 persons. It was found that seventy five men could be accomodated permanently at Prestwick, but at Stornoway there was temporary accomodation for about 100 men.

Tube Alloys, Manhattan and Colossus.
The American Embassy in London became heavily involved in dealing with the Tube Alloys/Manhattan Project , the latter being the code name for the American-led effort to develop a functional atomic weapon during World War Two. The controversial creation and eventual use of the nuclear bomb engaged some of the world's leading scientific minds, as well as the US military, and most of the work was done in Los Alamos, New Mexico, not the borough of New

York City for which it was named. The Manhattan Project came about in response to fears that German scientists had been working on a weapon using nuclear technology since the 1930s - and that Hitler was prepared to use it.

On 28 December 1942, President Roosevelt authorised the formation of the Manhattan Project to combine these various research efforts with the goal of weaponising nuclear energy. Facilities were set up in remote locations in New Mexico, Tennessee and Washington State, as well as sites in Canada, for this research and related atomic tests to be performed.

The British and Americans exchanged nuclear information but did not initially combine their efforts. Britain rebuffed attempts by Vannevar Bush, an American engineer, inventor and science administrator, who headed the US Office of Scientific Research and Development and James Conant an American chemist, a transformative President of Harvard University, and the first US ambassador to West Germany. In 1941 both these men made attempts to strengthen cooperation with its own project, codenamed Tube Alloys, because it was reluctant to share its technological lead and help the United States develop its own atomic bomb.

As a result - and through knowledge gained via the SPOBS and the Military Attachés - the USA decided as early as April 1942 that they should proceed alone. Also via the SPOBS, it became clear that he British, who had made significant contributions early in the war, did not now have the resources to carry through such a research programme while fighting for their survival. Tube Alloys was falling behind its American counterpart and on 30 July 1942, Sir John Anderson, the minister responsible for Tube Alloys, advised Churchill that: *'We must face the fact that... [our] pioneering work ... is a dwindling asset and that, unless we capitalise it quickly, we shall be outstripped. We now have a real contribution to make to a 'merger.' Soon we shall have little or none.'* That month Churchill and Roosevelt made an informal, unwritten agreement for atomic collaboration.

In 1942, and with the threat of invasion by Germany still apparent, the United Kingdom dispatched around twenty British scientists and technical staff to the USA to be involved in the Manhattan Project, along with their work, which had been carried out under the codename Tube Alloys, to prevent the potential for vital information falling into enemy hands.

The opportunity for an equal partnership no longer existed, however, as shown in August 1942 when the British unsuccessfully demanded substantial control over the project while paying none of the costs. By 1943 the roles of the two countries had reversed; in January Conant notified the British that they would no longer receive atomic information except in certain areas. While the British were shocked by the abrogation of the Churchill-Roosevelt agreement, head of the Canadian National Research Council C J Mackenzie was less surprised, writing *'I can't help feeling that the United Kingdom group [over] emphasises the importance of their contribution as compared with the Americans.'* As Conant and Bush told the British, the order came *'from the top'*.

The British bargaining position had worsened; the American scientists had decided that the United States no longer needed outside help, and they wanted to prevent Britain from exploiting post-war commercial applications of atomic energy. The committee supported, and Roosevelt agreed to, restricting the flow of information to what Britain could use during the war - especially not bomb design - even if doing so slowed down the American project. By early 1943 the British stopped sending research and scientists to America, and as a result, the Americans stopped all information sharing. The British considered ending the supply of Canadian uranium and heavy water to force the Americans to share again, but Canada needed American supplies to produce them. They investigated the possibility of an independent nuclear programme but determined that it could not be ready in time to affect the outcome of the war in Europe.

By March 1943 Conant decided that British help would benefit some areas of the project. James Chadwick and one or two other British scientists were important enough that the bomb design team at Los Alamos needed them, despite the risk of revealing weapon design secrets. In August 1943 Churchill and Roosevelt negotiated the Quebec Agreement, which resulted in a resumption of cooperation between scientists working on the same problem. Britain, however, agreed to restrictions on data on the building of large-scale production plants necessary for the bomb. The subsequent Hyde Park Agreement in September 1944 extended this cooperation to the postwar period. The Quebec Agreement established the Combined Policy Committee to coordinate the efforts of the United States, United Kingdom and Canada. Stimson, Bush and Conant served as the American members of the Combined Policy Committee, Field Marshal Sir John Dill and Colonel J J Llewellin were the British members, and C D Howe was the Canadian member.

One of the most significant advances the British made was in the area of code-breaking. Considerable information was transmitted from the UK to the US during and after World War Two relating to code-breaking methods, the codes themselves, cryptoanalyst visits, mechanical and digital devices for speeding code-breaking, etc. When the Atlantic convoys of war material from the US to the UK came under serious threat from U-boats, considerable encouragement and practical help were given by the US to accelerate the development of code-breaking machines. Subsequent co-operation led to significant success in Australia and the Far East for breaking encrypted Japanese messages.

'Ultra' was the designation adopted by British military intelligence in June 1941 for wartime signals intelligence obtained by breaking high-level encrypted enemy radio and teleprinter communications at the Government Code and Cypher School (GC&CS) at Bletchley Park.

Left: Vannevar Bush (*b*. 11 March 11, 1890, *d*. 28 June 1974)

Right: James Bryant Conant (*b*. 26 March 1893, *d*. 11 February 1978)

Both men were involved in the Manhattan Project and dealing with Tube Alloys in the UK.

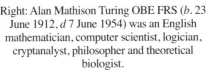

Left: Thomas Harold 'Tommy' Flowers, BSc, DSc ,MBE (*b*. 22 December 1905, *d*.28 October 1998) was an English engineer with the British Post Office.

Right: Alan Mathison Turing OBE FRS (*b*. 23 June 1912, *d* 7 June 1954) was an English mathematician, computer scientist, logician, cryptanalyst, philosopher and theoretical biologist.

Ultra eventually became the standard designation among the western Allies for all such intelligence. The name arose because the knowledge thus obtained was considered more important than that designated by the highest British security classification then used (Most Secret) and so was regarded as being Ultra secret.

Much of the German cypher traffic was encrypted on the Enigma machine. Used properly, the German military Enigma would have been virtually unbreakable; in practice, shortcomings in operation allowed it to be broken. The term Ultra has often been used almost synonymously with Enigma decrypts. However, Ultra also encompassed decrypts of the German Lorenz SZ 40/42 machines that were used by the German High Command and the Hagelin machine.

Colossus was a set of computers developed by British codebreakers in the years 1943–1945 to help in the cryptanalysis of the Lorenz cypher. Colossus used thermionic valves - commonly called vacuum tubes - to perform Boolean and counting operations. Colossus is thus regarded as the world's first programmable, electronic, digital computer, although it was programmed by switches and plugs and not by a stored programme.

Colossus was built by research telephone engineer Tommy Flowers to solve a problem posed by mathematician Max Newman at Bletchley Park. Alan Turing's use of probability in cryptanalysis contributed to its design. It has

sometimes been erroneously stated that Turing designed Colossus to aid the cryptanalysis of the Enigma. Turing's machine that helped decode Enigma was the electro-mechanical Bombe, not Colossus.

By all accounts, even the SPOBS and the Military Attachés never fully managed to get their hands on information about Bletchley Park, Ultra and Colossus. The prototype, Colossus Mark 1, was confirmed to be working in December 1943 and was in use at Bletchley Park by early 1944. An improved Colossus Mark 2 that used shift registers to quintuple the processing speed, first worked on 1 June 1944, just in time for the Normandy landings on D-Day. Ten Colossi were in use by the end of the war, and an eleventh was being commissioned. Bletchley Park's use of these machines allowed the Allies to obtain a vast amount of high-level military intelligence from intercepted radiotelegraphy messages between the German High Command and their army commands throughout occupied Europe.

The existence of the Colossus machines was kept secret until the mid-1970s, although some of its personnel and secret information undoubtedly fuelled further development in the US in the late 1940s; the devices and the plans for building them had previously been destroyed in the 1960s as part of the effort to maintain the secrecy of the project. This deprived most of those involved with Colossus of the credit for pioneering electronic digital computing during their lifetimes.

Chapter Eight

USAFBI becomes the ETOUSA.

When the Americans finally enter combat.

The SPOBS and the Military Attachés operating out of the American Embassy in Grosvenor Square had two levels of tasks: provide as much intelligence as possible back to Washington DC - and to make preparations for the American Armed Forces to arrive in the United Kingdom.

Gen. Chaney's memo to the Chief of Staff is a good summary of the actual plans and preparations made for the American installations in Great Britain.

Discussions by SPOBS with various organisations in reference to army G-4 services included:

1. *The War office. Subject: supply and transportation for US forces.*
2. *The joint planning staff. Subject: channels of trans-Atlantic communications.*
3. *The directorate of combined operations. Subject: materiel for landing operations.*
4. *The inter-service security committee. Subject: inter-service codes and ciphers.*
5. *The inter-service recognition committee. Subject: principles and techniques of inter-service land sea and air communications.*

The Special Observers were not authorised to make commitments of any nature and that all British construction was to be undertaken with a view to British utilisation and was not contingent upon US participation in the war. A base area was proposed containing all depots and shops with about 20,000 men.

No ports were to be allocated to the US for their use exclusively because of limited number of western ports and the likelihood of German attacks. It was decided that supply shipments were to be directed twenty-four hours prior to arrival to support available for utilisation at the time. Bristol and Liverpool were to be most frequently used. Northern Ireland troops were to be supplied through Belfast and Londonderry.

Suppliers were to move from ports to base depots by rail under British control. Almost all supplies required for the forces were to be brought from the US due to British shortages of food, gasoline, coal, hardware, motor parts and construction timber. The storage facilities were to be constructed, as were camps for QM troops. It was contemplated to locate a general Depot area in the central portion of Northern Ireland and the other in the Central Midlands portion of England. Gasoline, oil and coal would to be procured from the British, and replaced in kind by delivery at British ports of shiploads of these commodities.

It was determined that woollen outer garments be worn throughout the year, and that protective clothing being available due to the possible enemy use of gas.

It was proposed that an American officer would study British Movements Control, so that in the event of US entry in the war, this officer would become a coordinator between the US and British supply and troop movements.

It was decided that, although QM units technical orders provided that a large proportion of the personnel be armed with pistols, it was essential that every enlisted man be armed and trained with a rifle, as protection against parachute troops and similar enemy activity.

The engineering problems connected with US forces moving into the UK involved planning, constructing and maintaining installations. Roughly 110,000 personnel were to be located in four separate areas. It was recommended that civilian labour be used, the skilled component to be brought from the US, the unskilled portion to be provided by the British from the UK.

Concerning ordinance, it was decided that there were no problems requiring action which could not be provided by operating practice already employed or visualised in the Field Service Division of the Ordnance Department.

It was decided that insufficient medical units and fixed hospitals were included in the true basis of Rainbow 5. No provision had been made for the Chief Surgeons office, convalescent hospitals, nor the means of collecting and evacuating the sick and injured. Planning for construction of housing and hospitalisation with attendant water supplies and sanitary arrangements before the arrival of US troops constituted the biggest and most pressing problem.

The supply facilities were to provide space for only seventy-five days of supplies. It was proposed that the stockage of supplies all classes for proposed forces in the UK be determined by the Special Observer Group and that these be forwarded to the War Department for inclusion in basic logistics plans.

It was recommended that all housing and hospitalisation be completed before US troops enter the UK. During the summer and autumn of 1941 changes in the estimated number of American troops to be stationed in Great Britain were numerous. The tendency was to increase the proposed number which in turn increased the amount of research in and investigation required by the SPOBS.

Gen Chaney was designated as Commander of the United States Army forces in the British Isles (USAFBI) following a directive from the President on 8 January 1942 he retained his responsibilities as Special Observer. SPOBS was inactivated by HQ USAFBI on 31 May 1942.

After the headquarters of the USAFBI had been functioning for slightly less than two months, the War Department informed Maj Gen Chaney in a cable dated 26 February 1942 that *'your headquarters is not a mission, that is a theatre'.*

Meanwhile, the administrative capability was rapidly expanding. By 3 March, 24 offices and 239 enlisted men reached Euston Railway Station, London. A further two officers and fifty-five enlisted men were scheduled to arrive later by motor convoy. With the arrival of these troops for assignment to the London quarters USAFBI, on 20 March 1942, the Headquarters Command USAFBI was activated.

The term Headquarters Command came about after discussions by the General Staff Officers over the advisability of establishing a 'Post of London'. Colonel Summers, the Adjutant General HQ USAFBI was not in favour of the suggestion for the following reasons:

1a. Only the Secretary of War can designate the name of a military post.

b. Use of 'London' would be a violation of security regulations.

c. If the headquarters moved a new term would be needed.

2. Better use headquarters command.

The presence of a 'Headquarters Command' in London resulted in the appointment on 21 March of Col Clarence H. Brand JAGD as Acting Provost Marshall in addition to his other duties. Col Brand served for slightly over one month in the capacity when on 25 April 1942 he was relieved from his duties as Provost Marshall and Col Pleas B Rogers was appointed to the post.

On 1 May 1942 in conformance with the AGO cable #357, dated 17 April 1942, a detachment headquarters, and Headquarters Company, USAFBI would be organised, attached to the HQ Detachment SPOBS, pending the arrival of the Headquarters Company from the USA.

More and more officers were arriving. Col Carl L Marriott CWE became the USAFBI Chemical Warfare Officer, while around the same time a Special Services Section came into existence, concerning it itself with welfare, recreation, the operation of post exchanges, athletics, liaison with the American Red Cross. The special service officer was to be Lt Col Edmund M Barnum.

On 21 April 1942, the Quartermaster Service USAFBI was formally extended to include the Graves Registration Service, commanded by Col W E Middlemart.

The last general order, dated 31 May 1942, of the HQ USAFBI announced a system of base-censorship.

1. Effective 8 June 1942 censorship offices are established as follows:
   Base Censor Office #1: attached to USAFNI with station at Belfast.
   Base Censor Office #2: assigned to HQ Command with station at London.
2. The office of the chief military sensor USAFNI effective 8 June 1942 is really designated Base Censor Office #1.
3. Base Censor Office for postal censorship will operate under the Assistant Chief of Staff, G-2 this Headquarters.

On that same date, the command known as the United States Army Force of the British Isles became the European Theater of Operations (ETO), to include all United States Army Forces except those persons serving on the London

The dark days of the London Blitz may have been going on when the SPOBS first came into being, but by the time they were disbanded, it was not the end however. To quote Winston Churchill *'Now this is not the end. It is not even the beginning of the end. but it is, perhaps, the end of the beginning'*.

Munitions Assignment Board, the Military Attachés and personnel attached to Embassies. The jurisdiction of Headquarters, European Theater of Operations was to include staff of the United States Marine Corps assigned to military units in the Theater. Maj. Gen. Chaney was to be the first Commanding General, European Theater of Operations.

Boeing Stratoliner N-19908 seen here in TWA colours - it was used by Maj Gen Chaney to return to the USA on 20 June 1942. *(Simon Peters Collection)*

It was not until this time that the exact definition of the 'Special Observers' was questioned. The creation of the ETO indicated that the Special Observer group would continue. The dual responsibilities of Maj Gen. Chaney and other leading officers of the HQ USAFBI led to some confusion and misunderstanding as Chaney said in a cable, message #124, dated 9 March 1942: '...*continued use of the term Special Observer Group is causing confusion in administration. Personnel are still being assigned to duty Special Observer Group London. Recommend the use of the term Special Observer Group and that all personnel now carried on your records as SPOBS be transferred to HQ USAFBI and our orders for new personnel dispatched this theater read as assigned to USAFBI for duty. Officers arriving here with War Department orders placing them on temporary duty as Special Observers when in fact they are coming here for a permanent assignment. This is especially true of officers assigned for duty Air Force Bomber Command Headquarters.*'

A cablegram which Maj Gen Chaney sent to the War Department on 14 April included a possible reason for the continued use of the term 'Special Army Observer'. '...*the majority of the numbers of this group were classed as Special Army Observers. As such, they were reported by the State Department to the British Foreign Office through the American Embassy. This enabled them to be placed on the diplomatic list which recorded them certain diplomatic privileges*'.

Chaney continued to explain the difference between Special Army Observer and Military Observer. '...*The latter were regarded as local representatives of the State Department and not ordered by it to report to the British Foreign Office; hence they were denied such diplomatic privileges.*'

Gradually the duties of the SPOBS wound down. The Technical Services Coimmittee was abolished on 19 June, and its records, functions and responsibilities transferred to the main SPOBS section. Air Force Ferry Command was transferred to the Eighth Air Force on the same day.

The SPOBS Section itself lost its identity on 10 July 1942, with the publication of General Order 13, ETO, stating that the Special Observers Section had changed its name to the Air Technical Section and that the Special Observers Section had been deactivated.

So the Special Observer period of the ETO ended with the recall of Maj Gen Chaney to Washington DC. He was Commanding General of the ETO for just twelve days. The order, dated 20 June stated that he would return to his post once the period of temporary special duty was over, but his subsequent assignment was outside the ETO. Message # 2234 describes his departure the same day:

'... *Major General Chaney departed for Washington very promptly since this report was made of passengers leaving Prestwick on Stratoliner on 20 June 1942. 'Passengers on the Stratoliner N-19908 which departed Prestwick 1910 hours our time today are General Chaney, His Majesty King Peter II of Yugoslavia and party of six, also Sir Reginald Waterhouse, British courier.*'

Chapter Nine

Aftermath.

In which Attlee goes begging, Balls pays up, the CIA go full speed ahead worldwide, and Powell speaks his mind

What started as a plan for the destruction of the British Empire evolved into what at best could be called intelligence gathering and at worse, was called spying. It then developed into being allies, albeit reluctant ones. Then came the so-called 'Special Relationship'. Many critics deny the existence of this, calling it a myth and nothing but a public relations exercise, which has been used primarily by the British because the British have needed the Americans more than the Americans have required the British at a high level.

What began as a Churchillian public relations exercise as the UK statesman tried to whip up American support for the British position over Europe continued with mention of the Soviet Union in a tour that saw the cigar-chomping Churchill deliver his 'Iron Curtain' speech.

During the late 1950s and early 1960s, when UK Prime Minister Harold Macmillan had the tricky task of downsizing Britain, he cloaked it with the idea that Britain had a 'special relationship' with the Americans. Macmillan kept selling the idea that Britain was the brains to American brawn. Whatever the case, the 'Special Relationship' was and is only used when it suited the American point of view; history shows that it has often been discarded.

The Army Air Force went into combat on 29 June 1942, when Captain Charles Kegelman and crew from the 15th Bomb Squadron flew one of twelve Bostons from 226 Squadron RAF on an abortive attack on the Hazebrouck Marshalling Yards, thus becoming the first USAAF crew to maker a bombing attempt on enemy-occupied Europe. A few days later, one suspects in something of a propaganda exercise, on 4 July the 15th Bomb Squadron again 'borrowed' a number of aircraft from the RAF - this time six Bostons again from 226 Squadron to attack Dutch airfields. Two machines and

Members of Kegelman's Independence Day crew received the Distinguished Flying Cross from Gen Eaker at the same ceremony at Molesworth when Charles C Kegelman became the first member of the Eighth Air Force to receive the DFC for bringing home a badly damaged Boston on the 29 June mission. Seen posing with Kegelman in the picture of their left is Sgts, Cunningham, Golay and Lt Dorton. The two sergeants flew with Kegelman on the first Eighth Air Force bomber mission on 29 June. *(Simon Peters Collection)*

crews were listed as 'missing in action'.

The early days of the Eighth Air Force were far from being 'Mighty' - which was a late 1960's copywriters invention anyway - was in fact in the words of General Ira Eaker '... *a piddling little force*'. But that was to change and is outside the scope of this work.

Without doubt, the War Plan Red of 1930 was a scheme to destroy the British Empire. Some have claimed it was nothing but 'contingency planning' to give officers in the War Department 'something to do' during the dog days of the 1930s, and that the 'invasions' never happened. Even so, the British Empire was destroyed - and, in the main by the Americans. War Plan Red was about regime change by those who saw the USA as the world's only superpower. These 'plans' favoured the Americans, and there is a clear and direct linkage between that plan and America's activities of today.

Rebuilding for the future

'All forces under German control to cease active operations at 2301 hours Central European Time on 8 May 1945...'.

With that announcement, Churchill's fame as a war leader was became a very mixed blessing. The emphasis he gave for the need to finish the war against Japan suggested once more that war was his only real interest. The country was awash with rumours that he was also planning a war against Russia.

With the defeat of Germany, the Allies set about gaining as much technical intelligence, equipment, scientists and technicians from the Germans as possible, much of which has been described in *Operation Lusty - the Race for Hitler's Secret Technology* by the same author.

In the UK a General Election took place on 5 July, but the results were not announced until 26 July to enable those overseas in the forces to vote and have their results counted. The result took the country by surprise. With 48 per cent of the vote, Labour gained a Parliamentary majority of 146 seats, the largest in post-war British history. The swing of twelve points to the Labour Party was unprecedented. The vote represented more a rejection of the Conservative Party than of Winston Churchill's performance as a war-leader.

The notion that the Conservatives were defeated by 'the forces vote' is mistaken - as the opinion polls showed, the civilian vote was strongly pro-Labour. War weariness was a factor against Churchill among civilians and servicemen alike. The result plunged him into depression and his party into shock, but it was not quite as bad as it seemed. The first-past-the-post system gave an exaggerated picture of Labour's triumph, disguising the fact that just over half the electorate had voted against them.

'The Labour Party is a Socialist Party, and proud of it'. The sentence was buried in the party's 1945 election manifesto, which promised that Labour would take control of the economy and in particular of the manufacturing industry. The manifesto pledged nationalisation of the Bank of England, fuel and power industries, transport, and iron and steel. And with a majority of more than 150, the party could and would not be denied its aims.

One by one the industries fell into the public sector, where they became subject to elaborate planning controls. For the most part the takeovers were highly popular; none more so than the nationalisation of the coal mines. Other nationalisation operations were regarded more cynically. No sooner had British Railways taken over the old regional semi-private networks than jokes and sarcastic comments began to circulate about unreliable, crowded trains and crumbling stations.

After the initial

Clement Richard Attlee, 1st Earl Attlee, KG, OM, CH, PC, FRS (*b*. 3 January 1883, *d*. 8 October 1967); a British statesman and Labour Party politician who served as Prime Minister of the United Kingdom from 1945 to 1951.

Attlee shaking hands with US Secretary of State James F Byrnes upon his arrival at National Airport in Washington, 1945. *(NARA)*

euphoria of nationalisation, it wasn't long before doubts began to emerge. The state industries were smothered by bureaucracy and the demands of Labour's economic gurus, both amateur and professional. Their bolder ideas were often subsumed in the delicate balance between principle and pragmatism. It was clear that the lumbering machinery of economic planning could not deliver what the voters had demanded and Labour had promised: full employment, secure jobs with fair wages, an end to wartime rationing and decent homes for all.

It has been argued that the Attlee government's main disadvantage was that Britain had been on the winning side in the war. British cities and industries had certainly been on the receiving end of German air raids but had not suffered anything like the wholesale destruction which allowed the renascent German economy to start from a clean sheet. More importantly, the British economic class structures - and bitter the enmities - survived the war unscathed, in contrast to those countries which had been traumatised by

invasion and occupation into rethinking their economic cultures.

And even when the war was finally over, the victorious, but impoverished British nation maintained vast numbers of men and resources tied up in an empire on which the sun was about to set. In Europe, Britain paid for a huge army of occupation in Germany. The dawn of the nuclear age, and British pride demanded handsome investment in the new terrible weapons which would keep it allegedly a first-class power. The disarmament, which some in the Labour party craved, proved illusory as - in Churchill's words again - an iron curtain descended across Europe, and the cold war began.

The UK had not just spent World War Two 'giving away' its technology to the Americans - they continued it on into the post war years; and not just to the Americans. In a sparkling example of supreme commercial naiveté, the Labour government under Attlee made a so-called 'good-will' gesture that was later heavily criticised, which allowed the Soviet Union access, under the terms of a 1946 UK-USSR Trade Agreement, to several Rolls-Royce Nene jet engines. The Soviets, who at the time were well behind the west in jet technology, reverse-engineered the Nene and installed their own version in the MiG-15 interceptor, used to good effect against US-UK forces in the subsequent Korean War, as well as in several later MiG models.

There were other obstacles in the path of Labour's would-be revolutionaries. The country was, to put it brutally, bankrupt. It had poured its wealth into the war effort and in 1945 was groaning under a mountain of debt. It had pawned many of its most valuable assets, including a huge slice of overseas investments, to service that debt.

Once again they turned to the Americans. The Anglo-American Loan Agreement was a post World War Two loan made to the United Kingdom by the USA on 15 July 1946, negotiated by the economist John Maynard Keynes.

Supposedly, the loan was made primarily to support British overseas expenditure in the immediate post-war years and not to implement the Labour government's welfare reforms. British treasury officials believed they could achieve the Labour government's domestic reforms without the loan if Britain withdrew from all significant overseas commitments.

At the start of the war, Britain had spent the money that they did have in regular payments for materiel under the 'US cash-and-carry' scheme. The rights to place American bases in the UK were also traded for equipment, for example, the Destroyers for Bases Agreement, but by 1941 Britain was no longer able to finance cash payments, and Lend-Lease was introduced. Lend-Lease aid did not have to be paid back, but the other loans did.

Large quantities of goods were in Britain or transit when the USA unexpectedly and suddenly terminated Lend-Lease on 21 August 1945. The British economy had been heavily geared towards war production (around fifty-five per cent GDP) and had drastically reduced its exports. The UK, therefore, had come to rely on Lend-Lease imports to obtain essential consumer commodities such as food while it could no longer afford to pay for these items using export profits. The end of lend-lease thus came as a great economic shock. Britain needed

to retain some of this equipment in the immediate post war period. As a result, the Anglo-American loan came about. Lend-lease items kept were sold to Britain at the knockdown price of about 10 cents on the dollar giving an initial value of £1.075 billion.

Maynard Keynes, then in poor health, was sent by the UK to the US and Canada to obtain more funds. British politicians expected that given the UK's contribution to the war effort, especially for the lives lost before the United States entered the fight in 1941, America would offer favourable terms. However, instead of a grant or a gift, all Keynes was offered was a loan.

It seems that America did not realise - or care - that Britain was bankrupt. The loan was denounced in the House of Lords, but in the end, the country had no choice. The USA offered US$3.75bn (US$51 billion in 2018), and Canada contributed another US$1.19 bn (US$16bn in 2018), both at the rate of two per cent annual interest. The total amount repaid, including interest, was US$7.5bn (£3.8bn) to the US and US$2bn (£1bn) to Canada.

Of course, the loan was made subject to conditions, the most damaging of which was the convertibility of sterling. It may have not been the intention - although many are by no means sure of that - but the effect of convertibility was to worsen massively British post-war economic problems. International sterling balances became convertible one year after the loan was ratified, on 15 July 1947. Within a month, nations with sterling balances - that is pounds which they had earned from buying British exports, and which they were now permitted to sell to Britain in exchange for dollars - had drawn almost a billion dollars from British dollar reserves, forcing the British government to suspend convertibility and to begin immediate drastic cuts in domestic and overseas expenditure. The rapid loss of dollar reserves also highlighted the weakness of sterling, which was duly devalued in 1949 from $4.02 to $2.80.

In later years, the term of two per cent interest was rather less than the prevailing market interest rates, and was then seen as a 'very advantageous loan' by members of the British government.

Much of the loan had been earmarked for foreign military spending to maintain the United Kingdom's empire and payments to British allies before its passage, which had been concealed in negotiations through to the summer of 1946. Keynes had noted that a failure to pass the loan agreement would cause Britain to abandon its military outposts in the Middle Eastern, Asian and Mediterranean regions, as the alternative of reducing British standards of living was politically unfeasible. Here was yet another way that the Americans could implement a modified version of War Plan Red to destroy the British Empire without firing a single shot.

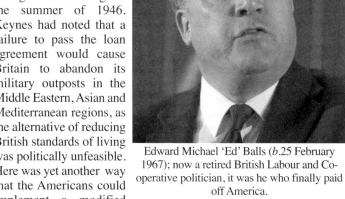

Edward Michael 'Ed' Balls (b.25 February 1967); now a retired British Labour and Co-operative politician, it was he who finally paid off America.

Britain's lend-lease balance was paid off for £650 million (US$900 million) in 2006. The last payment was made on 29 December 2006 for the sum of about $83m (£45.5m), the date being the last working day of the year. The final payment was six years late, the British government having suspended payments due in the years 1956, 1957, 1964, 1965, 1968 and 1976 because the exchange rates were seen as impractical. After this final payment, Edward Michael 'Ed' Balls, the Economic Secretary to the Treasury in Tony Blair's 'New Labour' government, formally thanked the US for its wartime support.

The CIA, proprietary companies and 'regime change'.

American subterfuge and covert operations did not end with World War Two. The Central Intelligence Agency (CIA) the successor to the Office of Strategic Services (OSS) quickly realised the excellent potential of using aviation to further its nefarious activities, although it took time before it gained strength. In simplistic terms, it was all about discovering 'Reds under the beds' overseas and doing everything it could to encourage 'regime change' - a concept that, as I have already stated seems to have originated with War Plan Red - in and against countries that the USA saw as its enemies.

It is remarkable that so much remained secret for so long, despite the air proprietaries - as these aviation companies were known - having their cover blown and the testimony on

their activities given by Lawrence R Houston, former CIA general counsel, to Frank Church's Senate Committee on Intelligence Activities in 1975. Possibly the most well-known of these was Air America. Much of this had came about in the early 1970s when a series of troubling revelations had appeared in the press concerning intelligence activities. First came the revelations by Army Intelligence Officer Christopher Pyle in January 1970 of the US Army's spying on the civilian population and Senator Sam Ervin's Senate investigations produced more revelations. Then, on 22 December 1974, the *New York Times* published a lengthy article by Seymour Hersh detailing operations engaged in by the CIA over the years dubbed the 'family jewels'. Covert action programmes involving assassination attempts on foreign leaders and covert attempts to subvert foreign governments were reported for the first time. In addition, the article discussed efforts by intelligence agencies to collect information on the political activities of US citizens.

Working through the corporate tangle of the Air America complex is as fascinating as it is frustrating. The scale of the CIA's air arm has been slowly revealed as one company connection led to another. Sometimes an airline would be wholly owned by the CIA, like Air America, sometimes it would be partially funded by the Agency, and sometimes it could just be counted on for favours. Amongst the airlines partly financed and set up by the CIA were Air Ethiopia, Air Jordan, and Iran Air. United Business Associates (UBA), a related proprietary to Southern Capital - the corporation central in the CIA's insurance complex - explained one of the methods the Agency used to win over foreign governments. A proprietary company is one whose shares may not be offered to the public for sale; a private company.

All of the airlines - and there were many - partially funded by the CIA would have a selection of aircraft available to the Agency at any time. The CIA also set up proprietaries for

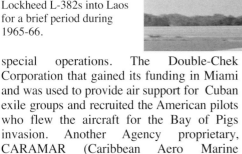

In April 1965 Continental Air Services Inc was formed as a subsidiary of Continental Airlines with a view to 'help' Air America with its commitments in Laos; in reality Continental wanted a share of the government's subsidies for such work. CASI operated Lockheed L-382s into Laos for a brief period during 1965-66.

special operations. The Double-Chek Corporation that gained its funding in Miami and was used to provide air support for Cuban exile groups and recruited the American pilots who flew the aircraft for the Bay of Pigs invasion. Another Agency proprietary, CARAMAR (Caribbean Aero Marine Corporation) hired the Cuban exile-pilots that flew B-26 bombers against Cuba.

The Agency's 'operating' companies carried out business as private companies, while its 'non-operating' companies were only prepared to do business. The latter varied in complexity according to their tasks, and the most elaborate were legally licensed to conduct business with nominee stockholders, directors, and officers overseen by one of the Agency's proprietary management specialists. Amongst their jobs was the purchase of Helio-Couriers and Pilatus PC-6 Porters and Turbo-Porters for which they provided cover.

In the mid-1960s Continental Airlines was awarded lucrative non-CIA MATS (Military Air Transport System) contracts to fly troops to Vietnam, and wanted a larger share of the profitable Southeast Asian business.

The CIA agreed to this on the basis that it could have back-up service if any country in Southeast Asia evicted Air America because of

its CIA connections. Continental created a wholly owned, Nevada-registered subsidiary, Continental Air Services in September 1965 after the Agency for International Development (AID) and CIA contractor William Bird and Son sold off its Vientiane, Laos operation. Continental announced that CIA veteran Robert Rousselot, who had seventeen years experience with CAT, was to be its president. Moreover, in August of the same year, Continental paid $4.5 million in cash to take over Bird Air, which had worked with and had contracts from the CIA for several years. Robert L 'Dutch' Brongersma, who had been manager of Bird Air and also had associations with CAT, became the general manager of Continental Air Services.

The company was not to regret its move. AID contracts alone totalled $24,288,000 when CAS ceased trading in July 1972, and Continental president Robert F Six could happily tell his stockholders that from 1965, the airline's operations in Laos, Thailand, and Vietnam had indeed very profitable.

In Panama, the Agency had a deal with Pan Am in the mid-1950s which allowed CIA men planted within the company to rummage through baggage during transit stops. The airline went as far as providing them with mechanics' overalls.

In the Far East, AA goes back to 1946 when

a so-called 'Chinese partnership' formed by Chennault and associates in October of that year was given a one-year CNRRA contract, commencing in January 1947 flying aircraft provided by the US government. The airline was called CNRRA Air Transport, but the name was changed to Civil Air Transport at the start of 1948 when the contract was not renewed.

In 1950, the CIA reorganised its air arm. The Far Eastern activities were grouped under the umbrella of The Pacific Corporation, initially incorporated in Delaware on 10 July 1950, as Airdale Corporation, which changed its name to Pacific on 7 October 1957. Within the CIA, the proprietaries were known euphemistically inside the Agency as 'The Delaware Corporations'. so called because the State of Delaware was chosen for their incorporation because of its lenient regulation of corporations. The Pacific Corporation became the holding company of Air America, Inc, Air Asia Co, Ltd., and Civil Air Transport Ltd.

During the early 1950s there were two struggles over the air proprietary inside the Agency: where control should lie inside the Agency itself, and what policies should apply to the operation of the company.

Civil Air Transport had several Douglas DC-4s and began modest operations between Hong Kong, Taipei, and Tokyo, and soon acquired DC-6s. As the overt side of the airline's operations grew, the problem of direct competition with private corporations arose for the first time.

Northwest Orient Airlines was then flying to Tokyo, Seoul and Manila, and an executive of the company, who was chairman of the Civil Aeronautics Board in the late 1940s and early 1950s, had noted the CIA's interest in the area and used to complain that CAT was interfering and was taking passengers from his airline.

In 1959 Northwest went to the Civil Aeronautics Board for a decision, maintaining that private industry should not be interfered with by government competition. The Agency argued the need for cover and said that they made every effort to restrict carriage to the minimum necessary to maintain it. Although some passengers travelled on CIA aircraft rather than Northwest machines, the impact was minimal and unavoidable, Houston claimed. The CAB came down on the side of the Agency.

Arizona Helicopters and Laos Air Development bolstered the CIA's Laotian air transport network, companies which also benefited from the rich pickings of USAID contracts put their way with the blessing of the Agency.

A smart-looking C-46 of Civil Air Transport, with five company air hostesses in front.

Douglas DC-4 N5519V of Seven Seas Airlines seen during a turn-around in Holland.
(Simon Peters Collection).

Just as the Air America complex was mostly the CIA's Far East air operation, Southern Air Transport became the Caribbean and South American clandestine air arm. Although the corporation was technically a separate entity, not involved with Air America, it was an integral part of the complex from a management perspective. All management decisions for Southern Air Transport were made by the same CIA consultant and advisory team that established Air America policy.

As in the case of Civil Air Transport, the CIA decided to buy an already existing company. Southern Air Transport had been founded in 1949, and for the next twelve years F C. 'Doc' Moor and Stanley G. Williams tried to make a success of the small Miami-based company. They owned one C-46 and leased two others, and business consisted of flying cargo from Florida to the Caribbean and the Bahamas. The company was losing money, in debt, and had assets of little over $100,000.

This unsatisfactory state of affairs was transformed overnight when the CIA paid $300,000 for the company, Moor and Williams remained officers of the corporation, and nominally owned fifty per cent of the company. The airline acquired two DC-6s from Air America when the CIA took over on October 1, 1960, and immediately began to fly international MATS contracts to undisclosed destinations. Profits jumped to $75,000 within three months of the CIA takeover, the balance sheet showed assets over $2.5 million, and the company was no longer in debt.

EXCOMAIR was an attempt to achieve overall coordination, conduct a thorough inventory of all the equipment that the Agency had in the aviation field, and keep track of who needed what. Lawrence Houston was appointed the chairman of the committee and representatives were selected from the Clandestine Services, the Support Directorate and the Agency's Executive Suite. The proceedings were so secret that the executive secretary was instructed to keep no notes or keep minutes.

In 1968, EXCOMAIR met to deal with a request from George Doole for several million dollars to modernise Southern Air Transport. He argued that as every major airline in the world was using jets, Southern needed to follow suit if it was to live its cover. He added that the airline should have the best and most effective equipment available in case the Agency needed to intervene in South America.

The request met with some opposition at the meeting from a CIA officer who quoted an intelligence estimate which had been presented to the President to the effect that open US intervention in the internal affairs of Latin America would damage an already bad American image. A Clandestine Services officer working in paramilitary affairs replied, in effect, that however accurate the intelligence estimate might be, they had a responsibility to be prepared for the worst possible contingency. Doole's request was approved and SAT received its several million dollars for jets.

Southern Air Transport was built up as a contingency against the possibility of future Latin-American interventions, and the Agency did not want to depend on the US Air Force. The precise analysis of the intelligence community had concluded that political, economic, and social conditions in Latin America had deteriorated so badly that a long period of instability was at hand. The Agency wanted to be sure that it had the assets for any contingency.

Southern Air Transport and Air America often overlapped in their activities in Africa, where the CIA's need for air support, especially in the Congo in the sixties, had been brisk. The CIA has had a financial interest in a plethora of companies, of which Pan African Airlines, based in Lagos, Nigeria, was a good example. Although not an outright proprietary, it did considerable business with the CIA, and eighty per cent of its revenues came from a single US government contract for air service to remote outposts in West Africa, and the CIA was a major participant in that contract to the tune of $575,000 a year.

An example of the 'smokescreen' of multi-ownership corporations was Seven Seas Airlines, supposedly created in October 1957 by two former employees of Slick Airways, the brothers Urban L and Earl L Drew. In Europe the demand for charters increased rapidly in 1959. In addition to the rising holiday transport to the sunny south of Europe, more and more ship's crews were transported around the globe, and more and more migrants chose not to stay on a ship for months to reach their new destination. Seven Seas Airlines was one of the first companies that saw this gap in the market and in June 1959 decided to open a European branch at Amsterdam-Schiphol. To carry out these flights, two C-54 Skymasters were 'purchased'.

Seven Seas Airlines SA a Luxembourg-based company created in Amsterdam in 1959 and who operated supply flights on behalf of the CIA to supporters of the Katanga province during the civil war in the Congo, with its aircraft temporarily based in Nairobi, Kenya.

Aircraft 'purchases' during this period was something of a dubious title. More than one

The Air America complex at Udorn, Thailand in 1973. Visible on the ramp are Fairchild C-123s, Pilatus Turbo-Porters and Beech 18 derivatives, along with assorted helicopters. *(via CIA)*

airline owner warned me that unless you were there to actually see the suitcases of money change hands, never ever say sold or bought - always say 'obtained'. The same applied to who actually owned the aircraft - and this is not discussing legitimate leases, instead refering to the web of parent/daughter companies, holding companies, and cut-out shell organisations that meant that the true owners could not be traced.

It is quite a regular occurance for this period to be able to trace aircraft back to the USA, only to have the trail go cold. Even aircraft registrations - supposedly sacroscant in order to preserve the machines identity - were not beyond manipulation. There are numerous accounts of different aircraft carrying the same registration or serial number - a good example being a number of Lockheed Constellations and Douglas DC-7s operated by the North American Aircraft Trading Company, an organisation operated by Hank Wharton and used for arms smuggling into Biafra. At least five of his aircraft 'wore' - often applied with just speedtape for one flight - the registration 5T-TAC or 5T-TAG during the conflict.

Pan African was set up in 1962 in close cooperation with the Agency and was considered to be a covert asset. It was the largest subsidiary of Africair, the holding company of a Miami man named Thomas R Green who ran a string of air companies in Florida, Africa, and the Caribbean. Green served on the board of

directors of Southern Capital, the CIA insurance proprietary, while Africair's Washington attorney was James Bastian, the longtime attorney for Air America and one-time secretary of Air Asia. The man who owned fifteen per cent of Africair, Marvin L. Evans, ran Southern Capital for the CIA until his retirement in 1973. There were minor air companies all over the world which shared this incestuous relationship with the CIA.

The CIA also leaned heavily on the USAF aircraft making the 'embassy run' all over Africa, and the world, when embassies have 'supplies' flown in. In Africa, the CIA code name for this was Project Eagle and it had limitless potential for nefarious activities.

Regime changes - the CIA frowned upon the use of the more obvious phrase 'government overthrows' - were a common feature in Africa where the USA and the Soviet Union was fighting World War Three by proxy. Older piston-powered aircraft - Douglas DC-3s, 4s, 6s and 7s, along with variants of the Boeing Stratocruiser and Lockheed Constellation - became common sights in many of the war zones. Along with them came men like Edwin 'Ed' Dearborn and Edwin Paul 'Ed' Wilson, South African Jack Malloch and German-American Henry 'Hank' Wharton.

Southern Air Transport needed the CIA because Air America had run into a technical difficulties. The airline had been deeply

In an effort to avoid paying Portuguese authorities a tax on exporting a cargo of Super Constellation tyres, to be used on arms smuggling flights from Sao Tomé into the Biafran airstrip of Ule, Hank Warton flew the cargo aboard L-1049G '5T-TAF' from Lisbon to Malta on 16 February 1968. The intention was then to fly back to Lisbon where he could argue that the cargo was now 'in transit' from Malta to his base at Bissau. An Air Traffic Controller at Luqa Airport, however, realised '5T-TAF' were marks that legally belonged to a Cessna 206. The aircraft was impounded and the crew of four were arrested. Within hours Warton and the aircraft's captain, Robert Major, were spirited to Catania aboard a fishing boat - courtesy of 'a friendly organisation based in Sicily'.

One of a number of clandestine B-17s seen at Clark Field in the Philippines during the late 1950s. A close study of the photograph shows a number of antennas and exhaust flame suppressors on the engines. *(Simon Peters Collection).*

involved in a Military Air Transport System (MATS) contract from the early 1950s. MATS contracts kept the proprietary's air fleets in constant use and paid good rates - some said suspiciously so. It was essential for Air America to get these contracts if it was to maintain such a large inventory during times of paramilitary and covert inaction.

MATS changed its policy in 1956, requiring that bidders on its contracts to be certified. As Air America could not become certificated because of a technicality, these contracts were switched to Southern Air Transport, so the money stayed within the family.

But the air proprietaries were becoming increasingly complicated, and the CIA was getting more and more involved in getting more and more aircraft, which were getting more and more expensive. It was felt inside the Agency that certain projects were demanding new and expensive equipment while in fact older aircraft were already available for the job.

It was decided that an amorphous group working on an informal basis should be created to keep abreast of the various air proprietaries. A 5 February 1963 memorandum entitled 'Establishment of Executive Committee for Air Proprietary Operations' (termed as EXCOMAIR) noted that the committee was *'...to provide general policy guidance for the management of air proprietary projects, and review final recommendations for approval of air proprietary project actions'.*

In addition to flying MATS contracts and covert missions, the airlines also fulfilled far-flung commercial charters such as one from AID to deliver relief supplies to Bangladesh. As a full member of CIA Air, Southern Air

Transport was able to benefit from the interchange of equipment, favourable loans, and government contracts, and bought, leased, and sold aircraft within the empire. Another organisation was Western Enterprises Inc. of Taiwan. Western Enterprises had been founded by the CIA in 1951 to funnel covert American assistance to the Republic of China in Taiwan. Their activities included airborne intelligence flights over mainland China as well as dropping agents, using B-17 aircraft and crews of Civil Air Transport.

In 1952, the CIA also trained five Taiwanese pilots and two mechanics in Japan in low-level flights and drop techniques, and in 1953, this new 'Special Mission Team' or 'Special Operations Unit' was supplied with two B-17s on loan from Western Enterprises – with more to follow. Between 1954 and 1959, three of these B-17s are known to have been shot down by the People's Liberation Army: - one over Fujian on 26 May 1954 by anti-aircraft artillery, killing four crew members. Another was shot down at in Jiangxi on 22 June 1956 by a PLA MIG-17, killing eleven people aboard. Also '835' of the 34th Squadron was destroyed over Guandong on 29 May 1959 by a PLA MIG-17PF, killing fourteen people aboard.

In 1957, the workhorse for covert China overflights from Taiwan still was the B-17. These CIA aircraft had been stripped of all weapons and national markings and had been painted black. In mid-September, one of these Taiwan-based B-17s was flown to Clark Air Force Base in the Philippines. Here two Polish five-man crews from Wiesbaden in Germany - code name 'Ostiary'- who normally flew penetrations of Soviet airspace, were trained on the aircraft for covert missions into Tibet. After the training had been completed, the B-17 was flown to Kadena, Okinawa, where training was continued with the Tibetan agents that had to be parachuted into their country. Two missions into Tibet are known to have been flown by the B-17: the first one in early October 1957, and the second one in early November, each time staging through Kurmitola airfield, East Pakistan, but in 1958 the programme was continued using a C-118A.

As far as can be ascertained the two aircraft were a pair of Boeing B-17Gs, 44-85531 and 44-83785, but in order to make the aircraft non-attributable during the missions into Tibet fake tail numbers were carried.

Another large Stateside air proprietary with very strong CIA links was Intermountain Aviation Inc - also called at various times Intermountain Airways and Intermountain Airlines - which operated from a former US Air Force base in Marana, Arizona, just outside of Tucson. A subsidiary of a Nevada holding company called Pan Aero Investment Corporation, Intermountain was founded, as far as can be ascertained, in the fall of 1961 as a direct result of the Agency's Bay of Pigs fiasco. Cuba had convinced the Agency that it could not depend on the US Air Force for air cover and needed its own strike force. Southern Air Transport had been formed to provide a long-haul heavy transport capability, while Intermountain was to provide close-in air support for covert guerrilla operations for the CIA in Southeast Asia and elsewhere during the Vietnam War era.

Intermountain's cover was that it acted as a storage base for the US and foreign aircraft, offered a full service and in-depth maintenance facility, and also provided a fire-fighting parachutist service for the US Forest Service. In promotional material, the company claimed to provide 'total air support for remote operations'. Publically, Intermountain helped train, supply, and deliver 'smoke jumpers', who were able to drop into the rough country from low altitudes to establish field camps from which remote operations could be carried out - activities which bore a very close resemblance to the activity of special services operations and spy teams. Intermountain also had STOL aircraft, developed a pinpoint parachute-drop system, and repainted and reconfigured aircraft to special requirements.

The company provided a service and maintenance facility for all sizes and kinds of aircraft and had a virtually unlimited capacity for the reconfiguration of airframe, engine, ordnance, avionics, fuel, cargo, and passenger capacity. Marana, with its dry Arizona climate, was a good place to mothball aircraft in between covert missions, and they would be ferried back to the US by AA pilots. Intermountain was a major operation.

The only area in which it was not equipped was helicopters, and this gap was filled by Arizona Helicopters, a subsidiary of a Delaware corporation called Air Services International which was based seventy-five miles away to the northwest in Scottsdale.

Although there was no formal connection between the two companies, Arizona acted as the rotary wing of the fixed-wing Intermountain fleet and advertised worldwide operations which included contracts in Laos and Nepal.

Eventually one of the two 'Tibetan' B-17s - 44-83785 - was ferried back to the USA - the date is not clear from surviving records, but it is thought that between May and August 1961, it was modified by Lockheed at Burbank to be able to carry the Fulton Skyhook recovery system.

The Fulton surface-to-air recovery system was used by the CIA, the USAF and United States Navy for retrieving persons on the earth's surface. It involved using an overall-type harness and a self-inflating balloon which carried an attached lift line. An aircraft engaged the line with its V-shaped yoke, and the individual was reeled on board. Recovery kits were designed for one and two-person retrievals.

This system was developed by inventor Robert Edison Fulton Jr for the CIA in the early 1950s. It was an evolution from a similar system that was used during World War Two by American and British forces.

Experiments began in 1950 using a weather balloon, nylon line, and ten to fifteen pound weights, Fulton made numerous pickup attempts as he sought to develop a reliable procedure. Successful at last, he had his son photograph the operation. Fulton then took the film to Admiral Luis de Florez, who had become the first director of technical research at the CIA. Believing that the programme could best be handled by the military, de Florez put Fulton in touch with the

Office of Naval Research (ONR). Thanks to de Florez's interest, Fulton received a development contract from ONR's Air Programs Division.

By 1958, the Fulton aerial retrieval system, or Skyhook, as it became known, had taken its final shape. A package that easily could be dropped from an aircraft contained the necessary ground equipment for a pickup. It featured a harness, for cargo or person, that was attached to a 500-foot high-strength, braided nylon line. A portable helium bottle inflated a dirigible-shaped balloon, raising the line to its full height.

The pickup aircraft sported two tubular steel 'horns' protruding from its nose, thirty feet long and spread at a seventy degree angle. The aircraft would fly into the line, aiming at a bright marker tag placed at the 425-foot level. As the line was caught between the forks on the nose of the aircraft, the balloon was released at the same time the spring-loaded trigger mechanism secured the line to the aircraft. As the line streamlined under the fuselage, it was snared by the pickup crew, using a J-hook. It was then attached to a powered winch and pulled on board. The aircraft also had cables strung from the nose to the wingtips to keep the balloon line away from the propellers, in case the catch was unsuccessful.

The stage was now set for the first operational use of Skyhook. What became known as Operation Coldfeet began when a naval aircraft flying an aeromagnetic survey over the Arctic Ocean reported sighting an abandoned Soviet drift station. A few days later, the Soviets announced that they had been forced to leave Station NP9 when the ice runway used to supply it had cracked by an ice pressure ridge.

The idea to use the drift ice for the exploration of nature in the high latitudes of the Arctic Ocean belongs to Fridtjof Nansen, who fulfilled it on Fram between 1893 and 1896. The first stations to use drift ice as means of scientific exploration of the Arctic originated in the Soviet Union in 1937, when the first such station in the world, North Pole-1, started operations.

North Pole-1 was established on 21 May 1937 some twenty kilometres from the North Pole by the expedition into the high latitudes.

Two views of the Intermountain Aviation N809Z was the former B-17G 95-DL 44-83785 and carried the Fulton Recovery System on its nose. The aircraft had a parachutist chute in the tail and doors in the nose through which the retrieved person was recovered.

Sever-1, led by Otto Schmidt. 'NP-1' operated for nine months, during which the ice floe travelled 2,850 kilometres. On 19 February 1938, Soviet icebreakers *Taimyr* and *Murman* took off four polar explorers from the station, who immediately became famous in the USSR and were awarded titles Hero of the Soviet Union: hydrobiologist Pyotr Shirshov, geophysicist Yevgeny Fyodorov, radioman Ernst Krenkel and their leader Ivan Papanin.

Since 1954 Soviet 'NP' stations worked continuously, with one to three such stations operating simultaneously each year. The total distance drifted between 1937 and 1973 was over 80,000 kilometres. North Pole-22 is particularly notable for its record drift, lasting nine years. On 28 June 1972, the ice floe with North Pole-19 passed over the North Pole for the first time.

For nearly six months CIA-contract pilots Connie W Siegrist and Douglas Price had perfected their technique using the SkyHook. Now the Defense Intelligence Agency made funding available for the project. Siegrist and Price later conducted demonstrations for the Forest Service and Air Force while training for a covert operation to extract fellow CIA-contract pilot Allen L. Pope from an Indonesian prison. Pope had been shot down on 18 May 1958, while flying a B-26 for the CIA-supported rebel group that was trying to topple the Sukarno government. The planned rescue attempt proved unnecessary after Attorney General Robert Kennedy obtained Pope's release in July 1962.

The prospect of examining an abandoned Soviet ice station attracted ONR's interest. ONR wanted to compare Soviet efforts on drift stations with US operations. The previous year, ONR had set an acoustical surveillance network on a US drift station used to monitor Soviet submarines. ONR assumed that the Soviets would have a similar system to keep track of American submarines as they transited the polar ice pack, but there was no direct evidence to support this. Also, ONR wanted to compare Soviet efforts on drift stations with American operations.

The problem was how to get to NP9. To Captain John Cadwalader - who was to command what became known as 'Operation Coldfeet' - it looked like a wonderful opportunity to make use of the Fulton surface-to-air recovery system. Following a recommendation by Dr Max Britton, head of the Arctic program in the Geography Branch of ONR, Rear Admiral L D Coates, Chief of Naval Research, authorised preliminary planning for the mission while he sought final approval from the Chief of Naval Operations. The mission was scheduled for September, a time of good weather and ample daylight. NP9 would be within 600 miles of the US Air Force base at Thule, Greenland, the planned launching point for the operation.

ONR selected two highly qualified investigators for the ground assignment. Major James Smith, USAF, was an experienced paratrooper and Russian linguist who had served on US Drift Stations Alpha and Charlie. Lt Leonard A LeSchack, USNR, a former Antarctic geophysicist, had set up the surveillance system on T-3 in 1960. During the summer, the two men trained on the Fulton retrieval system, working in Maryland with an experienced P2V Neptune crew at the Naval Air Test Center at NAS Patuxent River, Maryland.

On 26 May 1962, the Intermountain Aviation B-17 with Jerry Daniels as winch operator on board launched the operation from Point Barrow, Alaska, flying out over the ice to drop the two men not on NP9, but another station, NP8. After 72 hours at the site, a pick-up was made of the Soviet equipment that had been gathered and of both men. This mission required the use of three separate extractions - first for a 150-pound bundle of Soviet equipment, documents and exposed film, then of LeSchack and finally of Smith. It seems the same aircraft and system was used in 1963 again with Jerry Daniels as winch operator picked up the body of an American scientist who died of a heart attack on a US ice station.

Operation Coldfeet was a success - the mission yielded information on the Soviet Union's Arctic research activities, including evidence of advanced research on acoustical systems to detect under-ice US submarines and efforts to develop Arctic anti-submarine warfare techniques.

While the Skyhook system provided an essential asset for all manner of intelligence operations, its utility as a long-range pickup system was somewhat undermined during the 1960s by the development of an aerial refuelling capability for helicopters. Still, it appears likely that Fulton's Skyhook did find employment in

Right: John Richard 'Jeff' Hawke. Typical of the men who became involved with 'the spooks', Jeff was a larger-than-life adventurer embued with more than his fair share of derring-do. Also, like many of them, it was clear that he was never destined to die in his own bed.

Below: Portugal received a number of Douglas A-26 Invaders by somewhat dubious means almost all of which were flown over the Atlantic by Jeff Hawke. Here is 'D 7107' in full Força Aérea Portuguesa (FAP) colours. A number were used in Luanda. *(Both Simon Peters Collection)*

some specialised clandestine operations following Coldfeet, although its subsequent use by CIA and the military services remains shrouded in secrecy.

Remarkably, only three years later in 1965, N809Z, the CIA Fulton-equipped B-17, gave a full demonstration of the technique and equipment it used over the Arctic when was featured in the ending of the James Bond movie *Thunderball*.

Almost typical of these covert activities was that of Intermountain and one of its pilots which was used in 1965 as a conduit in the sale of A-26 bombers to Portugal for use in that country's colonial wars in Africa. Officially there was an explicit US government embargo on weapon exports for use in Angola, Mozambique, or Portuguese Guinea, but unofficially the government, at its highest level, had decided to sell twenty A-26s, and the CIA proprietary was following orders. The arms dealer, Luber SA in Geneva, signed an agreement with Aero

Associates of Arizona to supply twenty aircraft that would be refurbished by Hamilton Aircraft. The first A-26 would be delivered by 30 April 1965 and the last one by January 1966. Besides the aircraft, a lot of spare parts and accessories would also be included in the purchase. Seven A-26s were flown from Arizona to Lisbon by a rotund englishman, former RAF Flight Lieutenant John Richard 'Jeff' Hawke, hired by a company called Aero Associates.

It is not clear how the export licenses were obtained, but in May 1965 the first aircraft, piloted by Hawke, was ferried from Tucson to Tancos, Portugal, through Rochester, Torbay, Canada, and Santa Maria, Azores. As soon as he arrived in Tancos, the pilot was immediately transported to Lisbon Airport to take the first available flight back to the USA. By August 1965, seven aircraft had already been delivered.

Some sources say that when he was delivering the second aircraft was forced to land in Washington, and almost arrested, but when mentioning the code name 'Sparrow' was immediately released. By August 1965, when the seventh aircraft had already been delivered, the US Customs finally went into action and in September Hawke and other people involved were arrested in Florida and the authorities prevented a Curtiss C-46 freighter transporting spare parts to Portugal from leaving the USA.

The operation's cover was so thin that Soviet and Hungarian representatives at the United Nations attacked the transaction. Accused of violating its own official policy, the USA could do little but deny the charge and look for scapegoats. Jeff Hawke and Francois de Marin, a Frenchman who had acted as a middleman in the deal, were brought to trial in a federal court. The jury remained unconvinced that both men had deliberately broke the law, and so they were acquitted.

Jeff - who I knew - was a colourful, larger-than-life character; one of his more interesting incidents was that he allegedly recorded in his RAF logbook the attempted intercept of a Lockheed U-2 that had overflown Cyprus when he was based there. In 1968 he participated in the filming of the movie *The Battle of Britain* at Duxford, piloting *The Psychedelic Monster'*, the B-25 camera ship, which is where I first came across him.

Hawke was very much into locating and flying film aircraft. and was at one time President of American based company Euramericair, Jeff also worked on *633 Squadron, Empire of the Sun, Sky Bandits, White Nights, Sweet Dreams*, and *Hanover Street*. He was also heavily featured in the documentary *B-25 Mitchells Do Fly in IMC*.

The last time I saw him was over the far side at Coventry Airport around 1990 when he spent most of a Saturday getting a Ju.52 started, then flying it off across the grass and the main runway before disappearing into the distance!

At the time of his death, press reports said John Hawke had hired Piper Aztec G-OESX some months previously and was later fished up out of the Adriatic. The body on board carried a Miami driving licence in the name of John Hawke.

The aircraft was said to have had its undercarriage and flaps down and showed damage inconsistent with that expected during a ditching. In the period since it was first hired it had been repainted in 'anti-radar paint'. There

were several rumours going the rounds at the time that it had been shot down, as this was at the beginning of the troubles in Yugoslavia.

The accident report showed that on 21 November 1991 the aircraft was destroyed when crashed into the sea off Port Levante, in the Gulf of Venice, off the coast of Italy. It was scheduled to depart from Cannes, in the south of France, to fly to Aérodrome de Cerny-La-Ferté-Alais, near Paris.

Whilst the aircraft did indeed take off from Cannes-Mandelieu Airport, Cannes at 13:18 hours, instead of flying north-north-west towards the Paris area, it headed east, and was last seen on radar at 17:39 hours in the vicinity of Ca Negra, near Chioggia, which is in the Venice area.

At this point the aircraft disappeared from radar, and is presumed to have crashed at around 17:48 hours into the Gulf of Venice off Porto Levante at approximate co ordinates $45°19' 0''$ N, $13°0' 0''$ E. The Air Accident Investigation Board report concluded that the aircraft was probably heading - for unknown reasons - for Pula Airport then in Yugoslavia, now Croatia.

Only pieces of wreckage were found; the first being recovered by a fishing boat on 27 December some thirteen miles south east of Chioggia Harbour. An investigation was initiated by the Italian authorities when it transpired that the main door from the aircraft had been recovered on 18 December by another fishing boat. Subsequent sea searches by the Italian Navy took twenty-four days and recovered more than ninety per cent of the wreckage. In the view of the Italian Authorities, the possibilities of the aircraft accident being brought about by collision or explosion were specifically excluded. However, pilot incapacitation could not be ruled out.

What started with War Plan Red almost certainly continues to this day under the guise of false patriotism and massive ego that drives the desire of the world's only superpower. The only problem in discovering what has been happening is sorting through the rubble of mangled facts!

And finally...
Back in 1939, unfortunately - and fortunately - Adolf Hitler decided to declare war on most of the world, and the US apparently became best pals with the United Kingdom shortly thereafter

Right: Dwight David 'Ike' Eisenhower (*b*. 14 October 1890, *d*. 28 March 1969); an American five-star general and statesman who served as the 34th President of the United States from 1953 to 1961. Eisenhower was another American who had a severe dislike for some British, especially Field Marshal Montgomery.

- even while they still hated each other.

The level of dislike by the elite in political and military spheres on the American side is well documented. For example that Gen George S Patton and Dwight D Eisenhower loathed Field Marshal Bernard Montgomery, as well as having a very low opinion of Winston Churchill is embedded deeply in surviving documents. In the 1930s Churchill was regarded by many Americans as a brilliant, but burned out politican - a has-been who sought refuge in drink. Indeed, in the process of research for this work, I discovered a truly wonderful note from Sumner Welles, a foreign policy adviser to President Franklin D. Roosevelt who served as Under Secretary of State from 1936 to 1943, during FDR's presidency. Welles recalled a visit to Churchill in his office: '*Mr Churchill was sitting in front of the fire smoking a huge cigar and drinking whiskey and soda. It was quite obvious that he had consumed a good many whiskies before I had arrived*'.

But none of this hatred for the British was as much as they hated the Germans. Or the French, for that matter. But their attitudes and opinions percolated down the ranks and appears to be poorly concealed – something that became a source of endless friction.

After meeting and socially talking with some

Below left: George Smith Patton Jr. (*b*. 11 November 1885, *d*. 21 December 1945) It was well-known that Patton detested British Prime Minister Winston Churchill. *(NARA)*
Below right: Field Marshal Bernard Law Montgomery, 1st Viscount Montgomery of Alamein, KG, GCB, DSO, PC, DL (*b*. 17 November 1887, *d*. 24 March 1976), He was a target for dislike by a number of US military men.

senior American officials, and exploring their cultural views of the world, British Army officer and later politician Enoch Powell became convinced that one of America's covert war aims was to destroy the British Empire.

Writing home on 16 February 1943, Powell stated: *'The thought struck me for the first time today that our duty to our country may not terminate with the peace – apart, I mean, from the duty of begetting children to bear arms for the King in the next generation. To be more explicit, I see growing on the horizon the greater peril than Germany or Japan ever were; and if the present hostilities do not actually merge into a war with our terrible enemy, America, it will remain for those of us who have the necessary knowledge and insight to do what we can where we can to help Britain be victorious again in her next crisis'.*

John Enoch Powell MBE (*b*. 16 June 1912, *d*. 8 February 1998); a British politician, classical scholar, author, linguist, soldier, philologist and poet.

Today history seems to only remember Powell for his often mis-quoted but nevertheless notorious 'Rivers of Blood' speech - a term which, incidentally, never appeared in it - given on 20 April 1968 when he was the Conservative MP for Wolverhampton South West - addressing a meeting of the Conservative Political Centre in Birmingham - but Powell was much more than a politician.

During October 1939, almost a month after returning home from Australia, Powell enlisted in the Royal Warwickshire Regiment. In later years, Powell recorded his promotion from private to lance-corporal in his *Who's Who* entry, on other occasions describing it as a greater promotion than entering the Cabinet. Early in 1940, he was trained for a commission after, whilst working in a kitchen. He passed out as top entrant from his officer training.

Powell was commissioned on the General List in 1940 but almost immediately transferred to the Intelligence Corps. He was soon promoted to captain and posted as GSO3 (Intelligence) to the 1st (later 9th) Armoured Division. In October 1941, Powell was posted to Cairo and transferred back to the Royal Warwickshire Regiment. As secretary to the Joint Intelligence Committee, Middle East, he was soon doing work that would normally have been done by a more senior officer and was in May 1942, backdated to December 1941 was promoted to major. He was promoted to lieutenant-colonel in August 1942 and in that role helped plan the Second Battle of El Alamein, having previously helped plan the attack on Rommel's supply lines. The following year, he was honoured as a member of the Order of the British Empire for his military service.

Powell's suspicion of the anti-British Empire demeanor of the American Government's foreign policy continued for the remainder of the war and into his subsequent post-war political career. In a speech to the House of Commons on 5 November 1953 Powell continued this theme: *'I believe a second factor which has weighed heavily in this matter is the attitude, or supposed attitude, of the United States. I confess that I am not greatly moved by this. Whatever may be the attitude of the American Government and public to the United Kingdom as such, my view of American policy over the last decade has been that it has been steadily and relentlessly directed towards the weakening and the destruction of the links which bind the British Empire together. We can watch the events as they unfold and place our own interpretation on them. My interpretation is that the United States has for this country, considered separately, a very considerable economic and strategic use but that she sees little or no strategic use or economic value in the British Empire or the British Commonwealth as it has existed and as it still exists. Against the background I ask the House to consider the evidence of advancing American imperialism in this area from which they are helping to eliminate us.*

Bibliography and Resources

Selected books that have been useful in telling this story:

Beck, Alfred M. *'The Ambivalent Attache: Friedrich von Boetticher in America, 1933-1941.'* Ph.D. diss., Georgetown University, 1977 (unpublished).

Boston Series Reports and Related Records. Greg Bradsher, National Archives and Records Administration, College Park, Maryland, 2000.

Breitman, Richard, and Timothy Naftal. *'Report to the Interagency Working Group on Previously Classified OSS Records.'* National Archives, College Park, Maryland, 2000.

Complete Presidential Press Conferences of Franklin D. Roosevelt, 1933-1945. New York: Da Capo, 1972. Foreign Relations of the United States, 1939-1945. Washington, D.C.: US Government Printing Office, 1970.

Hearings on Proposed Legislation to Curb or Control the Communist Party Of the United States. Washington, D.C.: United States Government Printing Office, 1948.

Memorandum from Colonel Richard Park Jr. to President Harry S Truman, April 13, 1945. Harry S Truman Library.

Memorandum of Establishment of Service of Strategic Information. William J. Donovan to President Franklin D. Roosevelt June 10 1941 FDR Library.

For the President's Eyes Only: Secret Intelligence and the American Presidency from Washington to Bush. Christopher Andrew; Harper-Collins New York 1995.

Charles A Lindbergh and the Battle Against American Intervention in World War Two. Wayne S Cole, Harcourt Brace Jovanovich, New York 1974.

Conflict of Duty: The US Navy's Intelligence Dilemma, 1919-1945. Jeffrey M Dorwart, Naval Institute Press, Annapolis, 1983

Kennedy and Roosevelt: The Uneasy Alliance. Michael Beschloss; Norton, New York, 1980

The American FBI holds an eight-part, 428 page file on Joseph P Kennedy, that includes articles about Tyler Gatewood Kent.

By far the largest part of this work was completed using primary source documentation from the National Archives and Records Administration (NARA) in College Park, Maryland, USA. The main set of files used (along with the number of pages located in each file) are listed below:

NARA ADM No.001 – Administrative History Collection, Historical Section, ETOUSA – Accomodations, Assignment Section. (16 pages)

NARA ADM No.002 – Administrative History Collection, Historical Section, ETOUSA – Achievements, Service of Supply. (32 pages)

NARA ADM No.002a – Administrative History Collection, Historical Section, ETOUSA – Administrative Orders. (90 pages)

NARA ADM No.003 – Administrative History Collection, Historical Section, ETOUSA – Adjutant General Records. (118 pages)

NARA ADM No.004 – Administrative History Collection, Historical Section, ETOUSA – Adjutant General Section. (87 pages)

NARA ADM No.009 – Administrative History Collection, Historical Section, ETOUSA – Air Force. (225 pages)

NARA ADM No.010 – Administrative History Collection, Historical Section, ETOUSA – Air Force Division. (66 pages)

NARA ADM No.013 – Administrative History Collection, Historical Section, ETOUSA – Air Transport Command. (62 pages)

NARA ADM No.014 – Administrative History Collection, Historical Section, ETOUSA – Air technical Section. (33 pages)

NARA ADM No.020 – Administrative History Collection, Historical Section, ETOUSA – American Red Cross – 1. (222 pages)

NARA ADM No.020a – Administrative History Collection, Historical Section, ETOUSA – Amercian Red Cross – 2. (320 pages)

NARA ADM No.020b – Administrative History Collection, Historical Section, ETOUSA – American Red Cross – 3. (232 pages)

NARA ADM No.022 – Administrative History Collection, Historical Section, ETOUSA – Andrews, General Frank. (9 pages)

NARA ADM No.023 – Administrative History Collection, Historical Section, ETOUSA – Anglo-American Relations. (201 pages)

NARA ADM No.024 – Administrative History Collection, Historical Section, ETOUSA – Anglo-American Relations – letters, memoranda, press releases etc. (169 pages)

NARA ADM No.025 – Administrative History Collection, Historical Section, ETOUSA – Anti-Aircraft Section. (125 pages)

NARA ADM No.026 – Administrative History Collection, Historical Section, ETOUSA – Anti-Aircraft Section. (188 pages)

NARA ADM No.030 – Administrative History Collection, Historical Section, ETOUSA – Army Talks and Education. (26 pages)

NARA ADM No.031 – Administrative History Collection, Historical Section, ETOUSA – Army Exchange Service. (251 pages)

NARA ADM No.033 – Administrative History Collection, Historical Section, ETOUSA – Army Service Forces. (196 pages)

NARA ADM No.036 – Administrative History Collection, Historical Section, ETOUSA – Assembly Area Command. (22 pages)

NARA ADM No.038 – Administrative History Collection, Historical Section, ETOUSA – Awards & Decorations (366 pages)

NARA ADM No.039 – Administrative History Collection, Historical Section, ETOUSA – Baggage. (48 pages)

NARA ADM No.042 – Administrative History Collection, Historical Section, ETOUSA – Base Sections (48 pages)

NARA ADM No.042 – Administrative History Collection, Historical Section, ETOUSA – Base Sections (General) (33 pages)

NARA ADM No.043 – Administrative History Collection, Historical Section, ETOUSA – Base Sections – UK (33 pages)

NARA ADM No.047 – Administrative History Collection, Historical Section, ETOUSA – Billetting (33 pages)

NARA ADM No.048 – Administrative History Collection, Historical Section, ETOUSA – Biographies – American (248 pages)

NARA ADM No.049 – Administrative History Collection, Historical Section, ETOUSA – Biographies – United Kingdom (34 pages)

NARA ADM No.050 – Administrative History Collection, Historical Section, ETOUSA – Bomber Command Plan (110 pages)

NARA ADM No.054 – Administrative History Collection, Historical Section, ETOUSA – British Army (64 pages)

NARA ADM No.057 – Administrative History Collection, Historical Section, ETOUSA – Casualties (63 pages)

NARA ADM No.058 – Administrative History Collection, Historical Section, ETOUSA – Censorship (408 pages)

NARA ADM No.059 – Administrative History Collection, Historical Section, ETOUSA – Central Base Section (82 pages)

NARA ADM No.221 – Administrative History Collection, Historical Section, ETOUSA – Prisoners of War (432 pages)

NARA ADM No.318 – Administrative History Collection, Historical Section, ETOUSA – SPOBS (103 pages)

NARA ADM No.435 – Administrative History Collection, Historical Section, ETOUSA – Estimate of the Situation – Red and Tentative Joint Basic Plan Red. Original 8 May 1930. (84 pages)

NARA ADM No.490A – Administrative History Collection, Historical Section, ETOUSA – Lockheed Overseas Corporation (807 pages)

NARA NND 968133 – Navy Basic Plan Red WPL 22. Original Plans . Issued, February 1931. Released 2-2-2011

Index